2ND EDITION

BEHAVIOUR IN SCHOOLS

Behaviour in Schools 2e

Louise Porter

PhD, MA(hons), MGiftedEd, DipEd

Open University Press

Open University Press
McGraw-Hill Education
McGraw-Hill House
Shoppenhangers Road
Maidenhead
Berkshire
England
SL6 2QL

email: enquiries@openup.co.uk
world wide web: www.openup.co.uk

First published 2006

A catalogue record of this book is available from the British Library

ISBN 0 335 22001 0

Library of Congress Cataloging-in-Publication Data
CIP data has been applied for

Typeset by Bookhouse, Sydney
Printed by Ashford Colour Press Ltd., Gosport, Hants.

For Gerard,

who continues to tolerate my physical

and mental absences while I write

CONTENTS

FIGURES AND TABLES

Figures

Tables

Part 1 | THEORIES OF DISCIPLINE

A few years ago I met an old professor at the University of Notre Dame. Looking back on his long life of teaching he said, with a funny twinkle in his eyes, 'I have always complained that my work was constantly interrupted until I slowly discovered that my interruptions were my work'.

Henri Nouwen (in Rogers 2002: 5)

Teaching young people self-discipline is not a diversion from 'real' teaching but is integral to it: education must, first and foremost, be about teaching people to live together peaceably, for which they need to learn to consider others and to solve problems (Gartrell 2003). It is your professional responsibility to help young people become fully functioning members of society (Rodd 1996).

School-based behavioural difficulties are often blamed on students' disadvantaging home lives. However, young people spend 15 000 hours in school, which provides a significant time frame in which they can learn. This is verified by comprehensive research showing that differences in achievement outcomes, attitude to school and, to a lesser extent, rates of absenteeism and other behavioural difficulties are systematically related to schools' quality (Mortimore et al. 1988; Rutter 1983; Rutter & Maughan 2002). Indeed, school features have a more direct effect on students' academic progress and behaviour than does their family, accounting for between 20 and 25 per cent of the difference between schools in student progress, with family factors explaining only 5 per cent (Mortimore et al. 1988; Osterman 2000; Rutter & Maughan 2002; Sylva 1994). Classroom factors may be even more influential than aspects of the school (Sylva 1994), if only because there is probably more variation between classes than between schools. These findings confirm that teachers' influence over academic outcomes is stronger than parents' (Gonzalez-DeHass et al. 2005), with students' perceptions of the personal support they receive in school for academic achievement powerful in motivating them to put in the effort to learn (Marchant et al. 2001).

The conclusion is unequivocal: students' progress in school is more influenced by school quality than by their social backgrounds (Mortimore et al. 1988; Rutter & Maughan 2002). Student outcomes will never be equal, of course, as the only way to achieve this would be to lower the attainment levels of the more able students. Nevertheless, improving school quality can do much to alleviate individual difficulties by promoting in students a commitment to schooling and a sense of self-efficacy, which is their belief in their own ability to influence their life outcomes (Rutter 1983; Rutter & Maughan 2002; Sylva 1994).

Thus, while disadvantaging home factors create the *potential* for negative academic and behavioural outcomes, these will not be expressed when schools offer appropriate supports in the form of teacher involvement, effective teaching, high academic expectations, clear school organisation, surveillance to permit prompt intervention with difficulties, and noncoercive discipline (McEvoy & Welker 2000; Reinke & Herman 2002; Rutter 1983). To achieve this, schools need a clear rational (or theory) guiding their practice.

The value of theory

There is an old saying that advises: 'If you want to get ahead, get a theory'. This is because theories help us not only to know what to do, but also to be able to explain our practices. This is the essence of professionalism. Although theories might sound too abstract to be of practical use, they describe why and how things work as they do (Chibucos et al. 2005). They explain and predict events and, in doing so, guide practice.

Yet trainee teachers have many branches of knowledge to master, while practising teachers experience the imperative to 'just get on with it'. Neither can afford to 'waste time' theorising. The trouble is that 'getting on with it' can involve doing the same unsuccessful thing over and over—not because you are incompetent, but because the ideas (the theories) that drive your responses are not helping. Practice that lacks a coherent body of guiding ideas can leave you 'winging it', reacting to each disruption without the tools to reflect on which interventions have worked and which have failed. Not only is this less likely to result in effective action, but it adds to your work and stress loads as you are required to make decisions on the run, without the time to consider what you believe and to evaluate which actions correspond with those beliefs.

The abiding truth, of course, is that 'one cannot *not* theorize' (Fisch et al. 1982: 7). That is to say, we all do develop ideas (that is, theories) about events—in our case, about the behaviour of students in schools. Through experience and reflection, many teachers do arrive at clear theories about their practices. However, this process of personal theory building is more efficient and comprehensive when informed in advance by theoretical knowledge. To that end, this book aims to formalise your present knowledge about two bodies of theory: disciplinary practices in schools and educational theory about teaching and learning. The basic premise is that for your practice to be coherent these two sets of ideas must be congruent with each other.

Politics of discipline in schools

Before detailing in coming chapters the range of theories about school discipline, it must be acknowledged that each adopts a political stance, with inherent values, assumptions and contradictions (Johnson et al. 1994). Disciplinary practices typically reflect an imbalance of political power between teachers and students that is legitimised on the grounds of the developmental incompetence of children. As is always the case when power is distributed unevenly within society, some groups are served by the maintenance of this inequity; in schools, children are marginalised and disadvantaged by it (Johnson et al. 1994).

This power imbalance is reflected in the language used to discuss behavioural difficulties in schools. It is problematic in many ways. Sometimes the topic is referred to as *teaching discipline*, which is the term I use here, but because our society has such a long tradition of using controlling forms of discipline, the term itself is sometimes misconstrued as referring to punishment. Nevertheless, I prefer it to its alternative, *behaviour management*, because, in Western societies at least, the term *management* has overtones of controlling others, of doing something *to* them, rather than working *with* them (Kohn 1996a). Also, in educational circles, the term *behaviour management* is sometimes used synonymously with *behaviour modification*—that is, with an authoritarian rewards-and-punishment system. Other language that we employ in schools that implies that we (adults) will do something *to* children includes *observation*, *assessment* and *intervention*. Although our aim in using such language is to obey the scientific imperative to be *objective*, these top-down processes distance us from children's experience and overlook their frame of reference (Henning-Stout 1998), typically resulting in a 'laundry list' of what is wrong with children, subsequent to which we impose our own (often deficit-oriented) solutions (*treatments*) on them (McGlone 2001; Murphy & Duncan 1997).

This introduces the second issue to do with the terms *discipline* and *behaviour management*, which is that they have an interventive bias, overlooking the fact that by far the largest and most crucial component of any discipline program is the prevention of difficulties. Despite this, the preponderance of school policies on discipline are actually punishment policies (Lewis 1997). Their relative neglect of preventive measures will inevitably lead to failure and frustration as it is always more effective to prevent difficulties than to correct them once they have arisen (Maag 2001). Thus, as depicted in Figure I.1, school-based disciplinary measures must encompass three layers of practice, with those at the lower levels predominating. The first component is *primary* or *universal prevention* procedures, which focus on the larger environment and put in place protective mechanisms that safeguard all students and thus prevent behavioural difficulties on a school-wide basis (Algozzine & Kay 2002; Kerr & Nelson 2006). While universal preventive measures will meet the needs of a majority of students, creating fewer disciplinary issues and thereby releasing resources to direct towards specific difficulties, they will not be sufficient for all (Lewis et al. 2002). Therefore, you will also need to plan *secondary preventive* strategies. These are focused or *supportive* interventions aimed at avoiding future disruptions by providing specific skills and supports to students who are experiencing academic failure or behavioural difficulties. This form of prevention requires you to decide which students will be targeted (McConaughy & Leone 2002). The tertiary and final level of practice is enacting solutions—otherwise known as *intervention*. These methods are designed to prevent further deterioration of a problem (Algozzine & Kay 2002) and will encompass both immediate and longer-term actions.

A third issue with language is that terms such as 'misbehaviour' and 'unacceptable' or 'inappropriate' behaviour do not specify to whom those acts are 'inappropriate' (Kohn 1996a). They imply that adults' judgment on this issue is sacrosanct. Similarly, when a student's behaviour interrupts or disrupts the class, we often call this 'problem

FIGURE I.1   Levels of prevention and intervention with school behavioural difficulties

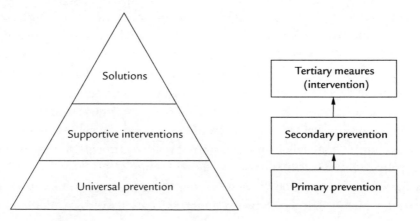

behaviour' or, taking this a step further declare that an individual student has or 'is' a behavioural problem. Using language such as 'disruptive child' suggests a character flaw—one, moreover, that either the child cannot help (so deserves pity) or one that he or she is indulging deliberately, which implies the need for authoritarian controls to make him or her stop (Docking 1982). Such language defines the behaviour as a quality of the student, while overlooking the contributions of the environment to the behaviour, and thus results in a deficit orientation to problems.

A medical or deficit orientation

Aside from the blaming character of diagnoses, individual explanations are linear: they contend that cause A leads to event B (Fisch et al. 1982). This linear explanation implies that, if only we could find out the 'real' or underlying cause of a problem, we could arrive at a solution. This mechanistic approach sounds logical, but is more relevant to the car repair industry than to people (Berg & Steiner 2003). With people, even if you could identify the cause, it may be virtually untreatable, such as a central auditory processing difficulty or social oppression. The fact that these causes are untreatable would generate hopelessness about the possibilities for improvement. However, this pessimism is unnecessary because many effective solutions are unrelated to their cause. You are willing to take painkillers for your headache, even though clearly the headache was not caused by a lack of painkillers. As de Shazer (1988: 10) observes:

> we end up searching for explanations believing that without explanation a solution is irrational, not recognizing that the solution itself is its own best explanation.

A purely pragmatic argument against prolonged searches for underlying causes is that this process will consume resources that could otherwise be used for intervention. In schools, this is particularly wasteful, given that the vast majority of disruptiveness will never qualify for a medical diagnosis anyway (Le Messurier 2004). Furthermore, even those behaviours that do get labelled (e.g. as ADHD, oppositional-defiance disorder or emotional-behavioural disturbance) will still have to be responded to by teachers in classrooms, regardless of their diagnosis (Rogers 2003). Even if stimulant medication improves the concentration and memory difficulties associated with ADHD, for example, the drug does not help affected children learn to put their hands up before answering or plan their activities: *they* still need to put in some effort to organise themselves (Rogers 2003). This can be made less likely when the diagnosis comes to excuse inept behaviour, both in the minds of teachers and the students themselves.

Moreover, we generally do not know enough to understand all the influences on others' actions. Teachers seldom have the training or are in a position to gain all the information they need to make accurate diagnoses, with the result that any intervention that follows may be misguided. To treat underlying learning difficulties or emotional trauma as simple behavioural problems would inflict further injustice on struggling children. Therefore, all theorists considered here (with the exception of the neo-Adlerians) agree that the most that teachers can legitimately do is observe and *describe* the behaviours of their students, rather than interpret or diagnose these.

A deeper objection is that labelling students blames them for what can often be natural reactions to an institutionalised setting that deprives them of power and dignity (Laws & Davies 2000). Their attempts to regain autonomy are defined as illegitimate attempts to 'eclipse power with power' (Butler 1997, in Laws & Davies 2000: 213). Talking about children as 'mad' or 'bad' causes us to assume either crazy or evil intent behind their actions, rather than assuming that they may have good reasons for what they do. Inexorably, this leads to attempts to make them desist.

Diagnoses (or a 'deficit discourse') also pose the broad ethical issue that, when people in authority (such as teachers) apply labels to others (to students or parents), their status as professionals ensures that their descriptions acquire the status of 'truth' and become irrefutable (Winslade & Monk 1999). Despite the fact that labels reflect only *some* of the qualities of individuals, the descriptions come to dominate outsiders' and recipients' own concept of their *whole* self and, furthermore, highlight their deficits rather than their competencies. Hence, rather than helping people to find solutions, negative descriptions commonly limit people's options in life and suggest that change is impossible. Seldom are the recipients of labels asked how *they* see themselves or would prefer others to see them, which results in their 'enfeeblement' at the same time as inflating the status of those who confer the labels (Winslade & Monk 1999).

Finally, even when not blamed for the problem, diagnostic labels can undermine teachers' and parents' confidence, because these define students as needing specialised expertise, which the adults believe they lack (Dicocco et al. 1987). While, on the one hand, labels can help you to understand the difficulties under which certain students are functioning, when you use diagnoses such as 'ADHD' or 'learning disabled' as *explanations* of children's difficulties, rather than mere shorthand *descriptions*, you may lower your academic and behavioural expectations for labelled children and may even use their difficulties as an explanation for their poor progress, without considering how teaching could improve that.

Conclusion

Examining the philosophical beliefs of the various theories of discipline will take both time and tolerance for uncertainty. It may liberate you from beliefs that do not withstand closer scrutiny, while also generating feelings of uncertainty about what to replace them with (Larrivee 2005).

You might find yourself disappointed that this book does not prescribe practices. It is not a practice manual with recipe-like instructions about how to respond to particular student behaviours, but a guide for thinking about what you believe, for examining whether those beliefs are useful and valid, and for recognising which practices align with your personal and professional beliefs. This analysis will allow you to 'infuse your personal beliefs and values into your professional identity' (Larrivee 2005: 15). When you emerge from the process of reflection with a new vision, it will be your own. And you will be enabled to solve your own dilemmas in an authentic and coherent way.

1 INFLUENCES ON DISCIPLINARY PRACTICES

Students are taught that they have choices about how to behave, and that their own recognisability as credible and competent students will depend on learning to make the right choices. They are coached in these right choices [about]...when to work, how to learn, when to be creative (and in what contexts), when to speak and what can be spoken, and when to be silent [p. 209]. The coercive practices through which most children are persuaded to take up [these] practices of being a 'good student' are themselves largely invisible to those with power to coerce [p. 207] and are not necessarily benign [p. 208].

Laws & Davies (2000: 207, 208, 209)

KEY POINTS

- Teachers' beliefs about children inform their educational and disciplinary decisions. When we regard children either as untrustworthy or in need of protection, we are most likely to impose both a curriculum and discipline on students, whereas when we see young people as competent, we are more inclined to give them some say in both their learning and discipline.
- The explanations that we generate about disruptions will induce either a controlling (authoritarian) or an educational response.
- Our values will govern which behaviours we define as problematical.
- These personal beliefs, explanations and values can be informed and extended by formal theories of discipline and teaching. The resulting collection of recommended

practices will then be attuned to the constraints and enabling features of the particular setting.

Introduction

Many ingredients contribute to your repertoire of responses to children's behaviour in schools. As depicted in Figure 1.1, fundamental to your practices are your beliefs about children and their behaviour; next are your personal and professional values; then your practices are informed by two bodies of knowledge, one pertaining to discipline and the other to education. Finally, your actual practices will be both constrained by the realities of your setting and enabled by its supports.

FIGURE 1.1   Components of teachers' disciplinary practices

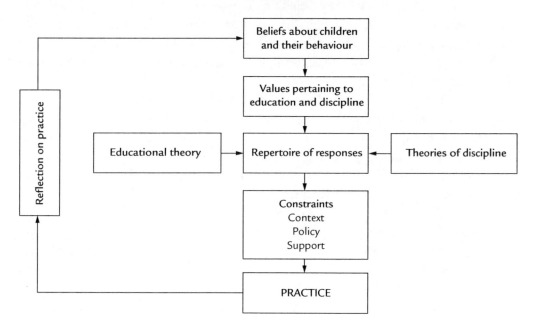

Beliefs about children

Your beliefs about children will colour everything that happens in your classroom, both educationally and in terms of student discipline (Kohn 1996a). These beliefs will centre on your view of children's inherent nature and their developmental status and of their development over time. Each has its own implications for practice, as detailed in Table 1.1.

The nature of children

The fundamental difference in beliefs about children concerns their nature. On the one hand is the puritanical view of children as wicked, evil, sinful and delinquents-in-waiting—that is, as the source of social disorder (Lee 2001). This view carries through the Abrahamic religions to more recent history, when it was espoused by Thomas Hobbes, famous for his characterisation of life (and perhaps children too) as 'nasty, brutish and short' (Montgomery 2003). The view that children are villainous and wild and have a bad influence on each other is particularly influential with respect to the topic of child discipline. It states that, to overcome children's inherent evil tendencies, adults must maintain strict control over them. This bleak perspective on human nature leads to notions that children need *socialising, taming, civilising* or *discipline* (equating this with punishment). This view underpins the use of rewards for behaviour of which we approve, as if children would not otherwise think to act thoughtfully again, and the advice that we must punish misdemeanours, which assumes that otherwise children will keep acting antisocially.

The opposite view is that children are innocents who need protection from the threats of the adult world. This romantic view of the wholesome child was first expounded by Rousseau (Montgomery 2003; W.S. Rogers 2003). According to this perspective, children start out life close to nature and will achieve virtue if uncorrupted by adult influences and if permitted free and playful self-expression. This implies that when children act disruptively, it is either because they do not understand, or they are misunderstood or mistreated (W.S. Rogers 2003).

The person-centred counselling style of Carl Rogers and its corresponding humanist approach to discipline arise from a more pragmatic version of this 'romantic' view. This perspective upholds that, in the choice between thinking of children as inherently wicked versus inherently good, given the lack of evidence either way, we might as well believe in humanity: that people are just as capable of behaving altruistically as they are of behaving selfishly (Kohn 1996a).

Children's developmental status

The second element of social understandings of children is beliefs about their skilfulness versus dependence. The first variant, originating with John Locke, sees children as bereft of useful knowledge, as *blank slates*, irrational and ignorant (Lee 2001; Montgomery 2003). Therefore, they need shaping, training and controlling—or, in other words, *schooling*. The task of adults is to fill children with the information and skills that we deem will be useful to them and to society. More recently, this passive view has evolved into regarding children as being more active in their own learning. From the perspective of children as passive learners, the teacher's task was to ensure orderly (passive) behaviour as a necessary condition for learning to occur; under the more modern, active perspective, the teacher's role is to enable children to learn for themselves. This can still imply a top-down approach to teaching, but one that can be child-focused—that is, focusing on what children need in order to learn and grow. This, however, is not the same as being child-centred, where the children are active and central participants in shaping their schooling.

At the heart of both the passive and active conceptions of children's skills is the notion that children are only becoming adult—in fact, only becoming *human*. They are not yet complete and therefore must not be afforded access to adult understandings and do not warrant respect (Buckingham 2000; Lee 2001). In comparison, adults (human *beings*) are responsible and fully competent—that is, stable, complete, 'grown up' and thus worthy of respect. Yet, Lee (2001: xiv) asks: 'Why is it that children and adults have ever been thought of as fundamentally different types of persons?'. Instead, humanism does not regard chronological age as an adequate criterion for distributing dignity and respect. It recognises that, like children, adults are still growing towards being all that they can be. Thus still being incomplete is not a reason to discriminate against children, as both adults and children have yet to finish their personal growth.

A time orientation

The third difference between conceptions of childhood is their perspective in time. Some views of children (usually espoused by politicians) proclaim that they are worth investing in, because our children are 'our future'. The educational parallel of this orientation towards the future is the emphasis on maximising children's personal 'potential', which is a particularly strident demand within the field of gifted education. This focus on the future leads to the concept of adults as gardeners—intervening at each stage of growth, taking deliberate control over the types of plants (children) that flourish, training and feeding them to 'maximise their potential'. This future orientation overlooks children's present needs. This means, for example, that when children protest an adult directive, their objections can be discounted; what is important is shaping their behaviour for the future ('He's *got* to learn . . .').

TABLE 1.1   Practical implications of views of childhood

	Children as threats to social order	Children as innocents
Children as empty vessels/blank slates	• Children are untrustworthy. • They need socialising. • Adults must censor their experiences and restrict their movement to prevent youth from perpetrating antisocial behaviour. • Top-down teaching model that is focused on training, rather than on education. • Authoritarian discipline.	• Innocence is equated with vulnerability. • Children are incomplete, still *becoming* human. • Censorship is needed to protect them from premature adulthood. • Child-focused but adult-directed curriculum (adult is a 'gardener'). • Mixed disciplinary styles.
Children as competent	• Children are blameworthy. • They must take legal and moral responsibility for their mistakes. • Top-down teaching model. • Autocratic discipline.	• Innocence is neutral: children are neither good nor bad, just human beings. • Child-centred (constructivist) teaching model. • Egalitarian discipline.

A second time perspective looks to the past to generate anxiety—if not episodic hysteria—about the apparent impending disappearance of childhood. It is assumed that children face more serious and varied risks from society at large than in the past although, to the extent that we can judge, it is likely that rates of child abuse, for instance, have remained unaltered for centuries. Based on a concept of threatened childhood innocence, this view is captured by lay people and eminent educators alike, the latter including David Elkind (2001), who mourns the speed at which children today grow up, pressured by media into consumerism and by ambitious parents seeking to skill them up to compete in a market economy. However, this nostalgia overlooks the fact that childhood is not a universal or unitary phenomenon. It is experienced differently in suburban Adelaide, Arnhem Land, metropolitan London and the slums of Calcutta. It is experienced differently today from a century ago and, no doubt, a century hence. Thus, Buckingham (2000) believes that what commentators are mourning when they decry the loss of childhood is in fact the decline in adults' *control* over childhood, over what children can experience. This has principally been a result of children's increased exposure to electronic media. Both the content and passive process involved in engaging with television and computer games may be an issue, but not one of the loss of childhood itself, only of the change in childhood as we in privileged societies have known it.

A present focus on skilled and trustworthy children

Humanism trusts that individuals are innately driven to grow and become all they can (Raskin & Rogers 2005). Maslow (1968) termed this *self-actualisation*. Combined with the notion of the inherent goodness of human nature, the view of children as competent feeds into a constructivist approach to education and egalitarian discipline (both of which will be defined shortly). It also encompasses the temporal dimension by graduating beyond developmental psychology, which studies how children develop into adults, to a sociology of childhood that appreciates how their lives are experienced in the present (Mayall 2002). This view leads to notions of teachers as caring facilitators who trust children to direct themselves and make appropriate choices when given the autonomy and support to do so.

Beliefs about children's behaviour

The second aspect of your beliefs concerning children is your perception of, and explanations for, disruptive behaviour.

Definition of 'problem' behaviour

Despite claims of a deterioration in student behaviour, evidence suggests that since the 1990s there has been a slight improvement in rates of school-based behavioural difficulties (Achenbach et al. 2002). Nevertheless, if you define as disruptive a large number of student behaviours, you will still feel overwhelmed. As an example of oversensitivity, a UK study found that teachers of four to seven year olds considered fully 16 per cent of their young charges to have 'definite' behavioural problems, with this incidence increasing by Grade 1, when teachers identified one-third of the children as having either mild or definite problems (Miller 2003; Roffey & O'Reirdan 2001). Prevalence rates for the attention deficit disorders also illustrate discrepant interpretations of what is considered normal behaviour in children. Reported rates range from 3 to 5 per cent in Australia, New Zealand and the United States, to a massive 19.8 per cent for boys and 12.3 per cent for girls in Columbia (Hallahan & Kauffman 2003). A third example of oversensitivity is that, when observing young children at group time, Arnold and colleagues (1998) identified an average number of 49 instances of 'misbehaviour' per fifteen-minute segment. Such high rates of reported behavioural difficulties imply that researchers may be defining misbehaviour too restrictively and including too many natural childhood behaviours in their definition. It thus seems that, like beauty, 'misbehaviour' is in the eye of the beholder.

Notwithstanding the rare but high-profile cases of school violence, the vast majority of teachers express concern about more everyday behavioural disruptions in their classes (Bibou-Nakou et al. 2000; Myers & Holland 2000). Of the everyday hassles, some writers define disengagement as a behavioural difficulty, whereas others see this as an educational issue (Glasser 1998a). The first view provokes attempts to change the child, while the second implies adjusting teaching and learning processes to make them more engaging.

Behaviours that do not violate anyone's rights are generally considered to be fairly minor. Some are accidental or result from normal childhood exuberance. While these behaviours can be inconvenient at times, even angering you, Grossman (2004) advises that you will cope better when you can adjust and accommodate to the nature of young people, accepting that at times their behaviour is 'par for the course', given their age and stage of development.

More serious are behaviours that disrupt the learning of others by interrupting the flow of an activity for the whole group. These disruptive behaviours are considered to be unacceptable because they violate the rights of surrounding students—and indeed of the individual miscreants, given that their actions interfere with their own learning as well as potentially provoking ostracism by peers. Most writers are clear that such inconsiderate behaviour requires a response that protects the rights of students to learn, supports the rights of teachers to teach and offers the student involved a chance to act more skilfully in the future.

Rogers (2002) distinguishes such (primary) disruptions from students' reactions to teacher correction behaviours such as an argumentative tone of voice, pouting, sighing and other nonverbal communications of protest are *secondary* to the original behaviour. They can be more disconcerting than the original infraction because they appear to challenge teacher authority. (This, of course, is a problem only if you believe that teachers *should* be in authority over children.)

Gordon (1970, 1974) and Porter (1999, 2003, 2006) also divide behaviours into two types: primary (or internally triggered) behaviours and reactive behaviours, which are students' negative response to adults' attempts to control the primary act. These reactive behaviours, resistance, rebellion and retaliation, were labelled by Gordon as the 'three Rs', to which he subsequently added two other reactions: escape and submission. In my doctoral research I found that these reactive behaviours were both more numerous and more disruptive than the original or primary behaviour (Porter 1999).

Explanations for school-based behavioural difficulties

Teachers typically attribute behavioural difficulties such as the above to characteristics of the children themselves, rather than to the nature of their teaching (Bibou-Nakou et al. 2000). One study found that in 66 per cent of cases, teachers blamed students' behavioural difficulties on home factors, with 30 per cent attributed to child factors and only 4 per cent to aspects of teaching (Croll & Moses 1985, in Miller 2003). For their part, students and parents blame teacher unfairness and student vulnerability, although parents do also recognise certain disadvantaging home factors (Miller et al. 2000, 2002). Teacher behaviours blamed by parents and students included favouritism and its opposite—'picking on' students—rudeness, shouting, not listening to students or noticing their good work, unfairly blaming students and being too lenient or too strict. Parents also blame too much homework and a lack of academic help for struggling students.

Meanwhile, the theoretical explanations for disruptiveness posed by each of the theories to be introduced in this text range from the authoritarian theories' focus on the child to the egalitarian theories' emphasis on the wider context. Flying in the face of the evidence cited in the introduction to Part One, assertive discipline claims that students behave disruptively in schools because of their home backgrounds (Canter & Canter 2001). The other theory occupying the authoritarian position—applied behaviour analysis and its variants—upholds that external events determine behaviour. However, this reductionist position is rejected by those espousing the egalitarian theories, among them Glasser (1998a), who says that external incentives and punishments only ever give individuals *information* about what might happen to us if we engage in a particular behaviour, but that we decide for ourselves whether we will abide by or defy a system of rewards and punishments. We make a choice, according to what actions will meet our needs.

These explanations for behavioural mistakes are often at odds with the explanations that we reserve for academic errors. Whereas we understand students' spelling mistakes as being inevitable—seldom thinking of them as deliberate misbehaviour, but responding by teaching the correct skill—we will often adopt a moralistic attitude to behavioural mistakes. In turn, this judgmental attitude makes it more likely that we will use coercive means to end the disruption. These different assumptions are listed in Box 1.1.

It is worth keeping in mind that almost all behaviours are functional at some time and in some contexts. Screaming or retaliating may be wise when under threat, but less suitable at school assembly. This tells us that the problem is not the behaviour, but our determination that it was inappropriate. In many instances, our judgment on

> **BOX 1.1**   ASSUMPTIONS ABOUT ACADEMIC VERSUS BEHAVIOURAL ERRORS
>
> | Academic errors | Behavioural errors |
> |---|---|
> | Errors are accidental. | Errors are deliberate. |
> | Errors are inevitable. | Errors should not happen. |
> | Errors signal the need for teaching. | Errors should be punished. |
> | Students with learning difficulties need modified teaching. | Students with behavioural difficulties need punishment. |

this issue is accurate; it may be, however, that the behaviour is just normal childhood exuberance.

Personal and professional values

As depicted in Figure 1.1, the second influence on your responses to students' disruptive behaviour is your values, which are your personal and professional standards for judging the goodness or worth of particular behaviours. Personal values align with preferences, such as for a quiet, tidy or orderly classroom, whereas your professional values pertaining to students' behaviour might include valuing students acting in ways that are trustworthy, fair and considerate of others (peers, yourself and colleagues). Although it is legitimate to *ask* students to consider your personal preferences, only your professional values can be actively taught.

Some values are intrinsic (valued for their own sake) and others are instrumental (that is, are the means to an end). This distinction implies that it is more legitimate to focus on intrinsic values. However, instrumental values can inadvertently become treated as if they were an end in themselves (Newman & Pollnitz 2005). For example, insisting that students work quietly to assist their concentration can accidentally become an insistence on quiet because there is a rule against speaking.

Theories of discipline

The third influence on your disciplinary practices is theories about school discipline. Each theory has been placed in Figure 1.2 along a continuum ranging from the political right (or authoritarian) position, where teachers exercise control over students, to the political middle ground, where teachers and students share power. This middle position has variously been termed an authoritative, democratic or egalitarian stance. None of these labels is ideal, however. The term *authoritative* means exercising authority that is based on expertise rather than the power to control. Although having been used now for some decades, it is prone to being confused with authoritarian (which means controlling), simply because of the two words' structural similarities. An alternative might be to call these theories *democratic*, but that is sometimes incorrectly thought to mean equality when, in any democracy, it signals only equal worth, not equal roles. Therefore, I have chosen to label as *egalitarian* those theories that advocate sharing power with children. This means that these theories regard all people as having equal worth. According to those theories occupying this middle ground on the continuum, age is not a criterion for apportioning human rights. Egalitarian practices are characterised by warmth and acceptance, support for students' autonomy and the provision of structure within which young people can be self-governed (Grolnick 2003; Grolnick & Ryan 1989). All three elements are aimed both at meeting young people's inherent needs and at enabling them to learn and behave prosocially.

FIGURE 1.2   The balance of power proposed by theories of student discipline

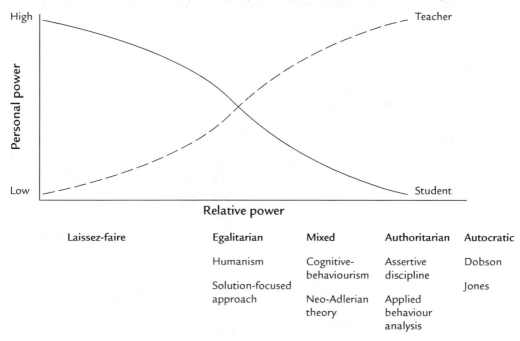

The power referred to in this continuum can take any of the following forms (Larrivee 2005; Schmuck & Schmuck 2001):

- role power—status conferred by the institution;
- coercive power—having the ability to punish students to gain compliance;
- reward power—the extent to which teachers are seen to acknowledge and celebrate student achievements;
- expert power—where students recognise teachers' knowledge and skill;
- referent power—when students identify with their teachers and wish to emulate their best qualities;
- connection power—achieved through close relationships with students.

Role power (status given to teachers by virtue of their *role*) upholds that it is teachers' right to dictate what goes on in their classrooms and is advocated by assertive discipline and other authoritarian theories (Canter & Canter 2001). Like coercive and reward power, it reflects teachers' ability to exercise power *over* students in an effort to control them (Schmuck & Schmuck 2001). The final three forms of power (expert, referent and connection power) are earned by the teacher and are the most effective basis for influencing student achievement and behaviour. This cluster is the power source in humanism. This theory will nevertheless, employ protective power to end a student's aggression, to protect both onlookers and the aggressor from the social ostracism that would result from continued assaults on others; but it contends that this protective use of power differs from the coercive use of power, where the aim is merely to gain compliance.

Assertive discipline

This approach was popularised in the mid-1970s by Lee and Marlene Canter (2001). It was born from an attempt to answer the practical problems that they encountered in their own teaching and, later, in the classrooms of teachers to whom they consulted. Assertive discipline upholds that teachers have the right to impose order on students and that students 'need' teachers to make it clear what is expected of them. To those ends, students' compliance is gained by the use of both positive and negative consequences for individual students or for the group as a whole.

Applied behaviour analysis

Applied behaviour analysis (ABA) and its more recent guises, functional behaviour assessment (FBA) and positive behaviour support (PBS), share a behaviourist philosophy which upholds that all behaviour is governed by the consequence it generates: if a behaviour earns students something that they want, they will repeat it; if the behaviour results in a negative consequence, they will desist in future. Therefore, to eliminate a behaviour, you must stop it from working. You can do this either by rewarding an alternative positive behaviour or by punishing the undesired behaviour.

Cognitive-behaviourism

As the double-barrelled title suggests, cognitive-behaviourism retains some of the beliefs of ABA, but takes account of individuals' thinking (cognitions) as well. This theory agrees that behaviour is controlled by its consequences, but also by students' values, emotions and thoughts, and by the social setting. Its interventions are directed both at the consequences (rewards and punishments) of behaviour and at altering students' thoughts and emotions.

Neo-Adlerian theory

Many modern writers have based their ideas on those of Alfred Adler, who wrote at the beginning of the 20th century. In the field of school discipline, the most well known of the modern writers are the authors of the *Systematic training for effective teaching* (or *parenting*) packages (STET and STEP) (Dinkmeyer et al. 1980, 1997; Dinkmeyer & McKay 1989). This theory believes that students act disruptively out of a discouragement that comes from feeling that they do not belong. Therefore, advocates of this approach suggest that you prevent student discouragement by building cooperative relationships in the classroom. When disruptive behaviour occurs, the theory advises you to diagnose which of four goals is motivating the behaviour. These goals are attention, power, revenge or withdrawal. Next, you are to find ways that students can meet their need in less disruptive ways.

Humanism

The humanist approach to school discipline has its roots in the progressive education movement, whose founders include John Dewey, Maria Montessori and Friedrich Froebel (who originated kindergartens). The humanist approach of these early educators was followed by the counselling theories of Carl Rogers and Tom Gordon and continues with the current emphasis on constructivism in education, which says that children actively construct their understandings of the world. It closely ties its disciplinary practices to this educational philosophy, placing the teacher in the role of facilitator of children's growing knowledge. Humanists contend that young people will both learn and desist disrupting when what they are being asked to learn meets their intellectual, social and emotional needs. This preventive aspect is supplemented by an interventive approach that uses no rewards and punishments but seeks instead to resolve disruptions by listening, being assertive and collaborating with students to resolve the issue.

The solution-focused approach

The solution-focused approach is probably the least widely known of the theories discussed in this book. It upholds that disruptive behaviours recur because present solutions are not working. Although this assertion is self-evident, this theory explains the failure as being due to the *interaction* between students and teachers who have become trapped in a 'dance' or an endless round of escalating disruptiveness and corrective measures. This is not due to the personal flaws of individual students or teachers—the problem is not the dancers; it's the dance. Therefore, you can change troublesome behaviour by changing these student–teacher interactions. Given that the only person whom one can control is oneself, this means that teachers will have to change their attempted solutions to ongoing problems, so that the 'dance' ends and the behaviour improves.

Theories not included

Theories of school-based discipline abound, so some limits needed to be placed on those covered here. One theory not included at the extreme right in figure 1.2 (the autocratic position) is that expounded in James Dobson's (1992) *Dare to discipline*. Dobson believes that teachers receive their authority from God (although it is not clear how this works for non-Christian teachers or societies). He claims that unless we punish children, they will not learn appropriate moral (by which he means sexual) standards of behaviour, and will be 'damned in hell'. He advises parents that when their child resists their directives, 'you had better take it out of him, and pain is a marvellous purifier' (Dobson 1970: 16) and that, 'The shoulder muscle is a surprisingly useful source of minor pain; actually it was created expressly for school teachers' (Dobson 1970: 27). His methods comprise rewards and punishments, so do not constitute a distinct approach from ABA, while his philosophy draws on biblical substantiation rather than evidence from the social sciences or education. This renders it a personal philosophy rather than a testable theory, so it is not included in this text.

At the other end of the continuum is the permissive or laissez-faire approach, which grants students a free rein with very few adult-imposed restrictions. This approach has never enjoyed endorsement in schools and, for that reason, it too is not covered in this text.

Another cluster of theories not included are those based on Freud's psychoanalysis. This theory has endured for over a century but, in my view, largely because it is untestable: any claim that sex is not the prime motivator in life merely proves how deeply repressed such emotions are and thus supports the theory. Freudian theory gained lay support in the 1970s with its modern manifestation, known as transactional analysis (TA), which was popularised in Harris's (1969) book, *I'm OK; you're OK*. Instead of Freud's superego, ego and id, TA speaks of the parent, adult and child ego states. I find this approach descriptive rather than explanatory, but if you are attracted to it, you can refer to Newell and Jeffery (2002) for its application to classroom management.

Included in the previous two editions of this book was Fred Jones's *Tools for teaching* (Jones et al. 2000). I had merged it with Canter and Canter's assertive discipline (2001), under the title 'limit-setting approaches'. However, as assertive discipline has softened in the interim, the blend now seems less tenable. Further, given that Jones's work is largely unknown outside of the United States and, as its title suggests, is a series of practical strategies rather than a comprehensive theory, it too is omitted from this edition.

Conclusion: theories of discipline

The six clusters of theories that have been included in this text differ in where they focus their intervention, as illustrated in Figure 1.3. Each theorist has a prime focus on either behaviour, thoughts, feelings or relationships. But, as with adding layers to an onion, as you move outwards the theories focus on that aspect plus all the inner dimensions. Thus, those on the outer are more multifaceted and social in their focus, with those represented in the inner circles being single-dimensional and focusing more individually than contextually.

Educational theory

The second body of theory that contributes to your repertoire of responses to students' behaviour is educational theory. Educational theory has two features that are relevant to the topic of student behaviour. The first is whether the theories aim to conserve or transform society. A conservative or *conformist* approach to teaching and student discipline aims for children to conform to cultural norms. In contrast, a *reforming* approach to education teaches independent thinking skills so the children are empowered to reform or advance society; while a *transforming* approach wants to enable young

FIGURE 1.3   Focus of each theory of discipline

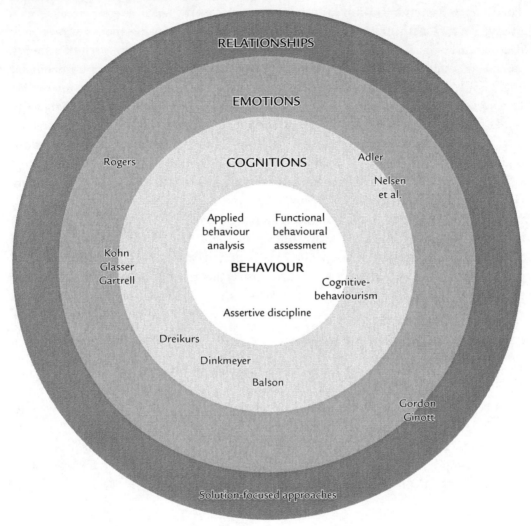

people to challenge social, political and economic inequalities and thus transform their culture (MacNaughton 2003).

The second distinguishing characteristic of educational theories is whether they are teacher-directed or child-centred. In the first—also known as a *top-down* model—adults determine which skills and information are of value to children and then set about teaching these. This approach is largely adult driven and, while not necessarily unresponsive to children's needs, is nevertheless largely originated by the educator. Of the theories described here, Canter and Canter's assertive discipline is the clearest example of a top-down approach to education and discipline in schools.

The contrasting constructivist, or *bottom-up*, approaches regard children as already enriched and vibrant human beings whose need to construct identities and generate understandings of the world is the starting point for, rather than an afterthought in, curriculum planning (Dahlberg et al. 1999). Rather than attempting to instil a predetermined curriculum, a bottom-up approach respects and responds reflectively to the skills and interests of children and their parents. It does not simply indulge these or rely on improvisation or chance, however; it utilises educators' expertise and active teaching while also engaging children's (and parents') competence (Fraser & Gestwicki 2002). It is 'child originated and teacher framed' (Forman & Fyfe 1998, in Fraser & Gestwicki 2002: 168). Of the theories covered in Part One of this book, humanism and the solution-focused approach are the clearest examples of this bottom-up stance.

Constraints on disciplinary practices

Having generated through your belief systems and theoretical knowledge a repertoire of disciplinary practices, your actual practices will inevitably be either constrained or enabled by your context. The first of these constraints is the self-evident observation that classrooms are complex places in which many activities are going on simultaneously, students' responses to even the best-planned activities can be unpredictable, you are called on to make hundreds of decisions per day, and all of your responses are public (Doyle 1986). These characteristics mean that you will continually have to make complex judgments about a particular behaviour, the individual student's history, and the circumstances prevailing in the classroom at the time, including both the teaching content and learning processes that are being fostered (Doyle 1986).

A second potential constraint is the duration of your relationship with the class. When your involvement is intended to be temporary (such as when relief teaching), you might feel obliged to adopt the approaches used by their regular teacher. On the other hand, it is obvious to everyone that you are a different person and, on the grounds that reasonable people can agree to differ, you can explain your own style and ask for consideration of this. Children adjust continually to new settings and tasks.

The students' ability levels might affect which behaviours you feel need a response, and how best to deal with it. Highly engaged students are less likely to be distracted by behavioural reminders being issued to their peers. On the other hand, less motivated students are more easily distracted; in which case, you might have to be more than ordinarily careful to direct instructions only to intended listeners, rather than to the whole class (Cangelosi 2004; Doyle 1986).

Although the students' ages might appear to constrain your use of egalitarian discipline, this does not seem to be the case, as evidenced by this style being more favoured in the early childhood sector than in high schools (Johnson et al. 1994; Lewis 1997). Although it has been assumed that young children do not have adequately sophisticated moral reasoning to profit from egalitarian discipline, it could be that their apparently limited reasoning skills are a *result* rather than a cause of adults' authoritarian disciplinary style and that, with appropriate support, all young people can solve problems without the need for authoritarian controls (Docking 1982).

Reflection

The final aspect of practice as depicted in Figure 1.1 (see p. 14) is your reflection on the effectiveness of your practices and the quality of the theory that spawns them. Given that with student disruptiveness your aim is to engender change, to be a useful tool for this purpose a theory must have the following characteristics (Haley 1980; Molnar & Lindquist 1989).

- On the grounds that a positive explanation is just as likely to be true as a negative one, and that change is less likely when people feel blamed or criticised, any theory aimed at encouraging change should be positive and generate hope that things can improve.
- The theory should suggest what to do, rather than what to think. It must focus directly on actions that could improve the problem.
- The explanation about a behaviour cannot blame past events for present difficulties, as the past cannot be changed. A focus on the past will lead to defeatist attitudes about the potential for change.
- A theory cannot impose on teachers practices that violate their values.

In other words, our theory must have the capacity to impel us towards change rather than immobilise us in despondency.

Eclecticism

As well as applying the criteria in the above list, another possibility for assessing the theories might be to select a blend of ideas and practices that concur with your own views. This is called eclecticism and can take one of three forms (Young 1992). The most basic is *atheoretical* eclecticism. This merges various approaches but, without a coherent theory base, results in practices with little more justification than that they 'seemed like a good idea at the time'. Atheoretical eclecticism is not an option for professionals. Corey (1996) calls it 'sloppy' and labels it the worst form of ill-discipline that provides an excuse for failing to understand the theories adequately and allows users merely to pick and choose elements of theories that support their preconceived notions. Without any overall rationale, it results in a recipe-like mindset that dictates, 'If students do this, teachers should do that', but ultimately will let you down as it cannot predict all student behaviours and will not help to suggest alternative responses for those occasions when your methods fail (Young 1992).

The next form, *technical* eclecticism, utilises one organising theory and borrows in some supplementary methods from other theories. It is deceptive in that it appears to make it possible to parcel together a few strategies but, if their underlying philosophies are incongruent, the various practices will in turn contradict and undermine each other, resulting in confusion for both your students and yourself.

The third and highest form of eclecticism is *synthetic*, which is an attempt to synthesise or integrate compatible approaches, resulting in a more complex and comprehensive blend than any of the original theories alone. To avoid the traps of the lower forms of eclecticism, I recommend blending only those methods that share similar philosophies, rationale and goals. Referring to Figure 1.2 (see p. 19), a useful guide would be to blend only those approaches that fall within the same category (authoritarian, mixed or egalitarian) or from one category to the right or left. Such an integrated synthesis would preserve the integrity of the original theories' philosophy, while leaving you free to employ a range of useful approaches rather than just those contained in the original theories. The hybrid will not create contradiction and confusion as long as the original philosophical principles have been preserved.

At the same time, it pays to be cautious about adopting an inflexible belief system that we come to regard as a higher form of truth rather than just one possible interpretation of reality (Fisch et al. 1982). A reified theory can bias our observations: we become subject to the theory, instead of using it as a tool for understanding our subject. A useful theory, then, is one that provides focus and direction without blinding us to other issues and to the individuality of each case (Young 1992).

Effectiveness

A further criterion for judging the theories is their effectiveness. All theories of discipline claim that they *work,* which usually means that a disruption ends. Achieving this is, of course, essential—but effectiveness entails more than this alone. For methods to be effective, they must also achieve the following outcomes.

- Disruptions in general need to be prevented from occurring.
- The particular disruption should be less likely in future to recur.
- Individuals should learn something positive during the process of correction, such as how to solve interpersonal disputes or regulate their emotions—not how to avoid detection, to tell lies to get out of trouble, to deny responsibility or to blame someone else.
- There must be no unintended emotional side-effects on the child, such as feeling intimidated or fearful, or being seen by peers as troublesome and therefore as someone to avoid or victimise.
- Surrounding children must continue to feel safe about how *they* would be treated if in future they were to make a mistake.
- Adults have to feel that they are abiding by their principles and doing a good job as teachers.
- The adult–child relationship must suffer no harm as a result of how the present disruption was handled. Children should be equally willing to interact with you after a corrective intervention, not least because you can have no influence on them if they avoid you.
- The methods that we use must in themselves convey our values, such as respect (for both students and teachers) and fairness of treatment (Rogers 2002).

As you read about the theories of discipline to be covered in the coming chapters, you will see that their goals span a range from managerial to educational aims.

- *Order.* The first goal of the various approaches to school discipline is to establish, maintain and reinstate order in an effort to create an environment in which learning is not only possible but probable. However, although order is necessary, it is not sufficient to promote high achievement (Doyle 1986). It can only ever be a means to an end, rather than an end in itself.
- *Compliance or obedience.* Like the quest for order, the aim that children obey adults is an instrumental goal, rather than an end in itself, although some advocates of the authoritarian approaches value compliance as a virtue (as an end in itself), equating it with responsibility. However, acting responsibly requires thought; compliance does not.
- *Self-discipline.* The aim of teaching students self-discipline is so they will be able to conduct themselves ethically, even when unsupervised. Self-discipline is professed

by all theories but has two different meanings, depending on their philosophical framework. The authoritarian theories regard self-discipline as teaching children to 'internalise' or learn the behaviours that we expect of them, whereas humanists aim to teach students to construct their own values and behave according to those even without adult surveillance (Kohn 1996a). This is termed *autonomous ethics*, in contrast to *internalised compliance*.

- *Emotional regulation.* Some of the theories covered in this text aim to teach students to express their feelings appropriately, without getting themselves distressed or upsetting surrounding people (Gartrell 2003). This protects surrounding individuals from their outbursts but, more importantly, teaches young people that they can recover from setbacks and regain their emotional balance (Porter 2003, 2006). This is the essence of resilience.
- *Cooperation.* In recognition that humans are a herding species and thus live and work in groups, a goal of all the theories of discipline is to teach children to cooperate with others. Although this goal is shared by all the theories, humanism extends the notion of cooperation by recognising that it must be mutual between students and teachers and must broaden beyond the here and now to balancing individual needs with those of communities (Goodman 1992).
- *Self-efficacy.* A final potential goal is to teach children that they are potent human beings who can make a difference to how they feel and behave by staying in charge of how they think.

Obviously, those theories supplying evidence that they achieve more comprehensive goals would be judged to be more effective than those that limit themselves to achieving compliance only.

Ethics

Effectiveness is not the only criterion by which we must judge the merits of disciplinary measures: our responses to children's disruptions also have to be ethical. As Walker et al. (2004: 15) observe:

> Any intervention can be misused and abused if the person using it lacks an ethical system of personal and professional values. Practitioners must never forget that knowledge is power and that with power comes the responsibility to apply that power for the benefit of all persons.

BOX 1.2 GOALS OF EACH THEORY OF DISCIPLINE

Assertive discipline
· order
· compliance/obedience

Applied behaviour analysis
· order
· compliance to external controls

Cognitive-behaviourism
· order
· self-discipline: internalised compliance

Neo-Adlerian theory
· order
· self-discipline: internalised compliance
· cooperation

Humanism
· self-discipline: autonomous ethics
· emotional regulation
· cooperation
· self-efficacy

Solution-focused approach
· self-discipline: autonomous ethics
· emotional regulation
· cooperation
· self-efficacy

As already flagged here, the main ethical distinction between the theories is their stance about adults' use of power over young people. This underpins the fundamental ethical principle that teachers must do what is right, just and good, rather than what is merely expedient, convenient or practical (Katz 1995). This generic value gives rise to some specific ethical guidelines. The first of these is *promoting the good of others*. This principle implies that, when trying to correct disruptive behaviour, any measures used must be aimed at improving the quality of life of the young people themselves.

The second principle is that you must *do no harm*. Given children's lack of power to advocate on their own behalf, you must use your influence over them in their best interests (Australian Early Childhood Association 1991). This means that you will engage only in practices that are respectful of, and provide security for, children and in no way 'degrade, endanger, exploit, intimidate, or harm them psychologically or physically' (AECA 1991: 4). You must avoid punitive, humiliating or frightening disciplinary strategies and should not place unnecessary restrictions on children—that is, apply controls for any reason other than safety (Doherty-Derkowski 1995; National Association for the Education of Young Children 1983).

The third principle is that everyone deserves *justice*—which means giving all children and families equal and fair treatment. Although this principle is usually applied with reference to characteristics such as culture, gender, religion and so on, it also applies to students with disruptive behaviour.

A fourth ethical principle requires that any behavioural intervention be delivered competently by staff with adequate training, experience and supervision. To abide by this principle, you will need not only to be fully informed of a range of management options but also to be aware of what you do *not* know—that is, to recognise your own limitations and refer students to specialists if you are not equipped to deal with their difficulties.

BOX 1.3 SELF-QUESTIONNAIRE
- As a child, how were you expected to behave?
- What happened when you did not meet those expectations?
- What behaviour do you now expect of the children with whom you live or work?
- What are your responses to children who do not meet those expectations?
- Do your expectations and responses differ for academic versus behavioural mistakes?
- Do you recall any times when as a child you, a sibling or classmate were reprimanded or otherwise punished unfairly?
- How many decades ago was that? What does the longevity of your memory about that incident tell you about how children feel about injustices?
- How could the injustice have been prevented? For example, were you asked for your side of the story? If you had been, would that have altered the adult's response and/or your feelings about it?
- How did the adult's response on that occasion subsequently affect your relationship with him or her? If the incident happened at school, did the way the adult responded have any influence on your attitude towards school itself?

Conclusion

Responding to student disruptions is clearly a practical matter of employing practices that both work and are ethically defensible. Judging this requires engagement with some deep questions concerning your beliefs about young people and how they learn, your goals of discipline, your beliefs about the causes of disruptive behaviour, and how much autonomy you trust students to exercise. Furthermore, your disciplinary measures cannot be divorced from your educational goals, as promoting student learning is, after all, the purpose of discipline (Manke 1997).

As someone who has solved many problems so far in your personal and professional life, you deserve better than being sold the latest fad for classroom management. By gaining knowledge of a range of theories, you will be enabled to decide on a framework that you can apply intelligently, wisely and coherently to guide your own practice. This allows you to break free from the role of a technocrat who employs methods that have been imposed on you to attain the 'pinnacle of professional competence' (Larrivee 2005: 11), where you not only know what to do, but why.

Discussion questions

1   What are your own goals for maintaining discipline in a class?
2   Which behaviours are a high priority for you to correct?
3   Think about the approaches you presently use or are familiar with for responding to students' disruptive behaviour. Which ones are most effective at meeting the goals that you specified when answering question 1? Which practices seem ineffective?
4   With which of the theories mentioned in this chapter are you already familiar? Which do you use, and which have you (so far) found unattractive? How do your personal beliefs influence your preferences?
5   If you are already teaching, do you have either a formal or informal discipline plan to guide you in responding to students' behaviour? If you have been teaching for some years, how have this plan, your beliefs, ideas and practices evolved over time?

ASSERTIVE DISCIPLINE

Proactive teachers don't wait for poor behavior to occur before developing a plan of action. They determine ahead of time the corrective actions they will use when students are disruptive. They also plan how to positively support students for appropriate behavior. Finally, they teach their students how they expect them to behave.

Canter & Canter (2001: 16)

KEY POINTS

- The assertive teacher has a right and a duty to enforce order, so that teaching and learning can be accomplished.
- To encourage students' cooperation, you will develop warm relationships with them.
- To maximise students' observance of rules, you will teach these to them.
- Positive recognition and incentives build cooperation.
- You will apply graded consequences for serious or repeated disruptions.

Introduction

In their earlier works, Canter and Canter (1976) highlighted the importance of teachers being assertive and setting limits, so that discipline becomes proactive rather than reactive. They defined assertiveness not only in terms of expressing disapproval, but also of communicating your pleasure clearly to students when they are behaving appropriately. This style was contrasted with that of timid teachers, who do not have their needs met because they do not state what they need clearly, or do not back up their words with action (Canter & Canter 1976). As a result, students feel frustrated, manipulated and angry, while timid teachers feel frustrated, inadequate and hostile towards students whom they 'cannot handle'. A second contrast is with hostile or aggressive teachers who have their own needs met, but at the expense of students' self-esteem—by putting students down, issuing threats or administering harsh consequences. Although students will comply in these circumstances, they do so only out of fear and, meanwhile, teachers feel guilty.

In their later writings, however, this assertive style is implied rather than being described explicitly. Yet the title remains for their theory, implying that the distinction still holds.

Philosophical assumptions

Lee and Marlene Canter (2001) define successful classrooms as those that are under firm teacher control. The clear message of this approach is that the classroom belongs to the teacher: it is *your* classroom (not the students'). You have an unquestioned right to determine expectations and consequences for your students. As Wolfgang et al. (1999: 77) state: 'The teacher is the adult and knows what is acceptable and unacceptable behaviour'. This external control is intended to teach students how to exercise control over themselves, although no specific management approaches are recommended for transferring control back to students. Therefore, this theory is placed at the authoritarian end of the continuum in Figure 1.2 (see p. 19).

Nature of childhood

This approach rests on the claim that children want and need clear limits on their behaviour, so that they know what they have to do to be successful and feel good when their achievements are acknowledged. They will respect the fair treatment that they receive from you and value the supportive feedback that they receive for attaining your standards (Canter & Canter 1976, 2001). Meanwhile, you benefit by having your needs met and achieving job satisfaction from discharging your professional duties well.

Reasons for disruptive behaviour

Canter and Canter (2001) assert that students no longer respect teachers and education because their homes lack stability, support and discipline. Consequently, many young people lack the self-esteem and impulse control needed to choose responsible behaviour.

Resulting disruptions in schools persist when teachers are too timid (by pleading or issuing threats that they do not follow through) or when they respond with hostility.

Goal of discipline

The assertive discipline approach upholds that, as a teacher, you have both a right and a responsibility to establish order in classrooms—that is, to maintain an effective and efficient learning environment through teaching obedience to authority. The goal of student compliance or obedience is to provide psychological safety, to protect children from performing behaviour that they would regret later, and to allow individuals to build on their positive skills. To achieve this, your job is to determine classroom rules and deliver positive consequences for compliant behaviour and negative consequences for rule violations.

Prevention of behavioural problems

You will prevent classroom behavioural problems by establishing and maintaining order. To that end, as an assertive teacher, you would ensure, first, that your teaching is of high quality. A good curriculum is necessary for maintaining order. You will establish order by your assertive demeanour and maintain that order through your lesson design and presentation, by giving supportive feedback and by offering incentives for diligence and excellence (Canter & Canter 1992).

Second, your relationships with students, while warm, will confirm your authority within the classroom. Warm, positive relationships in the classroom allow you to have an influence on students. Canter and Canter (2001: 21) advise that:

> your personal interest in your students' success may be the most important ingredient of your classroom management plan. Effective behavior management is defined by a balance between structure (rules and limits) and a genuine effort to reach out and establish cooperative relationships.

When you respect students, they will respect your values, rules and opinions. You will need to get to know students and their interests, encourage them to get to know each other, greet students by name daily, have fun together, give individuals a few special minutes, make home visits by arrangement and always help students to do their work—without, however, intensifying their dependence or generating delays for others while you give prolonged help.

The classroom discipline plan

The purpose of a classroom discipline plan is to avoid the need for you to make hasty, ill-considered or emotionally charged responses to students' disruptions, resulting in inconsistent or arbitrary reactions (Canter & Canter 2001). A plan also enables you to secure support from parents and school administrators. It will consist of the three elements of rules, supportive feedback and corrective actions for noncompliance.

Establish rules

The teacher determines how he or she expects students to behave and expresses these as rules. Little (2003) recommends rules that ensure safety and courtesy, while Canter and Canter (2001) suggest these general rules:

- follow directions;
- keep hands, feet and objects to yourself;
- use appropriate language—that is, no put-downs, teasing, name calling or swearing;
- for high school students, be in your seat when the bell rings.

The advantage of these rules is that they are immediate, observable, and apply throughout all classroom sessions. This is in contrast to goals (such as being courteous or respectful) that are long term, open to interpretation and are not readily observable. Students can contribute to determining rules, although you will need to guide them in not making their expectations too strict.

As well as these general rules, you are advised to institute rules for various academic activities (independent work, cooperative work, whole-group discussion, silent reading, taking tests, giving oral reports and so on) and for a range of procedures, including walking to, entering and leaving the classroom, beginning the day, passing out or collecting materials, making transitions between activities, getting and putting away equipment and moving between areas of the school. You will also need policies for the likes of using the pencil sharpener, going to the toilet, care of the work space, use of computers, assigning homework and dealing with interruptions (Canter & Canter 2001). Acceptable levels of noise and movement also need to be determined.

Deliver supportive feedback

Supportive feedback is driven by the slogan 'Catch them being good'. Canter and Canter (2001: 41) define feedback as 'the sincere and meaningful attention you give a student for behaving according to your expectations'. These educators contend that, by recognising students when they conform to your standards, you will motivate them to repeat appropriate behaviour. In turn, this will reduce disruptive behaviour, increase students' self-esteem and therefore result in improved effort, create a positive environment for the class and build positive relationships between you and each student. Supportive feedback is especially crucial during the first days of working with a class, but remains a high priority all year as it conveys the message that the way to gain your attention is to obey rather than to disrupt.

The first form of supportive feedback for individuals is verbal recognition or praise. This must be simple, direct, personal, genuine, specific and descriptive. Other ways to recognise observance of the rules include positive notes or phone calls to parents, giving students awards, bestowing special privileges and tangible rewards. Older students may be embarrassed by public positive recognition, so instead it can be delivered in private, perhaps followed with a statement such as 'You should be proud of yourself'.

When an individual is not following your directives, your supportive feedback can focus on those who are, using what Canter and Canter term *behavioural narration*. This involves identifying at least two students who are complying and naming both them and their appropriate behaviour. The aim of this method is to reinforce those who are complying, and indirectly remind others to do the same. For older students (who might resist being named as a 'goodie-goodie'), Canter and Canter advise awarding extra points to the whole class for individuals' compliance, so that the whole group benefits.

Once students are on task, you must continue to offer supportive feedback to reinforce this. Verbal recognition will be your main tool, involving naming the target child and offering sincere and specific praise that describes the appropriate behaviour. With younger children, you can write on the board the names of those who meet expectations, perhaps in a quest to see how many names can be accumulated.

As well as delivering individual rewards, the whole class can be rewarded with special privileges or free time. The aim of instituting these is to capitalise on peer pressure to correct a class-wide behavioural problem, to increase class unity and to create a feeling of belonging (Little 2003). Awarding bonus points to a whole group can avoid students' public embarrassment at individual recognition. These incentives are based on the principle that students will be more willing to complete something distasteful when doing so grants them access to something they like. When an individual's constant disruptions penalise the whole group, that young person can be placed on a personal incentive program with more frequent rewards and the team given points when he or she reaches an interim goal (Wolfgang et al. 1999).

The criteria and time frame for earning a reward need to be reasonable and realistic for the students' ages (Canter & Canter 2001). In the early years of primary school when, being young, the children will need more immediate reinforcement, the reward should be delivered within one day; children in middle and later primary classes (from Grade 3 onwards) can delay gratification for longer, in which case the reward can be earned over a time frame of two days to a week; whereas, by high school, the incentive can be offered up to two weeks in advance.

In the meantime, you will need to check that the reward has been earned by keeping score of the students' performances. For this task, you could use the blackboard or whiteboard at the front of the room, marbles in a jar, or a marker on a chart. Canter and Canter (2001) advise not to impose fines or deduct points for misbehaviour.

Administer corrective measures

The third component of your disciplinary plan (after establishing rules and providing supportive feedback) will be how to correct disruptive behaviour. On the grounds that consequences are imposed in the real world and classrooms should not be an exception, corrective discipline entails the use of consequences. Canter and Canter (2001) contend that these are not punishments (which are something teachers *do* to students) but are a natural outcome of students' behavioural choices. Corrective responses must be something that students do not like, without being embarrassing or physically or psychologically harmful to them.

Corrective actions are progressive, being graded from a mild response to more firm corrections. You can respond to a first infraction with a reminder or request to desist (Wolfgang et al. 1999). This will be delivered after moving in close to a disruptive student, because directives delivered from across the room will distract those who are on-task. This also avoids having the disruptive student challenge your authority to gain status with peers and your response exciting peer sympathy for the student even though they disapprove of his or her behaviour (Wolfgang et al. 1999).

The second and third infractions earn a consequence. Possible consequences include enforced practice of appropriate behaviour, a change of seating (e.g. being seated alone or moving a disruptive student close to you), being sent to the back of a line, being kept in at breaks, the imposition of additional work or extra time in class, removal from an activity (time out) and loss of points under a group incentive system (Canter & Canter 2001; Little 2003). For the fourth infraction on the same day (in primary school) or in the same lesson (in secondary school), you would contact the parents or have the student ring them. The final consequence (for the fifth violation) is being sent to the principal, with this having been planned in advance so that you know what support you will receive from the principal. For severe infractions such as aggression, you should bypass this hierarchy and instead send the student immediately to the principal. This is called the 'severe clause' (Canter & Canter 2001; Wolfgang et al. 1999).

Guidelines for using corrective measures

Consequences do not have to be severe, as it is their inevitability, not their severity, that has an impact (Canter & Canter 2001). The two basic principles are that, first, consequences must be delivered in a calm, matter-of-fact manner, whereby you do not threaten but only remind students about the consequences if they continue to behave inappropriately. Second, chosen sanctions cannot add to your workload and must be cost effective, as the process of management cannot become more important than teaching. The remaining guidelines are:

- To avoid humiliation of students, you should keep track of infractions on a clipboard rather than on the more public class board (Canter & Canter 2001).
- Corrective actions should not roll over into the next day. Each student must start each new day with a clean slate.
- Corrective actions must be applied consistently—that is, each and every time that students disrupt.
- You must follow a consequence with positive recognition when students return to appropriate behaviour.
- Misbehaviour that occurs outside the classroom comes under the school-wide discipline plan, which imposes its own sanctions. These are separate from your classroom system, with consequences imposed elsewhere not affecting the progression of corrective actions within the class.

Students will need an 'escape mechanism' that allows them to tell their story later, but not while a lesson is in progress. This may mean that you allow them to write down what they want to say, which you can discuss together at a later time.

Nondisruptive off-task behaviour

Even when they are not interfering with others, when students are not paying attention you cannot ignore this, as doing so would be tantamount to saying that it is all right in your class for students to learn nothing (Canter & Canter 2001). Their resulting lack of success would hurt students, while their off-task behaviour might grow into a disruption that interrupts teaching and learning.

However, imposing an immediate penalty is not the answer, as it will alienate students rather than return them to the task. Therefore, you should calmly redirect inattentive students back to the task. This can be done through directing a disapproving look towards the student, moving in close to him or her, naming the student while continuing with teaching, or praising those nearby students who *are* on-task. Once the student is back on-task, you should praise this. If students need repeated reminders to remain on-task, you would move up your hierarchy of sanctions and implement a corrective action.

Disruptive behaviour

While your class-wide plan is designed to apply to all students, on occasions modifications will be necessary for individuals whose behaviour is not improving. When students continually disrupt, move in close to them physically and remind them of the corrective actions that they have received so far and what will be the consequence if they continue to disrupt, expressing your concern that you want to protect them from that (Canter & Canter 2001). From a stance of empathy and concern, communicate that you are prepared to do whatever it takes to help the student succeed, while maintaining your firm resolve that the disruptions must cease. With older students, this conversation might be best conducted out of the classroom away from the gaze of their peers, as adolescents might stand up to the teacher in an effort not to lose face with their peers (Wolfgang et al. 1999).

If they defy your authority verbally or nonverbally, at the time be assertive (without getting angry) by repeating what you want them to do. If they have a reasonable grievance, listen and change what you are asking of them, but otherwise express understanding of their anger, then repeat the directive. When students are persistently disruptive, you will need to take a step back as well, making sure to see the value in them personally even when you disapprove of their behaviour. You will need to build trusting relationships with them, showing interest in them by means such as greeting them as they enter the classroom, initiating conversations with them about their lives and interests, giving supportive feedback for compliance, or calling them at home after a difficult day to talk through what went wrong and how you can jointly resolve the problem.

The next step is to collaborate with the student to develop an individualised behaviour plan. You can begin by asking the student what the problem is, then determine how you can help so that the behaviour improves and, finally, agree on a course of action. This will include both supportive feedback and corrective actions (consequences) for infractions. As always, these must be applied consistently and you must emphasise that they are not imposed by you, but that students choose them with their decision to misbehave. This teaches them to be accountable for their actions. Little (2003) advises that punishments be logically related to the misdemeanour and that if any one does not diminish the behavioural difficulty, another must be tried.

Teach the plan to students

Just as you teach academic subjects, using teaching techniques and aids that work for you, so too you will teach your discipline plan to your students, explaining the rules and reasons for them, the supportive feedback that you will be using and the corrective actions and reasons for these, while checking for understanding of each element. Discussion and role play can help young children to learn the rules (Little 2003), while older students have experienced rules already and therefore will need only a brief outline of each rule and its rationale. The purpose of explicit teaching is to empower students to abide by your expectations.

Obtain support from the school administration

No teacher can work successfully with each and every student; sometimes, support from the school administration is necessary. To give you assurance of this support, before you implement any disciplinary plan, you will need your principal to sign off on it. Then, should your attempts at resolving ongoing behavioural difficulties fail, your principal will need to be willing to counsel students and their parents, institute in-school suspensions and require parents to spend time in the class observing their son's or daughter's behaviour. More important even than these functions, however, is the principal's role of rewarding students when sent to him or her for recognition of improvements in their behaviour (Canter & Canter 2001).

If within-school support still does not resolve the disruptions, the principal may need to refer the family to social agencies; if the behaviour is criminal, the police and criminal justice system will need to be invoked.

Obtain support from parents

The first step for gaining parenting backing is to inform parents of your classroom discipline plan at the beginning of the school year and to make routine and positive contact through letters or phone calls with all parents (Canter & Canter 2001). Sending students' work home can also promote contact with their parents.

Once a behavioural problem arises, you will attempt to handle it yourself. If you ask too early for parents' or administrators' support, students will not have been given enough opportunity to overcome the problem themselves. In the meantime, you will document the steps that you have taken. Subsequently, you should contact parents at the first sign of the sort of difficulty that you would like to know about if you were the child's parent (Canter & Canter 2001). Such difficulties include violence, extreme emotional distress or repeated failure to complete work. When calling parents, you would open with a statement of concern for their child's interests, describe the behaviour that you believe disadvantages the child, outline what action you have taken so far, listen to the parents' view of the problem and suggestions for handling it, agree on what you will each do to solve it, and arrange for a follow-up call. Throughout, you should express confidence that the behaviour can be improved.

Summary

Canter and Canter (2001) detail a discipline plan that requires you to set limits on students' behaviour, so that order is maintained and teaching and learning can occur. You are advised to be assertive both in word and manner, while being warm and supportive with students. You must teach rules and reward compliance with personal and formal recognition and incentives.

If disruptive behaviour occurs you must enforce the limits, invoking backup sanctions as necessary. To help you tailor the plan to suit individual needs, you can counsel students (outside class time). You are empowered to seek support from parents and the school administration when faced with intractable disciplinary problems. Finally, Canter and Canter (1992) caution you to use the discipline plan as a tool rather than as a law, and to adjust it to individual students' circumstances as required.

Interim critique

This approach is not a comprehensive theory. It draws no links between classroom discipline and research into educational theory or the psychological needs of children. This approach's theoretical base is applied behaviour analysis (see Chapter 3), without the rigour. It overlooks the effects of school culture and practices on student behaviour. Furthermore, its assumptions cannot be tested. Probably for this reason, it attracts little research. The only reports of its effectiveness come from practitioners' accounts of its effects on classroom compliance, but these reports overlook potential side-effects on targeted children, classmates and on teachers themselves.

To this and other reviewers (e.g. Gartrell 1987a), the most troubling of its assumptions is its political stance. This takes for granted the teacher's right to impose the curriculum and rules on young people. The teacher's rights override those of the other 30 (young) people in the class, with the classroom defined as belonging to the teacher—never to students—with terms such as 'To successfully manage *your* classroom ...' (Canter &

Canter 2001: 33), '*your* classroom rules' (2001: 61) and so on. This reflects a basic distrust of children, as well as a failure to examine equity principles.

Second, in communication theory, the right to be assertive is mutual: one person's right to assert his or her needs guarantees the other's equal right to do the same. This reciprocity distinguishes assertiveness from aggression. Despite its title, this approach does not observe this principle.

Third, in considering only children's 'need' for limits, the approach misconstrues limits as being rules, when research clearly distinguishes these and finds that, in fact, children need structure, which is not the same thing (Grolnick 2003). Meanwhile, the core human need for autonomy is disregarded. Although assertive discipline advocates warm relationships with students, their experience of being under the control of someone else is unlikely to be received warmly by them which, in turn, will damage the student–teacher relationship and, according to humanists, give rise to further disruptiveness. Resulting behavioural difficulties *might* be suppressed by progressive sanctions, but cannot be cured by these. Meanwhile, just as students can be restricted by controlling discipline, teachers too are constrained by its methods, rendering the teacher a technocrat who dispenses predetermined consequences without the true professional's use of discretion (Curwin & Mendler 1988; Gartrell 1987a; Kohn 1996a).

CASE STUDY

Adam is seven. He has difficulty with reading, spelling and writing, although he enjoys and is capable at maths. During non-maths lessons he spends a considerable amount of time off-task, when he frequently disrupts the other students. This is worse in the afternoons than in the mornings.

He is in a composite class of six and seven year olds. He spends most of his play time with the younger children. Frequently, a pair including Adam is apprehended during play times doing such things as harassing passers-by from an out-of-bounds area of the playground that is close to the street, rifling through rubbish bins for food or cans to swap for other items with students, or engaging in fights in and around the toilets.

Adam seems bemused by the trouble he gets into, usually saying when challenged that he doesn't know why he behaves in these ways, that he couldn't remember that a given behaviour was against the rules, or that the other child was at fault for suggesting the activity.

Until a recent assessment, it was believed that Adam behaved as he did because of low academic ability. However, a battery of tests has shown his overall ability (IQ) to be average, with his maths skills in the high-normal range and his reading and spelling skills, while delayed, still within the lower range of normal limits. His teacher is now at a loss to find a new explanation for his behaviour.

Application of assertive discipline

In applying assertive discipline, you might take the following steps in response to Adam's behavioural difficulties.

Step 1: Adopt an assertive demeanour

You might start with realising that you have been nonassertive with Adam, sometimes virtually pleading with him to 'pull his socks up', but also at other times expressing some frustration at his behaviour and being punitive and almost hostile. Therefore, you will practise verbal assertion and make your body language convey more confidence, so that Adam learns that he has to take you seriously.

Step 2: Reduce Adam's dependence on supervision

You have been taking responsibility for Adam's behaviour by reminding him to bring required equipment to school or to do his homework, and by giving him excessive one-to-one guidance in class about his work. To teach Adam to work independently, you should give him only brief instructional help to convey to him that you are confident that he can work alone successfully.

Step 3: Foster a warm relationship

Your frustration and near-hostility to Adam will have harmed your relationship with him. Therefore, make some time to be alone with Adam to get to know him better and take an interest in what he enjoys. Until now, when Adam has worked appropriately, you have felt relieved that this has freed you to work with other students. From now on, increase your rate of positive recognitions of Adam's appropriate behaviour.

Step 4: Teach the rules

Adam clearly knows about the rules, but not how to observe them. In a class meeting, instruct all the students about what the rules are, why they are in place, how to abide by them, and the positive and negative consequences of infractions and the rationale for these. Give Adam and all students the opportunity to check their understanding of the rules and to role-play how to observe them.

Step 5: Distinguish between in-class and out-of-class infractions

Stop being responsible for infractions of the rules in the playground. This is the responsibility of the school as a whole, guided by its discipline policy. Meanwhile, in class, you will consistently enforce the limits that you taught the group in step 4.

Step 6: Use incentives
If Adam is just one of many disruptive students, set up a group incentive program. If Adam is the only student whose behaviour is seriously disruptive, establish an individual program, giving Adam the incentive of being allowed to spend time on a preferred activity.

Step 7: Invoke negative sanctions
If Adam disrupts repeatedly in the same day, invoke a series of consequences. You might begin with a request to desist then, for repeated misdemeanours, impose consequences such as time out from the class or staying in briefly during play breaks.

Step 8: Obtain support
If Adam displays numerous infractions on the same day, call his parents. Also, together with the principal, plan what you will do if Adam needs to be sent to the principal in the future. The two of you might decide that this final consequence will involve a conference with the principal, perhaps in conjunction with the parents.

Step 9: Revise the plan
If earlier steps prove unsuccessful, in consultation with Adam's parents and the principal, revise your responses to Adam's behaviour by refining, adapting or adding to the interventions that you have already tried. Monitor the plan and conduct follow-up meetings to discuss and reach agreement on any changes that might increase the plan's effectiveness.

Discussion questions

1   Do you agree with Canter and Canter's assertion that children *need* adults to exercise control over them?
2   Do you see any pitfalls in the assumption that external controls will teach children to exercise self-discipline?
3   If you are presently teaching, what forms of positive recognition do you routinely use, or which do you plan to use once you begin teaching? Are these intended for individuals or given to the class as a whole? How effective are they?
4   What do you think about the use of negative sanctions? Are they necessary? Effective? Practicable? Under what conditions would you apply negative sanctions?
5   Write your own case study. What responses would assertive discipline recommend for that student? What effect would the practices have on the student? On onlookers? On you?

Suggested further reading

Detailed description of assertive discipline

Canter, L. and Canter, M. 2001 *Assertive discipline: positive behavior management for today's classroom* Canter & Associates, Los Angeles, CA

Practical applications of Canter and Canter's ideas

Little, E. 2003 *Kids behaving badly: teacher strategies for classroom behaviour problems* Pearson Prentice Hall, Sydney

Wolfgang, C.H., Bennett, B.J. and Irvin, J.L. 1999 *Strategies for teaching self-discipline in the middle grades* Allyn & Bacon, Boston, MA

Website

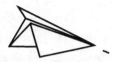

3 APPLIED BEHAVIOUR ANALYSIS

A major concern within the behavioural approach to teaching is with the identification of things and events which children find rewarding and to structure the teaching environment so as to make access to these rewards dependent upon behaviour which the teacher wants to encourage in his class.

Wheldall & Merrett (1984: 19)

KEY POINTS

- Behaviour is controlled by the response it receives (its consequence). Thus, if you want to increase the rate of a behaviour, you must follow it with a reinforcing consequence; whereas, if you want to reduce its rate, you must follow it with a punishing consequence.
- The environment (antecedents) can also make behaviours more or less likely to occur.
- Reinforcers and punishments vary in intrusiveness (which is the extent to which they interrupt teaching) and restrictiveness (the extent to which students are subjected to external control).

Introduction

The behaviourist philosophy underpinning this cluster of theories is the most well known of any to be covered in this book. Its three permutations share the philosophy of behaviourism, which maintains that all behaviour arises from environmental consequences rather than from hypothetical entities such as the mind or will (Gresham et al. 2001). The first variant, *applied behaviour analysis* (ABA), is the recent title for behaviour modification of which B.F. Skinner (1904–90) was the best-known proponent. Its basic tenet is that children learn to behave appropriately when adults reward them for desired behaviour and punish them for acting in ways of which we disapprove.

A recent refinement of ABA is known as *functional behaviour assessment* (FBA). It argues that applying general reinforcements and punishments to similar behaviours is less effective than adjusting the specific consequences at work with each behaviour (Ervin et al. 2001a; Myers & Holland 2000; Northup & Gulley 2001), although this is by no means proven (Nelson et al. 1999). Functional behavioural assessment involves detailed analysis of the particular conditions surrounding each behaviour, in recognition that the same outward behaviour—such as calling out in class—can be reinforced in different ways for different individuals. That is, the same behaviour can serve a variety of *functions*. Its related discipline, *functional behaviour analysis*, generates a range of potential hypotheses about the link between environmental events and the target behaviour, then systematically manipulates each in turn to prove which hypothesis is correct (Ervin et al. 2001b; Northup & Gulley 2001; Shriver et al. 2001). Given that such scientific experimentation is beyond the scope of most classroom teachers, its more simple counterpart will be discussed here.

A third variant is termed *positive behaviour support* (PBS), with differences from the other two alleged to be that PBS focuses more on individuals, their needs, preferences, values and requirement to be self-determining, has a greater emphasis on socially valid interventions, highlights prevention through environmental management, and has a central mission to improve the quality of life of individuals—that is, to bring about their desired living conditions (Wheeler & Richey 2005).

Philosophical assumptions

This cluster of theories is the second of those occupying the authoritarian position on the student–teacher status continuum shown in Figure 1.2 (see p. 19). Under this theory, teachers remain in control of students, manipulating their external environment to alter the probability that students will behave in certain ways. Nevertheless, in a slight softening of this authoritarian control, latest applications of ABA do consult students about their actions and the conditions that give rise to them.

Beliefs about childhood

As with all individuals, children are behaving beings. This means that their actions are governed by the same rules that apply to adults, which is to say that outside forces shape their actions.

Explanations for disruptive behaviour

All behaviours, appropriate or otherwise, begin randomly but subsequently persist because they are reinforced (or rewarded) more reliably and are easier to perform than alternative behaviours (Gresham et al. 2001). In other words, behaviours serve a 'function' of earning students something social (e.g. attention) or tangible that they want (which is termed *positive reinforcement*) or helping them to escape or avoid other people or to escape, avoid, delay or reduce aversive task demands (which is termed *negative reinforcement*) (Gresham et al. 2001; Macht 2005; Myers & Holland 2000).

Goal of discipline

According to behaviourism, the main purpose of discipline is the managerial goal of establishing, maintaining or reinstating order so that students can be successful at learning. It seeks to achieve this by teaching students to comply with outside controls. Educationally, behaviourism emphasises direct instruction on the grounds that, with a constructivist educational approach, teachers have too little control over what students are learning (Alberto & Troutman 2003). Indeed, so committed are these particular authors to a top-down teaching model that they even boast of not knowing what constructivism is.

Behaviourist principles

Behaviour can be of two types: reflexes, such as eye-blinking (which are termed *respondent* behaviours); and all other behaviours (termed *operant* behaviours) which are voluntary. The focus in schools, of course, is the latter. Whether these voluntary behaviours are new skills that you are asking students to learn, skills that you want them to display more often, or behaviours that you would like to see decreased, your intervention will be built on the following core behaviourist principles.

Principle 1: Verifiability

Behaviourists are interested only in descriptions of behaviour that can be verified through observation. This principle is in contrast with what they regard to be circular definitions of problems, whereby children are said to behave poorly because they have an emotional and behavioural disturbance and are diagnosed with this condition because they behave poorly. Behaviourists focus only on what events occur, not in generating such untestable 'explanatory fictions' (Alberto & Troutman 2003: 23).

Principle 2: Behaviour is controlled by its consequences

All voluntary behaviour (as distinct from reflexes) is lawful, which means that there is an orderly or predictable relationship between actions and their consequences (Alberto & Troutman 2003). This determinist view of human behaviour states that positive consequences will *reinforce* behaviour (result in its increase) and negative consequences will *punish* (result in a decrease in the behaviour). When consequences have no (or a *neutral)* effect, these are merely *subsequent events* (Kerr & Nelson 2006). It is important to highlight here that reinforcement and punishment are defined by their *effect* on a behaviour whereas the more colloquial terms, 'rewards' and 'punishers', are *things* that, despite the intent of their administrator, may or may not alter the rates of behaviour. Thus, if consequences do not have the desired effect in terms of changing behavioural rates this does not mean that reinforcement and punishment do not work, but merely that what adults *thought* would be rewarding or punitive are not for this particular student in this setting at this time (Maag 2001). Therefore, the key to effectiveness is to individualise your intervention for each student.

Principle 3: Contingency

The principle of contingency states that consequences must be delivered if, and only if, students display target behaviours. You must deliver the consequence only when the behaviour occurs and not when the behaviour is not displayed.

Principle 4: Least intrusive and restrictive methods

A key principle of ABA is that, while you must use effective methods, those you select must be the least intrusive and restrictive methods available. Intrusiveness (or invasiveness) is the extent to which interventions interrupt the educational process, while restrictiveness refers to how much external control is imposed on students (Kerr & Nelson 2006).

The principle of least restrictive treatment states that methods must curtail individuals' freedom no more than necessary to achieve desired behavioural changes (McDonnell 1993). Thus, your first priority must be to reduce the causes of disruptive behaviour by changing the antecedents that occasion it and by making natural conditions so highly reinforcing that students are motivated to behave appropriately (McDonnell 1993). Then, if a contrived intervention becomes necessary, reinforcement must be the first measure employed, with more restrictive methods applied only when it has failed (McDonnell 1993; Kerr & Nelson 2006). Punishment should be reserved only for those behaviours—such as self-abuse—that cannot be suppressed in other ways and must always be accompanied by positive reinforcement to strengthen alternative, desired behaviours.

Applying behaviourist principles to student behaviours

Behaviourist interventions begin by defining, in observable and measurable terms, the behaviour whose frequency needs to be increased or decreased. This is termed the *target behaviour*. Ethics demand that target behaviours be high-priority actions, which are those that violate someone's rights, rather than acts that are merely inconvenient to others (O'Leary 1972). Interventions must teach skills that will enhance students' quality of life (Wheeler & Richey 2005).

Having identified which behaviour needs altering, you then define, in positive terms, what modified form it will take as a result of successful intervention. This is called the *terminal behaviour*. The advice in formulating terminal behaviours or goals is to think small, keeping in mind that students with behavioural challenges cannot be expected to behave perfectly, nor better than children without difficulties (Maag 2001).

Subsequently, intervention occurs in four phases: assessment, altering the conditions where undesirable behaviour occurs, increasing the frequency of desired behaviours and finally, if necessary, decreasing undesired acts. These elements can be written into a behavioural contract that is negotiated with students. This will specify which behaviours you require, what rewards will be delivered for success and which punishments will be administered for noncompliance, with a final clause giving students a right to renegotiate this agreement and to correct failure.

Phase 1: Assessment

To establish how often a behaviour occurs, under what conditions, and what response it engenders, you will need systematically to observe and record the antecedent conditions and consequences that surround the behaviour. Functional behavioural assessment combines direct observation with interview data and a review of school records to arrive at a judgment of which specific reinforcers (positive or negative) are maintaining any given behaviour (Gresham et al. 2001).

Depending on the type of target behaviour, when observing and recording, you can focus on any or a combination of its following characteristics (Gresham et al. 2001; Rogers 2003):

- the *frequency* of the behaviour—the number of times it occurs;
- the *rate* of the behaviour—the number of times the behaviour occurs within a specified time period;
- the *interresponse time*—the amount of time that elapses between instances of the target behaviour;
- the *duration* of each instance of the behaviour;
- the *generality* of a behaviour—whether it occurs only in certain settings or more generally across many settings and with different teachers;
- the *intensity* or *severity* of disruptions;
- the *durability* of the problem—how long the student has been displaying the undesired behaviour;
- the *accuracy* of a behaviour—for example, the number of items a student gets correct on a series of tests over time;
- the *latency* of the behaviour—the amount of time it takes for a student to begin a task once instructed.

You can record every instance of the behaviour, which is termed *frequency* or *event recording*. Another method is *interval recording*, in which you divide an observation period into intervals and note whether the behaviour did or did not occur during, throughout, or at the end of each interval. Later intervention success is demonstrated when an undesired behaviour occurs in fewer and fewer intervals. The observation method that you choose will depend on the type of target behaviour, the context in which it is occurring, and how much time you have available for making observations.

Having observed the antecedent–behaviour–consequence (ABC) sequence, you would collate your results, perhaps in a graph or by performing the following calculation (Sterling-Turner et al. 2001: 215):

$$\frac{\text{number of target behaviours that are followed by a specific consequence}}{\text{total number of target behaviours}}$$

You would then use this information to generate a hypothesis about which type of positive or negative reinforcers are maintaining the behaviour.

Observation is also employed subsequently to evaluate whether an intervention is working. This data collection is essential because intuitive judgments about improvement or lack thereof may be inaccurate owing to discouragement or biased perceptions.

Phase 2: Adjust antecedents

The conditions under which a behaviour occurs are known as its *antecedents*. The three behaviourist traditions diverge a little with respect to consideration of antecedents: ABA takes stock of only the immediately preceding events; positive behaviour support (PBS) takes a wider view of potential triggers for behaviours; whereas functional behavioural assessment (FBA) places greater emphasis on the consequences of behaviours, as it contends that antecedents are important only inasmuch as they determine students' access to consequences (Gresham et al. 2001).

Identification of the antecedents that are salient for a given behaviour may be suggested by affirmative answers to any of the following questions (Bailey & Pyles 1989; Macht 2005; van Houten et al. 1988; Wheeler & Richey 2005).

- Are there any academic or nonacademic activities during which the behaviour *seldom* occurs?
- Are there any activities during which the behaviour *frequently* occurs?
- Do particular *routines* occasion disruptions?
- Does the behaviour occur at certain *times* of the day?
- Does the behaviour occur only with certain *people*?
- Could the behaviour be related to a *skills deficit*?
- Has a change in behaviour coincided with a *significant event* in the life of the student?
- Could the behaviour be a result of a *medical condition* or any form of physical discomfort or deprivation (e.g. hunger) or side-effects of medication?
- Does the behaviour occur as part of a *chain of behaviours*?
- Does the behaviour occur as a result of having another *ongoing behaviour terminated*?
- Does the behaviour allow the student to *gain attention*? If so, this may imply that there is insufficient attention in the normal setting.
- Does the behaviour have other *social pay-offs*?
- Does the behaviour allow students to *escape* learning? If so, some aspect of the curricular content or teaching process is aversive to them.

Adjustments to the environment can be suggested by noting when the behaviour is least prevalent and analysing which conditions make that possible. The next step is to put those environmental features in place more often and in more settings (Macht 2005).

Positive behaviour support upholds that, given that behaviours occur within specific contexts, it is not productive to blame disruptions on individual students and, in turn, to try to change them: instead, you need to adjust the contexts (Ervin et al. 2001a; Macht 2005; Wehmeyer et al. 2004). Environmental manipulations will include establishing a comfortable working environment, with adequate space and materials. Instructional changes may encompass offering an effective instructional program that maximises student engagement; altering schedules so that demanding tasks are not allocated late in the day; instituting breaks; interspersing easy with difficult tasks; reducing task difficulty or the duration of tasks; or changing the mode for student performances. Teaching and learning processes span the use of a high level of natural reinforcers, particularly positive attention; changing the size and composition of groups; expanding students' control and choices; building their self-esteem; and improving teachers' relationships with disruptive students (Gresham et al. 2001; Kamps 2002; Kerr & Nelson 2006; Wheeler & Richey 2005). Adjusting these elements is likely to avoid the need to intervene directly with individual students, has a better chance of preventing disruptions and thus is more humane than allowing students to get into trouble unnecessarily and makes it more likely that behavioural gains will be maintained (Bailey & Pyles 1989).

Phase 3: Increase reinforcement for desired behaviours

Whenever a student acts disruptively, it will be crucial to teach positive replacement behaviours (Wheeler & Richey 2005). However, the necessary skills must be within their repertoire. Therefore, if they lack certain abilities, you will need to teach these by *modelling* (that is, demonstrating) a behaviour and rewarding students for performing it, or giving *prompts* to help students complete a task, then gradually withdrawing these (in a process called *fading*) until students can complete the task alone. A familiar example of this process is where a teacher writes a letter of the alphabet for a child to trace over, then guides the child's tracings with only dashes, then with dots, until the child is able to write the letter without any visual prompts at all (Axelrod 1977). A third method is called *shaping*, which involves reinforcing less than optimal task performances, then requiring successive small improvements (or 'successive approximations') until students are performing the skill at a desirable level (Walker et al. 2004).

When students cannot complete a task that comprises many steps, you can break it down or *task analyse* it into a series of small steps that they can achieve serially. With *forward chaining*, you reinforce students for completing the first step successfully, then for completing the first two, then the first three, and so on until they have learnt the complete task. But for some tasks (such as tying shoelaces), the first step might seem irrelevant or out of context—in which case, you can reinforce students for performing the final step, then the final two, and so on, building up until they can complete the whole task. This is called *backward chaining*.

Having ensured that students are capable of performing alternative desired behaviours, these can then be strengthened by reinforcement—that is, by the delivery of a consequence that the student values. Reinforcement can be delivered to individuals or to the whole class. The former is difficult to manage in classrooms, as each target behaviour and reinforcer has to be determined and overseen individually for every child (Skinner et al. 2004). Moreover, if only specific students were targeted, it might seem unfair to peers that those with the poorest behaviour are receiving the most rewards. Therefore, Skinner and colleagues recommend delivering consequences to the entire group. To avoid satiation (that is, loss of potency of the reward) and to tailor the reinforcement to individual preferences, these writers suggest having a pool of potential rewards (written on slips of paper and posted in a receptacle) and selecting one once the group meets expectations. To avoid the provision of reinforcement for one specific academic activity (e.g. reading) causing students to reduce their performance in other areas (e.g. maths), the target behaviour and the performance level that will earn the reward can also be randomly selected (Skinner et al. 2004). Subsequently, maintenance can be fostered by fading reinforcement—by altering the pool of reinforcers to include more delayed reinforcers or fewer high-quality and more low-quality reinforcers, or by raising the performance criteria.

When an action results in the *presentation* of a consequence and, as a result, the behaviour occurs more often in the future, it has been *positively* reinforced. The range of positive reinforcers includes (from least to most intrusive) natural, task, social, activity, tangible, token, sensory and edible rewards.

Natural reinforcement

A formal intervention can sometimes be avoided by increasing the rate of natural reinforcers so that they occur at high enough levels to have a positive influence on students' behaviour.

Task reinforcement

When a long and daunting task is broken down into smaller sections, completion of each discrete section can in itself be reinforcing or occasion the delivery of a contrived reinforcer such as praise (Skinner et al. 2005).

Social reinforcement

Social reinforcement can maintain either disruptive or appropriate behaviour. Positive social reinforcers for *disruptive* acts can include recruiting teacher attention, gaining control, earning increased status with peers for defying adults, or being able to hang out with friends in the time-out area (Kamps 2002). Social reinforcement for *appropriate* behaviour typically entails verbal feedback (that is, praise) paired with social attention and approval (Kerr & Nelson 2006). To be effective, feedback must be contingent on the desired behaviour (which means that it is delivered if, and only if, the desired behaviour is displayed), must be specific, credible, high in quality, not overused and should not interrupt student attention (Wolery et al. 1988). Praise must also exceed reprimands by a ratio of at least 4:1, as otherwise the attention that accompanies reprimands can reinforce disruptiveness (Kerr & Nelson 2006).

Caring touch can also be a social reinforcer, although may be unwise in educational settings beyond the early childhood years. Other social reinforcers include appointing a child as student of the day or leader of an activity, allowing the child to be first in a line or activity, calling or writing to students' parent/s about their positive behaviour, or having a congratulatory visit from the principal (Mathieson & Price 2002; Zirpoli 2005).

Activity reinforcement

To encourage students to complete activities that they do not like, you can reward them with the chance to do an activity that they prefer. This is Premack's principle (Kerr & Nelson 2006), also known as 'Grandma's rule'. Preferred activities may include free time, time spent with you, an opportunity to hand out materials to the other students, use of the computer, feeding the class pet, bringing a toy to school, listening to music, or reading a story (Zirpoli 2005). Mathieson and Price (2002) list some naturalistic 'spirit lifters', many of which could be defined as activity reinforcers, such as playing music in the classroom, having dressing-up days, going for a walk, or attending special events such as fêtes or multicultural celebrations.

There are some limitations to the use of activity reinforcers, however. First, scheduling problems may mean that the preferred activity cannot immediately follow the target behaviour—in which case, the delay may render reinforcement ineffective, particularly for children with poor impulse control (Alberto & Troutman 2003; Neef et al. 1993, 2001). Second, some activities such as lunch time or music lessons should be available to students regardless of their performance in class.

Tangible reinforcement

Tangible reinforcers are non-edible items that students value for their own sake. Inappropriate behaviour can be reinforced tangibly when it allows students to acquire equipment (e.g. by stealing it or snatching an item off a peer). When used to encourage positive behaviour, tangibles include stars, stamps, stickers, points, toys or magazines (Zirpoli 2005). Tangible reinforcers differ from tokens in that they are valued in themselves and are not traded in for any other reinforcer. Determining a reinforcer for each student separately can make using tangible reinforcers intrusive (Kerr & Nelson 2006), while the public delivery of a tangible reinforcer to some students but not others could create differences in perceived status between peers (Skinner et al. 2005).

Token reinforcement

Under a token reinforcement system, you would give students points or a portable and durable token (such as a poker chip) when they display target behaviours. Later, they can trade these tokens in for pre-negotiated backup reinforcers. An example of a token economy is Canter and Canter's (2001) suggestion of placing a marble in a jar when any student does something that you want to reinforce then, once the number of marbles reaches a predetermined total, reinforcing the whole class.

The major advantage of token programs is that tokens can be exchanged for a variety of reinforcers, which avoids students tiring of a single reinforcer. The symbolic reinforcer (the token) can be delivered immediately, although the actual reinforcer itself is delayed. This may be sufficient for some students; others may not be able to delay gratification until the backup reinforcer is delivered, however.

A practical disadvantage of token economies is that they are vulnerable to sabotage by theft, swapping, loss and counterfeiting (Skinner et al. 2004; Walker et al. 2004). A second disadvantage is that, as with activity reinforcers, you must be careful in your selection of backup reinforcers. You cannot deprive students of activities that they have a right to access anyway, but neither can the backup reinforcer be a time waster. A third disadvantage is that setting up a token program is detailed and demanding. You need to determine how many tokens each desired behaviour earns, the costs of the various backup reinforcers, procedures for exchanging tokens for them and fines for misdemeanours. You will need a reliable recording system that seems fair to the students; otherwise, they will stop working within it. Finally, the reinforcers will need fading out once the program has achieved success, which will take skilful handling lest the behaviour deteriorates again.

Tactile and sensory reinforcers

Students with sensory integration difficulties (as found either alone or as part of the autism spectrum of disorders) will often engage in self-injurious behaviour because it increases their sensory stimulation or provides some sensory comfort (Kamps 2002). To replace self-stimulation with a less dangerous or more appropriate form of stimulation,

VIGNETTE 3.1 PITFALLS WITH TOKEN REINFORCEMENT

At a recent presentation where I was discussing the discouraging effects of reinforcement systems (star and sticker charts) on many children, a mother showed me a letter that her son, aged nine, had received the day before from his teacher:

> Dear Nathan
> On the last day of term, the class is having a pizza party to celebrate the end of the school term. To be invited you will need 72 points.
> Mrs x

Nathan had six points: in two terms of the school year, he had managed to be awarded six points, yet in the next two weeks, he was supposed to earn another 66. Knowing the impossibility of doing so, Nathan said to his mother after she had read the letter, 'So I won't be going, will I, Mum?' The inevitable happened and Nathan was sent to a different classroom during the class party, on the grounds that he had not earned enough points to be given access to the backup reinforcer (the party).

This illustrates that, while reward programs are ordinarily thought to be benign, they will necessarily involve withholding a reinforcer that adults deem has not been earned. Thus, they are punitive. Loss of a hoped-for reward feels like a punishment. Furthermore, Nathan's exclusion sends a message to his classmates about his acceptability as a person and about their own safety should they fail to meet expectations in future. Meanwhile, rather than being emboldened to try harder in future, there is a risk that Nathan will feel so disheartened at this injustice that he will disengage from school altogether.

you can use an alternative sensory reinforcer which meets the same sensory need (Piazza et al. 2000).

Edible reinforcers

Food is a reinforcer for everyone, as it satisfies a basic physiological need. However, edible reinforcers are unwise in schools, as they do not work unless students are hungry, teachers cannot take account of each student's food preferences and potential food intolerances, and there are nutritional concerns such as obesity and tooth decay (Kerr & Nelson 2006). Even more troubling would be teaching a link between food and emotional comfort, when eating should instead be a response to hunger.

Negative reinforcement

Instead of administering something positive that students like, you can increase the frequency of a desired behaviour by *removing* something negative. This is termed *negative reinforcement*. An example is allocating no homework—removing the imperative to do homework (which most students do not like)—to reward their diligence in class. (Note that negative reinforcement is the opposite of punishment: negative reinforcement *increases* a desirable behaviour by withdrawing something negative; punishment *decreases* an undesirable behaviour.)

Selection of reinforcers

For reinforcers to be effective, they must be individually tailored to each student. You can base your selection on your knowledge of reinforcers that generally work, of those that have worked in the past and of students' preferences (Martin & Pear 2003; Wheeler & Richey 2005). To gauge the last of these, you can ask students to write a list of their interests and preferences and select one of these, reserving the right to veto any item that you deem to be unsuitable or that might embarrass students (e.g. because it is delivered in public). Once a reinforcer is in place, you will observe its effects and abandon it if it does not increase the frequency of the desired behaviour.

Reinforcement schedules

Several properties of reinforcement can alter its influence over behaviour. One of these is the reinforcement *schedule*. This refers to how much time must elapse or how often students have to display desired behaviour before they receive some reinforcement. In classroom settings (as opposed to research laboratories), it is not possible to be exact about schedules, but a few research results can be borne in mind. The first of these is that, when behaviours are reinforced on each and every occasion (which is termed *continuous reinforcement*), students will learn them quickly. However, these behaviours also extinguish quickly once reinforcement ceases, as it is easy to detect the sudden absence of reinforcement. (It does not take many flickings of the light switch during a power blackout before you realise that the light no longer works.) On the other hand, behaviours that are seldom reinforced are slow to be acquired but are very resistant to extinction, as illustrated by gambling. This is termed *intermittent reinforcement*. This difference means that high levels of reinforcement are needed when students are learning a new skill, while intermittent reinforcement is more appropriate for maintaining skills (Wheeler & Richey 2005).

For discrete acts, you will reinforce students when they have displayed a specified number of target behaviours, such as completing a given number of maths equations. This is called a *ratio schedule*. For continuous behaviours (e.g. staying in their seats), you would reinforce students after a specified time period. This is called an *interval schedule*. Both can be difficult to administer within classrooms, as ratio schedules require you to count all instances of a behaviour, while interval schedules require that you keep time records. This is especially demanding when each interval is brief, resulting in the need to reinforce as frequently as every 30 seconds, for example.

BOX 3.1 GUIDELINES FOR ADMINISTERING REWARDS

The behavioural gains produced by reinforcement are more likely when you abide by the following guidelines for its administration (Kaplan & Carter 1995; Martin & Pear 2003; Walker et al. 2004; Wheeler & Richey 2005; Zirpoli 2005).

1 *Tell students in advance* exactly what behaviours you expect and which consequences will follow both their observance or noncompliance.
2 Allow students to *choose* from a range of suggested reinforcers.
3 The chosen reinforcer must be more attractive than naturally occurring alternatives. For example, when behaviour allows students to escape the learning task altogether, your replacement reinforcer has to be both more powerful and reasonably immediate (Dixon et al. 1998; Zarcone et al. 1994).
4 Students with impulsive behaviour choose the most immediate reinforcer, even when it is less attractive (Binder et al. 2000; Neef et al. 1993, 2001), which implies that for these students in particular you will need to deliver a high-quality reinforcer *immediately* if it is to be more potent than competing reinforcers.
5 Reinforce *often* at first, so that behaviour is learned quickly, but gradually reduce reinforcement to natural levels so that the new behaviour is maintained.
6 Reinforcement must be *systematic*: its delivery must be contingent on the occurrence of the behaviour.
7 For a reinforcer to be effective at increasing behaviour, students must have been *deprived* of it initially.
8 It will be important to *vary* reinforcers, because they lose their reinforcing capacity if overused. This process is termed *satiation*.
9 It can help to *pair* an activity, tangible or token reinforcer with social reinforcement such as praise.
10 Improvement and *generalisation* will be most easily assured if you employ reinforcers that are commonly and readily available in the environment.
11 If behaviour improves but then deteriorates, this may be because reinforcement has become too inconsistent and infrequent, so will need increasing once more (Foxx 1982).
12 At the end of an intervention you should strengthen natural reinforcers, so that the acquired behaviour itself becomes intrinsically rewarding, allowing you gradually to withdraw (or fade) external rewards altogether.

Phase 4: Punish undesired behaviours

Once students' desired behaviours have been strengthened, any remaining undesirable actions can be reduced or weakened by *punishment*. There are three rules guiding the decision to use punishment: first is the ethical principle that punishment must be applied only to behaviours that cannot be suppressed in other ways. Second, these behaviours must be serious enough to warrant the use of such a restrictive method. The undesired behaviour should be potentially dangerous; interfere with students' ability to learn essential skills or limit their participation in activities or the community; or result in students being unnecessarily dependent on others (Schloss & Smith 1998). Third, punishment must follow or be paired with the use of reinforcement for desired behaviour, so that students have something else to do in place of an inappropriate behaviour. This is known as the 'fair pair' principle, which states that when you target a behaviour for reduction, you must simultaneously select an appropriate behaviour to increase (Zirpoli 2005).

As is the case when increasing desirable behaviours, it is important to specify precisely in behavioural, rather than diagnostic, terms which behaviours you wish to see reduced in frequency. You must describe what actually *happens* (for instance, Sam hits Cody during library session) rather than by labelling the behaviour or the student (e.g. Sam is aggressive). It is also crucial to re-examine your preventive measures and the part that your own behaviour might be playing in inducing undesirable behaviour in your students (Zirpoli 2005).

Again, it must be said that what seems to be a punishment may not be so for a given individual. As with reinforcement, punishment is defined simply by its effect, not by your intentions. In ABA terms, punishment results in a decrease in the behaviour, whereas the colloquial use refers to the administration of something unpleasant in response to undesired behaviour, which may or may not alter the rate of the behaviour.

To reduce undesirable behaviour, you can deliver an aversive consequence (*Type 1 punishment*) or withdraw a positive one (*Type 2 punishment*). Behaviour can also be decreased by removing the specific consequence that maintains it. This is termed *extinction*. Other strategies for decreasing inappropriate behaviour include overcorrection and negative practice, but these are less relevant in schools and so will not be described here. The remainder can be ranked in order from the least to the most restrictive methods (which you might recall refers to how much external control is imposed on students), thus:

- discrimination training;
- simple correction;
- self-punishment;

- differential reinforcement;
- stimulus satiation;
- extinction;
- withdrawal of positive stimuli (Type 2 punishment);
- presentation of aversive stimuli (Type 1 punishment).

Discrimination training

The same act can be appropriate in one venue (e.g. shouting at a sporting match) and inappropriate elsewhere (e.g. during school assembly). Providing cues and administering consequences differently in different circumstances will help students learn which behaviours are appropriate in various settings. In this way, students achieve some measure of self-control or learning.

Simple correction

As the name implies, simple correction requires students simply to undo or correct the results of their behaviour (Wolery et al. 1988). The restrictiveness of this approach depends on the extent to which students correct their behaviour willingly when asked. If no other punishment is delivered, it is one of the least restrictive (and intrusive) methods available.

Self-punishment

Although self-punishment affords students more control than adult-administered punishment, it can have a negative effect on students' motivation because it highlights their errors and so may activate a fear of failure. For this reason, self-reinforcement for desired behaviours is preferred over self-punishment for undesired ones.

Differential reinforcement

Differential reinforcement procedures involve reinforcing a positive behaviour while simultaneously withholding reinforcement of an undesirable target behaviour (Kerr & Nelson 2006; Vollmer et al. 1993). Differential reinforcement is less restrictive than other reductive methods, as it focuses on reinforcement rather than punishment (Alberto & Troutman 2003; Sulzer-Azaroff & Mayer 1991). On the other hand, for reasons to be discussed in a coming section, the extinction component can reduce its effectiveness (Vollmer et al. 1993).

There are five main types of differential reinforcement (Zirpoli 2005). The first is differential reinforcement of *higher rates of behaviour* (DRH), in which you reinforce students for displaying a rare desirable behaviour more often. The second is differential reinforcement of *lower rates of behaviour* (DRL), in which you reinforce students when their undesirable behaviour occurs less frequently. You would specify how many instances of the behaviour they may display within a given time period and deliver a reinforcer if they do not exceed this number. Gradually, you would decrease the number of behaviours that you permit, or increase the duration of time, until the behaviour occurs at a tolerable level. This approach can take time to achieve results and relies on careful measurement of the frequency of the behaviour. It has the advantage that students continue to receive reinforcement, although your focus is on undesirable behaviour rather than its positive alternatives (Sulzer-Azaroff & Mayer 1991). It has been used with swearing (Kerr & Nelson 2006) but would be inappropriate for behaviours such as aggression, which cannot be tolerated at any rate.

While ceasing reinforcement of the undesired behaviour, in a process called differential reinforcement of *incompatible behaviours* (DRI) you can reinforce incompatible behaviours, such as staying seated when the target behaviour is out-of-seat behaviour. Or you can reinforce alternative (not opposite) behaviours, such as putting up a hand rather than calling out. This is differential reinforcement of *alternative behaviours* (DRA). DRI and DRA have the advantage of teaching students what *to* do, rather than what *not* to do, although reinforcement can be effective only if they perform the alternative behaviour often (Sulzer-Azaroff & Mayer 1991; Wheeler & Richey 2005). In real situations, it can be difficult to withhold all reinforcement of the undesired behaviour and always to reinforce its alternative, although perfect accuracy is not essential (Vollmer et al. 1999).

Less positive in its approach is differential reinforcement of *zero rates of behaviour* (DRO), in which you give students reinforcement for not displaying the target behaviour at all during a given time interval, which can be lengthened as the behaviour improves. When using this approach, it makes sense to use Reset-DRO, in which the timer is restarted if the behaviour is displayed (Zirpoli 2005). The method can be used for verbal or physical aggression and destruction of property (Walker et al. 2004). Although this can achieve rapid results, it is less educational than the other methods, as you do not teach any alternative, replacement behaviours (Sulzer-Azaroff & Mayer 1991).

Stimulus satiation

Stimulus satiation entails giving students so much of the antecedent to the behaviour that they tire of it. An example is giving dozens of pencils to a student who frequently steals these from classmates. The theory predicts that the student will eventually become overloaded with pencils and will no longer choose to steal them.

Extinction

Extinction involves identifying and then withholding the particular reinforcer that is maintaining the target undesired behaviour, resulting in its reduction. The most common application of extinction procedures is when teacher attention is thought to be reinforcing children's disruptiveness—in which case, you should discontinue giving the disruptive behaviour your attention (by becoming engaged with another student or task) while ensuring that you reinforce alternative, more appropriate behaviours at other times (Alberto & Troutman 2003).

Extinction works only gradually and there are many instances where it will not be effective at all. First, it will not eliminate *self-reinforcing behaviours* such as rocking or thumb sucking by children with sensory integration difficulties; or behaviours that permit students to escape work demands (Mace & Wacker 1994; Zarcone et al. 1994); or when students' conversation is itself reinforcing and has no additional reinforcer that you can withhold. A second category of behaviours for which extinction might be ineffective is when *you are not in control of the reinforcement* students receive, such as when their clowning in class attracts the mirth or admiration of their peers. A third is with *self-injurious or violent behaviours*: you cannot allow students to accumulate injuries while you wait for extinction to work (Kerr & Nelson 2006; Zirpoli 2005). Fourth, its slow effects mean that it would be unwise to use it for behaviours that may be *contagious*.

Three problems emerge with the use of extinction with all other behaviours. First, it can be difficult for you to notice how your own actions might inadvertently be reinforcing a disruptive behaviour and thus to apply extinction procedures to yourself. Second, it might not be possible to tolerate the behaviour while extinction takes effect and, meanwhile, in your exasperation you may accidentally reinforce it intermittently, which will prolong it further. Third, in what has been called an 'extinction burst', the target behaviours may initially deteriorate before they get better, or new antisocial behaviours such as aggression or agitation may emerge (Alberto & Troutman 2003; Lerman & Iwata 1996; Lerman et al. 1999; Wheeler & Richey 2005; Zirpoli 2005). If peers copy the behaviour or if it becomes too dangerous or disruptive, you may no longer be able to ignore it—that is, to apply the extinction procedure. Finally, behaviour that has been extinguished in one setting is still likely to occur elsewhere: gains made with extinction do not generalise readily (Alberto & Troutman 2003).

Withdrawal of positive stimuli (Type 2 punishment)

As the name implies, withdrawal of positive stimuli entails withdrawing something the student likes when the undesirable behaviour is displayed, with the expectation that this will decrease the rate of the undesired behaviour. The two main types of this form of punishment are *response-cost procedures* and *time out*. For each of these, there must be a high level of reinforcement in the natural situation, so that the punishing condition is noticeably less positive than the usual setting.

Response-cost procedures

With response-cost procedures, you remove a reinforcer when students act inappropriately. The consequence that is forfeited might be a privilege (such as free time) or, under a token economy system, you could impose a penalty or fine, such as the loss of points. The latter has the advantage that you can withdraw points at your discretion rather than, say, having physically to confiscate tokens within a token economy system (Alberto & Troutman 2003).

One difficulty with response-cost approaches is establishing the magnitude of fines. If these are too severe and a day's gains can be wiped out with one misdeed, the students will resist the program or feel that they have 'nothing to lose' by further disruptions. Also, you cannot exact further punishment from bankrupted students and thus will have no further influence over their behaviour. On the other hand, if fines are too lenient, they will have no punitive effect. For these reasons, under response-cost procedures reinforcement for appropriate behaviour must far exceed fines for disruptiveness (Zirpoli 2005).

Time out from positive reinforcement

This procedure involves removing students' access to reinforcement following an unacceptable behaviour. Two factors are essential for time out to be effective. First, the natural setting must be very reinforcing, so that removal from it is indeed a punishment. Second, reinforcement cannot be available in the time-out condition. This means that, while time out cannot be punitive (e.g. by causing students embarrassment or anxiety at their confinement), neither can it be positive; it must be a neutral. The method works best with behaviours that are maintained by social (e.g. teacher attention) or tangible reinforcers, as these are the most easily withheld during time out (Wheeler & Richey 2005).

There are many types of time out (Alberto & Troutman 2003; Kerr & Nelson 2006; Sterling-Turner & Watson 1999). The most naturalistic is variously termed 'planned', 'deliberate' or 'tactical' ignoring, which is probably indistinguishable from extinction and thus has all of its shortcomings, such as the potential for contagion and escalation of the disruption (Kerr & Nelson 2006; Rogers 2002; Sterling-Turner & Watson 1999).

A more formal version is *nonseclusionary* time out, in which students remain where they are but are deprived of reinforcers such as attention, work materials or the right to earn rewards such as points or tokens. You might, for example, direct disruptive individuals to place their heads in their folded arms on their desks. The next form is *exclusionary*, when you remove students from the activity and set them apart within the classroom, such as at an isolated desk. The final form of time out is *seclusionary*, whereby you confine students to an isolated area for a specified and brief period of time. The room must be of a reasonable size, with adequate ventilation and lighting, should be free of objects with which students could hurt themselves and should allow you to monitor the student continuously.

Time out has some practical difficulties. Most concerning is that all forms result in a loss of instruction time, which could further disadvantage those students who have learning difficulties and result in increased disruptiveness when they return to class. Practical difficulties include: the necessity for a functional assessment to be conducted, because time out in the form of ignoring will work for behaviours that are maintained by teacher attention; exclusionary time out would be needed if peer attention were the reinforcer; and time out should not be used at all for behaviours that are reinforced by avoidance of task demands, as it will be ineffective or, worse still, disruptiveness may actually be reinforced by the opportunity it provides for escape (Myers & Holland 2000; Sterling-Turner & Watson 1999; Wheeler & Richey 2005). Unintended outcomes also need to be considered during the assessment phase—for example, nonseclusionary and exclusionary time out may embarrass students and engender defiance.

Such an assessment, however, is time consuming and this is compounded by the demands of supervising time out. With seclusionary time out in particular, your surveillance will be essential to ensure that students are both safe and not forgotten. To that end, you will have to determine an appropriate duration. On this issue, most advocates suggest a duration measured in minutes; any longer could justifiably be termed solitary confinement (Alberto & Troutman 2003). Next, you will need to be able to prevent escapes. Although the most effective method to prevent escapes is to lock the student in the room (Sterling-Turner & Watson 1999), this raises ethical objections. Exiting criteria have to be established, which will require a decision about whether you will return students from time out at the end of a specified time period, or whether you will require them to have calmed down before exiting time out. This raises the issue of how to respond if a student is still disrupting at the end of the specified time-out period. You could extend the time until he or she has settled, but this can prolong the isolation for too long and appears to make little difference to the effectiveness of the procedure anyway (Sterling-Turner & Watson 1999). A more effective strategy is to reinforce the first appropriate behaviour displayed once the child has returned to time in (Sterling-Turner & Watson 1999).

Despite these practical demands on teachers, the removal of a troublesome student is a powerful reinforcer for them, thus giving rise to the potential for overuse (Maag 2001; Zirpoli 2005).

Presentation of aversive stimuli (Type 1 punishment)

With Type 2 punishment, the teacher removes something positive in an effort to decrease undesired behaviour. In contrast, Type 1 punishment has the same aim of reducing inappropriate behaviour but involves administering an aversive consequence. Two such aversive punishments are available. The first is *verbal reprimands* in the form of brief, immediate feedback to students that their behaviour is unacceptable (Kerr & Nelson 2006). As long as these are delivered in private and do not humiliate or embarrass students, reprimands can be very effective with mild behavioural difficulties, but are less successful with more severe problems (Kerr & Nelson 2006), partly because being reprimanded can raise students' status among their peers.

The second type of aversive punishment is physical or *corporal punishment*. In many jurisdictions, the use of physical punishment by professionals (and, in some countries, by parents) is illegal. Even when permitted by law, there can be no justification morally for striking children. Not only is the method unethical, but less aversive approaches are equally, if not more, effective (Zirpoli 2005).

Disadvantages of punishment

The colloquial use of the term *punishment* disguises the fact that surprisingly little is known about its effective use in everyday settings (Johnston 1972; Lerman & Vorndran 2002). Most research has focused in laboratories on rats, pigeons and monkeys being exposed to electric shocks, sprays of water, blasts of air, squirts of lemon juice, ammonia odour and physical restraint, none of which are applicable in classrooms.

The conditions that make punishment effective in laboratory settings include that punishers must be fairly intense and delivered both immediately (within seconds) and every time the inappropriate behaviour occurs, while any competing reinforcement (e.g. teacher attention for inappropriate behaviour or during delivery of the punishment) must be eliminated (Johnston 1972; Lerman & Vorndran 2002). These conditions are seldom manageable in classrooms, not least because many misbehaviours occur in a teacher's absence, with the result that many are not detected and thus cannot be punished, while it is seldom possible to set aside all other activities to deliver immediate punishment. Moreover, the very conditions that make punishment effective—particularly its intensity—are unlikely to be judged as ethical or justifiable in schools and may provoke aggressive reactions, resistance and escape in recipients (Johnston 1972; Lerman & Vorndran 2002; Martin & Pear 2003).

Furthermore, there is considerable doubt whether changes brought about by punishment transfer to other settings (generalise) or are maintained, probably because punishment on its own does not teach a desirable behaviour but only suppresses an undesired one (Lerman & Vorndran 2002; McDonnell 1993). In one rare naturalistic study of response-cost and DRO procedures in a preschool, for example, behavioural disruptions returned to pre-punishment levels once two months of treatment ceased (Conyers et al. 2004). This means that, once instituted, punishment would need to be in place virtually permanently, which is undesirable within schools where it is important that students outgrow the need for interventions.

The conclusion from many behaviourists is that punishment is effective for the 95 per cent of students who do not need it and who would therefore respond to lesser methods; for the remainder, punishment seldom works (Maag 2001). Its disadvantages far outweigh its advantages and, other than signalling who is in charge, fails to promote any lasting educational or behavioural improvements (Wheeler & Richey 2005).

Generalisation

Behaviourist methods have demonstrated limited success at having students maintain improvements in behaviour over time or transfer gains to other settings or other teachers, particularly for children with severe disabilities (Alberto & Troutman 2003). This lack of generalisation is a serious flaw, as you are unlikely to have the time to oversee permanent behavioural management programs for numbers of your students. Given this, training for generalisation will have to be specifically included in a behavioural program (Alberto & Troutman 2003; Martin & Pear 2003; Schloss & Smith 1998). The most basic means to foster skill maintenance and transfer are to enhance motivation by teaching only relevant skills in naturalistic settings using naturally occurring reinforcers. In classroom settings, using a variety of teachers and teaching methods will give students the flexibility needed to adjust to and transfer their skills into various environments. Finally, you will need to ensure that students have mastered targeted skills fluently before ceasing training, as only reliably performed skills have a chance of being maintained.

Summary

Applied behaviourism in schools begins by defining, observing and recording the outward behaviour of students, so that a judgment can be made about which environmental events trigger a disruption (the antecedents) and which are maintaining (reinforcing) it. Subsequently, teachers will adjust salient antecedents and intensify reinforcement of appropriate behaviour to increase its occurrence, using a range of reinforcers from natural to edible, and reinforce fewer instances of a negative behaviour (differential reinforcement). If dangerous behaviour persists, under strict conditions you could use punishing or reductive procedures, such as response-cost procedures or time out from positive reinforcement.

Interim critique

The abiding contribution of this theory is its insistence on objective observation of others' behaviour, both prior to and during the implementation of a program. This avoids teachers' subjective judgments and emotions clouding their judgment about the severity of a behaviour or about program effectiveness. This impartial observation is the gold ribbon standard to which all approaches should aspire. However, under FBA each and every case must be individually assessed, as the reinforcers operating at one time for one particular student will differ for others. The lesser option under ABA of administering general consequences can be ineffective or even exacerbate disruptiveness, because the specific reinforcers in operation have not been identified (Gresham et al. 2001; Myers & Holland 2000; Sterling-Turner et al. 2001).

The costs and time involved—with consequent delays in delivering an intervention—may be untenable in schools. When trying to identify your own role in a behavioural sequence consultants could be employed, but waiting lists for their services may delay intervention still further. Even when consultants can be utilised, their observations are still prone to error. This is because teachers and students can change their behaviour while being observed, the wrong reinforcer might be identified (e.g. when behaviour is reinforced later by peer admiration, which the observer does not see), and because cause–effect links between behaviours and their consequences are difficult to detect, especially for low-incidence behaviours (Gresham et al. 2001).

The intricacies of this method raise concerns that it may be difficult—if not impossible—to enact the approach accurately, as demanded by ethical principles. This theory is more complex than it first appears and takes considerable competence, sophisticated training and a huge investment of time to use appropriately (Alberto & Troutman 2003).

A second ethical issue arises because behaviourist interventions involve doing something *to* students in the form of administration of consequences. This means that student consent is required. This must be both informed and voluntary. *Informed* consent requires that you have considered a range of viable treatment options and have discussed these with students and their parents (Martin & Pear 2003). *Voluntary* consent implies that you cannot threaten students or their parents with any unfair consequences— such as school suspension or refusal to teach a student—if they withheld consent to the program (Rekers 1984), but neither can you promise extravagant benefits for their participation (Alberto & Troutman 2003). Your professional status may put parents or students under subtle pressure to consent, and thus the onus is on you to ensure that what they are agreeing to represents best practice (Rekers 1984).

CASE STUDY

Adam is seven. He has difficulty with reading, spelling and writing, although he enjoys and is capable at maths. During non-maths lessons he spends a considerable amount of time off-task, when he frequently disrupts the other students. This is worse in the afternoons than in the mornings.

He is in a composite class of six and seven year olds. He spends most of his play time with the younger children. Frequently, a pair including Adam is apprehended during play times doing such things as harassing passers-by from an out-of-bounds area of the playground that is close to the street, rifling through rubbish bins for food or cans to swap for other items with students, or engaging in fights in and around the toilets.

Adam seems bemused by the trouble he gets into, usually saying when challenged that he doesn't know why he behaves in these ways, that he couldn't remember that a given behaviour was against the rules, or that the other child was at fault for suggesting the activity.

Until a recent assessment, it was believed that Adam behaved as he did because of low academic ability. However, a battery of tests has shown his overall ability (IQ) to be average, with his maths skills in the high-normal range and his reading and spelling skills, while delayed, still within the lower range of normal limits. His teacher is now at a loss to find a new explanation for his behaviour.

An application based on applied behaviour analysis

Given that Adam's behavioural difficulties are not serious enough to warrant a functional behaviour assessment, this case study will illustrate an ABA approach to his behaviour.

Step 1: Observe the conditions

You will need to observe Adam in a range of settings and record in behavioural terms the conditions (antecedents) that occasion his inappropriate behaviour and the consequences that follow it. In language-based activities you might notice, for instance, that Adam remains on-task for only two minutes, following which he chats to a neighbour or leaves his desk for spurious reasons, such as wanting to sharpen an already sharp pencil. In so doing, he frequently speaks to or touches other students, who in turn become distracted by him.

Step 2: Define a target behaviour

Next, you would select the behaviour that is of most concern to you (the target behaviour) and define it operationally in precise terms. Let's say that you are most concerned with Adam's off-task behaviour, because it interferes with other students' learning. In that case, you will decide to target his disruptive acts, such as chatting to other students or moving about the room unnecessarily during desk activities.

Step 3: Define goals (the terminal behaviour)

Next, you would define what improvement you are aiming for in the target behaviour. You might decide that you want Adam, instead of distracting after two minutes in language-based activities, to remain on-task for five minutes, following which his distractions are not to disrupt others. You will define what on-task means.

Step 4: Change antecedents

Next, you will turn your attention to changing the antecedents. For example, you might determine that the teaching methods in maths are more visual, whereas those in reading and spelling are auditory. Given that Adam does better in maths, this could be because he is more capable at visual thinking—in which case, reading and spelling lessons will be adjusted to include more visual instruction.

Step 5: Choose a recording method

You must record systematically to assess whether Adam's behaviour is improving. Given that event recording is unsuitable for continuous acts such as the target behaviour, you might decide to observe Adam for three five-minute periods during a desk exercise, and record for each minute of that five-minute span whether Adam was on-task throughout the one-minute interval or not. (It is likely that this observation regime will be incompatible with your other teaching duties, so you may need to have an assistant perform this.)

Step 6: Plan a reinforcement regime
Next, you will plan a reinforcement program. Using differential reinforcement of higher rates of behaviour, you might decide to deliver a reinforcer if Adam is predominantly on-task for two of the one-minute time intervals per five-minute observation period. After one week, you will increase your demand to three one-minute intervals before he receives reinforcement, increasing by a minute per week until he must be on-task for five minutes to earn reinforcement.

You could select an activity or tangible reinforcer by asking Adam about his preferences and choosing one of these, changing them regularly to avoid satiation. Alternatively, you might institute a token economy system that allowed Adam to gain points each time his behaviour met the criterion. Once sufficient points were earned, he could receive a pre-negotiated social reinforcer, such as collecting the class's lunch orders or being team leader in a sporting activity; or earn an activity reinforcer, such as having extra time on the school computer, which he enjoys.

Step 7: Evaluation
You will need to maintain continuous records to evaluate the effectiveness of the program.

Step 8: Reduce undesirable behaviour
If Adam's on-task behaviour did not improve significantly with the reinforcement regime, even when a range of reinforcers was tried and the criteria for success refined, you would need to institute a reductive procedure. Extinction is unsuitable, because you cannot prevent Adam's peers from responding to him when he distracts them. You might determine that response-cost procedures (such as loss of points) are too discouraging for him. Therefore you might select time out. Because there is no separate time-out room in the school where exclusionary time out could be supervised, you will elect to use nonseclusionary time out within the classroom.

Step 9: Repeat the steps for other behaviours
Finally, you would turn your attention to residual behavioural difficulties and design successive interventions for each of these.

Discussion questions

1   Does ABA take a wide enough view of antecedents? Are there any potential triggers that it ignores?

2   In your opinion, what ethical issues are raised by behaviourist approaches, and how could they be resolved?

3   Re-apply the case study that you generated in Chapter 2, this time using ABA principles and practices. What are the differences in recommended practices? What effect would these differences have on the individual student? On the whole class? On you?

Suggested further reading

Alberto, P.A. and Troutman, A.C. 2003 *Applied behavior analysis for teachers* 6th edn, Merrill Prentice Hall, Upper Saddle River, NJ

Kerr, M.M. and Nelson, C.M. 2006 *Strategies for addressing behavior problems in the classroom* 5th edn, Pearson Merrill Prentice Hall, Upper Saddle River, NJ

Walker, J.E., Shea, T.M. and Bauer, A.M. 2004 *Behavior management: a practical approach for educators* 8th edn, Pearson Merrill Prentice Hall, Upper Saddle River, NJ

Wheeler, J.J. and Richey, D.D. 2005 *Behavior management: principles and practices of positive behavior support* Pearson Merrill Prentice Hall, Upper Saddle River, NJ

Zirpoli, T.J. 2005 *Behavior management: applications for teachers* 4th edn, Pearson Merrill Prentice Hall, Upper Saddle River, NJ

For parents

Green, C. 2001 *Toddler taming: a guide to your child from one to four,* Doubleday, Sydney

Sanders, M. 2004 *Every parent: a positive approach to children's behaviour* Penguin, Melbourne

4 COGNITIVE BEHAVIOURISM

The cognitive-behavioral approaches [are] a purposeful attempt to preserve the demonstrated positive effects of behavioral therapy within a less doctrinaire context and to incorporate the cognitive activities of the [student] into the efforts to produce therapeutic change.

Kendall (2000: 6)

KEY POINTS

- Cognitive approaches aim to teach students effective ways of dealing with problems independently.
- Success at any task depends on the environment, students' emotions and beliefs about themselves and the task, their problem-solving skills, ability to do the task and ability to organise themselves to complete it.
- Learning constructive thinking habits can help both teachers and students remain in control of their own behaviour and emotions, thus reducing stress and increasing their personal effectiveness.

Introduction

Cognition is another word for thinking; you have already been introduced to the term *behaviourism*. When the two are combined into the cognitive-behavioural approaches, their aim is to support students to control their own thinking so that they can understand what they are doing and why they are doing it and can judge if it is what they really want (Le Messurier 2004). Whereas applied behaviour analysis concentrates on what students *do*, cognitive theory focuses more on their thinking *processes*. And whereas ABA says that external control of students will give them the skills to control themselves (although it is not entirely clear how this transfer from outer to inner control would take place), cognitive theory systematically *teaches* self-regulatory skills. Advocates claim that this has greater potential to prevent a recurrence of disruptiveness (Yell et al. 2005). At the same time, the second half of its double-barrelled title, *behaviourism*, signals the retention of some purely behaviourist strategies, such as the use of rewards and punishments.

Philosophical assumptions

The behavioural elements of this theory, such as the imposition of consequences, maintain the authoritarian overtones of ABA. On the other hand, cognitive training is more egalitarian when it involves collaboration with students to decide the goals for their behaviour and the steps to achieve these. Rogers (2002: 75) quotes Thomas Szasz's statement that 'A teacher should have maximal authority and minimal power', which is to say that their expert and referent power (as described in Chapter 1) should exceed their role authority (Rogers 2002). This authority is based on purposefulness rather than power. At the heart of this is respect, but teachers *earn* this by having respect for students rather than being accorded it automatically because of their role. Given this stance, cognitive-behaviourism is placed between the authoritarian and egalitarian positions on the continuum of theories in Figure 1.2 (see page 19).

Nature of childhood

Bernard (1986) argues that people are neither good nor bad: they are just alive and do some good and some bad things. This implies that the cognitive theorists see individuals as possessing the capacity for both good and evil and that they make choices about their behaviour.

Explanations for disruptive behaviour

Cognitivists believe that people are self-directive and not merely passive recipients of external incentives (Bandura 2001). They are active and intentional agents in shaping their experiences. Thus, cognitive theorists believe that individuals are influenced to make behavioural choices not only by the consequences of behaviour, but also by the following elements (Bandura 2001; Kendall 2000; Meyers et al. 1989):

- their context, particularly its social relationships;
- their values;
- their motivation, as affected by their self-efficacy and expectations of success;
- their information-processing and problem-solving skills;
- their self-organisational skills, which allow them to direct their actions to achieve their goals;
- their interpretation of feedback about their performances.

Given these multiple influences (as illustrated in Figure 4.1), cognitive theorists will attempt to alter students' maladaptive behaviour by retraining their thinking and feelings. In contrast, the purer behaviourists believe that change is achieved in reverse—that is, that a change in students' behaviour will lead to improvement in their thoughts and emotions (Agran & Martin 1987).

Goal of discipline

Discipline has both a managerial function of creating order so that learning can occur and an educational function of promoting student self-discipline in the form of internalised compliance. In an effort to achieve these aims, Rogers (2002, 2004) explains that the teacher's job is not to control students but to control or manage their *situation* in order to lead, motivate, guide, encourage and support students to manage themselves.

Components of cognitive training

Cognitive theory is implicit in teaching any skill. When applied to school-based behavioural difficulties, it is commonly used to guide the teaching of social skills in general or of aggression and anger management in particular, teaching students to compensate for their attention deficits (ADD or ADHD), and teaching students self-restraint skills, which Rogers (2003) terms *academic survival skills*. In each of these domains, cognitive training entails the three phases of analysing the task to determine what skills and strategies are needed for success, analysing students' skills to diagnose which requisite abilities they lack, and implementation of a training program to teach these (Cleary & Zimmerman 2004; Yell et al. 2005). Training programs typically teach by demonstrating the required skill and having children rehearse it in training sessions. This is the cognitive component. The behaviourist component of this approach then administers reinforcement for the children's performance both in training sessions and

FIGURE 4.1   Phases of task completion

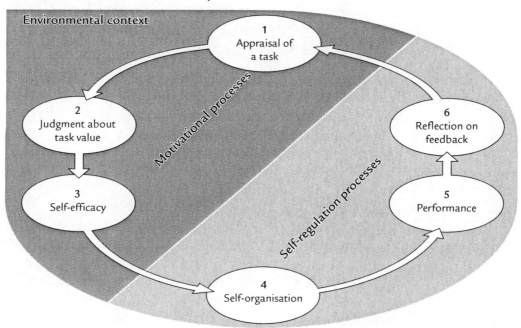

when they transfer that skill into the regular work or play settings of the classroom or playground.

Depending on which skills the assessment has shown the student to lack, cognitive training will encompass any or all of the phases depicted in Figure 4.1. The first three phases are motivational, demonstrated in the exercise asking you to identify the number of triangles in Figure 4.2 (Napier & Gershenfeld 2004: 4). You will have had previous experience with similar tasks and your emotional and intellectual reaction to those will affect how deeply you engage with this one. Napier and Gershenfeld assert that some individuals attempt the task half-heartedly because they assume it is a trick or because (on the basis of past failure at such activities) they do not expect to be able to get it right; or do not engage with it at all because there is little to be gained from working at it; some are trained to be competitive (with themselves or others) and so persist with the task for an unduly long time to make sure they get their answer right; while those working in groups wait to see how other group members answer and agree with those who they assess are likely to be correct. (You will find the puzzle answer at the end of this chapter.)

This exercise demonstrates that three factors affect individuals' motivation to invest effort in a task: their expectation that they can be successful, the benefits they anticipate

FIGURE 4.2   Exercise in the perception of task demands

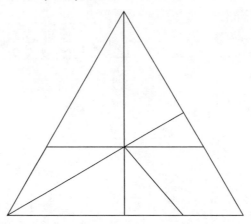

Source: Napier & Gershenfeld (2004: 4)

that success will earn them, and the social context in which they are working (e.g. its competitiveness). Together, then, these three elements constitute motivation. This makes the greatest contribution to success, because even if individuals have the ability to do the task but are not invested in doing so, they will not engage with it.

Environmental interventions

The social context has a powerful influence on behaviour (Burden & Fraser 1993). The quality of the relationships between teachers and students and among peers affects the way students view the academic and behavioural tasks that they are being asked to complete and determines which resources are available to support their performances. A highly competitive social climate, for example, will cause students to fear getting things wrong and may block them from even attempting tasks, as when bullying causes students to withdraw and cease asking to join the group. Therefore, a cognitive approach to students' behavioural difficulties will begin by establishing or repairing the warmth of students' relationships with teachers and with each other, not least because students will find it difficult to act disruptively for someone whom they care about (Le Messurier 2004).

Phase I: Appraisal of a task

Individuals' ultimate success at any task will be reliant on their ability to detect or be sensitive to the need to employ their abilities: they have to notice when a task calls for a particular skill (Perkins et al. 2000). Selective attention will limit the breadth of cues to which students attend (Bye & Jussim 1993). Some (e.g. those who have been abused) will be overly alert to signs of danger and therefore to protect themselves may either withdraw or lash out, while aggressive children are more likely to misinterpret even ambiguous social cues as hostile (Lochman et al. 2000; Nelson & Finch 2000; Wragg 1989). Urbain and Kendall (1980) give an example of training in perspective taking where children wrote and videotaped skits of events involving people their age, with all the group members acting out each role in turn to improve their ability to perceive another's point of view.

Phase 2: Judgment about task value

Individuals will be interested in attempting tasks or behaviours that they believe will help them meet their goals. This defines for them whether they value the task. If they see no value in what they are being asked to do, it is less likely that they will attempt it, especially when this judgment is combined in the next phase with maladaptive attributions about their ability to perform it. (In the exercise for Figure 4.2, you might have determined that you could do it if you wanted to but were unwilling to interrupt your reading to attempt it for so little gain.)

For a behavioural task, students need to value the general principles that govern behaviour, such as consideration of others and acceding to reasonable requests. This valuing of prosocial behaviour is not guaranteed, however. For example, snatching an item from a peer may be antisocial but it secures the contested item, which outcome may be more attractive to the child than its more prosocial alternative of waiting for a turn.

Phase 3: Self-efficacy

The third motivational aspect of task completion (as depicted in Figure 4.1) is self-efficacy. This is our sense of personal potency, or ability to influence events in our lives. Self-efficacy answers the question 'How effective, competent or powerful am I in my life?'. Having felt empowered in the past to surmount obstacles and achieve success, individuals expect that they will be able to do so again and thus are willing to confront challenges and persist at tasks.

This sense of self-efficacy results from judgments that we make about how influential we have felt in the past to influence events like the present task. When we have succeeded previously—and particularly when we have failed—we will have generated explanations (or 'attributions') about the cause of these failures and successes. These attributions have four properties (Weiner 2000):

- where we *locate* the cause of events—whether we believe them to be due to internal versus external forces;
- whether we see these forces as *durable* (e.g. personal traits such as ability) or *temporary* events (e.g. lack of effort);
- whether the causes are *pervasive* (e.g. inability) or *specific* (e.g. not understanding fractions);
- how *controllable* we believe events to be.

The most adaptive attributions—the ones that will encourage us to engage and persist—will explain causes as being due to internal, temporary, specific and controllable events, whereas maladaptive attributions blame external sources that are permanent, pervasive and uncontrollable (Weiner 2000). Such attributions generate low self-efficacy, as a result of which students might not attempt to manage their own actions because they feel powerless to affect what happens to them anyway. They believe that they are at the mercy of uncontrollable or outside forces. When maladaptive attributions lead to a lack of engagement and effort and to poor self-regulatory skills, failure becomes habitual and is entrenched. In its extreme form, this pattern has been called *learned helplessness* (Seligman 1975).

There is some crossover in these attributional styles, however. For example, children might blame their behaviour on inability or ADHD which, although caused internally, is nevertheless defined by them to be uncontrollable. These children might thus fit the pattern called 'robot thinkers' in Table 4.1.

Correcting faulty internal attributions

Students' internal attributions about the causes of their failures will typically refer either to *inability* or lack of *effort*. Given that ability is a durable, pervasive and uncontrollable trait, it is maladaptive to cite it as a reason for failure. It might therefore seem better for students to attribute failure to lack of effort, as that is temporary, specific and controllable. However, children aged over ten years tend to believe that highly able individuals do not need to exert effort. Although this is patently untrue (as evidenced, for example, by elite athletes' extensive training), when students experience the need to put in more effort or are admonished by adults to 'try harder', they take this as meaning that they lack ability (Tollefson 2000; Weiner 2000). Thus, attributions about effort degenerate into durable, pervasive and uncontrollable attributions after all, resulting in students feeling discouraged and being less likely to exert effort.

Therefore, attribution training must direct students' focus on to something that is internal, temporary, specific and controllable—namely, strategy use (Robertson 2000).

Teaching students to attribute failure to their use of an ineffective strategy transfers their focus from *themselves* as failures to their specific *actions* and assures them that a change in strategy will produce better results.

Correcting external attributions

Although emerging before terms such as 'self-efficacy' were being used in cognitive theory, the first structured program for teaching people an internal locus of causality appeared in the late 1950s in the form of Albert Ellis's *rational-emotive behaviour therapy* (REBT) (Ellis 1962). It upholds that individuals with emotional difficulties share a common fallacy: that events or other people *make* us feel as we do. In contrast, REBT claims that emotional upsets arise, not from external events themselves, but from our faulty thinking about those events (Gonzalez et al. 2004). In other words, the source of our emotions is *internal*. This distinction is illustrated by an example developed by Ellis:

> Imagine that as you are driving, you pass a lifelong friend who, upon seeing you, leans out her window and hurls a long tirade of abuse at you for some wrong that you have apparently done but of which you were unaware. If your friend were leaning out of her car window you would feel distressed and mortified at her vitriol, with no idea what you had done to upset her. However, if she were leaning out of a mental hospital window, you would probably think, 'The poor dear: she's clearly disturbed and in the best place to get the help that she needs'.

In this scenario, your friend's behaviour was the same, but your differing emotional response resulted from your *interpretation* of what the behaviour meant. This shows that other people's actions might be the stimulus for our feelings, but they do not *cause* these. Our own thinking generates our feelings.

The next error made when people have an external locus of causality is to conclude that they cannot feel better until other people cease doing what is making them unhappy. Their demands with respect to others often contain the words *must*, *should* and *should not* (which thinking Ellis provocatively calls '*must*urbating'). These demands, however, do not (and cannot) make others change their behaviour and thus we feel helpless to improve our circumstances. The fallacy of an *external* locus of causality has thus been combined with an *uncontrollable* attribution for our negative circumstances.

A third and final error adds to our misery. This entails exaggerating the negative consequences of our own or others' failures to obey these rigid standards (termed 'awfulising' or 'catastrophising' thoughts). (For children, this is called 'doomsday thinking'—see Table 4.1.) This thought pattern is often accompanied by defeatist thinking about ourselves that comprises words such as *always*, *never* or *can't* and blocks us from taking steps to improve our own lives (Ellis 2005; Rogers 2003).

The result of this series of errors in thinking is that, rather than feeling healthy emotions such as sadness, regret, sorrow, annoyance or frustration, we generate feelings that are excessive, illogical, self-defeating and upsetting (Ellis 2005; Gonzalez et al. 2004). To overcome this, REBT teaches individuals to adopt internal and controllable attributions. To that end, it employs behaviourism's ABC (antecedent–behaviour–consequence) analysis of behavioural sequences, but defines each element slightly differently and adds two new steps, thus:

A   Activating event (or Adversity)
B   Belief
C   Emotional Consequence
D   Disputing absolutist thinking and external attributions
E   Generating a more Effective outlook

For children, the place to start is to teach them that their emotions are generated by their thoughts. When they are becoming overly aroused emotionally or acting in ways that get them into trouble, this signals that they need to change their thinking. The first step is to identify which circumstances are triggering overreactions and which thought pattern they use at such times (selecting from the dysfunctional attributions listed in Table 4.1). The children can learn to dispute these thinking habits, guided by the following questions, using the acronym AFROG (Kaplan & Carter 1995: 407):

• Does this thinking keep me *alive*?
• Does this thinking make me *feel* better?
• Is this thinking based on *reality*?
• Does this thinking help me get along with *others*?
• Does this thinking help me to reach my own *goals*?

Once the children can acknowledge that their thinking is not working for them, they can practise more self-efficacious thoughts that will, in turn, generate more adaptive feelings and behaviour. Students may require some prompts or secret signals from you to remind them to employ more helpful attributions and will need to practise their new thoughts as ardently as they previously asserted their dysfunctional thinking. They will also need encouragement during rehearsal time and specific feedback about their progress (Rogers 2003).

TABLE 4.1   Children's common dysfunctional attributions

Inaccurate thinking	Attributional style	Common theme	Examples	Resulting emotion
Robot thinking	Internal Durable Specific Uncontrollable	It's not my fault.	I can't help it: I've got ADHD.	Feelings of failure
I'm awful	Internal Durable Pervasive Uncontrollable	It's all my fault. I can't do anything right.	People are mean to me because I'm no good.	Avoidance of risk
You're awful	External Durable Pervasive Uncontrollable	It's all your fault.	I'd behave better if you weren't so mean.	Belligerence
Fairy-tale thinking	External Temporary Specific Controllable by others	It's not fair.	I wish they wouldn't be mean to me.	Hurt, anger
Wussy (defeatist) thinking	Internal Durable Specific Uncontrollable by me; controllable by others	I can't stand it.	Performing in front of others is scary.	Anxiety, shyness, overreaction to threats
Doomsday thinking	External Durable Pervasive Uncontrollable	Things are always awful. They'll never get any better.	I'll never have any friends.	Depression

Source: adapted from Roush 1984 (in Kaplan & Carter 1995: 396)

VIGNETTE 4.1 A CASE OF DYSFUNCTIONAL ATTRIBUTIONS
A six-year-old, intellectually gifted child was refusing to go to school on the grounds that every day was 'awful'. On a scale of 1 to 10, every day was a zero. In other words, her attributions about school were external, durable, pervasive and uncontrollable. To challenge these qualities, I expressed incredulity at this consistent rating, given that on some days she had computer, some days she had music, on others there was physical education. So, given that the days differed, how could it be that their ratings were identical? In my disbelief, I described the six patterns of dysfunctional thinking and she recognised that she was doomsday thinking.

I gave her the task that, upon arriving home from school each day for the next two weeks, she was to record on her calendar a rating for the day and report back to me what she had discovered. She returned a fortnight later to report that there had, surprisingly, been no zero-rated days, but a handful of fours, fives and sixes, which indicated that she had indeed been doomsday thinking. But then as an afterthought she added 'But I don't think I'll ever be able to stop it'. Her insight allowed her to recognise immediately and confess, 'I just doomsday thought about my doomsday thinking!'

Phase 4: Self-organisation

The fourth phase of the model in Figure 4.1 (see p. 77) requires that students organise how they go about completing a task. To be effective and independent managers of their own behaviour, students need the following several skills (Alberto & Troutman 2003; Whitman et al. 1991):

- ability to focus and sustain their attention;
- ability to monitor their own actions;
- impulse control—that is, the ability to delay responding;
- skills at goal setting;
- the verbal skills necessary for self-instruction;
- continuous decision making;
- to recognise their own accomplishments;
- to set appropriate standards or criteria by which to judge their performances;
- ability to delay gratification.

These abilities entail using self-organisation skills as well as being able to restrain maladaptive responses (Bandura 2001). This requires self-regulation of both our emotions and cognitions, which is often referred to as *metacognitive skills*.

Goal setting

Students perform better when they can set their own goals for their learning and behaviour, rather than having these imposed on them by others (Alberto & Troutman 2003). These goals need to be specific, fairly immediate and challenging but achievable (Alberto & Troutman 2003). To that end, you can guide students to set goals that are an improvement on their typical behaviour, but lower than their best performance (as no one can constantly achieve his or her best). Once students achieve one goal, they can be encouraged to raise their expectations until both of you are satisfied with their performances.

Self-recording skills

You will need to teach students how to record their own behaviour. In so doing, they can focus on the *outcomes* of their behaviour (in terms of quantity, quality or rate of a behaviour) or their thinking *processes* (Bandura 1986; Maag et al. 1993; Reid & Harris 1993). It is likely that students will be most successful when they are able to choose which aspect of their behaviour to monitor.

During self-recording training, you might need to use prompts to remind students to record their own actions. Recording methods include simple tally sheets (perhaps with pictures for younger students) or counting devices. Any such self-recording devices need to be portable, easy to use, inexpensive and obtrusive enough to remind students to record their behaviour while being undetectable by someone else (Shapiro 1984). The simplest form of recording is counting the number of times a behaviour occurs (Kaplan & Carter 1995). Students can do this by having their class time divided into intervals on their recording sheet and then noting on the sheet whether they did or did not perform the target behaviour during each interval. A less structured self-monitoring approach could entail simply asking students whether they are complying with class rules at the time a violation begins, thus: 'What are you doing? What is the rule about that?'.

The act of self-recording itself can produce a change in the behaviour, particularly when students are focusing on successes rather than failures (Alberto & Troutman 2003; Bandura 1986; Shapiro 1984). Perhaps surprisingly, self-recording still works even if it is not accurate (Alberto & Troutman 2003; Kaplan & Carter 1995; Whitman et al. 1991). However, you can enhance students' accuracy by initially recording their behaviour separately and rewarding them when their observations match your own, and subsequently fading this procedure once they are clear about which behaviours they need to be taking note of and thus can record independently.

Self-instruction

Self-instruction, or self-talk, is simply personal verbal prompts that we use to guide our own behaviour. When a task is new or challenging to us, we talk about it out loud to ourselves; then our self-talk becomes covert; and, finally, we no longer need to self-instruct because we have become competent at the task. You can teach these same steps using modelling, rehearsing and feedback—that is, you can complete an activity while commenting on the processes that you are using; then have students complete the task accompanied by your commentary; then have them instruct themselves, first out loud and then silently, as they complete the activity (Alberto & Troutman 2003). Eventually, they will learn to self-instruct quietly in their heads.

However, students may already have their own personal way of structuring tasks which, although not what you might use, is successful for them. Therefore, when using this process, it pays to ask them how they are structuring the task so that you do not impose on them your own self-instructions that do not make sense to them. This can be especially crucial when you teach auditorally but students learn visually.

Self-evaluation (self-assessment)

In this phase of self-regulation, students compare their performance against a preset standard to determine whether it meets this criterion. You will need to guide students to set appropriate performance standards, as this may be the most crucial phase of the self-management process (Whitman et al. 1991). Some students may set themselves very lenient standards, while others either do not give themselves enough reinforcement or are too demanding in their self-assessments (Alberto & Troutman 2003; Kaplan & Carter 1995).

Self-reinforcement or self-punishment

Once external reinforcers are working, you can fade them out and instead give students the opportunity to administer their own reinforcers. Self-reinforcement is likely to produce better results than external reinforcers (Alberto & Troutman 2003), particularly when students can select their own reinforcers. These can be administered both for improvement in the target behaviour and for the use of self-organisational strategies.

An alternative is to set up a self-punishment regime involving response-cost procedures or loss of tokens within a token economy system. However, these have two disadvantages.

First, students can find it more difficult to do the arithmetic involved in subtracting tokens in a self-punishment procedure than to add tokens in a self-reinforcement process. Second, self-punishment procedures may increase students' awareness of failure and consequently reduce their motivation (Alberto & Troutman 2003). Therefore, self-reinforcement procedures are preferable.

Phase 5: Performance

Phase 5 of the model for task success in Figure 4.1 (see p. 77) comprises taking action. Self-evidently, the required action needs to be within students' capabilities. One key skill that students need for academic or behavioural success is problem solving. Given that in the course of living problems are inevitable, human adjustment relies on the ability to identify and then solve difficulties (Kendall 2000). In order to surmount obstacles, students need to examine what has to be done, scan a range of behavioural options, and select one that they think will be most successful. To achieve this, they need to be capable of paying attention, pacing themselves, persisting and noting feedback, among other skills. Most fundamental of all will be their ability to use self-talk to guide their problem solving. The following explicit steps may be written or drawn on cue cards as reminders (Ashman & Conway 1989; Kaplan & Carter 1995; Yell et al. 2005).

1 *Pause.*
2 Ask: 'What is the problem?' This step *defines* the task to be accomplished.
3 Ask: 'What do I want?' This is the *identification of goals* step, which calls for examination of their own needs as well as those of others.
4 Ask: 'Is what I'm doing helpful to me?' This is the *self-assessment* phase.
5 If not, *plan solutions*: 'What else could I do?' It can be helpful at this point for students to generate a number of potential solutions, so that subsequently they do not become frustrated if their first one does not work out.
6 Choose what to do and do it. This requires *decision making*, wherein students select one of the alternative solutions on the basis of whether it is feasible and will meet their goal without making new problems for them. It also requires them to *devise a plan* for implementing their chosen solution. This calls for consequential thinking, which is the ability to consider the potential outcomes of a proposed behaviour.
7 *Evaluate the results.* (Go back to step 4.)
8 *Self-reinforce.*

The cognitive strand of cognitive-behaviourism teaches problem solving by instructing students how to structure problems in this sequence and providing practice at the analytical and reflective skills involved. The behaviourist strand advises you to strengthen students' resulting appropriate behaviour with the delivery of reinforcement.

Phase 6: Reflection on feedback

Feedback comes from two sources: from within and from others. Evaluating their own performances is essential to sustain motivation and to empower students to adjust their learning strategies on future tasks (Cleary & Zimmerman 2004). Evaluations that attribute failures to their inaccurate strategy use will be integral to this. You can also guide them to regard failure as *information* about what does not work, rather than as evidence of their inadequacies. Meanwhile, feedback from others needs to be authentic—students need to receive *accurate* information about what they have achieved and information that is *specific* enough to enable them to recognise their achievements and correct their errors. This introduces the debate between evaluative (or judgmental) and informative feedback, which is expanded on in Chapter 5 and applied in Chapter 12.

Conclusion: Cognitive-behavioural interventions

The cognitive route to enhancing motivation is to teach students to appraise tasks accurately, to value becoming skilful and to make adaptive attributions about their influence over their successes and failures. Students' motivation to participate will be improved when you involve them from the outset in developing the goals, defining the criteria for success, and planning the contingencies involved in the training.

This cognitive intervention is supplemented from the behaviourist tradition with the administration of rewards for engagement, strategy use and self-regulation. During the early phases of a program, these might be extrinsic rewards (such as ticks on a chart) that can later be traded in for activity reinforcers such as free time, a canteen voucher or a whole-class reward (Rogers 2003). However, cognitivists recognise that self-regulation is intrinsically more rewarding than externally imposed controls, so any rewards must be framed as celebrations of children's achievements and activity reinforcers must not be set up as bribes (Rogers 2003). In a departure from pure behaviourist principles, cognitive theory upholds that your belief in the children, encouragement to recover from setbacks and pleasure in their progress will ultimately be more meaningful to them than contrived reinforcers.

Applied cognitive-behavioural interventions

With behavioural (in contrast with academic) difficulties, training can focus on all phases of performance or specifically target only those aspects that are most deficient. For example, young people who are depressed will need to make more internal and controllable attributions, which is a *self-efficacy* issue. Where students feel that aggression works for them, they might not be *motivated* to change their behaviour, so training might focus on both the social context and all three motivational aspects. With impulsive children, the self-regulation processes will be the major issue.

Aggression

Cognitive theory represents aggression as the end result of faulty thinking at all six phases of performance that are depicted in Figure 4.1 (see p. 77):

- in terms of their *appraisals* of social tasks, children who are habitually aggressive attend to fewer relevant social cues;
- at phase 2, they often *value* coercive behaviour and have competitive goals, with little appreciation of the negative effects of their aggression on others;
- they have low *self-efficacy* as a result of maladaptive attributions whereby they appraise events from a hostile frame of reference, often being biased in interpreting others' behaviour as hostile even when it is ambiguous, while their locus of causality is external in that they tend to blame others for provoking them, with the result that they are not disposed towards exercising self-control;
- in terms of *self-organisation* skills, they become overly aroused emotionally (that is, angry), with the result that their responses often become disorganised;
- with respect to *performance*, they have an inadequate repertoire of problem-solving skills, particularly when faced with conflict; and
- finally their *reflection* on their own behaviour is inaccurate, resulting in an underestimation of their own aggressiveness (Asher 1983; Katsurada & Sugawara 1998; Lochman et al. 2000; Miller et al. 1998; Nelson & Finch 2000; Yoon et al. 2000).

Cognitive interventions for these students must be multifaceted, therefore, typically entailing a general social skills program and perhaps anger-management training.

Social skills training

Structured social skills training comprises giving demonstrations and practice of each skill during training sessions, employment of teacher and peer feedback about students' performance and, finally, natural reinforcement for using the skill in real situations (Cartledge & Milburn 1995; Ducharme & Holborn 1997; McGrath 1998; Noble 2006).

The content of social skills training describes to students the range of social skills (such as those listed in Box 4.1). To motivate them to expand their skills, you will need to provide a rationale for learning these by describing how particular behaviours will benefit themselves and others. The second component is teaching students to *value* prosocial behaviours such as cooperating, sharing, participating and validating peers.

Third, students need to know about feelings, starting with how to recognise and then deal constructively with common emotions such as anxiety or stress, embarrassment, responding to success and failure and dealing with provocation (Cartledge & Milburn 1995). Subsequently, they can learn empathy by practising how to identify others' feelings by looking, listening and asking (see Gesten et al. 1979; McGrath & Francey 1991; MacMullin et al. 1992; Petersen & Ganoni 1989).

The next cluster of prosocial skills is the self-management or planning skills of social goal setting, gathering information, making decisions about alternative behaviours, problem solving and negotiation (Caplan & Weissberg 1989; Goldstein et al. 1995; LeCroy 1983). Petersen and Ganoni's (1989) social problem-solving program teaches planning skills using the steps 'stop', 'think', and 'do'.

The final skill involves reflecting on other people's reactions to their behaviour so that students can judge whether their own actions are suitable. Some students do not pay enough attention to relevant social feedback, while others underestimate the extent to which their own behaviour influences the reactions of others.

BOX 4.1 SOCIAL SKILLS
To work cooperatively and competently together, students need the following social skills.
Personal qualities
- outgoing and friendly
- positive disposition
- sense of humour

Social behaviour
- listen and show empathy for others
- open to others' ideas and opinions
- negotiate differences in opinion
- compromise
- be respectful of others and their property
- not verbally hurt others

- be loyal, trustworthy and fair
- achieve what they want without hurting anyone else
- establish accepting relationships with peers of the same and other gender
- resist peer pressure to take dangerous risks
- give and receive both positive and negative feedback
- share resources
- take turns
- share friends with others: are not jealous or possessive
- communicate their feelings
- tactful
- able to apologise
- express affection
- assist others

Self-management
- know their own feelings
- manage their own feelings
- respond non-provocatively to teasing or bullying
- cope with failure and success and feelings of frustration without becoming angry or hostile

Relating to groups
- gain entry without disrupting the ongoing activity of the group
- respond positively when others are initiating interaction
- moderate their own behaviour to match the group
- aware of how their actions affect others
- cooperate with the group
- able to lead diplomatically by making suggestions rather than issuing orders
- manage conflict constructively and assertively—that is, without aggression
- avoid acceding to unreasonable demands, citing a rationale and offering an alternative suggestion

Relating to adults
- give information
- ask for information or help
- evoke favourable responses from other people
- scholastic competence (as this affects social acceptance) and responding to teacher expectations
- gaining independence from adult authority

Sources: Kamps & Kay 2002; Putallaz & Gottman 1981; Putallaz & Wasserman 1990; Rogers 2003; Trawick-Smith 1988; Warnes et al. 2005

The attention deficit disorders

Although the attention deficit (ADD) and attention deficit hyperactivity (ADHD) disorders are commonly regarded in the lay community as behavioural problems, this theory has focused on the cognitive impairments that underlie children's disruptive behaviours. An early conception was that impulsivity—that is, poor self-regulatory mechanisms—was at the heart of both the inattentive and hyperactive forms of the disorders (Anastopoulos & Barkley 1992). Children were thought to be less able to inhibit their impulses to distract and respond to competing stimuli. This was said to result in specific impairments in social judgment (phase 1), low self-efficacy (phase 3), problems with self-regulation and a lack of both emotional regulation and organisational skills (phase 4). The external manifestations of impulsive responding include a high rate of accidental injuries and impaired relationships with peers and family, while associated internal difficulties span emotional problems, including depression and anxiety, and learning difficulties such as poor phonological awareness (despite having average intellectual abilities overall) (Goldstein 1995; Hinshaw 2000).

Early cognitive interventions focused on teaching children with ADHD to self-instruct to overcome their impulsive tendencies. However, these researchers found that in fact children with the conditions talk to themselves *more* than same-aged peers (Berk & Landau 1993; Berk & Potts 1991; Diaz & Berk 1995). They concluded that this was because, whereas beyond the first year or two of school peers have been able to internalise their self-talk (to think quietly), children with ADHD are still having to guide themselves overtly—often using self-talk that is audible to others—in an attempt to overcome the disorganisation in their heads. This is the same mechanism that causes adults to talk out loud to themselves when they feel disorganised, even though ordinarily their thoughts (self-instructions) are covert.

Today there is an indication that the conditions may be due not to impulsiveness as such but instead to an impaired working memory (Tannock 2004). This is the memory that allows us to hold, store, evaluate and compare various pieces of information at once. Colloquially speaking, these children have difficulty 'keeping many balls in the air' simultaneously. The results are that affected children can have an idea but, before it is solidified, other ideas crowd in and they lose their original thought. Or they will have difficulty waiting to consider all information before responding, which leads to impulsive acts.

Aside from their learning difficulties, the social impairments of these children are the second aspect that most concerns schools. Although their number of prosocial interactions is the same as for children without the condition, children with ADHD display ten times more negative verbalisations directed at other children and three times more aggressive acts than typical children (Goldstein 1995). Not surprisingly, this behaviour leads to a difficulty establishing friendships but, even more importantly, to a difficulty with sustaining friendships. Also not surprising is these children's tendency to make friends with other children who are similarly experiencing difficulties (Barkley 1988).

These two aspects indicate the need in schools for two strands to cognitive-behavioural training for children with ADHD, the first focusing on their impaired social relationships and the second on the types of instruction needed to circumvent their memory impairments. The former entails social skills training and the latter will include, for example, giving simplified instructions, delivering these in short bursts and supplementing spoken directives with visual cues (e.g. drawings or photos of the tasks they need to do before the bell rings at the start of the school day). The thrust of these adjustments is to ensure that the students' restricted working memory space is not employed with processing complex instructions, thus leaving the children more capacity available to manage their completion of the task.

Self-restraint skills

As well as focusing on skills for solving academic and other problems you will need to teach certain students some practical skills, which Rogers (2003) calls *academic survival skills* (as listed in Box 4.2). These can be construed as self-restraint skills.

An example of a program for teaching these self-restraint skills is Bill Rogers's (2003) *behaviour recovery* program. This entails withdrawing targeted students from the group for training sessions. These start out by explaining, in a relaxed and warm manner, the behaviours that concern you, so that the students become clear about which of their actions are a problem and why. With young children in particular you can use a technique that Rogers calls *mirroring*, in which you briefly act out the behaviours of concern to illustrate these (as long as it is physically possible for you to do so; otherwise, gestures will suffice). Line drawings depicting the troublesome behaviour can also be useful. Then you can question the children about what they are doing in the demonstration or picture (not why they are doing it). This needs to be a description of their actions, not a label such as 'being naughty'. If they cannot or will not answer, you can provide the description yourself. If such questioning would be too confronting, you could act out the behaviour of hypothetical children, leading into your demonstration with 'Sometimes children do *this* when they get angry . . .', and subsequently posing the

BOX 4.2 A SAMPLE OF SELF-RESTRAINT SKILLS
· entering and leaving the classroom without violating the personal space of others
· settling down during group instruction, so that teaching and learning are not disrupted
· getting teacher attention during instruction time (e.g. raising a hand)
· movement
· settling to a task
· maintaining focus on the task
· desisting from interrupting others during their work
· maintaining a 'partner voice' during work

Source: Rogers 2003

same questions about what they see but maintaining the ruse that this talk is hypothetical (Rogers 2003).

The next step is to demonstrate or depict in illustration an alternative, more appropriate behaviour. Once again, you will ask the child to describe what actions are now being depicted. Picture cues keep the behavioural plan concrete, immediate and specific and are a memory aid. There will be one picture cue (or one pair depicting both old and new behaviours) for each troublesome behaviour.

At the next phase of the program, young children in particular will need to *rehearse* the alternative behaviours. Initially, you will demonstrate the new skill, then talk them through all aspects of their performance of it. Meanwhile, you will offer encouraging *feedback* for their efforts. This can include a demonstration as well as verbal information about the improvements in their performance. During this phase, you can introduce the children to privately understood cues and signals that you can deliver in the classroom to remind them to use their new behaviours in the regular setting. In subsequent training sessions, you would offer feedback and encourage self-reflection on how they have been performing there.

Applying cognitive theory to teachers

Your ability to regulate your own actions—and, in turn, to manage the class—is influenced by your own thinking, which includes your beliefs or attributions about your students and yourself, both personally and professionally.

Teacher self-efficacy

Professional self-efficacy is the extent to which you feel able to influence your students and work circumstances (Friedman 2003). This has three aspects: your sense of professional efficacy about teaching itself and classroom discipline, about your relationships with students, and about your influence within your school (Friedman 2003). Teachers with low professional efficacy are more likely to become overwhelmed by teaching, stressed by student disruptiveness (Martin et al. 1999) and more concerned with conveying the curriculum than with meeting students' needs. In contrast, those with high self-efficacy not only become less stressed but, when faced with challenges, take action to resolve the problems rather than avoiding them or using emotion-focused coping methods, such as alcohol or drug taking (Friedman 2003). Confident of their ability to generate solutions rather than feeling helpless, teachers with high self-efficacy implement an array of teaching methods, modify tasks to make them achievable by students and create a classroom climate that expects and supports high achievement (Tollefson 2000).

Teacher attributions

Teachers' attributions about their students and about themselves affect how they respond to disruptive behaviour. First, with respect to attributions about students, when teachers regard the cause as being located outside of students (due, say, to their disadvantaging family circumstances), they expect less of these students and, as a result, are less likely to expend the effort needed to ensure student success, thus depressing student outcomes and in turn confirming their external attributions (Tollefson 2000).

In contrast, when teachers view the source of disruptions as being *internal* to students, controllability becomes the issue. If the cause is seen to be something internal that students cannot control (e.g. a disability), teachers are more likely to be sympathetic, warm and supportive which, while positively intended, further entrenches students' own attributions about their personal incapacities. On the other hand, when teachers regard students as voluntarily making little effort or deliberately failing to control their own behaviour, they may become angry and, in turn, be less willing to help, provide more negative feedback and administer more punitive discipline in retribution (Martin et al. 1999; Scott-Little & Holloway 1992; Stormont 2002; Tollefson 2000; Weiner 2000). Students will either internalise this attribution and develop guilt, or withdraw from learning.

With respect to your attributions about your own role in managing disruptive behaviour, teachers with an external locus of causality who blame students or their parents for controllable behavioural difficulties in the classroom will perform the same three-step fallacious thinking already described for others: namely, 'It's their fault; my job will not be tolerable until they stop it; so I have to make them stop it'. This will lead to unproductive, authoritarian—even autocratic—behaviour management strategies.

However, you cannot blame students' disruptive behaviour on uncontrollable sources such as their nature, their family or social disadvantage. And you cannot blame behavioural difficulties on your own internal but uncontrollable qualities, be these durable (e.g. your personality) or temporary (e.g. your stress levels), as the ensuing self-criticism will be maladaptive. The conclusion, therefore, is the same as was drawn earlier with respect to students: you need to focus on the preventive and interventive *strategies* that you can employ to help students to function more successfully. According to this attributional style, if problems persist this merely indicates the need to change strategy.

Summary

Cognitive-behaviourism focuses on student self-management and also offers some advice to teachers about managing their own thinking and consequent approach to teaching. The aim of cognitive instruction is for students to become independent in managing their own behaviour, thus freeing teachers from the need to manage this for them. The rationale for promoting self-management is to increase students' motivation to comply with expectations, to ensure consistency (as students are always present to monitor their own behaviour, whereas teachers are not), to improve generalisation of skills, and to enhance the effectiveness of a behavioural program (Alberto & Troutman 2003; Kaplan & Carter 1995; Yell et al. 2005). Furthermore, when you teach students to think accurately, you are also contributing to their mental health as well as their ability to observe the norms of the classroom (Kaplan & Carter 1995).

Interim critique

In theory, the cognitive approach offers an efficient intervention for the many students who experience a common constellation of school-based difficulties: namely, low school achievement, disruptive behaviour and low self-esteem. As depicted in Figure 4.3, the use of self-instruction, self-monitoring and self-evaluation respectively would teach the self-discipline that is pivotal for resolving all three aspects. Self-management skills and students' resulting improved self-efficacy are more relevant than many other skills that

FIGURE 4.3   Cognitivists' view of the interrelatedness of achievement, behaviour and self-esteem

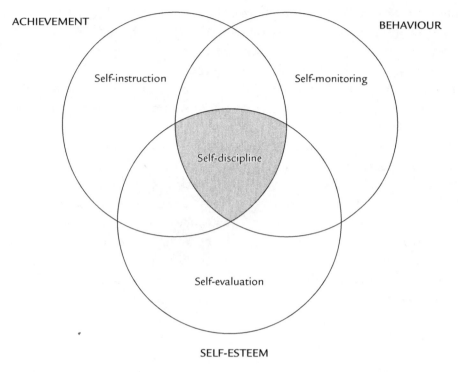

we teach students and are more likely to generalise (Kaplan & Carter 1995). Thus, cognitive techniques may be more suitable for older and more able students than behaviourism alone (Kaplan & Carter 1995), and have the advantage of including students more actively in their intervention (Braswell 1995).

However, the cognitive-behavioural approach has a dual personality: its cognitive arm advocates teaching an internal locus of causality, but its behaviourist strand employs external controls in the forms of rewards and punishments, which may both undermine self-efficacy and negate the aim of engaging students more actively in their own intervention.

Second, cognitive theory focuses mainly on the self-regulation processes and relatively neglects the motivational aspects (as depicted in Figure 4.1 on p. 77); and, while focusing on thinking and behaviour, it overlooks the role of emotions, with the result that it says little about how to motivate students to participate in the program in the first place. This is acknowledged by Rogers (2003) in his recognition that, if students resist committing to a cognitive-behavioural program, you cannot force them to do so as, by definition, self-management requires self-directedness.

Although the significance of cognitive skills has been clearly shown by research, the effectiveness of cognitive training to overcome skill deficits has not been verified. Social skills training, for example, has been found to increase children's knowledge about prosocial behaviour, while their attitudes and behaviours change minimally, if at all (Arnold & Hughes 1999). Part of the difficulty is determining which skills student lack, as teaching a skill they already possess (but perhaps are choosing not to employ) will obviously be ineffective. For example, attribution training works for students with maladaptive attributional styles; self-regulation and self-restraint skills are appropriate instructional targets for students with deficits in these; and a combination of these approaches is needed for students with both deficits (Robertson 2000).

While cognitive programs are taking effect, cognitive-behaviourism continues to employ a purely behaviourist delivery of punishments in response to rule violations. However, these behavioural interventions will be no more effective under the umbrella of cognitive theory than they are under pure behaviourism (as critiqued in Chapter 3). Those students whose behaviour most needs improvement are the ones who are least likely to cooperate with an intervention.

CASE STUDY

Adam is seven. He has difficulty with reading, spelling and writing, although he enjoys and is capable at maths. During non-maths lessons he spends a considerable amount of time off-task, when he frequently disrupts the other students. This is worse in the afternoons than in the mornings.

He is in a composite class of six and seven year olds. He spends most of his play time with the younger children. Frequently a pair including Adam is apprehended during play times doing such things as harassing passers-by from an out-of-bounds area of the playground that is close to the street, rifling through rubbish bins for food or cans to swap for other items with students, or engaging in fights in and around the toilets.

Adam seems bemused by the trouble he gets into, usually saying when challenged that he doesn't know why he behaves in these ways, that he couldn't remember that a given behaviour was against the rules, or that the other child was at fault for suggesting the activity.

Until a recent assessment, it was believed that Adam behaved as he did because of low academic ability. However, a battery of tests has shown his overall ability (IQ) to be average, with his maths skills in the high-normal range and his reading and spelling skills, while delayed, still within the lower range of normal limits. His teacher is now at a loss to find a new explanation for his behaviour.

A cognitive-behavioural response

If you endorsed the cognitive-behavioural approach, you might respond to Adam's behaviour in the following steps.

Step 1: Define a target behaviour

Just as an ABA practitioner would decide which behaviour is of most concern and describe that in clear terms, so too you need to begin a cognitive-behavioural intervention with this step (Carter 1993). You might start by targeting Adam's disruptive off-task behaviour and out-of-bounds play.

Step 2: Specify goals

You will negotiate goals with Adam, stating your expectations for his on-task behaviour and specifying an activity reinforcer (e.g. computer time) that he will earn if he satisfies this criterion. Wragg (1989) advises teachers to require a 25 to 50 per cent improvement in the target behaviour, so this would be your initial criterion, adjusted later if necessary.

Step 3: Adjust the environment

To help Adam meet these raised expectations, you would examine how relevant the curriculum seems to Adam (and other students), including assessing its level of difficulty. As part of your reflection, you should examine possible differences in teaching style between subjects because, while Adam's better performance at maths may be due to his greater interest in and ability at maths (as indicated by his assessment results), it may also be due to a closer match between the teaching methods used in that subject and Adam's learning style. This step is similar to the behaviourists' attention to antecedents, although it takes a wider view of contextual features that could lead to troublesome behaviour.

Step 4: Teach the rationale for rules

To make the rules more relevant for Adam and others, you would institute a class meeting in which the group nominated some rules and consequences for their infringement. During this discussion, you would explain why certain areas of the playground are out of bounds (which will be for safety reasons, such as the potential for abduction by passers-by and the risk that children who are injured beyond teachers' surveillance will not receive timely first aid). In terms of Adam's in-class behaviour, you might have peers explain to him, in a non-confronting way, how his disruptiveness makes it difficult for them to concentrate. The aim of these explanations is to help him value keeping the rules.

Step 5: Enhance self-efficacy

You would teach Adam to attribute the outcomes of his work to his own strategy use. This would entail three phases: teaching strategies; teaching him to make internal, specific, temporary and controllable self-statements about the causes of his success and failure; and giving specific and authentic feedback that highlighted the strategies he had employed, rather than necessarily commenting on the product itself.

This can then carry over to his behaviour where, rather than asking why he has broken a rule and thus inviting an external attribution, using a cognitive framework you can assume that the reason is internal and controllable and ask Adam how he might manage to control the impulse better next time. You can ask him what could be done now to help him remember in future. If you were to use a behavioural framework at this point, you would institute a punishment such as seclusionary time out. (You would have to be aware that application of external sanctions is risky in that it might undermine the concept that you are trying to convey to Adam—namely, that he is in control of what happens to him.)

Step 6: Teach self-recording skills

Together with Adam, you could generate a recording method whereby he can note his concentration span and resistance to impulses to play beyond the bounds of the official play areas. You will negotiate the delivery of reinforcers, both for the act of recording and for specified levels of improvement in his behaviour. You will simultaneously record his behaviour and reinforce him for accurate record-keeping, until the two records are similar enough that recording can be done by Adam alone.

Step 7: Teach self-instruction skills

You will need to teach Adam how to give himself positive instructions about his task-attack skills. His use of these will be reinforced according to the initial contract or agreement, with reinforcement administered first by you, then by the two of you, until Adam can reinforce his own improvements independently.

Step 8: Teach self-restraint skills

To guide Adam to overcome his impulses, you will need to teach him to apply his self-instruction skills to restraining his impulses. You will write verbal prompts on cards, with cartoons to give visual cues. At first, you will prompt Adam to use these cards to guide his thinking and then will gradually guide him to use them independently.

Step 9: Teach social skills if necessary

If Adam's social isolation does not improve subsequently to the improvement in his behaviour, you could teach the skills that appear to be restraining his positive involvement with his peers. These may be social or developmental. For example, if Adam's play is inhibited by an inability at the activities that his peers enjoy (e.g. ball games), assisting his inclusion could entail something as simple as teaching him ball skills yourself or recommending relevant extracurricular activities where he could practise these.

Discussion questions

1   Cognitive-behaviourists say that internal factors (as well as external consequences) influence behaviour. Is this a significant change from applied behaviour analysis?
2   How could you motivate a reluctant student to participate in a self-management program?
3   Select a behaviour of interest, such as aggression, attention deficit disorder or depression, and describe how you would address it using a cognitive-behavioural approach.
4   Reapply the case study you generated in Chapter 2, this time using cognitive-behavioural principles and practices. What new features are introduced into the recommended practices? What effect would these differences have on the individual student? On the whole class? On you?

Suggested further reading

Kaplan, J.S. and Carter, J. 1995 *Beyond behavior modification: a cognitive-behavioral approach to behavior management in the school* 3rd edn, Pro-Ed, Austin, TX

Practical programs are outlined by:

Rogers, W. 2003 *Behaviour recovery: practical programs for challenging behaviour* 2nd edn, ACER, Melbourne
Wragg, J. 1989 *Talk sense to yourself: a program for children and adolescents* ACER, Melbourne

Cognitive interventions for aggressiveness, anger, depression and ADHD

Kendall, P.C. (ed) 2000 *Child and adolescent therapy: cognitive-behavioral procedures* 2nd edn, Guilford, New York

Puzzle answer

The puzzle contains fifteen triangles: the large one, and six single triangles (which excludes the shape marked x, as it has four sides) plus eight triangles formed from two or more singles: 1+2, 1+2+3, 2+3+4, 3+4, 3+4+5, 5+6, 5+6+x+1 and 6+x+1+2 (see Figure 4.4).

FIGURE 4.4   Puzzle answer

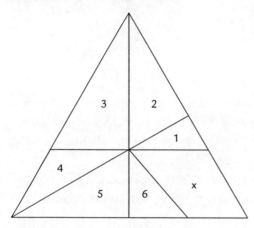

Source: Napier & Gershenfeld (2004: 4)

5 NEO-ADLERIAN THEORY

> ...each child needs encouragement like a plant needs water. Without it, his growth
> is stunted and his potential sapped.
>
> Dinkmeyer & Dreikurs (1963: 3)

KEY POINTS

- The neo-Adlerians aim to increase students' sense of belonging and consequent appropriate behaviour by establishing democratic relationships within the classroom that are based on mutual respect, cooperation and encouragement.
- Disruptive behaviour arises from faulty decision making; disruptive students have selected an inappropriate way to meet their legitimate goal of seeking to belong in the group.
- You can identify the goals of students' disruptive behaviour by noting how you feel and respond to the behaviour, and how students respond to correction. Following this, your aim will be to guide students to satisfy the same goal through more appropriate behaviour.

Introduction

Two differences distinguish the theories of Alfred Adler (1870–1937) from those of his contemporaries. First, whereas the dominant Freudian theory of the day analysed individuals' (internal) forces, Adler regarded individuals and their difficulties as embedded within their *relationships* or social contexts. Second, Adler was interested in individuals' present rather than their past (Goldenberg & Goldenberg 2005; Mosak 2005). Some modern writers have adapted Adler's beliefs, giving rise to my characterisation of them as neo-Adlerians. In the domain of discipline in schools, these writers include Rudolf Dreikurs (1897–1972), Don Dinkmeyer senior (1924–2001) and Don Dinkmeyer (junior), who were the principal authors of the *Systematic training for effective parenting* and *effective teaching* programs (Dinkmeyer & McKay 1989; Dinkmeyer et al. 1997; Dinkmeyer et al. 1980), and subsequently Jane Nelsen and colleagues (1998, 2000). In Australia, this theory is advocated by Maurice Balson (1992, 1994) and Jeannette Harrison for the early childhood years (2004).

Philosophical assumptions

The neo-Adlerian preventive approaches are based on democratic relationships in schools—that is, on the belief in the equal worth and dignity of all human beings (Harrison 2004). These aim to foster individual freedom while maintaining limits (Harrison 2004). Nevertheless, on the student–teacher power continuum shown in Figure 1.2 (see p. 19), this theory appears between the authoritarian and egalitarian positions because, although its preventive approaches are egalitarian, its interventions are authoritarian.

Nature of childhood

As with cognitive theory (discussed in the previous chapter) neo-Adlerian theory rejects the determinism of applied behaviour analysis, contending that individuals do more than merely respond to stimuli in predetermined ways: they actively assign meaning to events and make choices to meet their needs for significance (or a place in the world), security and self-esteem (Mosak 2005). Individuals strive for success and are creative in overcoming life's challenges (Chew 1998; Mosak 2005). While acknowledging the reality of biological limitations on children's academic achievements, Adler believes that 'It is not what you have that counts, but rather what you do with what you have' (Chew 1998: 9). This yields an optimistic view that young people can overcome difficulties in school and elsewhere.

Reasons for disruptive behaviour

The neo-Adlerians believe that all behaviour is goal-directed and purposive, that it is aimed at satisfying individuals' goals. These relate to the future rather than the past. Because children actively interpret their surroundings, their actions are not determined by consequences, the past, heredity or even emotions (Mosak 2005). Instead, individuals generate feelings to help them attain their goals.

Adler's original understanding of children's disruptive behaviours was that they were incited by feelings of inadequacy. He regarded these feelings as both natural and healthy in that they cause individuals to strive to achieve a unique identity and significance to others (Chew 1998). However, unhealthy levels of inferiority can result from excessive demands, negative competition at home and school, discouragement of risk taking, ridiculing children, and not taking them seriously because they are children (which Adler said was especially true for girls). These parenting and disciplinary practices stifle creativity, self-confidence and spontaneity (Adler 1957; Dreikurs & Cassel 1990). In their ensuing discouragement, children discover that they cannot find a 'place' for themselves where they can use their attributes and abilities, and therefore become discouraged. Purposeful activity will be replaced by disturbed thinking and behaviour (Mosak 2005).

In contrast with Adler's early focus on feelings of inferiority, the modern writers emphasise the need to belong, whereby children strive to gain acceptance in the groups of which they are a member (Chew 1998). If their prosocial behaviours are not acknowledged, they become discouraged and so seek to belong in any way they can, even if their resulting behaviour is antisocial.

Goal of discipline

Neo-Adlerian discipline is intended to create the order that is necessary for learning to occur, to guide students to exercise self-discipline (in the form of internalised compliance) and to promote cooperation within the group. The more recent writers mention potency as well and argue that these life skills are more important than any academic teaching that is conducted in schools (Nelsen et al. 2000).

Prevention of behavioural problems

The basic tool for preventing disruptions is to recognise that the only person we can control is ourselves. We do not have power to make other people change. To attempt this would be disrespectful, as we must honour others' right to control themselves (Nelsen et al. 2000). This means that your task is to decide what *you* will do to prevent and respond to student disruptiveness, rather than how students must act. You must enable students to take responsibility for their own actions by enhancing their sense of self-worth, taking advantage of positive forces within the group and responding non-punitively to disruptive behaviour (Chew 1998). Perhaps in a blend of Adler's focus on inferiority feelings and Dreikurs's focus on the need to belong, Albert (2003) proposes *three C's* of discipline for conveying to students that they are significant: capability, connection and contribution.

The first C: Capability

Students need to know that their worth does not depend on how successful they are (Harrison 2004). To give them a belief in their own capabilities, you will need to communicate to them your faith that they can achieve. To that end, mistakes have to be treated as a natural part of learning, conveying that it is better to try and make mistakes than to do nothing and learn nothing. You should accept a good attempt and show confidence in students' ability to improve on it another time. Thus, neo-Adlerians seek improvement, not perfection in their students (Nelsen et al. 2000).

Reduce competition

Neo-Adlerian principles suggest that schools abandon competition, as it does not motivate students for long and even then motivates only those who can succeed. Competition cuts across cooperation, leads to a lack of respect for the intrinsic worth of individuals and detracts from the satisfaction that is gained from mastering skills (Dreikurs & Cassel 1990).

Encourage but do not praise

Your feedback needs to be based on realistically achievable standards, for which knowledge of child development is fundamental (Nelsen et al. 1998). It is also crucial to employ encouragement rather than praise, so that students do not learn to rely on external judgments of their efforts, but instead trust their own wisdom and self-evaluation (Nelsen et al. 2000). The disadvantages of praise are listed in Box 5.1, key among which is that praise fosters conformity, whereas encouragement aims for understanding (Nelsen et al. 2000). Other features that distinguish the two forms of feedback are the following.

- Unlike praise, encouragement *does not judge* students, their work or behaviour. Using self-disclosure, it describes how their behaviour affects you or what you admire about their achievements. It *gives information*, not an evaluation.
- Encouragement invites students to evaluate their own efforts: 'What do you think of *that*? . . . Was that fun? . . . Are you pleased with yourself? . . . You seem proud that you did that so well.' Making independent evaluations of their own performances allows students to strive for standards that are relevant to themselves, rather than

having these imposed on them by others. In turn, this fosters an internal locus of causality (self-efficacy) and teaches students how to think, rather than what to think.

- Encouragement focuses on the *process* rather than the *outcome*. This enables teachers to equalise feedback between students of differing abilities; all students can each concentrate, persist or be creative according to their own capacities, even when their work products differ considerably.
- This allows encouragement to *avoid comparisons and competition* but to focus on individual students' progress.
- Encouragement is a *private* event that does not show students up in public or try to manipulate others into copying someone who is behaving to expectations.

BOX 5.1 DISADVANTAGES OF PRAISE

Praise and other rewards signify an inequality of power between adults and young people, implying that you have a right and some special competence to judge whether others' achievements are adequate.

Effects on students' self-esteem

- Praise tells students that they are being judged, raising anxiety that on a future occasion your judgment might be negative—thus communicating a lack of acceptance of them.
- Praise can set up unrealistic standards for students' performances, implying that they must be perfect, lowering their self-esteem when they realise that perfection is impossible.
- Praise teaches students that other people's opinions of them are more important than their own. This can stifle self-reliance.

Praise can impede learning

- Praise can be intrusive, interrupting students' absorption in their activity (Biederman et al. 1994).
- Praise causes students to focus on external rather than intrinsic rewards. It inhibits self-motivation and fosters an external locus of causality, impairing self-efficacy.
- Praise and other rewards may limit students' learning, as they confine themselves to tasks that they feel sure they will be able to achieve; they may do more work, but it is of a lower quality and less creative.

Praise can provoke disruptive behaviour

- Discouragement about being unable to meet unrealistic expectations may cause some students to behave disruptively.
- Praise does not teach students to monitor, and thus regulate, their own behaviour.

- Praise and other rewards might teach students how to manipulate their peers.

Praise can be ineffective

- Praise can be automatic for teachers and delivered, therefore, in a meaningless way.
- Teachers and their praise will lose credibility if the students' evaluations of their work do not match those of their teacher.

Praise can be unfair

- Teachers need a high level of technical expertise to use praise well.
- While some students can 'pull' praise from teachers, others cannot and therefore will receive less.
- Praise increases competitiveness between students.
- Their experience that praise is unfair causes some students to resent teachers who administer it.
- Individuals dislike being manipulated, even by methods (such as praise) that seem benign.

Sources: Balson 1992; Chew 1998; Dinkmeyer & Dreikurs 1963; Dinkmeyer & McKay 1989; Dinkmeyer et al. 1980, 1997; Dreikurs & Cassel 1990; Harrison 2004; Hitz & Driscoll 1988; Larrivee 2002, 2005; Nelsen et al. 2000

VIGNETTE 5.1 UNINTENDED OUTCOMES OF PRAISE

Sarah was twelve and academically gifted. Up until two years ago, she had been top of her class in almost all subjects. However, for the past two years she had been earning only C grades at best.

In conversation with her parents, we traced the beginning of her academic decline to an event two years ago when she had completed a superlative school project, which the principal displayed at assembly. This was probably an attempt to 'reinforce' Sarah's good study habits and encourage her peers to apply themselves equally conscientiously.

However, Sarah realised that if she did not wish to be made a spectacle of in front of the whole school, she should never do good work again. Moreover, as Sarah was gifted (which means that her skills fall in the top 3 to 5 per cent of the population), 95 to 97 per cent of the children looking on that day were not gifted and probably recognised that they could not achieve at that level, no matter how they tried. Some of them might have reacted to this comparison by becoming discouraged. And, feeling worse about themselves now than they did before, they might also resent Sarah and show this in hostility towards her in future.

Rewards do not always have these unintended outcomes, but *they can*. And there is no need to run the risk because, if the principal had wanted to encourage Sarah's efforts, he could have called her into his office and had a private conversation with her that went something like this: 'Sarah, thanks for coming over. I asked you here because your teacher showed me your school project and I just had to tell you that I think it is *extraordinary* and I hope you do too. I hope you're proud of what you've achieved, because I believe you deserve to be. I just wanted to congratulate you and shake your hand'.

The neo-Adlerians argue that this encouraging feedback would have *at least* as good a chance of 'reinforcing' Sarah's studiousness, with none of the risks of praise.

The second C: Connection

Students need connection both with their teachers and peers. As Bayton (in Nelsen et al. 2000: 27) states 'You have to reach the heart before you can teach the head'. Albert (2003) details five aspects of communication that let students know that you care for them: acceptance, attention, appreciation, affirmation and affection. The last entails kindness, which by definition is freely given rather than earned. Your caring is communicated by your tone of voice, by listening to young people, by honouring their emotions, appreciating their uniqueness, respecting their outside interests, enjoying your job and having a sense of humour (Nelsen et al. 2000).

Communication skills

The neo-Adlerians detail some communication skills for interacting with students individually and in class meetings. Like Gordon's communication roadblocks, to be discussed in Chapter 6, Dinkmeyer and colleagues (1997) also describe some ineffective listening styles, which they list as: the commander-in-chief, the moralist, the judge, the critic, the amateur psychologist and the consoler. These writers detail alternatives to these counterproductive styles, including your nonverbal communication that you are comfortable with engaging interpersonally with students and the verbal skills of reflective listening, assertiveness and collaborative problem solving. These writers acknowledge Thomas Gordon (1970, 1974) as the source of many of these concepts, and therefore the skills will be detailed in Chapter 6.

Class meetings
Like the humanists to be discussed in Chapter 6, Dreikurs and Cassel (1990: 78) advocate the use of regular class discussion groups on the basis that:

> . . . any problem child is a problem for the whole class, and the solution to the problem grows most naturally out of the helpful involvement of all class members.

The process of solving problems in the group is a real-life application of skills. Students take both ownership of their own difficulties and responsibility for finding a solution to them.

Students will generate most of the topics for the meetings, with communication skills used in an atmosphere of cooperation and orderliness to achieve win-win (or nonpunitive) solutions (Nelsen et al. 2000). When a student places on the agenda a complaint about a peer's behaviour, you can ask 'How is that a problem for you?', so that the focus is on fixing the effects of the behaviour, not blaming the actor. Now that the problem is clarified, students can brainstorm suggestions for solving it, then have those involved select one that they prefer. For whole-group issues, such as deciding on an excursion, voting is appropriate unless this would leave a disgruntled minority— in which case finding a consensus is more useful (Nelsen et al. 2000). Holding brief daily meetings rather than conducting these only when problems arise prevents the escalation of conflict and allows students to anticipate that problems will be solved promptly.

The third C: Contribution

You need faith in students' abilities to make meaningful contributions to their class, school, community, the environment and each other (Albert 2003). This entails involving them in making decisions that affect them by inviting rather than directing their actions and exploring with students what choice they might make rather than explaining to them what they should do (Nelsen et al. 2000). Students can contribute to generating rules governing their conduct to reflect their vision of how their ideal class would function (Albert 2003).

Intervention with disruptive behaviour

When disruptions occur, you would begin by checking students' understanding of the code of conduct by questioning whether their behaviour is on the 'appropriate' or 'inappropriate' list (Albert 2003). Next, you and the students will seek to understand why they are violating the code. Young children's motivation will entail one of four behavioural goals, whereas adolescents have more complex motivations (Chew 1998).

Behavioural goals

The goals and their behavioural expressions are listed in Table 5.1. The first three of these have a healthy manifestation, but when students feel discouraged by previous unsuccessful attempts to achieve significance and belonging their behaviour becomes either passive and defensive or actively antisocial and attacking (Balson 1992).

Striving for undue attention

Adler said that children need affection and power (autonomy) to overcome their feelings of inferiority. The later writers restated this goal as a need for attention. Thus was born the concept of *attention-seeking* behaviour. Neo-Adlerians explain such behaviour as a way to seek recognition. This is a legitimate goal, but when the need for attention becomes unhealthy—namely, when children come to believe that they have to be the focus of attention or have adults acting in their service (Harrison 2004)—they require ever-increasing amounts of attention, are constantly dissatisfied with the attention levels they receive and constantly display inappropriate behaviour to get more.

Misguided power

The need for power reflects children's requirement for control over their environment (Dinkmeyer & McKay 1989; Harrison 2004). However, antisocial behaviours result from the power struggle that ensues when adults try to control children—a battle the adults will inevitably lose (Chew 1998). Not to be confused with momentary attention seeking, children who want power want their own way all the time (Edwards & Watts 2004). Students who seek to dominate others have come to believe that the only thing that they can control is the pleasure or displeasure of the adults in their lives.

Justice or revenge

Seeking revenge results when an extreme power struggle between adults and children produces antagonism, or when students become so deeply discouraged because of being disliked and not belonging that they believe that they must hurt other people in return (Chew 1998; Dreikurs & Cassel 1990). They blame others for their problems (Balson 1992) and believe that justice therefore is served by getting back at them. This occurs even when the perceived wrong has not been committed against themselves but against a peer (Tileston 2004). Particularly when they behave in an attacking mode, these

TABLE 5.1   Behavioural manifestations of children's goals

Goal	Positive expression	Passive, defensive antisocial expression	Active, attacking antisocial expression
Attention	Desire to be involved Willingness to contribute	Engage adults unnecessarily by being untidy, cute, shy, fearful, tired, frivolous, in need of help	Provoke adults in ways that cannot be ignored, e.g. showing off, clowning, making mischief, pencil twiddling, arriving late
Power	Quest for autonomy, exercise responsibility for self	Uncooperative, stubborn, forgetful, weak, apathetic or uncooperative behaviours that send the message 'You can't make me'	Rebellious, defiant, angry, aggressive, bullying and dominant acts that convey the message 'You can't stop me'
Revenge	Seek social justice	Sullen, moody, refuse to participate	Delinquent lifestyle demonstrated in vicious, destructive acts, including stealing and vandalism
Withdrawal from demands	Healthy levels of feelings of inadequacy cause individuals to strive to achieve and surmount challenges	Acting hopeless and helpless by being idle, feigning stupidity, being isolated, not mixing with others, playing in babyish ways	This goal has no active, attacking behavioural expression

Source: adapted from Albert 2003; Balson 1992

students seem unlovable and it is difficult for teachers to convince them that others like them, as they do not like their behaviour (Balson 1992). Dreikurs and Cassel (1990: 49) extend this point further:

> Unfortunately those who need encouragement most, get it the least because they behave in such a way that our reaction to them pushes them further into discouragement and rebellion.

Withdrawal

All individuals must feel inadequate to some extent, as this feeling provides the motivation for learning. However, those who are too ambitious, competitive or sensitive to pressure are vulnerable to becoming deeply discouraged about their chances of securing their goals and therefore withdraw in an effort to avoid humiliation (Edwards & Watts 2004). The short-term goal of avoiding difficulties comes to override the long-term goal of achieving success. Teachers interpret such students' displays of inadequacy as either a need for help or as a signal to give up teaching them, as they are not making any effort to succeed.

Diagnosis of the student's goals

Intervention centres on diagnosing which of these goals is driving students' behaviour, a process that Dreikurs and Cassel (1990) assert is fairly simple given that there are only four goals for disruptive behaviour. As summarised in Table 5.2, diagnosis is based on three clues: noting your own emotional reactions and behavioural responses and observing how the student reacts to your attempts at correction.

Confrontation

The neo-Adlerians contend that, while individuals are aware of their behaviour, they are not always conversant with their goals and thus gaining awareness of the reasons for their behaviour (achieving insight) may induce students to change how they act. Therefore, once you have generated a hypothesis about individuals' goals, you can confirm your diagnosis by discussing these with them. You are to do this by asking students whether they know why they behave as they do and, if not, whether they would like to hear your ideas. Then, you are to ask in a matter-of-fact way one question (judged to be the most salient) out of each of the following categories (Dreikurs & Cassel 1990; Edwards & Watts 2004: 117):

- *Attention seeking.* Could it be that you want me to notice you more; that you want special attention; that you want me to do something special for you; that you want to be special to the group?
- *Power seeking.* Could it be that you want to be boss; that you want your own way; that you want to do what you want; that you want me to admit that I can't control you?
- *Revenge seeking.* Could it be that you want to punish me; that you want to hurt others as much as you feel hurt by them; that you want to get even with me?

TABLE 5.2   Clues to diagnosing the goals of disruptive behaviour

If the teacher feels	and responds by	and the student's response to correction is to	this means that the student's goal is
Annoyed Irritated Worried Guilty	Reminding, coaxing, ignoring, helping students do things that they could do for themselves	Desist temporarily, but then resume the behaviour	Undue attention ('Notice me; involve me')
Angry Challenged Threatened Defeated	Fighting power with power Confronting Giving in Self-righteousness	Escalate defiance or comply, but is smug at making the adult upset	Misguided power ('You can't make me; I'm the boss of me')
Hurt Disappointed Disgusted	Retaliating to get even	Retaliate back, become devious, violent or hostile	Revenge ('I will hurt you as you hurt me')
Despairing Hopeless Helpless Inadequate	Agreeing with the student that nothing can be done, pitying, giving up, being overly helpful	Refuse to participate or cooperate, retreat further, be apathetic, helpless	Withdrawal from demands ('Don't expect anything from me; leave me alone; there's no use trying as I won't get it right anyway')

Sources: adapted from Albert 2003; Balson 1992; Nelsen et al. 2000: 85

- *Withdrawal from demands.* Could it be that you want to be left alone because you think you can't do anything; because you want to be the best but don't think you can; because you want me to stop asking you to do things?

In case students are motivated by more than one goal, you should ask at least one question pertaining to each. Those who seek attention or power are seldom aware of their motivation, whereas those seeking revenge are often aware of their goals but do not notice their own role in provoking others (Edwards & Watts 2004). Clarifying their motives through questioning is said to produce a 'recognition reflex'—e.g. a peculiar smile, glint in the eye, or posture adjustment—that indicates when students recognise their own motivation (Chew 1998; Nelsen et al. 2000). The resulting insight into their goals and into the effects of their behaviour on others might bring about a spontaneous change in a student's behaviour (Dreikurs & Cassel 1990; Nelsen et al. 2000). If not, you will need to intensify your encouragement at the same time as instituting the following corrective measures, whose aim is not to force children into submission but to motivate them to make responsible choices (Chew 1998).

Convert negative behaviours into positive behaviours

Once you are aware of a student's goal, you should act to make sure that the need is met through more appropriate behaviour, while ensuring that the misbehaviour does not achieve its desired end. A positive first response is listening to *attention-seeking* students, reflecting what they might be feeling (Nelsen et al. 1998). Subsequently, you should ignore attention-seeking behaviour whenever possible and instead give students attention in unexpected ways when they are not making a bid for it. Encouraging them when they are behaving appropriately teaches them that they have a place in the group without needing to resort to the antisocial behaviour. You are also advised to refuse to remind, punish, reward or coax.

When students are seeking *power*, you should refuse to play the authoritarian role, withdrawing from the conflict in the knowledge that fighting will only escalate their rebellion. During teaching, you could stop instruction altogether, so that in persisting with the behaviour the student is confronting the whole class rather than just you (Edwards & Watts 2004). Some time out might be beneficial here (Nelsen et al. 1998). You will need to give power-seeking students appropriate choices, solicit their help, cooperation or leadership in appropriate ways, and agree to solve the problem collaboratively (Nelsen et al. 1998). The aim is to teach these students to use power constructively.

When students want *revenge*, you must avoid feeling hurt and must not punish or retaliate, but once again listen to their feelings and recognise that a child who is hurtful is 'a hurting child' (Nelsen et al. 1998: 279). Feeling that they are in the right, they will regard anyone who disagrees as their enemy (Edwards & Watts 2004). Therefore, you must listen to their outrage at a perceived injustice (Tileston 2004). Nevertheless, when someone else has been harmed, you will need to help the perpetrator to make amends (Nelsen et al. 1998). In the longer term you will need to build a trusting relationship with students who want revenge, in order to convince them that they can be accepted without resorting to antisocial behaviour. Punishment is ineffective with revenge-seeking students, as it will only provoke further rebellion and will confirm their belief that they do not belong in school (Ansbacher & Ansbacher 1956). If they are so discouraged that they no longer care whether or not they are accepted at school, you may need to refer them for specialist help. Otherwise, you can institute class meetings to reaffirm rules and confirm these students' place in the group.

When discouraged students *withdraw* through displays of inadequacy, you need a sincere conviction that they are capable and can succeed. You must refuse to give up. Instead, you must recognise their deep discouragement and stop all criticism, acknowledge all positive effort, and not get hooked into pity or into agreeing that they are incompetent and that there is no hope. You will need to break tasks into small, achievable steps to encourage risk taking, allow students to try—even if that involves failure—and teach them the task-attack skills that they will need for success, such as problem solving, positive self-instruction and sequencing (Albert 2003; Nelsen et al. 1998).

Apply natural and logical consequences

Should the preventive and earlier interventive methods fail to bring about enough improvement in students' behaviour, most neo-Adlerians recommend using natural or logical consequences for offences that violate the needs of others. The exception is Nelsen and colleagues (2000), who recant the advice in the earlier edition of their book to use consequences, claiming (as do the humanists) that these are just a euphemism for punishment. Again in keeping with the humanists, they dispute the assumption behind punishment that teachers have to make children feel worse to motivate them to do better. In recognition of its negative effects—namely rebellion, low self-esteem, avoidance of risk and blind compliance—and that it is better for children to learn from their mistakes than to pay for them, Nelsen and colleagues advise looking for a solution rather than imposing a punishment, employing class meetings for doing so. They caution that such meetings can function only in a nurturing environment, which would be damaged by the imposition of punishment.

Nevertheless, the remaining neo-Adlerian writers advocate the use of both natural and logical consequences. A *natural consequence* is the natural outcome of an individual's actions that occurs without adult intervention, such as getting wet when you stand in the rain (Harrison 2004). Although letting natural events take their course sounds reasonable, you cannot do so in dangerous situations (such as allowing children to run onto a road, the natural consequence of which can be injury), while students deserve protection from some natural consequences, such as the peer rejection that can result from antisocial behaviour. Their rejection might be natural, but it is too high a price to pay.

Logical consequences are arranged by you but, unlike punishment, have a logical, cause-and-effect link with the student's actions. For example, if a student draws on a wall, the logical consequence is to clean the wall. The difference between this and a punishment is that you are objective about guiding students to take responsibility for their actions, with no disguised aim of forcing them to change their decision. Experiencing the results of their choices teaches students that, while they can behave as they choose, they must still be responsible for their decisions. (The exception is physical danger.) Reality replaces the authority of the teacher (Dreikurs & Cassel 1990).

BOX 5.2 GUIDELINES FOR ADMINISTERING LOGICAL CONSEQUENCES

Consequences include a loss or delay of privileges, loss of freedom of interaction, restitution or reteaching an appropriate behaviour (Albert 2003). These will be effective when they are logically related to the misdemeanour; are reasonable—which means that they are proportional to the severity of the disruptive behaviour; are respectful inasmuch as they do not convey a judgment of the student; and are reliably enforced (Albert 2003). Even so, logical consequences are to be used only for attention-seeking behaviour, with natural consequences employed for power and revenge seeking and neither for displays of inadequacy (Dreikurs & Cassel 1990).

These core guidelines for delivering effective consequences are supplemented by the following recommendations.

- Logical consequences work only if students care. Therefore, for consequences to be effective, preventive measures must already be in place (Dreikurs & Cassel 1990).
- There is not a logical consequence for every problem. Look first for solutions and use consequences only if solution attempts fail.
- If you have to struggle to identify a logical consequence, this is a clue that you are planning a punishment; if the consequence is not obvious, it is not logical or appropriate (Nelsen et al. 2000).
- The consequence should be helpful, rather than hurtful (Nelsen et al. 2000). For example, apologising to a peer helps the aggrieved party to feel better; cleaning up a mess results in a clean space. As long as students are not blamed or shamed in the process of restitution, both consequences *help*. In other words, they are solutions as well as consequences.
- Involve students in generating consequences in advance. Although students have a wealth of wisdom to apply to this task, they have also learned about punishment by receiving it themselves. Therefore, during the phase of selecting which consequence to apply (after brainstorming a range of alternatives), you will need to guide them to avoid punitive suggestions.
- Focus on what will prevent future incidents, rather than making students pay for their past mistakes (Nelsen et al. 2000).
- Teach the link between opportunities, responsibilities and consequences (Nelsen et al. 2000). Opportunities (e.g. to use sporting equipment) can be made available to students only when they can exercise responsibility

(to use the equipment safely). When their unsafe behaviour demonstrates that they are not ready to take responsibility, ask them how long they need to cool down before being given the opportunity to use the equipment once more (Nelsen et al. 2000).

- During a disruption, give students choices about what would help them most. You might ask 'What will help you most right now? Would you like to call an emergency class meeting, have some time out on your own till you feel better, or talk with someone?'.

- Finally, logical consequences must be delivered in a matter-of-fact manner, be related to the circumstances at the time, and be applied only for harmful behaviour that cannot be solved in other ways.

Alternatives to punishment

Nelsen and colleagues (2000) recommend that class meetings be employed to have students brainstorm a list of consequences for misdemeanours and then a list of solutions. You will then ask students to reflect on which responses they prefer and which have the better chance of being effective. These writers report that students always choose the solutions. Suggested solutions might include apologising, walking away, putting the issue on the agenda for a class meeting, being assertive, telling a peer to stop, counting to ten to cool off, and so on. These strategies can be illustrated on what these writers term 'a wheel of choice' and displayed in the classroom, with an instruction to students to use two of these solutions before approaching teachers for help (unless in an emergency).

Recovery from mistakes

Nelsen and colleagues (2000) point out that, when playing video games, students are willing to see mistakes as information that they need to try a different strategy, rather than a reprimand for being incompetent. This same attitude needs to be applied by teachers and students to behavioural mistakes. Starting from acceptance that what you do is separate from who you are, these writers enunciate three steps for recovering from such mistakes: *recognise* that you are responsible (but not to blame) for the error; *reconcile* by apologising to the person you have offended; *resolve* the problem by brainstorming a solution.

Positive time out

Becoming upset is not inappropriate and therefore students should not be punished for it. However, there will be times when, before they can *behave* better, they will need to take some time out of the setting to calm down—that is, *feel* better. An analogy is a time out during a sports match, during which players can catch their breath and come up with a new game plan (Nelsen et al. 2000). For this purpose, you and your students can together design a positive time-out area that will help soothe their feelings. The area might include some comfortable cushions, music with headphones, a window through which students can gaze outside. Collectively, you might determine a time limit (e.g. ten minutes), or you might decide that students can remain in time out for as long as they need to recover their emotional equilibrium. A friend might be invited to accompany students to time out to listen to their feelings about the incident that has disturbed them.

If students exploit this opportunity to withdraw by using it to escape commitments or work demands, you would solve this by diagnosing which of the four goals is motivating their behaviour and solve that (Nelsen et al. 2000). However, Nelsen and colleagues find that, when students are involved in designing the positive time-out area, they seldom take advantage of it.

Parent–teacher–student conferences

Students need to be involved in any meetings where they will be discussed. These joint meetings between yourself, students and their parents should be encouraging. To that end, Nelsen and colleagues (2000) suggest writing four questions on a form that students, parents and yourself fill out prior to your meeting. These questions will ask them to report on what is going well for the student, what will encourage continued success, what needs improvement and what would support that improvement. Then in the meeting you can compare your answers, beginning with the student's.

Nelsen and colleagues remind us that students will be encouraged by success in their best or favourite activities. They cannot be good at everything; therefore, rather than focusing on eliminating their difficulties, excellence will be fostered only by focusing on students' strengths while supporting them to manage (not overcome) their weaknesses.

Teachers helping teachers

A final intervention recommended by Nelsen and colleagues (2000) is based on awareness that, while challenging students need more than the usual levels of encouragement and support, so too do their teachers. To that end, teaching staff should hold regular meetings where they can encourage each other's efforts. In such meetings, a facilitator will guide teachers to describe a problem that has arisen in their class and detail how they felt about it. This will allow the staff group to diagnose the student's mistaken goal, following which they can brainstorm potential solutions, one of which the affected teacher will select. Nelsen and colleagues recommend role playing at each stage to enact the problem, the teacher's feelings at the time, and the chosen solution.

Summary

The neo-Adlerian writers base their approach on the belief that children strive to belong and that, if they become discouraged about their ability to feel significant to others through prosocial behaviour, they will resort to antisocial behaviour to meet this fundamental need. Your preventive role as a teacher is to enhance students' beliefs in their own capabilities through minimising competition and giving encouraging feedback, enhancing their connectedness to each other and yourself by communicating individually and as a group in meetings, and enabling students to contribute meaningfully to decisions about themselves, their class and their school. The goals behind disruptive behaviours are diagnosed, and students are encouraged to translate their needs into more positive expressions. As a last resort, you would impose natural or logical consequences.

Interim critique

The main contribution of this theory is its distinction between encouragement (informative feedback) and judgmental feedback in the form of praise and other rewards. However, it violates its humanist preventive methods with its behaviourist interventions.

The main issues pertain to its diagnosis of the goals for disruptive behaviour. First, the process of diagnosing based on your own feelings defies the theories both to the political right and left of neo-Adlerianism: it flouts the behaviourist edict to be impartial in observing others' behaviour; it violates cognitive understandings that the cause of our emotions are our own thoughts, not other people's behaviour; and it defies the humanist (and its own) contention that diagnosing others ('mind-reading') blocks communication with them. It should be self-evident that we cannot diagnose another's intent based on our own reactions, not least because the same behaviour can evoke different emotional reactions from different observers and from the same observer at different times.

Moreover, diagnosis of the goals is an error in logic that confuses the *outcome* of a behaviour (e.g. the teacher's emotions) with the student's *intent*. When disruptive behaviour diminishes upon being ignored (an outcome), that is not evidence that the behaviour was 'attention seeking' (an intent) any more than criminals' cessation of lawbreaking after being imprisoned proves that their former criminal behaviour was 'prison seeking'.

Not only is the process for goal diagnosis problematic, but the notion that there are only four goals for all human behaviour is preposterous. It seems absurd to claim that 'For some children, attention for negative behaviour is better than no attention at all' (Roffey & O'Reirdan 2003: 41) when adults would prefer to be ignored than reprimanded by their supervisor. Surely, children cannot be so deranged that their preference is the opposite. Not only is it inhumane, it is inept psychology and intellectually lazy to blame children by calling their behaviour attention seeking or a misguided quest for power when they are reacting to extreme trauma (such as from emotional neglect, abuse, war or detention), are grieving the death of or separation from their parent, are being tormented by school bullies, or they have been made responsible for the welfare of their siblings or incapacitated parents, to name but a few common experiences for children. Overlooking these injustices to diagnose some glib motive adds yet another injury to thus misunderstood children.

Furthermore, although Adler and Dreikurs contended that individuals' behaviours are a natural and valid response to discouragement, this theory describes children's motives in negative terms. More respectful ways to label the goals could be, for example:

- attention seeking could have been called a quest for *confirmation*;
- power seeking could be referred to as a need for *autonomy*;
- the goal of revenge could instead be seen to reflect a desire to pursue *justice*;
- withdrawal could be more positively framed as a feeling of *hopelessness*.

This lack of respect for students is mirrored in a lack of respect for parents, who are said to be the cause of their children's difficulties (Balson 1992). The belief that problems will be resolved if parents received the 'right' training conveys an undemocratic disrespect for the skills that parents already possess.

Furthermore, this negative characterisation of children's motives almost inevitably gives rise to authoritarian interventions. First, despite emphasising students' social needs in its preventive measures, its intervention applies consequences to individuals with scant regard for their social context. Second, regardless of whether they are logical rather than arbitrary, its 'consequences' are still punishments in disguise, as acknowledged by Nelsen and colleagues (2000).

Even if its diagnosis of goals were accurate, I do not share the neo-Adlerians' faith in the power of students' insight to influence their behaviour. Attitudinal research tells us that there can be little link between attitudes, information and behaviours, as illustrated by the fact that cigarette smokers are aware of (have insight into) the risks from smoking and yet they continue to smoke. Indeed, rather than preceding a change in behaviour, insight often *follows* it (Ullman & Krasner 1975), as demonstrated by the anti-tobacco vehemence of the *ex*-smoker.

Finally, the fact that this approach attracts no research activity might be a clue that it cannot withstand rigorous evidence-based scrutiny. Other than the edict that punishments be logical rather than arbitrary, it adds nothing to behaviourism and does not augment the preventive elements that it imported from humanism. Therefore it is redundant.

CASE STUDY

Adam is seven. He has difficulty with reading, spelling and writing, although he enjoys and is capable at maths. During non-maths lessons he spends a considerable amount of time off-task, when he frequently disrupts the other students. This is worse in the afternoons than in the mornings.

He is in a composite class of six and seven year olds. He spends most of his play time with the younger children. Frequently, a pair including Adam is apprehended during play times doing such things as harassing passers-by from an out-of-bounds area of the playground that is close to the street, rifling through rubbish bins for food or cans to swap for other items with students, or engaging in fights in and around the toilets.

Adam seems bemused by the trouble he gets into, usually saying when challenged that he doesn't know why he behaves in these ways, that he couldn't remember a given behaviour was against the rules, or that the other child was at fault for suggesting the activity.

Until a recent assessment, it was believed that Adam behaved as he did because of low academic ability. However, a battery of tests has shown his overall ability (IQ) to be average, with his maths skills in the high-normal range and his reading and spelling skills, while delayed, still within the lower range of normal limits. His teacher is now at a loss to find a new explanation for his behaviour.

A neo-Adlerian application

As a neo-Adlerian teacher, you might use the following approach with Adam.

Step 1: Encouragement
You would establish democratic relationships with Adam and all students, making particular effort to encourage him to see himself as capable.

Step 2: Connection
Adam often gets into trouble with younger collaborators and does not seem to mix socially with his age mates. To assist his social inclusion, you could place the issue on the agenda for a class meeting, so that all can contribute to its solution.

Step 3: Contribution
You would discuss Adam's behaviour with him individually, listening to him and seeking his ideas for solving it. At this point, you will negotiate with him some natural or logical consequences that might be administered for future infractions.

Step 4: Diagnosis of goals
If the disruptive behaviours persist, you would analyse the goals for his behaviour by noting that you frequently feel annoyed and often coax Adam to improve his work output and behaviour. He is a good-natured lad and he desists from his disruptiveness temporarily, but then resumes it. Therefore, you diagnose his goal to be seeking undue attention.

Step 5: Confrontation
You would then ask Adam if he knows why he acts as he does and, if he answers in the negative, would ask if he would like to hear your ideas. You would follow with one question pertaining to each goal, observing for a 'recognition reflex' that signals that Adam has just gained insight into his motives.

Step 6: Goal redirection
Assuming that his goal does turn out to be attention seeking, you would ignore his disruptive behaviour whenever possible and instead make a special effort to give Adam your attention when his behaviour was neutral or appropriate. You would cease reminding, coaxing, rewarding and punishing him.

Step 7: Administration of consequences
If these measures were unsuccessful, Adam would need to experience the natural and logical consequences of his choice of behaviour, as previously negotiated with him. For example, failure to confine himself to in-bounds areas of the playground would result in his opportunities to play being restricted, perhaps with the imposition of

time out or being required to accompany the duty teacher at play times for a limited period. If he insists on rifling through rubbish bins, you might give him playground litter duty for a specified period. His disruptive off-task behaviour would result in non-seclusionary time out (being seated at a distant desk) in the classroom until he can work without interfering with others.

Discussion questions

1   What do you think of the arguments against praising students? Does encouragement overcome these?
2   Can you identify reasons for students' misbehaviour besides the ones identified by this theory?
3   What do you think of the three sets of clues that neo-Adlerian teachers use to diagnose the student's goals?
4   What are your thoughts about the similarities and differences between punishments and logical consequences?
5   Re-apply the case study that you generated in Chapter 2, this time using neo-Adlerian principles and practices. What new features are introduced into the recommended practices? What effect would these differences have on the individual student? On the whole class? On you?

Suggested further reading

For teachers

Albert, L. 2003 *Cooperative discipline: teacher's handbook* AGS Publishing, Circle Pines, MN
Balson, M. 1992 *Understanding classroom behaviour* 3rd edn, ACER, Melbourne
Dinkmeyer, D., McKay, G. and Dinkmeyer, D. 1980 *Systematic training for effective teaching* American Guidance Service, Circle Pines, MN
Nelsen, J., Lott, L. and Glenn, H.S. 2000 *Positive discipline in the classroom* 3rd edn, Prima Publishing, Roseville, CA

For early childhood practitioners

Harrison, J. 2004 *Understanding children: foundations for quality* 3rd edn, ACER, Melbourne
Nelsen, J., Erwin, C. and Duffy, R. 1998 *Positive discipline for preschoolers: for their early years—raising children who are responsible, respectful, and resourceful* rev 2nd edn, Prima Publishing, Rocklin, CA

For parents

Balson, M. 1994 *Becoming better parents* 4th edn, ACER, Melbourne
Dinkmeyer, D. Sr, McKay, G.D., Dinkmeyer, J.S., Dinkmeyer, D. Jr and McKay, J.L. 1997 *Parenting young children: systematic training for effective parenting (STEP) of children under six* American Guidance Service, Circle Pines, MN
Dinkmeyer, D. and McKay, G. 1989 *Systematic training for effective parenting* 3rd edn, American Guidance Service, Circle Pines, MN

Websites

Nelsen, Lott and Glenn's site: <www.empoweringpeople.com>
Linda Albert's site: <www.cooperativediscipline.com>

6 HUMANISM

We need young adults who can think and act creatively, who value human life, are able to make discerning decisions, and know how to communicate and negotiate rather than fight. It is our responsibility as guardians of these values to establish learning environments that foster freedom and responsibility.

N. Rogers (1994: iv)

KEY POINTS

- You will promote both high achievement and considerate behaviour in students when you nurture their emotional needs and curiosity about learning.
- You can do this by establishing egalitarian relationships with students and by facilitating rather than directing their learning.
- Intervention with disruptive behaviour comprises communicating to solve the problem, rather than any attempt to punish a miscreant.

Introduction

In counselling, the person-centred or humanist approach was first identified with Carl Rogers (1902–87). Within education, it is based on the progressive education movement whose founders, such as Friedrich Froebel (1782–1852) and John Dewey (1859–1952), abhorred traditional teaching methods where children sat passively behind desks and were required to learn by rote information of little meaning in their lives (Gartrell 2003). This educational philosophy is carried into humanists' beliefs about discipline; the two are inseparable.

Following those first pioneers of progressive education, early humanistic writers within education were Tom Gordon (1918–2002), who wrote the *Parent* and *Teacher effectiveness training* texts (1970, 1974), and Haim Ginott (1922–73). In this chapter, Bill Glasser's choice theory is also subsumed under the humanist heading because, although written about quite separately and with little reference to a humanist heritage, its philosophy is compatible and its practices are so similar that it would be repetitive to devote a separate chapter to it.

Subsequent generations of humanist educators include writers such as Covaleskie (1992), Kohn (1996a, 1999, 2004), Gartrell (2003) and Porter (2003, 2006). Although not necessarily referred to explicitly in the early childhood literature, many early educators also endorse humanist philosophies with respect to discipline (e.g. Fields & Boesser 2002; Reynolds 2001).

Philosophical assumptions

Humanism is the quintessential egalitarian theory. It allocates equal worth to all people and bases teachers' status on being skilled at what they do (authority based on *expertise*) rather than from having *power* over students (Gordon 1991). Although Glasser places teachers in a leadership role, humanism goes beyond this by advising that teachers *facilitate* student achievement. The distinction is that 'Leadership requires followers, but facilitating requires standing among others rather than standing apart' (Rogers & Freiberg 1994: 103).

At the same time as respecting students, humanistic teachers also respect themselves and therefore will not allow their students to override their needs (Rogers 1978). Thus, egalitarian principles give young people freedom, but not licence (Mintz 2003; Rogers & Freiberg 1994).

Nature of childhood

Three strands inform the humanist view of children. First, in a constructivist understanding of children's learning, humanism trusts children's innate *capacity for growth* as they strive to become all they can be (Raskin & Rogers 2005). All children want to learn skills that are useful in their lives and therefore, when adults do not threaten them with punishment or bribe them with incentives, they will be motivated in school and will make constructive choices (Rogers 1951; Rogers & Freiberg 1994).

The second strand is a statement about children's *goodness*: humanism contends that children are equally capable of considerate behaviour as they are of looking out for themselves (Kohn 1996a). Humanism does not accept the 'sour' (Kohn 1996a) or bleak view of human nature adopted by authoritarian theories, that children need to feel pain before they will behave well or that they will not think to act thoughtfully unless manipulated by rewards into doing so.

Third, it believes in children's *status* as human beings. Supported by concepts emerging from the sociology of childhood (as introduced in Chapter 1), humanism asserts that age is no barrier to human rights. Children are of inherent value now, not for who they may become or what they may achieve in the future.

Explanations for disruptive behaviour

Humanism and choice theory reject the premise of applied behaviour analysis, which states that external events dictate our behaviour. Glasser (1998a, 1998b, 1998c) explains that all that the outside world can ever give us is information; we choose what we do with it. Thus, all behaviour is instigated from within.

Exploration

Students learn by exploring the rules of their social environment in just the same way as they explore their physical world. They sometimes act in ways that allow them to gain social understandings by discovering what you stand for and what you will not stand.

Mistakes

Just as we understand that spelling errors are inevitable, so too we need to accept that in childhood (and beyond) individuals will make occasional behavioural errors (Gartrell 1987b, 2003). While an opportunity to learn, mistakes may come about because:

- children are yet too young to have acquired and practised the required skill (which probably applies mainly to the early childhood years);
- as a result of having become emotionally overwhelmed, children have temporarily lost control of themselves and therefore, although they possess the requisite skill, cannot oversee their execution of it;
- children sometimes get excitable, especially in each other's company and, in their exuberance, accidents can happen (Porter 2003, 2006).
- not always having the skills to predict outcomes in advance, at times children will act without realising that their actions could negatively affect someone else (Gartrell 1987b; 2003);
- a behaviour in one setting proves to be inappropriate elsewhere;

- young people are emulating an adult who has displayed inappropriate behaviour (e.g. violence) in their presence (Gartrell 2003).

Unmet intellectual or emotional needs

Glasser (1998a: 44) says that 'No human being is unmotivated', but that students will be motivated to do high-quality school work only when it meets their needs. Their apathy does not mean that they have lost their drive to learn, but that learning *this* material in *this* manner does not satisfy them. Apathy is not the problem; it is a symptom of the problem, of the irrelevance of their schooling to their lives (Gordon 1974).

Emotionally, when students have trouble in their lives that is beyond their ability to understand and cope with, they display repeated dysfunctional behaviour that has strong emotional undertones (Gartrell 1987b, 2003). Their disruptiveness can take the form of doing whatever it takes to survive emotionally.

Reactive behavioural problems

By school age, the most common reason for ongoing disruptions by individual students is that they are reacting against the violation of their autonomy by authoritarian attempts to control them. These reactions take the form of resistance, rebellion, retaliation, escape and submission (Gordon 1970, 1974). The first three of these responses give rise to further punishment; escape and withdrawal lead to alienation from school; while submission leads to problems with peers, who typically denigrate compliant, dutiful children.

Goals of discipline

Disciplinary and educational goals are integrated under humanist philosophy. That is to say, disciplinary methods must be in keeping with schools' educational aims of preparing students to live by the values of equality and social justice for all members of society (Goodman 1992; Knight 1991; Kohn 1996a; McCaslin & Good 1992). Therefore, rather than mandating self-discipline, humanism aims to *develop* it in children. Self-discipline is 'knowledge about oneself and the actions needed to grow and develop as a person' (Rogers & Freiberg 1994: 221). Thus, when humanists talk of self-discipline they do not mean internalised compliance, as with the authoritarian theories, but instead they aim to create humane and compassionate students who can act in accord with their own high values. They want students to develop a system of *autonomous ethics*; to use their emotions to enrich rather than hinder their lives; to cooperate with others; both in the immediate setting and in the wider community, by balancing their own needs with the needs of the group; and to have a strong sense of self-efficacy that enables them to enact such values (Ginott 1972; Goodman 1992; Knight 1991; Kohn 1996a; Porter 2003, 2006).

Compliance should not be a goal of educators, as controlling others is unethical, ineffective and dangerous (Curwin & Mendler 1988; Gartrell 1987a; Gordon 1991; Kohn 1996a; Porter 2003, 2006). The ethics are debatable, as ethical presuppositions are not factual but matters of opinion (Strike & Soltis 2004). In terms of effectiveness, the humanists contend that, just as learning facts does not teach students how to think, so too making students conform does not help them to become good people who can think about the effects of their actions on others (Kohn 1996a).

In terms of its inherent danger, teaching obedience renders individual children vulnerable to sexual abuse, as those who are trained to do what adults tell them are less empowered to resist their assaults (Briggs & McVeity 2000); it places surrounding children at risk when onlookers fail to resist bullying because they feel obliged to follow the directives of its powerful instigator; and whole societies become unsafe, as shown in Milgram's (1963) experiments on conformity to authority, where subjects obeyed the expert researcher's directives to administer what they thought to be dangerous levels of electric shocks to others, demonstrating that genocide is made possible when people do not disobey despotic leaders.

Preventive approaches

Humanism emphasises universal prevention which, as you might recall from the introductory chapter, encompasses school-wide approaches that encourage the full participation of all students. This is a valued end in itself, but is also instrumental in disinclining students to behave disruptively.

The core universal principle of humanism is that students will work productively and act thoughtfully when their needs are met by what we are asking them to do and how we are asking them to do it. This, then, requires an explication of these needs. In an adaptation of Maslow's (1968) description, I have proposed a model that links the emotional needs (Porter 2005, 2006). It is fashioned on a tree, as illustrated in Figure 6.1. As indicated by the upward arrow to the left of the tree trunk, like Maslow's this model is hierarchical, which means that the lower-level needs have to be satisfied before individuals can focus on meeting their higher needs.

The most basic human need—fundamental for all growth and so depicted in Figure 6.1 as the roots of the tree—is the need for physical *survival*: for food, shelter, warmth and (in adulthood) procreation. Although these survival needs are not the core business of teachers, we all know that hungry children will think of food rather than the academic

FIGURE 6.1   A humanist model of individual needs

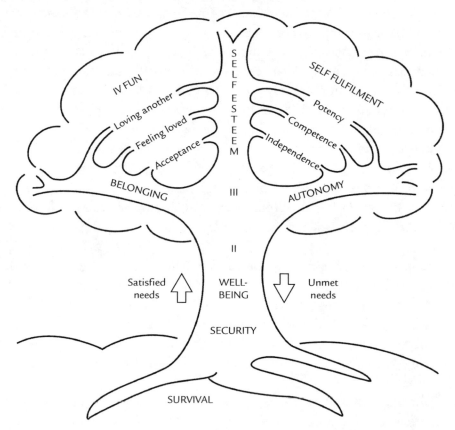

Source: Porter (2006: 41)

fare that is in front of them and thus by default these survival needs do sometimes become the purview of teachers.

At the second level are the dual needs for *security* and *wellbeing*, depicted as the trunk of the tree in Figure 6.1. As we know from children reared in orphanages, it is not enough that they simply be fed and watered: children also need to feel *secure* that they will be nurtured and that adults will be sensitive to and alleviate their discomfort or pain.

The next level of needs are the core emotional needs, depicted in Figure 6.1 as the tree's three limbs. These comprise:

- self-esteem—the need to value oneself;
- belonging—the need to love and be loved;
- autonomy—the need to be self-determining.

In the model, self-esteem is the central emotional need, but it cannot exist in isolation: individuals cannot feel positively about themselves without being connected to others and feeling in command of themselves. Early in life, infants' self-esteem relies almost entirely on whether they feel loved and accepted: it is most reliant on their belonging needs. After the age of two, young children feel pleased with themselves when they can exercise control of themselves. Thus, their self-esteem starts to be aligned with their need for autonomy. Ultimately, different personalities will end up with their self-esteem allied more strongly to either belonging or autonomy. Students who want you to like them (whose self-esteem is allied most with their need to belong) will seldom act disruptively at school; whereas those with autonomy contributing most to their self-esteem are willing to risk your displeasure to prove that they cannot be controlled by others. This is the group who most display behavioural difficulties in reaction to the imposition of external controls.

The final level of need is depicted in Figure 6.1 as the tree's foliage and encompasses the requirements for self-fulfilment and for fun. The need for self-fulfilment means that young people cannot live out others' ambitions for them, but have to fulfil their own mission in life. The need for fun, according to Glasser (1988: 30), is the 'intangible joy' that we feel when all our lower needs are being met. As such, fun cannot be experienced in a vacuum, but only within contexts that provide for our physical needs, are nurturing, affirming (self-esteem), emotionally close (foster belonging) and free (permit autonomy).

The following measures are based on meeting these needs. The most fundamental of these measures is egalitarian teaching and discipline.

Egalitarian teaching and discipline

A basic difference between the authoritarian and egalitarian theories is their view about the locus of causality of human behaviour. Proponents of ABA believe that humans are not free to choose, but are subjected to external manipulation from their environment. In contrast, humanism believes that the 'laws' linking a behaviour to an antecedent or consequence only *describe* individuals' actions, but do not *prescribe* these. Even if their behaviour is lawful in the sense of being predictable, individuals are not *compelled* to behave as they do in the way that a stone, once kicked, is compelled to move (Schlick 1966). Although behaviourists (e.g. Alberto & Troutman 2003) claim that external control is the way of the 'real world', when their survival needs are met and thus they can afford it adults select employment for its job satisfaction, not its salary; and many volunteer for community agencies for no pay but instead for the inherent satisfaction of knowing that they are making a contribution. In short, when free to do so, adults *choose* intrinsic reinforcers.

This discussion about locus of causality is basic to the humanists' claims that authoritarian discipline (i.e. the use of external controls) is both ineffective and destructive in the following ways.

- No one *can* control someone else's behaviour. It simply does not work that way; the only person we can control is ourselves (Glasser 1998c). Individuals make their own choices based on their judgment about what will meet their needs and, if their need is great enough, will defy any regime of rewards and punishments that others impose.
- Although external controls can engender obedience while students are dependent on teachers, by the time students reach adolescence teachers run out of the power to coerce compliance. Gordon (1991: 94) states this argument: 'It's a paradox: Use power, lose influence'. As evidence that controlling approaches are ineffective, Kohn (1996a) notes that they remain in place throughout the school years, yielding the observation that if they were going to work, they would have by now.
- This means that external controls are largely *irrelevant,* as the children who most appear to need their behaviour to be adjusted are already showing by their nonconformist behaviour that they will defy external controls, while those students who are already cooperating do not need manipulation in order to do so—lesser means will be successful with them.
- The administration of rewards and punishments is educationally *ineffective,* as consequences focus children's minds on what *they* will get out of behaving in a particular way, whereas egalitarian discipline wants them to focus on the effects of their behaviours *on others.* The result is that, when students do comply with coercion, they do so in their own interests, not others', which will not teach them right from wrong. The goal should be to give children a moral compass to guide their living an ethical life: *why* we act is as important as *how* we act (Covaleskie 1992).
- Controlling methods are *counterproductive*, as they incite more difficulties than they solve. Reactive behavioural difficulties are typically severe and prolonged and thus very difficult to deal with while, in terms of their education, students' resentment of being coerced will cause them to do the absolute minimum of what they have been asked (Glasser 1998a).
- Coercion *damages relationships*. The contest between teachers and their students uses much of the energies of both (Glasser 1998a). And because schools have very few rewards available to them for coercing students positively, external controlling methods are frequently negative, with the result that students come to ridicule or ignore their teachers or regard them as adversaries who are obstacles to need

satisfaction (Glasser 1998a). Many leave school altogether; many more drop out psychologically.

- Authoritarian methods are *risky to individuals*, as they cause recipients and administrators to feel dehumanised.
- Controlling methods *heighten rivalry* and competitiveness with peers as they compete with each other for the limited amount of teacher approval and incentives that are available.
- Authoritarianism is based on a *negative view of children* that is seldom the actual view of teachers. The inconsistency will both trouble teachers and provoke unauthentic practice.

A sense of community

Humanists aim to create a caring school community in which students feel cared for and are encouraged to care about each other (Kohn 1996a). Within such a setting, students will be more likely to take intellectual risks—and thus will learn more—as they know that they will not be humiliated or punished for mistakes (Kohn 1996a). A sense of cohesiveness allows students to accept each other and trust other class members with their ideas and feelings. As well as classroom activities that encourage this, student participation in the running of the school allows them to experience—rather than only learn about—their democratic rights and the corresponding responsibilities that they will need to exercise as adult citizens (Knight 1991). However, participation alone is not enough; the issues addressed must be real and debate must produce socially useful results (Knight 1991).

Student involvement is matched by teacher participation in decisions about school policy and procedures (Ginott 1972; Rogers & Freiberg 1994). You have a right to limit intrusions of your work into your personal life and to demand respect and dignified treatment from school administrators (Ginott 1972).

The third members of the school community are parents. Just as humanist teachers aim to work *with* students, so too you would aim to collaborate with parents, recognising their skills and expertise and not imposing your own ideas on them. These partnerships need to be ongoing, not just activated in times of crisis, with parents regularly receiving positive information from their child's teachers. Glasser's (1998a) advice on parent collaboration is somewhat controversial, suggesting that teachers collaborate with parents to solve nondisciplinary issues, such as their son or daughter's difficulty with making friends, but not to involve them when behavioural disturbances arise. His rationale is that this sends two messages to students: first, that you believe that you both can solve the problem independently of their parents; second, that you want to solve the problem, not punish students, and you do not want their parents to punish them either. Perhaps the advice is warranted more for adolescents than their younger counterparts, and perhaps only for nascent rather than entrenched problems.

Involvement with teachers

A core component of a caring community is for teachers to relate to students with acceptance, respect, empathy, humanity and as a real person, rather than hiding behind your role or professional façade (Rogers & Freiberg 1994). More important than these qualities, however, is honesty, with yourself and your students. This involves *owning* your feelings—that is, accepting personal responsibility for them—and being assertive when your needs conflict with your students'.

A conducive physical environment

To prevent disruptiveness, you can modify the classroom so that you facilitate learning and cooperation (Gordon 1974). Measures include *enriching* the environment—for example, by having a variety of activities and multimedia teaching—or, conversely, *impoverishing* or *restricting* it, to aid the concentration of distractable students. For example, you can restrict particular activities to certain areas in the classroom, so that those who are working there can concentrate. To *simplify* the demands placed on students, you can break complex tasks into small steps that enable success. Keeping the area safe and preparing students in advance for upcoming changes in routines all prevent disruptions arising out of stress.

Relevant curriculum

Instead of asking 'How can we make children conform to our expectations?', the humanist writers ask 'How can we provide what children need so that they can learn?' (Kohn 1996a). In order to answer that question we need to recognise that, rather than being a type of orderly cognitive, left-brain activity, meaningful learning involves both thinking and feeling (Rogers & Freiberg 1994). This implies that you will promote learning when your curricula have emotional as well as cognitive content and when you establish a non-threatening, accepting, person-oriented climate in which students can learn information and skills that will make a difference to their lives (Rogers 1951, 1978; Rogers & Freiberg 1994). Both the content and process of education must meet their needs for autonomy, relatedness and competence (Deci et al. 1991).

To ensure that the curriculum has emotional as well as intellectual meaning for students, humanists recommend the following measures.

- In light of your students' ages, examine whether what you are teaching is relevant to them at this time in their lives (Fields & Boesser 2002).
- Teaching is not a matter of instructing students in the skills and information that you and others have decided they need to know, but instead you should discover what interests your students and use those topics as a vehicle for facilitating the expansion of their skills and knowledge and to enrich what they learn at school. Respecting the opinions, experience, interests and observations that they bring from home by incorporating these into your teaching also fosters the inclusion of students from non-dominant cultures.
- Incorporate your own interests and passions into your teaching so that, rather than explaining your vision to students, you invite them to stand beside you and see it for themselves.
- Explain how the task will help students to meet their goals, detailing why, when, where and how they could use the information now or in the future (Glasser 1992b, 1998b).
- Make real problems the subject matter of your classes (Rogers & Freiberg 1994). You might begin by asking students what issues confront them, or posing questions that they will need to deal with later in life. This fosters an attitude of inquiry.
- Cover less ground in academic subjects, so that students have more time to learn worthwhile content in greater depth and thus become competent (Glasser 1998a). Glasser (1992b: 694) justifies this suggestion by saying that 'We should never forget that people, not curriculum, are the desired outcomes of schooling'.
- Teach students *how* to learn, so that they become producers of ideas rather than mere consumers of information (Rogers & Freiberg 1994).
- Provide opportunities for experimentation and reflection rather than transmitting information, as knowledge that is discovered is more meaningful and better retained than knowledge that is transmitted.
- Refuse to require students to memorise facts, as this involves no thinking and generates 'throwaway information' that students forget almost as quickly as they learn (Glasser 1969, 1992b).
- Provide for the social needs of students by enacting group-based learning, where appropriate for the task.

If students are not responding to the curriculum, you will interpret this as a sign that it is not meeting their needs and will adjust it accordingly. In what may seem to many to be a bold recommendation, but one that provides teachers with valuable feedback about their teaching, a core approach employed within democratic schools is for all classes to be optional (Mintz 2003). Competing theories assume that, under such a regime, students would not choose to attend and humanism agrees that there is no way to motivate students to do something that is futile (Glasser 1998a). However, it also believes in students' motivation to learn when the content and processes are relevant for them. This is evidenced by the fact that class attendance is high in democratic schools (Mintz 2003).

The process of learning is more important than curricular content. The only content that is indispensable to an education is learning to read, write, do arithmetic (but not higher mathematics, as that is not useful in life) and to speak in public (Glasser 1969, 1998b). Learning processes, however, are vital. These include using initiative, taking responsibility for decisions, evaluating outcomes, garnering useful knowledge through research, adapting flexibly to new situations, tolerating uncertainty and ambiguity, solving relevant problems, and working cooperatively with others (Rogers 1951).

Even so, if students are to be free to learn, they will also need to be free to choose *how* they learn (Rogers & Freiberg 1994). Some will prefer to be guided by you, while others will flourish under self-direction (Rogers & Freiberg 1994). Therefore, you can divide students into groups of self-directed and outer-directed learners, so that all have the opportunity to work within their preferred style.

Authentic assessment

The practice of coercing students through tests to memorise irrelevant information discourages independent thinking and causes students to cheat, not because they lack ethics but because they realise that 'there is no virtue in learning nonsense' (Glasser 1992a: 217). More important, enforcing memorisation of isolated facts causes many students to detest the subject matter, which 'is worse than just not knowing it' (Glasser 1992a: 231). It would be better for young people to emerge from the education system ignorant than hating to learn. Therefore, any tests should be open-book and examine students' skills rather than memorisation of facts. Closed-book examinations are based, Glasser (1969: 72) maintains, on the fallacy that 'knowledge remembered is better than knowledge looked up', when in fact rote learning is suitable for a relatively small range of material. He states that ideal practice would be to have students nominate when they are ready to take tests (Glasser 1998a, 1998b).

When testing and grades are imposed on you, this can become just one more problem for the students and you to solve jointly. For example, they might choose to submit questions that they think should be included in a test, or you could supplement their formal results with their own self-evaluations. This safeguards society's need for an accountable education system, while still promoting students' growth. Those who achieved well on the test would proceed to new material; those who did not would be given the opportunity to practise further until they had mastered the content. Glasser (1998a) defends this suggestion with the observation that there is no point assessing students' skills if we are not going to give them a chance to improve these.

Authentic feedback

Just as humanists refuse to punish, so too they refuse to reward. Loss of a hoped-for reward feels like a punishment (Fields & Boesser 2002), illustrating that the two are reverse sides of the same coin—and the coin buys very little: merely temporary compliance, which is accompanied by some risks, as already outlined (Kohn 1996a). Therefore, feedback within classrooms will offer information that describes to students— or asks them to reflect on—what they have achieved and what their next goal might be. Elsewhere, I have termed this 'acknowledgment' (Porter 2003, 2006). It will involve the cessation of all rewards in the forms of praise (judgments or evaluations of students, their work or their behaviour) and tangible or token rewards, such as merit certificates, stars, school awards or grades. The reasons to cease delivering grades are detailed in Box 6.1. Instead of using grades, humanism advocates teaching students to assess their own learning. Only their own judgment about their grasp of useful skills (that is, self-evaluation of a relevant curriculum) will motivate them to invest continued effort in their work. Nevertheless, while some will experience self-assessment as an opportunity for growth, those who are accustomed to authoritarian methods may at first need guidance in how to be self-accepting, rather than self-critical, when they are assessing their own work.

Eliminate compulsory homework

Compulsory homework is a fundamental source of coercion and irrelevance in schools. For this and the additional reasons listed in Box 6.2, you would not assign compulsory homework, although in the following instances you might invite students to complete some home-based activities voluntarily:

- if the work can only be done at home and is not just an extension of class work— such as when students need to watch a particular TV program or interview relatives;
- if students choose not to apply themselves to their work during the school day, thus electing to complete it in their own time;
- if students choose to revise and practise in order to improve their skills by completing extra work at home (Glasser 1998a).

BOX 6.1 NEGATIVE EFFECTS OF GRADES

Contribution to low-quality work

- Grades distort the curriculum, so that only those things that can be counted are measured. The resulting focus on discrete facts reduces curricular relevance.
- Grades may encourage the academically successful students to learn but the remainder, who may not care about your opinion of them or their work, will become even more disenchanted with school.
- The anxiety that grading engenders in students will impair their ability to study and reduce the quality of their work.
- Setting and marking assignments uses teacher time that could be spent on facilitating more authentic learning.

Unfairness

- While grades are supposed to be an objective measure of students' progress, it is hard to make any finer distinction than pass or fail. Attempts to do so are subjective, inaccurate, unfair, unreliable and phoney.
- Grades are not a good indicator of success at anything other than school work, and are poor indicators of students' ability at work or higher education.
- There is no recognition of late maturing and no second chance to redeem a poor school record; school failure commonly damns one to failure for life.

Damage to relationships

- Grades increase competitiveness between classmates, particularly when they are allocated on a normal curve, and thus the higher grades are scarce.
- Grades reduce human involvement between teachers and students.

Sources: Glasser 1998a; Kohn 1999, 2004

Freed from policing and marking the unnecessary homework of your entire class group, you could assess the needs of the handful of students with learning difficulties, plan individual remedial homework activities for them and deliver specific and personalised feedback that helped them to improve their skills.

Class meetings

Meetings are an excellent venue for airing issues that concern members of the class (Kohn 1996a). They will be most effective when conducted daily in primary school and twice weekly in high school (Glasser 1969, 1998a, 1998b). It is crucial that class meetings do not become an exercise in control where you impose your views on the

BOX 6.2 DISADVANTAGES OF COMPULSORY HOMEWORK

Reduction of student motivation and achievement

- Compulsory homework reduces the quality of students' lives: it does not meet their needs.
- Homework is irrelevant, especially until the most senior years of high school.
- Students have no choice about doing it, which makes them unmotivated.
- Homework allows students to make the same mistakes over and over when studying at home without teacher supervision.
- Most homework is more easily and better done at school.

Contribution to student drop-out and burn-out (stress)

- Homework is excessive and tedious and causes students to detest school and learning.
- Homework eats into relaxation time, which would offset stress.
- Bright students who are conscientious about doing homework have no time left to pursue other recreational activities; less able students do not do the homework, but because this defines them as failures they do little else either. Thus, both groups of students are denied other learning and enjoyable activities. And by adulthood, they have not developed ways to enjoy their leisure time.

Exacerbation of demarcations between students

- Students from privileged homes have the facilities for quiet study, whereas students from disadvantaged homes have not, leading to a widening of the differences between their academic achievement levels.
- Just as it contributes to academic differences between students, homework highlights differences in their social status, as only academically able students complete their homework while the remainder are defined as disruptive.

Interference with high-quality teaching

- Assigning compulsory homework prevents teachers from planning exciting instruction.
- Homework must be graded, with all the disadvantages of grading.
- Failure to do homework must be punished, which violates egalitarian principles.
- To avoid arguments, teachers (and parents) accept low-quality homework, sending the message that it is acceptable to do poor work.

Contribution to antagonistic relationships with young people

- Compulsory homework leads to conflict between students and teachers.
- Voluntary homework that involved talking to adults could help bring

parents and children together, whereas compulsory homework only creates antagonism between them, as parents frequently believe that it is their role to ensure that their children complete their homework. (Instead, if the school sets the work, it should supervise it.)

Sources: Glasser 1969, 1998a

students, but instead support them in generating their own ideas and solutions, even running the meeting themselves (Kohn 1996a). Therefore, you will need to give your opinions sparingly and they should carry equal weight with students' views. When making decisions, students could vote on their options, although a more sophisticated task is for them to discuss an issue until they can reach a consensus, because this requires them to fashion creative solutions to accommodate other people's points of view (Kohn 1996a).

Class meetings can be of three types. The first, *social problem-solving* meetings attempt to solve behavioural issues that concern any student, teacher or parent. These meetings should focus on generating solutions rather than finding fault with individuals (Glasser 1969).

Open-ended meetings allow the students to discuss any issue that is relevant to their lives, including any dissatisfaction with school. They can be a vehicle for sharing news, deciding anything from how to arrange the classroom to how to raise funds for people in need, or jointly planning field trips or other class activities (Kohn 1996a).

The third type of meeting, *educational-diagnostic* meetings, are related to what the class is studying. In these meetings, students will discuss the rationale for curricular content and classroom procedures in order to determine whether these are effective in producing in the students a living, working understanding of the concepts being taught, rather than purely theoretical or fact-based learning.

Create cooperative working teams

Most learning should take place within cooperative groups, as learning together within a small team satisfies students' need to belong and to be independent of their teacher. For this recommendation, humanists draw on educational research on collaborative learning, which is presented in Chapter 11.

Intervention

Humanism is not permissive; indeed, it has rigorous standards for children's personal conduct. Nevertheless, to institute rules to enforce personal behaviour would create a rule-driven rather than value-driven setting (Wien 2004). Teaching unthinking obedience without an understanding of the basis of rules fails to teach students the ethical thinking that is the essence of responsible behaviour (Bear et al. 2003; Covaleskie 1992). Rules also typically have predetermined consequences attached, enforcement of which requires you to use coercion, which engenders defiance in students. The consistency with which rules and consequences must be applied also enshrines unfairness, as there is nothing so unfair as treating unequals equally. Instead, teachers need permission to exercise their professional discretion and respond wisely in the circumstances, not acting as mere technicians dictated to by an inflexible system of discipline based on rule enforcement (Gartrell 2003). Finally, the expectation that students comply behaviourally will undermine the educational aim of encouraging them to solve problems and be creative and adventurous intellectually (McCaslin & Good 1992).

Therefore, the only guidelines that you will need to negotiate with students would pertain to basic courtesy, such as that no one can hurt another emotionally or physically. Subsequently, violation of this norm will not attract penalties, but will merely activate problem solving.

VIGNETTE 6.1 THE REDUNDANCY OF RULES

Wanting to keep routines consistent for the children, a relief preschool teacher asked her young charges about the rules in their centre. Despite her framing the question in various ways, the children seemed puzzled by her questions and could not answer. Finally, she decided that being specific would help: 'What about the toilet? What's the rule for using the toilet?'. One of the children was now delighted to be able to answer. 'I know!' he declared. 'When you go to the toilet, you do a wee.'

The regular teacher had no need for rules. She had only ever used conflict or disturbances to activate problem solving, and therefore the children had no knowledge of a system of expectations or of consequences for failing to attain them.

Communicate to solve problems

The aim of humanism is to find a solution rather than a culprit (Gordon 1991). As punishment solves nothing, it is not employed and instead communication is used to resolve problems, which are defined as any behaviour that violates someone's rights. When students' unmet needs are impeding their own learning or violating their own social or emotional needs, this calls for the communication skill of *listening*. When your own needs or other students' needs are being violated, this becomes your problem and requires the communication skill of *assertiveness*. By far the most common occurrence, however, will be when both you and one or more students are being inconvenienced by a behaviour, when *collaborative problem solving* will be required. Finally, a problem may seem apparent, but it actually requires no resolution. There are two main instances of this. The first is when the individual affected can set aside something that is troubling him or her to focus on teaching or learning; the second is when students' actions violate your values (e.g. by their dress code). In such cases, you can ask that they respect your preferences but, as their failure to do so has no material effect on you, you cannot impose your values on them.

The student has a need: Listening

Some behaviours will interfere with students' own ability to access learning or to get along with others. Therefore, you will need to listen to disruptive behaviour and solve the problem that it signals. This listening is more than mere hearing; it is an active process whose skills require practice. True listening requires generosity, as it is something we do for someone else. It takes willingness to see another's point of view. It takes courage, as we might hear something that causes us some discomfort. And it takes sensitivity in order to decipher more than the verbal messages alone. Ginott (1972: 77) says that the chronological and psychological distance between adults and young people can be bridged only by listening with genuine empathy, which he describes as 'the capacity to respond accurately to a child's needs, without being infected by them'.

Listening entails, first and foremost, paying attention. While attending, it pays to ask very few questions—especially those that call for yes/no answers—because these direct, rather than follow, what the children are telling you and can make them feel that they are being subjected to an inquisition. The next component is *reflecting* others' feelings. This can be a particular challenge when children are expressing strong emotions; but emotions, like rivers, cannot be stopped—only channelled (Ginott et al. 2003). To help children understand their feelings, you can reflect back not only the content but also the emotions that underlie their words using paraphrasing, which is a concise response that rephrases the essence of what they are saying in your own words (Bolton 1993).

Despite attempting to listen effectively, we sometimes unwittingly use communication 'roadblocks' that discourage others from talking about what matters to them (Gordon 1970). These roadblocks fall into three categories: judging, sending solutions and avoiding other people's feelings.

Judgmental responses include *criticising*, *blaming* or *name calling*, which students are likely to regard as unfair, generating resentment and rejection of both you and what you are saying (Ginott 1972; Gordon 1974). Another type of judgment is *praising* (whose many negative effects were detailed in Chapter 5). The final forms are *diagnosing* or *interpreting*, which are both attempts to tell students that their stated problem is not the 'real' issue. This ignores or deprecates their own perceptions.

Solutions are often delivered in the forms of *directing* students to stop their present behaviour, giving *orders* or *preaching* about what to do instead, or issuing *threats* about what will happen to them if they do not. *Interrogating* is a means of probing that suggests that you are about to find a solution for students. Finally, *advising* treats students as if they cannot solve their own problems. The main problem with all these means of imposing solutions is that the timing is wrong: when individuals are distressed, their feelings need to be honoured before they will be able to focus on solving the problem. These responses tell them that you think their ideas and needs are not important, and that what you want is paramount. Moreover, they are patronising, implying that students cannot solve their own problems.

The third cluster of communication road blocks, avoiding students' feelings, can arise because we are uncomfortable with unpleasant emotions in others. The first form of avoidance is *distracting*, which tries to take students' minds off their worries but instead your lack of understanding discourages them from talking with you. A second form of avoidance, *logical argument*, tells students: 'Don't feel, think'. And, finally, another avoidance method that looks harmless on the surface but which ignores the depth of students' feelings is *reassuring*. Like the other avoidance responses, reassurance tells students that they are not allowed to feel as they do because you are uncomfortable with their emotions.

The teacher has a need: Assertiveness
Although the discussion of rules indicated that you do not need to respond consistently (that is, in an identical fashion) to each disruption, you do have to be consistent (that is, unswerving) in your resolve to uphold your own needs and those of any students who are inconvenienced by their peers' disruptiveness. This will require the use of assertive skills. In using these, you must demonstrate the same standards of courtesy and self-discipline that you want your students to observe (Ginott 1972). You may act spontaneously, but not impulsively; you cannot use verbal violence to discipline students,

even when angry. Anger indicates that we are judging students (thinking to ourselves that they *shouldn't* behave that way) or criticising ourselves (for not knowing how to handle it). Instead, we need to channel the energy behind the anger into expressing our feelings and needs (Rosenberg 2003). Regulating and communicating your own feelings fairly can teach students constructive ways to resolve their own feelings, which will be particularly valuable for those students who have been exposed to inappropriate and terrifying ways of handling their emotions (Fields & Boesser 2002).

The best-known assertive message describes the action–feeling–effect sequence, using the formula: 'When you (*do such and such*), I feel (*x*) because (*my rights are being interfered with in this way*)'. However, listeners can misconstrue this as confrontive or accusatory, while messages in this format defy the cornerstone principle of assertiveness, which is that individuals must accept responsibility for their own emotions and needs; no one else is to blame for our feelings.

This means, first, that we must avoid using victim language that blames others for how we feel and obscures awareness that we make our own choices. A second principle is to avoid words that are interpretations of others' actions, in the guise of describing our feelings. For example, we might say that we are feeling manipulated, pressured, overworked, put down or taken for granted, when in fact the words that express our actual *feelings* (rather than others' actions) include annoyed, bitter, disappointed, disgruntled, tired, frustrated, irritated, overwhelmed and resentful (Rosenberg 2003).

To avoid accusing others and to ensure that you talk about feelings rather than thoughts, in place of the action–feeling–effect message you can name the need that leads to your feelings. Unlike aggression that contains the word *you* and criticises others' behaviour, this assertive message follows the format: *I feel…because I need…* This message is more likely to receive a compassionate hearing from others. Nevertheless, listeners still might misread it as a criticism or an attempt to impose a solution on them and, as a result, react defensively or aggressively. These reactions indicate that *they* now have the problem, so you need to revert to listening, followed by repeating your assertive message, until the two of you can agree on a resolution.

Collaboration to solve mutual problems

Gordon's third category of classroom difficulties is when both you and a student have unmet needs. Of the three occasions for problem solving, these shared problems are the most common. Conflict is a natural part of human relationships but many of us fear it, especially if we define good teachers as people who never experience conflict in their classrooms or if we feel that there are only two possible solutions: *either* students win *or* teachers win (Gordon 1974). Instead, we can regard conflict as inevitable and use its energy to generate workable solutions that protect all participants (Knight 1991). Collaborative problem solving involves the following steps.

- *Step 1: Agree to talk it over together.* In this way, the two of you can define the problem. Begin by finding out what the student needs and then state your own needs, in order to establish where the conflict lies.
- *Step 2: Generate possible solutions.* Generate what you could do to meet both your needs. At this stage, do not evaluate how practical the suggestions are, just brainstorm all possibilities—even those that seem ridiculous—and write them down.
- *Step 3: Select a solution.* Next, evaluate the options and discard those that would not be workable or which would represent a compromise that meets no one's needs.
- *Step 4: Determine implementation.* Plan when and how to carry out your chosen solution. Everyone must be able to agree to try the solution, even if not yet convinced that it will work.
- *Step 5: Check that it is working.* Once it is in place, check whether the solution is working. Be on the lookout for commitments that were made with initial enthusiasm but that later turn out to be unrealistic or unworkable. Be prepared to discard or amend solutions that are not working.

With simple, everyday problems, the steps do not have to be this regimented, although solving even minor issues will always entail listening to each other.

Collaboration increases the likelihood of finding a high-quality solution, because two heads are always better than one and it enhances students' motivation to abide by the agreed solution, given that they participated in devising it. Meanwhile, helping to decide what should be done develops their thinking skills. On the other hand, collaborative problem solving will not work when there is time pressure to get something done or when children are in danger, such as being about to run out in front of traffic. In these instances, you will need to take charge without consulting with them and explain your reasons later. This is the protective use of force, which has the aim of protecting children from harm. In contrast, a punitive use of force is intended to ensure compliance (Rosenberg 2003).

Another occasion where negotiation will not work is when the children are out of command of their feelings. As Faber and colleagues (1995) observe, when a person is drowning that is not the time to give swimming lessons. In short, when young people are drowning in emotion, they will be temporarily too overwhelmed to listen to reason and therefore need time to regain their composure.

Institute time away (sanctuary)

In a method that bears resemblance to the 'positive time out' recommended by Nelsen and colleagues (2000) and discussed in Chapter 5, time away would entail allowing students to withdraw to a pleasant area, perhaps taking a friend with them, or taking advantage of some solitary time.

A special case is ongoing, chronic and repeated aggression which, by definition, is violating the needs of peers by tormenting and terrifying them and restricting their ability to learn. Time away for chronic aggression would not be voluntary, but instead the humanists would impose it while perpetrators think of a way to desist. This is another instance of the protective use of power. The clear implication is that adults will not (because they *cannot*) force the student to change the behaviour, but they will enforce the principle that when people cannot be sociable, they cannot be social. Nevertheless, anyone coming into contact with students who are partaking of either voluntary or involuntary time away for repeated aggression will be warm and pleasant, happy to engage with them on any issue (without broaching the subject of their behaviour), and will allow them to accompany them on their duties as appropriate. But students must remain apart from their *peers* until they generate a specific plan for resolving the behaviour (Porter 2006) or, in Glasser's (1998a) terms, are willing to 'work it out'. To do so, they can take all the time they need. However, if they disrupt seriously while isolated, Glasser advises that they should be sent home, as schools do not have the resources to assist young people while they are unwilling to act thoughtfully. This would be an extremely rare event in a school where a student wanted to be.

Counsel students with chronic disruptiveness

If the school has resources for doing so, a member of staff can counsel students with chronically disruptive behaviour, to guide them to question whether what they are doing is in reality helping them to achieve their personal goals. This does not have to take a long time, as you will already have an ongoing, positive relationship with students, which will be a good basis for a therapeutic discussion. Having secured their willingness to talk the issue through, you will guide them to identify the triggers for their disruptive behaviour (Hammel 1989). In so doing, while demonstrating empathy for their difficult home life or past traumatic events, this discussion will not permit excuses as these treat students as helpless victims, which is not a kindness (Glasser 1998c). Similarly, it does not pay to focus on students' feelings as they have no direct control over those. While sensitive to their distress, you need to focus instead on what they can *do* or how they can *think* differently, subsequent to which their feelings will improve (Glasser 1998a).

In the next phase, you will help them to identify what they want from school, examine dispassionately whether their present behaviour is helping them to secure this and, once they realise that it is not, gain a commitment from them to pursue alternative ways of meeting their needs.

Negotiate reciprocal contracts

It should be self-evident that the term 'reciprocal', when paired with the word 'contract', is a tautology. By their nature, contracts are reciprocal—for example, when buying your house, I pay you the asking price and, in exchange, you hand over the title to the property. But when it comes to contracts about students' behaviour, authoritarian contracts usually list what students must do and detail what will happen to them if they do not. There is no reciprocity. In contrast, humanist contracts would negotiate with students not only what you need them to achieve, but also how you will help them to achieve that. This is the same approach as we might use for students with additional educational needs—for example, we do not instruct a student with a severe vision impairment to 'Use your eyes!', but adjust the environment (e.g. lighting, size of print and distance from the teacher) to enable the child who cannot see to function in a seeing world. Similarly, when a child has difficulties behaving thoughtfully, we need to adjust the demands and supports that we provide, to make it easier for the child to function in the setting.

Summary

Humanists recommend some fundamental changes in the philosophy that governs the organisation of schools and classrooms and the relationships within them. As a teacher, you are advised to abandon being an expert who holds all knowledge, to become a facilitator who encourages critical inquiry in your students. When your curricular content and learning processes meet students' needs, you would rarely need to intervene with disruptive behaviour. On occasions when individuals' needs come into conflict (as is inevitable in social settings), you will listen to those affected, be assertive when you are disturbed by another's behaviour and use these two skills alongside collaborative problem solving to resolve instances when both you and others are perturbed by the outcomes of a behaviour. Should this fail, students will need time to calm down, during which they can generate a plan for preventing a recurrence.

Interim critique

The main distinction between humanism and the earlier theories is encapsulated in the debate about authoritarianism, which has to be held over until Chapter 8, once all the theories have been detailed. The crux of the debate, however, is humanists' criticism that behaviourism has a narrow view of the precursors to behavioural disruptions and that this represents a callous and unethical disregard of the broader social context and the effects that teaching content and methods may be having on students' behaviour (Jones & Jones 2004). In the vein of Calvin Coolidge's declaration that 'There is no right way to do the wrong thing' (Sapon-Shevin 1996: 196), the humanists contend that we cannot teach students to be humane by using inhumane methods, which is how they characterise external controls.

In practical terms, humanism is sometimes criticised for not *doing* anything when students disrupt. This is probably true, to the extent that humanism does not do anything *to* students but rather works *with* them to solve the problem. Furthermore, its universal preventive measure of establishing egalitarian relationships with students enhances their emotional wellbeing and improves their motivation to learn (Rogers 1951; Rogers & Freiberg 1994), while safeguarding your own rights and those of other class members. Although some criticise this approach for demanding that teachers practise sophisticated communication skills (Edwards & Watts 2004), communication is at the heart of all teaching. Therefore it is legitimate to expect teachers to master it.

CASE STUDY

Adam is seven. He has difficulty with reading, spelling and writing, although he enjoys and is capable at maths. During non-maths lessons he spends a considerable amount of time off-task, when he frequently disrupts the other students. This is worse in the afternoons than in the mornings.

He is in a composite class of six and seven year olds. He spends most of his play time with the younger children. Frequently, a pair including Adam is apprehended during play times doing such things as harassing passers-by from an out-of-bounds area of the playground that is close to the street, rifling through rubbish bins for food or cans to swap for other items with students, or engaging in fights in and around the toilets.

Adam seems bemused by the trouble he gets into, usually saying when challenged that he doesn't know why he behaves in these ways, that he couldn't remember that a given behaviour was against the rules, or that the other child was at fault for suggesting the activity.

Until a recent assessment, it was believed that Adam behaved as he did because of low academic ability. However, a battery of tests has shown his overall ability (IQ) to be average, with his maths skills in the high-normal range and his reading and spelling skills, while delayed, still within the lower range of normal limits. His teacher is now at a loss to find a new explanation for his behaviour.

A humanist response

As a humanist, your measures would be designed to enhance a sense of community that would support Adam and all members of the class to participate fully in learning and social activities.

Step 1: Involve students in decision making
Engage Adam and all students in making decisions about the operation of the class and school. This will enable Adam to understand the reason that certain areas of the playground have been restricted.

Step 2: Enhance curriculum relevance
In a series of class meetings, discover what sense the children are making of their present curriculum and have them nominate ways that they would prefer to work and topics they are interested in covering. New learning processes may entail the formation of cooperative learning groups or the use of peer tutoring, for example. Adam could gain self-confidence and status among his peers for tutoring the less able students in maths, while being a tutor may encourage him to accept similar support from his peers in his own weaker subject areas. Enriched learning content is aimed at engaging Adam (and others) so that he voluntarily attends to his work, rather than distracting others to escape it.

Step 3: Use authentic feedback
Cease awarding grades and any other prizes or incentives that you may have been giving for desired work performances or behaviours and instead institute informative feedback (acknowledgment) for both. Teach Adam and all his classmates to evaluate their own work, appreciate their own achievements and set their own learning goals.

Step 4: Cease allocating homework
Announce to your parent group and students that you will not be imposing homework. Then, if supported by Adam's parents, suggest that in the spare time he now has available, he engage in an extracurricular activity where he could practise a sport favoured by his classmates at play time. If the activity is also attended by one or two of his peers, they might befriend him during the sessions and carry this into school time. This would improve his social isolation at school.

Step 5: Conduct problem-solving class meetings
If Adam's social isolation does not improve with the prior primary preventive measures, place on the agenda of a class meeting a request for the group to suggest ways to help Adam be less lonely at school. Your rationale for this step would be the hope that, once more fully included, Adam would have no need to resort to antisocial activity at play times.

Step 6: Collaborate to solve the problem
Ask Adam if there is anything else you can do to help him achieve at school. Do not ask why he behaves as he does, as young children can seldom articulate reasons and such a question can sound either pleading ('*please* help me understand') or accusatory (as if, once you hear the reason, you are about to deliver a lecture to set him straight). You will then be assertive about what you need and the two of you will collaborate to find a resolution that satisfies you both.

Step 7: Reciprocal contract
Your decision could be written into a reciprocal contract that states what Adam hopes to achieve and how you will help him to attain that.

Step 8: Use time away
Adam's behaviour is not violent and therefore does not warrant enforced time away, but when he seems too bewildered or upset to control his own actions, invite him to enjoy some time alone or with a friend in a designated part of the classroom (or outside it, if a supervisor is provided by the school) until he feels better.

Step 9: Collaborate with Adam's parents
If Adam's behaviour is not resolved by these measures, ask his parents for their suggestions of what you might do to help him.

Discussion questions

1 What do the humanists' goals for discipline imply for day-to-day instructional practice? What do they imply for intervention with disruptive behaviours?
2 Contrast the humanists' practices with those of the neo-Adlerians. Do you see any significant differences? Is your answer different for their preventive versus interventive approaches?
3 Reapply the case study that you generated in Chapter 2, this time using humanist principles and practices. What new features are introduced into the recommended

practices? What effect would these differences have on the individual student? On the whole class? On you?

Suggested further reading

Ginott, H.G. 1972 *Teacher and child* Macmillan, New York
Gordon, T. 1974 *Teacher effectiveness training* Peter H. Wyden, New York
——1991 *Teaching children self-discipline at home and at school* Random House, Sydney
Kohn, A. 1996 *Beyond discipline: from compliance to community* Association for Supervision and Curriculum Development, Alexandria, VA
——1999 *Punished by rewards: the trouble with gold stars, incentive plans, A's, praise, and other bribes* 2nd edn, Houghton Mifflin, Boston, MA

Choice theory

In this chapter, choice theory was subsumed under a humanist approach, but it has its own body of literature, which you might want to consult separately:

Glasser, W. 1969 *Schools without failure* Harper & Row, New York
——1988 *Choice theory in the classroom* rev edn, HarperCollins, New York
——1998a *The quality school: managing students without coercion* rev edn, HarperPerennial, New York
——1998b *The quality school teacher* rev edn, HarperPerennial, New York
——1998c *Choice theory: a new psychology of personal freedom* HarperCollins, New York

Democratic schools

Mintz, J. 2003 *No homework and recess all day: how to have freedom and democracy in education* Bravura, New York

Communication skills

Bolton, R. 1993 *People skills* Simon and Schuster, Sydney
Faber, A., Mazlish, E., Nyberg, L. and Templeton, R.A. 1995 *How to talk so kids can learn at home and in school* Fireside, New York
Rosenberg, M.B. 2003 *Nonviolent communication: a language of life* 2nd edn, Puddle Dancer Press, Encinitas, CA

For early childhood practitioners

Fields, M. and Boesser, C. 2002 *Constructive guidance and discipline* 3rd edn, Merrill Prentice Hall, Upper Saddle River, NJ
Gartrell, D. 2003 *A guidance approach for the encouraging classroom* 3rd edn, Delmar, New York
Porter, L. 2003 *Young children's behaviour: practical approaches for caregivers and teachers* 2nd edn, Elsevier, Sydney/Paul Chapman, London/Brookes, Baltimore, MD

For parents

Ginott, H.G., Ginott, A. and Goddard, H.W. 2003 *Between parent and child* 2nd ed, Three Rivers Press, New York
Gordon, T. 2000 *Parent effectiveness training* 2nd edn, Three Rivers Press, New York
Kohn, A. 2005 *Unconditional parenting: moving from rewards and punishments to love and reason* Atria Books, New York
Porter, L. 2006 *Children are people too: a parent's guide to young children's behaviour* 4th edn, East Street Publications, Adelaide, SA

Websites

Gordon Training International: <www.gordontraining.com>
Effectiveness Training Institute of Australia: <www.etia.org>
The Alternative Education Resource Organisation: <www.educationrevolution.org>
International Democratic Education Network: <www.idenetwork.org>
Choice theory: <www.wglasser.com>

7 SOLUTION-FOCUSED APPROACH

My passion for consulting with children, including young people in conversations, and honouring their perspectives and rights to make decisions about the course of their lives . . . was fuelled by my own childhood and the intervention of a myriad of institutional systems into my family and into our lives as children. Like flakes of snow we melted in their hands. I learnt first-hand of how children get spoken about and then get spoken to as a result of being spoken about.

Perry (1999: 128)

KEY POINTS

- The solution-focused approach recognises the self-evident truth that behavioural problems persist when attempted solutions have not worked.
- Change, then, is brought about by altering the way in which the behaviour is handled. To do this, you need to identify previous solution attempts, recognise which of these have worked, even partially, and repeat these, while ceasing to employ those methods that have failed.

Introduction

The solution-focused approach sprang from systems theory, which upholds that any individuals who are in ongoing contact unavoidably influence each other (Fisch &

Schlanger 1999). When students have behavioural difficulties at school, adults will have tried to influence them to improve their behaviour. The persistence of the behavioural difficulty is evidence that these efforts have been unsuccessful. Therefore, it is these attempts to influence the problem—that is, the interaction between teachers and students around the problem—that must change.

Solution-focused theory represents at least three fundamental shifts in focus from individualist theories. First, instead of examining individuals, it addresses how they are interacting. Second, rather than examining the past for causes of a problem, it seeks to intervene in the present. Third, the intervention is driven by the perceptions of those experiencing the problem, rather than by a counsellor's theoretical understandings (Duncan et al. 2003). This means that, although the following sections and Figure 7.2 may imply that the approach is linear, it actually flows from recursive conversation among those experiencing a difficulty (Carey & Russell 2003).

Philosophical assumptions

Solution-focused theory was classified in Figure 1.2 (see page 19) as egalitarian because it affirms the equal status of all individuals. It does not elevate 'adults' rights, feelings and convenience over the needs of children' (Joy 1999: 149). In practical terms the theory states that, when people have problems that undermine their functioning, they are more familiar with those problems than outsiders can ever be (Selekman 1997). These people are the experts on how the problem affects their lives and, often without knowing it, are the experts on how they can affect it. In this way, then, the adult–child hierarchy is upturned, with young people and their expertise at solving their own problems being at the centre of interventions. Educationally, this view of children as actively constructing solutions to their own problems aligns with a constructivist educational paradigm, rather than a teacher-directed or top-down approach to curricula.

Beliefs about children

The core credo of solution-focused approaches is (Winslade & Monk 1999: 2):

> The person is not the problem; the problem is the problem.

Rather than looking for what is wrong with children and how to fix it, a solution orientation searches for what is right and how to use it (Berg & Miller 1992, in Davis & Osborn 2000). To focus in this way on people's competencies instead of their presumed pathologies is a choice, not an issue of fact (Durrant & Kowalski 1995, in Murphy & Duncan 1997).

In light of this focus on competencies, Berg and Steiner (2003: 18) declare their assumptions that children want to please their parents and make their parents proud of them; to be active and involved and learn new skills; to be accepted by and belong in their social group; for their opinions and choices to be honoured; and to be surprised and to surprise others. Adolescents, in particular, want to be respected for who they are now, rather than who they have been (Davis & Osborn 2000).

Explanations for disruptive behaviour

Problems are not one-off events but are difficulties that are occurring repeatedly, causing those involved to become distressed or incapacitated (Fisch et al. 1982). Serious problems are not a sign of individual pathology but merely signal that those involved are intimidated by the potential outcomes of the difficulty, such as the fear of suicide by someone who is depressed (Fisch & Schlanger 1999). In other words, problems signal that people are stuck, rather than sick (Murphy 2006). Solution-focused approaches take little interest in how people got stuck in the first place, but focus instead on how solutions can be developed (Nichols & Schwartz 1995). As such, they have a future orientation, rather than an interest in the past (De Jong & Berg 2002; Molnar & de Shazer 1987; Murphy 1994).

According to the solution-focused approach, problematic behaviour persists when everyday developmental challenges or crises are accidentally mishandled. Subsequently, when the problem worsens people try harder to solve it, but the harder they try the worse it gets (Murphy 2006). Their methods—which were aimed at solving the problem— unintentionally maintain or intensify it (Amatea 1988; Amatea & Sherrard 1991; Fisch et al. 1982). This leads to a recursive cycle of problems and attempted solutions (as illustrated in Figure 7.1), whereby the student disrupts, you attempt to correct the behaviour, the student resists your correction, you respond to that reaction, and so on. You each have been caught up in doing 'the same damn thing over and over' (de Shazer et al. 1986: 210). This is no one's fault; it just *happens*. Thus, the problem is not the dancers, but the dance in which they are engaging.

Despite the failure of their solution attempts, participants nevertheless repeat these, not because they are deranged, foolish or illogical but because their responses seem sensible and correct (Fisch & Schlanger 1999). They conscientiously follow the wrong advice—namely, that 'If at first you don't succeed, try, try again' (Fisch et al. 1982: 18). Instead, Murphy (2006: 119) endorses W.C. Fields's suggestion: 'If at first you don't succeed, try again. Then quit. There's no use being a damn fool about it'.

FIGURE 7.1   A recursive cycle of escalating disruptiveness and corresponding escalating attempts at correction

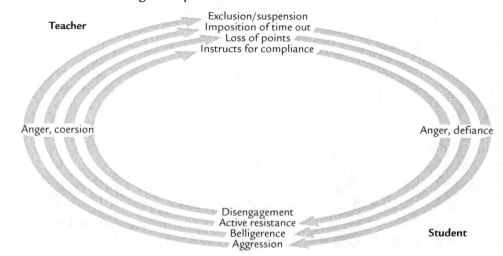

Source: adapted from Dallos & Draper (2005: 70)

When students and teachers are caught up over a long time in these repetitive cycles of action and reaction, they both feel victimised by the other's behaviour. Students complain of being picked on and that it is 'unfair'. Teachers do likewise (although perhaps using more mature terms). Both parties to this interaction believe that their behaviour is justified in light of the behaviour of the other person, but this self-righteousness does not help to resolve the problem (Cooper & Upton 1991) and may even block them from enacting a new solution on the grounds that *they* are not the one with the problem.

Instead, finding a solution will involve changing how individuals are presently responding to the behaviour. This will not entail searching for an initial cause in the cycle surrounding the behaviour, as this is both fruitless and unnecessary, given that there *is* no beginning or end in a circle. As the starting point does not matter, the place to intervene in this repetitive cycle is with *yourself*, as explained by an analogy suggested by Fisch and colleagues (1982), who observe that if you wanted to put an end to a tennis rally, the simplest way would be for one of the players to put down his or her racquet. In school-based behavioural difficulties, it is virtually impossible for adults to convince students to be the one to discard their racquet; the adults have to initiate the change. This is because no one can make anyone else change.

Having described that problems persist because of unsuccessful solution attempts, solution-focused thinking does recognise that neurological impairments and other limitations can lead to learning difficulties. Nevertheless, the approach can help students to harness the benefits of other interventions, such as remedial classes or medication (Murphy 2006).

Goal of discipline

The goal of the solution-focused approach is determined by those experiencing the problem. It does not empower them, as outsiders can never give others something that they do not already have (Murphy 2006), but it does aim to increase their awareness of their personal resources and wider supports so that they can use these to achieve a better quality of life for themselves (De Jong & Berg 2002). The approach believes that, no matter what problems they are experiencing, all individuals have strengths that can be harnessed to improve their functioning and that all environments, no matter how bleak, have resources to support their efforts at doing so (De Jong & Berg 2002). Nevertheless, solution-focused theory recognises that oppressive social forces, such as poverty and racial or sexual discrimination, marginalise individuals and limit their options. To ensure that discipline does not compound such injustices, it must not be repressive—that is, it cannot aim to correct and suppress troublesome behaviour by forcing students to conform (Winslade & Monk 1999).

Building solutions with students

On the assumption that two heads are better than one, particularly when one of those heads belongs to the person who will have to implement changes, the search for a solution requires you to collaborate and consult with students and others involved in school problems (Murphy & Duncan 1997). They know best how the problem affects their lives and what solutions are available to them, while the sense of achievement inherent in designing their own solution ensures that they will be motivated to carry it out.

In its belief that children have the wisdom to solve their own problems, solution-focused work relieves you of the responsibility to be the expert with all the answers. You will need to quiet your own assumptions and 'expert' frame of reference and instead respect what others want for their life and affirm their skills for attaining this (De Jong & Berg 2002). Your task is not to assess what is wrong, but to listen to their accounts of what is working (Murphy 2006), to help them to know what they don't know they know. To that end, while adopting a stance of inquiry or curiosity, you will ask about the problem and their resources (internal and supportive network) for solving it using open-ended *who*, *what*, *where*, *when* and *how* questions but not *why*, because *why* questions invite analysis and a search for someone to blame (De Jong & Berg 2002). Students' answers (rather than your own frame of reference or assumptions) will provoke your next question. Their answers to these will generate the next step (Kay 2001).

Such problem-solving discussions can be opportunistic, taking advantage of brief moments during the day to have an incidental conversation, can occur during a scheduled meeting time, or can be formalised as a counselling process. If you are the child's teacher and therefore an active participant in the cycle of problem behaviour and its attempted solution, it might be difficult for you to direct such counselling yourself—in which case it can be useful to recruit an outside facilitator, such as a colleague, the principal or a student counsellor.

Recruit the engagement of young people

It is self-evident that an intervention is no intervention at all if those involved are not willing to use it (Murphy 2006). However, young people rarely volunteer that they need help with their behaviour at school and thus are usually unmotivated to enact others' recommended solutions. They have typically received much advice and endured many reprimands and scoldings about what is wrong with them (De Jong & Berg 2002). Naturally, they are unwilling to be blamed and need to defend their autonomy and sense of themselves as capable rather than damaged (De Jong & Berg 2002). As a result, they are likely to be reluctant participants in the problem-solving process.

Students may have had their perceptions discounted in the past, so you could begin by asking them what they think would be helpful to them. Any anger they display is a reaction to fear or hurt, and thus is a message about how hopeless or desperate they feel (Berg & Steiner 2003). In their angry comments will be a clear message about what is important to them (De Jong & Berg 2002). You could ask about their reluctance to engage with you, thus: 'You must have a very good reason for believing that it's a waste of time to talk with me. Can you tell me what it is?' or 'It sounds like you've had some bad experiences with other people talking with you about this. What could they have done differently that would have been more useful to you?' (De Jong & Berg 2002).

Phase 1: Define the problem

When eliciting details of the problem, your purpose is not to establish the facts or to work towards a consensus of opinion about these; it is enough to understand how participants *perceive* the problem, because they act as if their perceptions are reality. Perceptions are all there ever is (Fisch et al. 1982). Therefore, you do not have to agree

FIGURE 7.2   Phases of the solution-focused approach

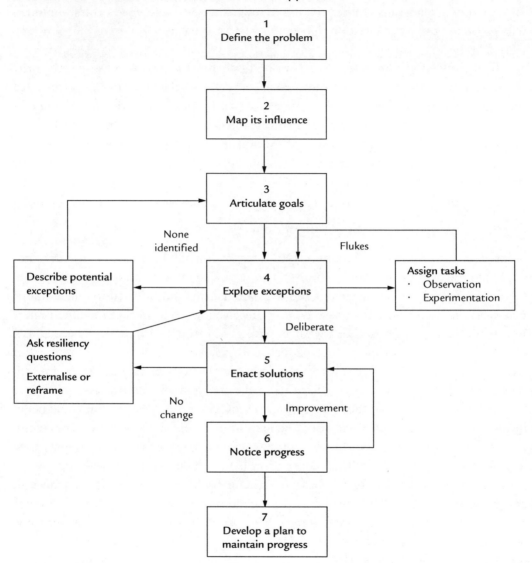

that their view is the only possible one, but merely recognise that it is the one from which they are operating.

Thus, recognising their frame of reference is not the same as approval (De Jong & Berg 2002). When the problem entails antisocial behaviour, you still need to start from the assumption that young people have good reasons for acting in these ways (Berg &

Steiner 2003), while explicitly challenging choices that are detrimental to themselves and others by asking 'You must have good reasons to tell lies/steal/become aggressive. Can you tell me what they are? What is happening that tells you that skipping classes helps you? How does fighting with your classmates make the situation better for you? In what ways does taking drugs help you get what you want from life?' (Berg & Steiner 2003; De Jong & Berg 2002). In their answers, you will listen to the need that is driving the behaviour and subsequently guide them to come up with solutions that meet those same needs through less destructive acts.

Students' description of the sequence of events that occur when the problem is happening and specific information about who does what will yield their history or 'story' of the problem. However, when problems have endured for some time, people's whole identity can come to be defined by 'the problem'. The image that others have of them (and often the image they hold of themselves) becomes saturated with incidents of problematic behaviour. They are seen in terms of being mad, bad or sad, while their many other skills and qualities are often overlooked (Perry 1999).

To avoid this, early in the conversation you must turn the discussion towards getting to know what matters to students personally by talking with them about their interests and asking questions about their lives to which you do not know the answers. Even if you already know individual students well, you can ask them to tell you something about themselves that would surprise you, that you might not know. This focus on aspects other than the problem is not merely to build rapport or ease into talking about difficult issues, but to gather information about their skills and personal attributes that can become part of the solution that you will jointly generate. Those skills to look out for include actions that indicate courage, strength, dedication, effort, wise judgment, loyalty, cooperation and caring for others, to name but a few (De Jong & Berg 2002; Sklare 2005).

The next step will be to discuss non-problem times (as described shortly). However, this can seem premature in instances when the problem seems insurmountable. In that case, one of two methods may first be needed to deflect their despair—namely, externalising the problem or reframing it.

Externalise the problem

One way to avoid locating blame *within* students is to give the problem a name and speak about it as if it were *external* to them. Narrative therapy calls this *externalising* the problem. It can be particularly useful when the problem seems to have a life of its own, or when the young person reports feeling helpless to control it. The name allocated to the problem is decided on in discussion with the children, using their language or having them select from a list of potential labels that you generate, such as calling outbursts of anger 'Temper', 'Trouble', 'the Agitation' or 'the Rage'; sadness might be labelled as the Misery; for those with learning difficulties, it could be that 'Squirmies', 'Rushing' or 'Guessing' make them unsuccessful, for example (Huntley 1999). And sometimes these problems have allies that team up with them and cause further oppression, such as 'Self-doubt' or 'Self-criticism' (Morgan 2000).

Redefine (reframe) the problem

When externalising the problem seems too frivolous to those involved, a second type of redefinition, called *reframing*, might prove useful. This begins with describing the problem and previous corrective measures. Any such descriptions of our own or others' behaviour are always partial in the two senses of being incomplete and of being biased. Although this is true of all descriptions, when our purpose is to facilitate change in ourselves or others some portrayals will be more useful than others, just as road maps are more suited to planning a road trip whereas geophysical maps give better guidance about the location of mineral deposits. Our verbal 'maps' or explanations of our own or others' behaviours—such as diagnoses of mental illnesses, for example—can intimidate those involved and imply constancy rather than the ability to change. But, as Einstein (in de Shazer 1993: 84) said 'You cannot solve the problem with the same kind of thinking that has created the problem'. Therefore, you will need to describe the behaviours in ways that suggest possibilities of change. This will begin by modifying the present explanation for the problem. Typically, these have one of the following two themes:

- The first theme, which centres on the belief that a student is 'doing it deliberately', is usually employed when young people are aggressive or lack remorse for their antisocial behaviour (Morgenson 1989). Teachers typically find such an attitude intolerable and feel victimised, angry and frustrated by the behaviour (Amatea & Sherrard 1989), and thus use a range of escalating punishments that, although different on the face of it, all have the same intention of making the students cease the behaviour.
- The second belief, that students 'cannot help themselves', is most common with passive behaviours, such as mood disturbances, phobic reactions or learning disabilities (Amatea & Sherrard 1989), and when students seem remorseful about their behaviour (Morgenson 1989). When students believe that they are helpless, they do not attempt to take charge of the problem; when *you* believe that they are helpless, you will by turns be too solicitous or patient, or experience frustration and make exasperated demands that they 'pull their socks up'. Neither response will be effective, as students alternate between feeling so comfortable that they are not motivated to change and feeling victimised and misunderstood, against which they rebel.

Given that the behavioural difficulty has persisted, the present explanation for the behaviour is not helping to find a solution. Therefore, you need to generate a new way of viewing the problem, as illustrated in Vignette 7.1. This new view activates a change in solution.

VIGNETTE 7.1 AN EXAMPLE OF REFRAMING
A boy in his last year of primary school frequently became violent at school, to the point where his mother would be asked to come to school and settle him down. This had been occurring around twice a week for the past three years.

The school's explanation for the behaviour was that the boy was emotionally disturbed as a result of sexual abuse by his father. This sympathetic understanding might have been accurate, but *it wasn't helping*. Therefore, we needed an alternative explanation (a reframe).

The mother reported that, when she had discovered that her husband was abusing his sons (then aged six and four years), she expelled him from the household. Subsequently, she experienced what she characterised as a nervous breakdown. Her elder son's problems began at this time. His mother was now well in command of her life—and yet the problems with her son continued, verifying to the individually focused adults that he was emotionally scarred by his early experiences.

In generating a reframe, I was aware that there is always one well-meaning but misguided relative who, when a child's father leaves the family, tries to placate the eldest son with the notion that he 'is the man of the house' now. Instead of comforting a child, however, this platitude results in the theft of his childhood. When his father left, this young lad was aged six, at which time he began taking care of his mother.

Considering that the sequence in this case was that the boy acted up at school and his mother was called in to sort him out, the reframe generated was as follows. When your job is to look after your mother, the two of you have to be together. But when you are a school student, you are not allowed to leave the school grounds. Therefore, your only alternative is to ensure that your mother visits the school, so that you can check that she is okay. Once you have done that, she is free to leave again.

Thus, the reframe was that the boy was maintaining the habit of looking after his mother, even though it was no longer necessary.

The final step was to act in a new way suggested by the reframe. In this case, the mother thanked her son for sacrificing his childhood to look after her. He was clearly an honourable and loyal son and would grow into a fine and gentle man. Next, she told him that she was able to look after herself again now and wanted to look after him too. And, as he did not have a father who could teach him how to grow up to be an honourable young man, as an adolescent he would need now to devote himself to this task.

Meanwhile, at school, the teachers developed a new respect for the boy and could understand his perspective better. Their increased care and respect for him was, in turn, communicated to him indirectly and supported him in his efforts to change.

Comment

This reframe is no more 'true' than the prior explanation that the child was emotionally disturbed. But we could not change past events or cure an emotional disturbance, even with access to trained counsellors. And meanwhile, his teachers would still have to deal with his disruptions. The alternative explanation implied that the young person was not emotionally disabled by the earlier abuse as such, but burdened by his ongoing feeling of responsibility for his mother. Thus, our task was to reduce his responsibilities (allow him to 'grow down'), so that he was thus freed to assume appropriate responsibilities for himself (and thus 'grow up').

Phase 2: Map the problem's influence

So that you appreciate the gravity of the problem, you can ask how long it has been in the student's life, whether it has been getting worse or better, and how it might develop in the future. This maps the problem's *length*. You also need to understand to what *depth* or intensity the problem is felt. Does it weigh heavily on the child? Does its severity vary? When is it hardest to handle? (Winslade & Monk 1999). Third, its *breadth* refers to how widely the problem has affected students' lives (Winslade & Monk 1999). Does it affect school life only, or spread into their family, peer and other relationships? Has it interfered with their school work, career plans, social life, extracurricular activities? Does it affect how they think about themselves, making them seem younger than they are by bossing them around and making them make mistakes? (Freeman et al. 1997; Morgan 2000).

These questions are aimed at acknowledging the distress that the problem has wrought. You might summarise this effect as taking the fun out of life, interfering with the students' relationships or causing them to do poorly in class. Next, you will inquire what *tactics* it uses to achieve this: 'How does it speak to you? Does *self-doubt* shout at you or only whisper nasty things in your ear about how hopeless you are? What sorts of things does it tell you?' You could then ask students how they *feel* about the influence of the problem and the strategies it uses to maintain its hold over them, querying whether it is fair that the problem uses these tactics to take the fun out of life, or what they did to the problem to deserve being spoken to like this. Such questions will get them in touch with their motivation to manage the problem and thus reduce its impact on their lives.

Phase 3: Articulate goals

To provide a clear direction for change, goals must be concrete, realistic and measurable, so that improvement can be recognised. Even more important, goals must be meaningful to those having to make changes, so that they are motivated to do so. You can elicit the goals of those involved by asking them what they would like to get out of your conversation or how they would know things were improving. The 'miracle question' is fundamental here (de Shazer 1988). This asks those involved to imagine that tonight, while they were sleeping, a miracle happened and their problem was fixed. You follow this up by asking what will have changed in their life, who will be doing what differently. This question can be less formal by asking 'If tomorrow turned out to be a good day for you, what would be happening?' (Ajmal 2001). Or, you can ask them to pretend that there are two movies of their life, one with the problem as it is now and one without the problem: 'What does the second movie look like?' (Murphy 2006). Their answers will tell you what is important to them in life, what they value and how they would like to live. This is their goal.

The aim is for the students to enunciate positive goals that state what they want to happen in their lives (De Jong & Berg 2002; Sklare 2005). When they declare that they want a given behaviour to cease or for other people to change, these negative goals will have to be translated into something positive that *they* can do—for example 'If you weren't losing your temper, what would you be doing instead...? If your teacher were being nicer to you, what would you be doing differently to make that happen...?'. If, even with the miracle question, young people still say that they do not know what they want, you can ask hypothetical questions such as 'If you did know...? If you had to take a guess, what might it be?' or distal questions such as 'What would your mum tell me was the most important thing to you?'. When they identify *impossible* goals, such as for their parents to reunite, you can respond to such wishes by asking 'That means a lot to you because...?' (Sklare 2005: 30), which allows you then to focus on finding ways to meet the underlying need. The same approach lies behind instances where their goal is to leave school or to take up a delinquent lifestyle, when you can ask how that will help them so that you can detect the need (goal) that their chosen behaviour is intended to satisfy.

Once goals are framed in achievable terms, scaling questions can ask students to rate where they are presently on a scale of 1 to 10 (with 1 being the worst it has ever been and 10 being the day after the miracle), so they can assess how close they already are to achieving their goal. Being concrete, the use of numbers suits children well (Berg & Steiner 2003). The following questions can be useful (Kral & Kowalski 1989; Rhodes 1993; Wagner & Gillies 2001).

- At what number is your life at the moment?
- How happy are you with that number? (This will tell you how motivated they are to change their behaviour.)
- What number would you prefer to be at?
- What will life be like at $x + 1$? What will you be doing differently?
- Have you ever been at $x + 1$ before? If so, what was happening then?
- What do you think are the chances that you will reach (the goal number)? (This allows you to gauge how confident they are about the possibility of change.)
- How will you know that you are making progress? What will be the first sign?
- When this problem is entirely solved, what will be happening that is different from what is happening now?

Phase 4: Explore exceptions

The basic assumption guiding the next phase is that, although an enduring problem can appear to be 'always' happening, this is an illusion: change is inevitable. There *will* be times when the problem is not occurring, is happening less often, or is less intense. These occasions are called *exceptions*. To uncover what needs to happen for students to achieve their goals, you will need to gain an understanding of what they have done in the past to bring about these exceptions. You can begin by asking generally which solutions they have tried, listening out for four types of these: those that have failed, those that have worked, those which they have been considered but not implemented, and those that others have advised (Murphy & Duncan 1997). Finding out what has failed tells you what not to try again, while finding out what has worked, even partially, gives you clues to what may work again and what strengths they have already brought to bear on the problem and thus could use again. This focus on their attempts is powerful, as it implies that you see them as having the capacity to make things happen and gives them hope about their future (De Jong & Berg 2002).

Specific questions that will identify what they have done to generate these exceptions include (Carey & Russell 2003):

- Are you aware of how you got that to happen?
- Did you take any steps leading up to it?
- What did you do to pull that off?
- What were you thinking at the time that helped you do that?

A second class of questions implies something about the person's identity (Carey & Russell 2003):

- What does this tell us about your ability to control the problem?
- What does it tell us about what is important to you in life, that you were willing to work to control it?
- Can you tell me about other times you have acted to give yourself a better life?

Phase 5: Generate tasks that contain solutions

Once young people can describe their goal and the skills they have used on occasion to achieve at least part of what they want, you need to 'build a bridge' between their past successes and future solutions (De Jong & Berg 2002). The first step for providing such links is to ask those involved what they think will work, as they have proven (through the exceptions) that they can do it (Murphy & Duncan 1997). You might support their ideas with some suggested tasks aimed at transferring their solutions to other situations or increasing their frequency (Murphy 2006).

- When those involved can identify their previously successful strategies, ask what it would take for the exceptions to happen again and invite them to do that or, if they doubt their ability to do so, merely have them observe what is different about those times when they *do* manage to create an exception (de Shazer 1988).
- When those involved believe that the exceptions were just flukes, to heighten their awareness that these are not in fact mere accidents but happen as a result of something *they* do (Carey 1999) you could, for example, inquire about their heroes and then ask: 'What do you think (their hero's name) would do if faced with this problem? Would that be something you'd be willing to try?' (Murphy 2006). Alternatively, they could *pretend* that the miracle/solution/goal has been achieved. Durrant (1995) gives the example of inviting a student to act *as if* he did not feel like throwing things at his peers, was having fun and was enjoying his work. Meanwhile, his teacher was to guess whether he was pretending or was 'for real'.

This helped the teacher to notice those occasions when the student's behaviour had improved instead of naturally focusing on the disruptions.

- When those involved are convinced that the problem always happens, you can suggest observational tasks such as 'Next time we meet, I want you to describe to me one thing in your life that you want to continue to have happen' (De Jong & Berg 2002: 130). Or you can ask them to think about how come their problem is no worse than it is—what is keeping it from becoming even more serious? (Molnar & de Shazer 1987). You might activate problem solving by having them act as a consultant, asking questions such as 'What advice would you give to someone else having this kind of problem?' (Murphy 2006).

Phase 6: Notice progress

In the next review meeting, you will begin with the question 'What's better/different since last time we spoke?'. This conveys confidence that those involved are competent to have taken some steps towards improving their life (De Jong & Berg 2002). You will not ask if they performed the task you suggested, because if they have not done so they will be embarrassed or despondent. Besides, the task is irrelevant if they came up with a different strategy altogether or improvements are happening anyway.

In a process represented by the acronym EARS, you need to *e*licit exceptions, *a*mplify these, *r*einforce (celebrate) students' successes, and *s*tart again by asking about other exceptions (De Jong & Berg 2002). As students recount changes, it is crucial to notice even those that do not appear to be related to the problem or its solution. Furthermore, each improvement needs to be appreciated for its own sake, not just as a step towards further advances.

Next, you will highlight (or *amplify*) the changes, investigating the ripple effect that changes in students' behaviour have wrought on the behaviour of others (Sklare 2005). In examining these effects, you will highlight the skills that the students have used to bring them about, not out of any attempt to flatter them but in an effort to help them recognise their own skills. One technique that is termed 'positive blame' asks 'How did you get that to happen? Where did you get such a useful idea? What did you tell yourself that helped you do that? Is that something different for you?'. Further amplification can be achieved by asking 'What does that tell you about yourself? What did the problem have you thinking about yourself before? What do you think about yourself now?'. If you are the child's teacher and need to examine your own role in the changes, you might have to ask the student what he or she has noticed you doing differently. These changes can then be summarised using the rating or scaling system used earlier.

When there appears to all those involved to have been no change, or even a deterioration in the problem, you will need to listen to their despondency. Having acknowledged their discouragement, you can then compare bad days with worse days and ask what creates the difference (McLeod 1989). You can then ask resiliency questions, such as 'how come they have not given up?', 'what keeps them hanging in there and trying?', or 'how come the problem is no worse than it is?'. If you have not already done so, it could be helpful to externalise or reframe the problem so that it seems more manageable.

Phase 7: Develop a plan to maintain progress

One specific way to reduce the chances of old habits taking hold again is to engage as wide an audience as possible in celebrating and supporting students' success at overcoming their problematic behaviour. This is especially important within schools, where teachers' or other students' scepticism can make it difficult for students to overcome their negative reputation. One way to do this is to formulate lists, charts, diaries, letters, certificates of achievement, art and poetry to document their progress. With their consent, you can circulate these to selected readers, such as their parents, the principal or other teachers, as appropriate. This audience can even be hypothetical, such as deceased or absent relatives or friends, the child's pet or stuffed toy, or imaginary friends.

A second audience for these documents can be the students themselves. Whereas conversations are ephemeral, documents endure and can reaffirm children's knowledges and successes at times when they are discouraged (Fox 2003).

A crucial means to maintain progress is to develop with the student ahead of time a plan for coping with obstacles and any new or unfamiliar experiences that might flow from changing their behaviour (Murphy 2006). This helps them be realistic about the work ahead of them and prevents their being caught off guard by unforseen challenges (Sklare 2005). For example, you might have to ask whether their new behaviour will disrupt their friendship groupings and, if so, how they can deal with that.

Those involved can become particularly discouraged if they revert to displaying instances of the old patterns of behaviour. To avoid despondency, you can frame relapses as ways that the problem tests them to see if they can 'get back on track', or that these relapses provide extra information about the tricks and tactics that the problem uses to take over their lives (Morgan 1999). Next, you can remind the students of the strategies that they originally used to overcome the problem and encourage them to resume using those (Kowalski 1990). Alternatively, even a failure contains a partial success. When the alcoholic who is trying to be abstinent takes six drinks, she used a strategy not to have a seventh; when a student has been verbally abusive towards a peer or teacher, you can ask what he did to stop himself lashing out physically as well. When students are deeply discouraged, you could try coping questions such as 'What have you done since the outburst to calm yourself down? How did you find the courage to come and speak with me about this? On a scale of 1 to 10, how badly did you feel at the time? How does that compare with how you feel now? What did you do to bring about the improvement?'. This highlights that, even in the face of failure, the students are still using some skills to recover from the setback.

If you are in a position to do so, you might negotiate an agreement with the principal that, except for outright violence, the student will not be suspended from school as long as there is an overall trend of improvement, so that there is not a systemic overreaction to a relapse.

Conclusion: Building solutions with whole-class groups

This action-oriented approach works equally with individuals or with groups of students (Davis & Osborn 2000; Sklare 2005). When whole classes are highly disruptive, a class meeting can be convened to discuss ways to improve how the class functions. You or an outside facilitator will ask students what they like about or are proud of in their class, its achievements, what they do to play or work well together and, moving towards enunciation of goals, what they would like to see happening more (Cullen & Ramoutar 2003). In subsequent meetings, their efforts to achieve these goals are highlighted and expanded.

Changing your own solution

Circumstances might preclude your working directly with a student whose behaviour is a problem. Given that problems (and their solutions) are circular, this is not an impediment, as you can instead focus on changing your side of the interactions that surround the disruptive behaviour. To that end, the following methods may prove useful.

Storm the back door

In order to build constructive relationships with troublesome students, in everyday interactions you can use a method known as 'storming the back door', which involves acknowledging something positive or neutral about their behaviour without focusing at all on the problem (Molnar & Lindquist 1989). Because all interactions are linked,

changing any one interaction—even when it has nothing to do with the problem—
alters your relationship with the students and in turn changes the problem.

Record exceptions

When frustrations with ongoing behavioural difficulties are high, it is easy to overlook
the times when the problem could have occurred but did not. Therefore, in contrast
with a deficit orientation that assesses problems by recording how often they happen,
you can record instances when students challenged their difficulties or behaved in ways
that tell you that things are changing (McGlone 2001).

Interrupt the pattern

Let's say that the simple reframe of the young man's situation in Vignette 7.1 (see p.
163) did not produce improvement in his behaviour. Or perhaps you do not have
access to enough information about what might be going on for a particular student
and thus cannot generate a reframe. In that case, you could instead use *pattern interruption*
(Durrant 1995). This approach is based on the understanding that the student has
good reasons for the behaviour, even though you do not know what these might be.
In line with this theory's egalitarian principles, you cannot frustrate a student's legitimate
need, but you *can* insist that the resulting behaviour is modified in some way so that
it becomes less disruptive to others (Molnar & Lindquist 1989).

There is an old saying that a chain is only as strong as its weakest link. This tells us
that to change a behaviour, we can disrupt the usual sequence of events that gives rise
to it by (de Shazer et al. 1986; Durrant 1995; Murphy 2006; Murphy & Duncan 1997):

- changing its location;
- changing who is involved;
- changing the sequence of the steps involved;
- interrupting the sequence in its initial stages ('derailing');
- introducing random starting and stopping;
- increasing the frequency of the behaviour.

The pattern (or sequence of events) in Vignette 7.1 was that, when the child disrupted
in class, his teacher tried to settle him, and when this proved impossible the teacher
called his mother in; she calmed the child and then left. Without detailing all the
options, possibilities for pattern interruption include: having everyone leave the classroom
as soon as the student became agitated (interrupting the sequence in its initial stages);
allowing him to go home at lunch time to check on his mother (change the location);

insisting that he phone at both recess and lunch times to check on her until he realises that there was no need to verify her safety (increasing the frequency of the behaviour); allowing him to invite his mother by phone into the school at times when his behaviour was fine, so that he could still check on her without having to behave disruptively to do so (changing the sequence of the steps); or, with the same aim, asking his mother to visit the school whenever she was passing by (introducing random starting and stopping).

A more everyday example would be to invite active students to move about prior to a desk activity or assign them two desks, so their movement from one desk to another seems legitimate while, at the same time, temporarily relieving nearby students of their disruptiveness. This would help the engagement of surrounding students and lead to their reduced exasperation with, and perhaps improved social acceptance of, highly active students.

Reversals

Unlike reframing, which is based on changing how those involved *think* about the problem, reversals merely involve *doing* the opposite of previous responses, regardless of whether you understand how that might help. You might imagine the last thing that the student would expect you to do, and do that. Sometimes this will be something that was recommended to you or that you thought of already but rejected as it seemed implausible. This use of reversals is based on the belief that, if present solutions were going to work, they would have by now. Given that they have not, in the words of Fisch and colleagues (1982: 88) you will need to 'change a losing game' or, more simply, obey the self-evident truth that if something isn't working, you should stop doing it and do something else instead.

Teach specific skills

Once children are willing to conquer or tame their problem you might, on their invitation, teach them some specific skills and strategies that will help them to do so. These can include teaching constructive self-talk to assist children to weaken the influence of the problem when it is trying to divert them from their goal, teaching emotional regulation or conflict management skills so that they do not inflame peer conflicts, or providing remedial tutoring for those whose rushing or guessing has been a way to mask gaps in their learning, for example.

However, a solution-focused approach would adjust any teaching methods that are borrowed in from other theories. For example, whereas cognitive training works on the assumption that maladaptive attributions result from deficits in children's thinking, a solution-focused approach might assume that students are able to frame adaptive attributions in other domains. For example, if they excel at football, they will have some adaptive attributions that foster their skill development. In that case, you can capitalise on their skills by suggesting that they transfer this positive attributional style into their school work and behaviour.

A second example pertains to children diagnosed with learning difficulties such as dyslexia. With such problems, it is worth keeping two things in mind. First, for every child with dyslexia who cannot read, there are plenty more who can (Wagner & Watkins 2005). Second, instead of equating learning with being taught, which downplays the role of the learner, we need to see it as individual sense making (Wagner & Watkins 2005). With these two thoughts counteracting the 'thin' description represented by a diagnosis, a solution-focused intervention might employ traditional tutoring, but at the same time it would highlight the attributes that students use to help them learn other skills (the exceptions) and support them to transfer these learning skills to the tasks that they are finding difficult (Wagner & Watkins 2005).

Collaborate with colleagues

It can be necessary for all teachers of a given student to meet to plan a solution to chronic disruptiveness. Whereas most case conferences merely confirm a student's negative reputation and entrench teachers' feelings of hopelessness through their almost exclusive focus on problems, solution-focused case conferences within schools can follow the same format as used with the students themselves (Harker 2001). That is, they will describe the problem, formulate goals, discuss present interventions and identify which of these have worked by highlighting exceptions and noting what is happening when the student is not behaving disruptively, and then plan to do more of what is working. Each teacher can rate the student's behaviour on a scale of 1 to 10 before, during and after a planned intervention. The different ratings by various teachers and by the same teacher in different contexts help to identify what contributes to the higher ratings, can clarify what goal is realistic ('What rating would you settle for?') and, later, can document progress (Harker 2001).

Refer on

If an intervention is failing, your first option is to check whether you might have overlooked injustices to which a child is legitimately reacting, such as child abuse, racial or gender discrimination or bullying (from teachers or peers). Depending on your role within the school, some of these and other serious difficulties will be beyond your expertise—in which case, referral to a relevant specialist is the only ethical option.

Summary

The success of interventions depends on individuals' characteristics, the quality of their relationship with their counsellor, and hope (Duncan et al. 2003; Murphy 2006; Murphy & Duncan 1997). The solution-focused approach aims to capitalise on all three. In contrast to approaches where the practitioner is the hero and those with problems are regarded as fragile and ineffective, the solution-focused approach *chooses* to see young people and others involved in school problems as the heroes in their own story, the creators of their own solutions (Murphy & Duncan 1997). Nevertheless, as Murphy and Duncan (1997: 49) state:

> This does not mean that the practitioner ignores suffering or assumes a pollyannish [sic], 'hear no evil, see no evil' attitude, but rather that he or she listens to the whole story: the confusion *and* the clarity, the suffering *and* the endurance, the pain *and* the coping, the desperation *and* the desire.

Distilled down to its simplest notions, solution-focused approaches advise that when present solutions are not working, you either view something differently or do something differently (Murphy & Duncan 1997). *Viewing* differently encompasses noticing non-problems (exceptions) as well as the problems, externalising, or reframing problems. In the words of de Shazer and colleagues (1986: 212), *doing* something differently obeys the maxims:

> If something works, do more of it. (Look for exceptions.)
> If something isn't working, stop it. (Do less of the same.)
> If something isn't working, do something else. (Do something different.)

Interim critique

Like humanism, the solution-focused approach builds on individuals' strengths rather than diagnosing their deficiencies. This communicates respect for students, their parents and their teachers and, in so doing, conveys optimism about the potential for progress. It encourages creativity, light-heartedness and open-mindedness in the face of chronic problems (Molnar & Lindquist 1989), making its approaches particularly attractive to children (Combrinck-Graham 1991; Heins 1988). With their engagement comes a fund of information to which adults do not otherwise have access, which is useful in devising an intervention.

Liberated from a need to search for causes, the solution-focused approach can quickly produce significant changes in school problems. Its focus on the present is particularly useful, given that those involved are looking for relief from present, not past, difficulties (Dicocco et al. 1987). However, some criticise its techniques of reframing and focusing on exceptions as being overly optimistic and dismissive of people's distress (Piercy et al. 2000; Nichols & Schwartz 1995; Schwartz & Johnson 2000). In answer, advocates of solution-focused approaches contend that these honour others' distress in two ways: first, by listening to and validating their feelings about the problem's influence in their lives (Winslade & Monk 1999); second, by recognising that people's distress is about the problem, so the surest way of reducing their pain is to solve the problem (Fisch & Schlanger 1999). As long as practitioners focus on rather than force a solution, emotions are respected (Murphy 2006). A third rebuttal is that emotions are not the problem to be solved; they merely signal that there *is* a problem to be solved (Miller & de Shazer 2000).

In providing clear direction and purpose, solution-focused approaches run the risk of appearing to be highly structured and restrictive, while their questions could seem to be mere formularised techniques (Lowe 2005). Yet, McGlone (2001: 123) cautions that:

> To view solution-focused approaches to problem behaviour as a quick fix or another strategy to be used from a 'bag of tricks' undervalues the contribution of language in the deconstruction of a 'deviant' identity and its role in creating more hopeful alternatives.

Instead, when questions are employed as 'tools for listening', the conversation will *follow* rather than direct the perceptions of those experiencing the problem (Lowe 2005). The disadvantage of this collaborative approach is that interventions are not prescribed in a 'cookbook' fashion, which can lead to a lack of confidence by practitioners. The advantage is that it provokes an inquiring frame of mind where we *ask* rather than tell others about solutions to their problems (Selekman 1997). This one-down position is particularly useful when working with children because it avoids generating resistance to your authority, as *they* (not you) will be the ones to generate solutions.

CASE STUDY

Adam is seven. He has difficulty with reading, spelling and writing, although he enjoys and is capable at maths. During non-maths lessons he spends a considerable amount of time off-task, when he frequently disrupts the other students. This is worse in the afternoons than in the mornings.

He is in a composite class of six and seven year olds. He spends most of his play time with the younger children. Frequently, a pair including Adam is apprehended during play times doing such things as harassing passers-by from an out-of-bounds area of the playground that is close to the street, rifling through rubbish bins for food or cans to swap for other items with students, or engaging in fights in and around the toilets.

Adam seems bemused by the trouble he gets into, usually saying when challenged that he doesn't know why he behaves in these ways, that he couldn't remember that a given behaviour was against the rules, or that the other child was at fault for suggesting the activity.

Until a recent assessment, it was believed that Adam behaved as he did because of low academic ability. However, a battery of tests has shown his overall ability (IQ) to be average, with his maths skills in the high-normal range and his reading and spelling skills, while delayed, still within the lower range of normal limits. His teacher is now at a loss to find a new explanation for his behaviour.

A solution-focused response

In collaboration with and guided by Adam (and his parents when indicated), a solution-focused approach would entail the following steps.

Step 1: Engage with Adam
Conduct a conversation with Adam, getting to know and commenting on his interests and skills. Ask his permission to talk with him about the trouble he is getting into.

Step 2: Define the problem
Ask Adam what he sees as the problem. For the sake of demonstration of this method, we will assume that he reports that his teachers are 'mean' and unfairly 'picking on him'.

Step 3: Map the problem's influence
Adam will report that the problem with his teachers has been going on for some time and affects his school performance, while angering his mother but otherwise not affecting his relationship with peers. He has a couple of peer 'collaborators in crime' and gets along well with them.

Step 4: Identify goals

On inquiry, Adam says that he wants his teachers to 'stop picking on him'. This negative goal needs to be transformed into a positive one, however, by asking what his teachers would be doing at times when they are not being mean to him, then asking what he would be doing at those times that would cause his teachers to act more fairly towards him. He may recognise that he would need to obey rules about staying in safe areas of the school, avoiding fights and completing more work in class.

Step 5: Examine exceptions

Adam remembers his swimming gear (and Adam loves swimming), and yet cannot remember school rules. He also remembers to play in designated play areas when there is an organised game such as soccer (at which he is skilled). As to his school work, he seldom distracts during maths. All these examples indicate that he is able to generate exceptions to problems.

Step 6: Identify his role in creating the exceptions

Let's say that, during your discussion with Adam, he recognises the above exceptions but cannot explain why they occur. He thinks that they 'just happen'.

Step 7: Allocate a task

In that case, following the path in Figure 7.2 (see p. 160), you would ask him to observe over the next week what he does differently during the exceptions compared to the times when the problem occurs. You could ask Adam each morning to predict what sort of a day he will have at school that day (on a scale of 1 to 10) and then, if his prediction is on target, ask him to note that afternoon what he did to make the prediction come true.

Step 8: Notice progress

At a subsequent meeting, ask Adam what has been different since the last time you spoke. Use scaling to depict his progress and highlight his efforts at achieving this. Ask what effect the improvements have had on his teachers' behaviour. Is his mother pleased with his progress? What does he think of it? What difference is his new behaviour making in his life? How confident is he that he can continue to make it happen? Who is most surprised by his new behaviour?

Step 9: Flag obstacles

Discuss with Adam what difficulties might arise from continued progress. Would his old friends still want to be friends with him when he gets into less trouble at school? Would they try to convince him to break the rules again? What could he tell himself to help resist the temptation? Do his teachers believe that he can keep it up? What could he do that would surprise them?

Step 10: Termination
In subsequent conversations, continue to elicit, amplify and highlight his achievements. Once he is confident that he is achieving his goals, terminate conversations about his problems, thus leaving him to remain in charge, but leave the door open for him to approach you again in future if he wants to.

Discussion questions

1   What is the significance of searching for solutions rather than trying to locate the causes of problems?
2   Looking back on your experience in schools, think about a student's behaviour that was not solved. What methods were used to respond to it? Which ones worked and which failed? Which methods were contemplated but never enacted? How would teachers using a solution-focused approach respond differently?
3   How would the solution-focused approach recommend you respond to the student in the case study that you generated for Chapter 2? What effect would its unique recommendations have on the individual student? On the whole class? On you?

Suggested further reading

Solution-focused approach

Ajmal, Y. & Rees, I. (eds) 2001 *Solutions in schools* BT Press, London

Amatea, E.S. 1989 *Brief strategic intervention for school behavior problems* Jossey-Bass, San Francisco, CA

Berg, I.K. and Steiner, T. 2003 *Children's solution work* Norton, New York

De Jong, P. and Berg, I.K. 2002 *Interviewing for solutions* 2nd edn, Brooks/Cole Thomson, Pacific Grove, CA

Durrant, M. 1995 *Creative strategies for school problems* Eastwood Family Therapy Centre, Epping, NSW/Norton, New York

Molnar, A. and Lindquist, B. 1989 *Changing problem behavior in schools* Jossey-Bass, San Francisco, CA

Murphy, J.J. 2006 *Solution-focused counseling in middle and high schools* Pearson Merrill Prentice Hall, Upper Saddle River, NJ

Selekman, M.D. 1997 *Solution-focused therapy with children* Guilford, New York

Sklare, G.B. 2005 *Brief counseling that works: a solution-focused approach for school counselors and administrators* 2nd edn, Corwin Press, Thousand Oaks, CA

Narrative therapy

Freeman, J., Epston, D. and Lobovits, D. 1997 *Playful approaches to serious problems: narrative therapy with children and their families* Norton, New York
Morgan, A. (ed) 1999 *Once upon a time... narrative therapy with children and their families* Dulwich Centre Publications, Adelaide, SA
Morgan, A. 2000 *What is narrative therapy?: an easy-to-read introduction* Dulwich Centre Publications, Adelaide, SA
Winslade, J. and Monk, G. 1999 *Narrative counseling in schools* Corwin Press, Thousand Oaks, CA

Websites

<www.brieftherapysydney.com.au>
<www.brieftherapy.org.uk>
<www.sycol.co.uk>
<www.brief-therapy.org>
<www.solutions-centre.org>

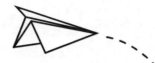

8 CRITIQUE OF THE THEORIES

There is a time to admire the grace and persuasive power of an influential idea, and there is a time to fear its hold over us. The time to worry is when the idea is so widely shared that we no longer even notice it, when it is so deeply rooted that it feels to us like plain common sense. At the point when objections are not answered anymore because they are no longer even raised, we are not in control: we do not have the idea; it has us.

Kohn (1999: 3)

KEY POINTS

- One can give the illusion of a lively debate by asking and attempting to answer questions about the merits of the various theories covered here, by examining evidence of their effectiveness. Meanwhile, however, the presuppositions of the field itself typically go unnoticed and unexamined.
- Disciplinary policies and practices in schools are not selected in a vacuum, but within the context of a society that marginalises and silences powerless groups— in this case, young people. This necessitates a scrutiny of the politics of the ideas themselves.
- Practices must also be judged by both their ethics and effectiveness, which encompasses not only ending a disruption but also promoting positive learning and respectful relationships within the classroom.

Political stance

Every aspect of life is political and disciplinary practices in schools are no exception. They are a clear example of applied politics—that is, of the imposition of power upon the marginalised and silenced (Johnson et al. 1994). It is in this political sphere that humanism and the authoritarian theories most diverge, and they do so on two levels. The first level pertains to the authoritarian methods themselves, which critics claim are abusive inasmuch as the imposition of external controls on others is dehumanising and denies them their basic human need for autonomy. In answer, behaviourists acknowledge that authoritarian methods deny students freedom of choice but argue that, if we do not restrict their choice to fail, their options later in life will be restricted for them (Alberto & Troutman 2003; Bailey 1991; Kaplan & Carter 1995). These writers claim that applied behaviour anaylsis expands students' options and personal freedom, avoids ostracism by peers and gives them the dignity of success while also avoiding other more intrusive interventions (such as drug therapy), meaning that it not only helps individuals to achieve their goals, but also does so efficiently and without unnecessary suffering (Schloss & Smith 1998). In other words, the ends justify the means. Furthermore, behaviourists claim that their laws linking behaviour to its antecedents and consequences are neutral (or amoral). Therefore, if behaviourist methods do not advance children's interests, this cannot be a fault of the theory but instead is plain malpractice. Exploitation of the vulnerable will be prevented by practitioners' own practical ethics, rather than by behaviourist laws as such (Martin & Pear 2003).

Humanists agree that we must protect children from behaviours that will disadvantage them and others, but contend that the same ends can be achieved by less damaging means. They believe that people learn all kinds of knowledge without direct experience of behavioural consequences and thus can make valid behavioural choices for themselves without being manipulated by others. Humanists claim that you cannot teach people to be humane by using inhumane methods, that you cannot teach people to be self-governing by controlling them externally. The means, they say, are as important as the ends. And the ends (self-disciplined individuals) can be achieved without violating children's autonomy.

This introduces the second and deeper level of dispute between humanism and the authoritarian theories, which is encapsulated in humanism's contention that it is *im*moral to be *a*moral, to take no moral stand. In this case, the moral stand they seek is a rejection of social inequities, including those between adults and children. At this philosophical level is the criticism that authoritarian theories assume that an imbalance of power between adults and children is not only inevitable but *right* and, in turn, this 'right' of adults to control children is often elevated into a *duty*. School discipline then becomes a matter of doing things to children rather than *with* them, which critics conclude refutes behaviourism's contention that it is apolitical (Kaplan & Carter 1995). Indeed, Kohn (1999: 30) claims that it is 'a profoundly conservative doctrine posing as a value-free technique'.

According to humanists, the failure of authoritarian theories to examine this political dimension of discipline in schools means that controlling discipline is often employed to coerce children into accepting the status quo and adjusting to established power structures, rather than questioning the system and its power relationships (Winett & Winkler 1972). Thus, the humanist objection is not only to authoritarian methods themselves but also to the fact that their application entrenches social inequalities. Even rewards, which are often justified as being harmless or even positive in their effects on children, manipulate students into doing as teachers want and thus it is the adults who actually benefit (Kohn 1999). This makes the term *benevolent dictatorship* a quintessential oxymoron, as it is never benign to be manipulated by others no matter how 'positive' their methods.

A second result of a failure to consider the political implications of practices is that many advocates of authoritarian theories of school discipline (e.g. Manning & Bucher 2003; Wolfgang et al. 1999) regard teachers' use of power as merely a practical issue. On the purely pragmatic grounds that teachers' corrective interventions should not be more intrusive than the original behaviour, such writers advise using a continuum of graded responses (drawing on any of the theories covered here), with teachers exercising the minimum of power for minor disruptions and applying increasing control to repress more serious disruptions. However, this results in an atheoretically eclectic blend of incompatible approaches and overlooks the ethical and political issues inherent in imposing power over people who are defenceless against it. The primacy of the institution is not questioned. The 'influential idea' which Kohn (1999) criticises in the opening quote to this chapter is the idea, embedded and seldom questioned within society's institutions, that the powerful have a right to control the vulnerable.

Not only do humanist theorists object to the imposition of adult control over children, but when the children themselves are asked they report it to be a central issue for them at school (Mayall 2002). The general injustice for all children is further compounded when disciplinary technologies are imposed in schools on members of socially disadvantaged groups by those who are both more powerful and more privileged. One such group is those young people who come to school oppressed by and underfunctioning as a result of coercive discipline at home. Their reactions against the injustices in their lives are typically met at school with still more coercion, with the result that these students are rejected by both their parents and teachers (Reinke & Herman 2002). They consequently gravitate towards other malcontents within the school—and an antisocial peer group is born (Reinke & Herman 2002). Thus, instead of ameliorating social disadvantage, schools' authoritarian disciplinary methods entrench it.

In addition to antisocial youth, schools also fail those from minority cultures. Across many Western countries, including Britain, the United States, Australia and New Zealand, minority cultural students figure disproportionately in the statistics for school suspension and exclusion and for special education referrals (Osler & Vincent 2003; R. Slee 1995). Other than the solution-focused approach, the theories of discipline introduced here seldom question this inequity.

Boys are a third group to be disadvantaged by the power imbalance in schools, where there is a well-documented negative perception of boys and higher rates of teacher negative feedback to them (Birch & Ladd 1997; Childs & McKay 2001; Jones & Dindia 2004; Stuhlman & Pianta 2001). Boys are disproportionately the focus of school disciplinary measures and suspension. It is usually assumed that this is due to their inherent nature. However, even if boys *were* inherently more troublesome (which research has been unable to prove), schools have a responsibility to honour and adjust to their needs. Instead, in a tendency that has been termed 'petticoat tyranny', a largely female teaching profession denigrates and attempts to suppress boys' more active nature and, when it cannot, pathologises their behaviour by blaming the children themselves.

As for girls, their lives and needs are often overlooked in educational research and in schools themselves (Henning-Stout 1998). Perhaps their superior academic performance as a group (relative to boys') is partly why individual girls' behavioural and learning difficulties are so often neglected, both within classrooms and in the official statistics that foster accountability of the education system (Osler & Vincent 2003; R. Slee 1995). For example, girls with the attention deficit disorders are outliers (and often outcasts) compared with other girls, but do not stand out as obviously within a mixed-gender group and thus tend to have less access than boys to remedial support (Arnold 1996; Hallahan & Kauffman 2003). A second example is that, while one in four students permanently excluded from British schools is female, we have limited tools for assessing girls' adjustment (Henning-Stout 1998) and thus we know little about the causes of girls' disaffection with school or about the resulting social exclusion that follows school expulsion (Osler & Vincent 2003). Meanwhile, patriarchal values impose a compliance on girls that allows them to do well in their school work but produces a conventionality that disadvantages them in adult life (Kerr 1996; Kline & Short 1991; Loeb & Jay 1987). Their docility in the classroom can result in a progressive decline in girls' hopes, aspirations, self-esteem and achievements during adolescence and adulthood (Butler-Por 1993; Freeman 1996; Kerr 1996, 1997; Reis & Callahan 1989).

As you will have gleaned, this humanist critique of authoritarianism centres on the belief that all human beings have equal worth, regardless of any distinguishing features, including age. Like all ethical debates, its starting point is an assumption, not a fact (Strike & Soltis 2004): the equal worth of children is a philosophical choice that is not amenable to evidential proof (N. Rogers 1994). However, inequitable or authoritarian *practices* have been comprehensively researched and these findings do allow us to draw conclusions about their effects.

Effects of authoritarian practices

The fundamental difference between the theories presented in Part One of this book is their position on the authoritarian–egalitarian continuum (as represented in Figure 1.2—see page 19) with corresponding contrasting beliefs (as listed in Box 8.1—see p. 187). In examining the different outcomes of these two styles across domains of young people's functioning, the minimal research on the issue within schools can be supplemented by a robust body of research into parenting styles. Findings that students benefit from the same kinds of relationships with teachers as with parents (Wentzel 1997) indicate that this parenting literature is relevant to the debate about discipline in schools.

The authoritarian parenting style comprises both psychological control, which intrudes into the psychological or emotional life of children, and behavioural control, which uses rewards and punishment to pressure children to comply with parents' expectations. In contrast, egalitarian practices encourage independence and individuality and are characterised by warmth and acceptance, support for children's autonomy and the provision of structure (Grolnick 2003; Grolnick & Ryan 1989). While low on psychological control or intrusiveness into children's lives, a jointly generated structure of behavioural expectations provides a framework within which young people can initiate their own actions (Grolnick 2003). It comprises both vertical aspects of influence and horizontal dimensions, including mutual warmth and joint decision making, with the actual content of these decisions naturally differing according to children's ages (Grolnick 2003).

In terms of outcomes of the two parenting styles on children's *behaviour*, a seminal series of studies by Baumrind (1967, 1971) found that when mothers exercise restrictive control over their children, the children become defiant and uncooperative; in contrast, parents using egalitarian methods tend to produce children who are more cooperative, self-controlled and independent. Other researchers found similarly that children were more likely to cooperate with mothers' directives when the mothers had previously been responsive to their needs (Parpal & Maccoby 1985). Indeed, mothers' responsiveness caused ordinarily nonconformist children to be as cooperative as their more typically well-behaved counterparts. A further study found that mothers' negative control over children—in the forms of threats, criticism, physical intervention and anger—induced defiance in their children and reduced cooperation, while mothers' use of egalitarian discipline was more likely to elicit cooperation and self-assertion (Crockenberg & Litman 1990). Moreover, these researchers concluded that those mothers who used restrictive control did not do so out of frustration at their child's higher rates of behavioural difficulties, as these did not differ across the children studied.

These findings on the behavioural outcomes of the two parenting styles were replicated by my own research in centre-based care (Porter 1999). This study found that centres and caregivers using behaviourist methods experienced far higher rates of behavioural disruptions in the children in their care than did those using egalitarian disciplinary methods. It could not have been that the adults' behaviourist methods were a response to a higher rate of behavioural problems in the children, as the difference held for two caregivers (one authoritarian and the other egalitarian) who were team-teaching the same group (Porter 1999). The conclusion, then, was that—as predicted by Gordon (1970, 1974)—the children resisted, rebelled and retaliated against controlling forms of discipline. These reactive behavioural difficulties were typically both more serious and more challenging to resolve than had been the original disruption (Porter 1999).

While authoritarian discipline can achieve child compliance in the short term, it is less likely that children reared under rewards and punishments will internalise adults' *values* (Sears et al. 1957, in Spera 2005). Children are more willing to abide voluntarily by their parents' guidelines when these are not imposed externally but are self-generated or independently endorsed by the children on the grounds that they are legitimate (Grusec & Goodnow 1994).

Emotionally, Baumrind's observations (1967, 1971) that children of authoritarian parents were withdrawn, anxious, unhappy and hostile when frustrated contrasted with the emotional profile of children of egalitarian parents, who were self-confident and socially outgoing (Baumrind 1967, 1971). Grolnick and colleagues (1996) extended these findings with their research showing that mothers' autonomy support for their toddlers led to the children being better able to regulate their distress than was the case for children subjected to authoritarian parenting. Later in life, under egalitarian parental discipline, adolescents develop greater psychosocial maturity, sense of autonomy, self-efficacy and positive self-esteem about their achievements and experience reduced emotional distress, all of which result in a healthy orientation towards their school work and less antisocial behaviour (Dekovic et al. 2003; McClun & Merrell 1998; Steinberg et al. 1989, 1992; Wentzel 1994). In turn, this enhanced maturity persuades their parents to grant their adolescents further increments of autonomy. This is probably why researchers have found that, over time, academic self-concept increases and behavioural difficulties decline in adolescents with egalitarian parents, whereas emotional and somatic problems increase significantly for those raised by authoritarian parents (Steinberg et al. 1994).

In terms of their *learning styles*, Baumrind's studies (1967, 1971) and those of Grolnick and colleagues (1984) found that infants of controlling mothers were less persistent in their play when compared with children whose mothers supported their autonomous interaction with toys, while Deci et al. (1993) found a decline in intrinsic motivation in children of mothers whose interactions were controlling. Such findings extend into performance at school, where it has been found that when teachers support young people's autonomy, students engage with tasks more, perform better, are more creative and feel better about themselves as learners (Grolnick 2003; Grolnick et al. 2002).

Learning outcomes are also differentially affected by authoritarian versus egalitarian parenting. A series of extensive studies has shown that an egalitarian parenting style is associated with adolescents' internal locus of causality, higher intrinsic motivation, improved willingness to seek challenge and higher achievement in school (Dornbusch et al. 1987; Gonzalez-DeHass et al. 2005; Grolnick & Ryan 1989; Paulson et al. 1998; Steinberg et al. 1989, 1992, 1994). These outcomes are partly due to parental support of their children's self-regulation in the home, which the young people carry over into the school sphere (Grolnick 2003) and partly to parental involvement in their children's schooling. But again, the effects of parental involvement depend on how controlling it is (Grolnick & Ryan 1989; Steinberg et al. 1992). Authoritarian surveillance by parents of their children's homework and administration of rewards for high grades produces students who are extrinsically motivated, dependent on external sources for academic guidance and lacking initiative and persistence, resulting in turn in lowered school grades (Ginsberg & Bronstein 1993; Gottfried et al. 1994). These findings are paralleled in the early childhood years, where one study found that egalitarian discipline and parental responsiveness to their children's interests during play improved the children's school readiness, whereas demanding or didactic parental instruction produced in children poorer task orientation and greater negativity towards school work (Parker et al. 1999).

Other benefits of egalitarian parenting are *social*, extending into peer relationships. Egalitarian parent–child relationships give children experience of, and teach them the skills for, maintaining reciprocal interactions that involve power sharing, mutual influence, making suggestions, persuasion, negotiation, compromise, collaboration, intimacy and positive emotion. In addition to the self-esteem and autonomy afforded young people by egalitarian parenting, it is likely that these 'horizontal' social skills can be directly imported into peer relationships, thus embellishing the children's social competence (Russell et al. 1998).

In summation, egalitarian parenting—and, with a less comprehensive research base, egalitarian teaching—has been shown uniformly to produce beneficial outcomes for children across all developmental domains: behavioural, emotional, intellectual and social. Moreover, with the exception of Steinberg and colleagues (1992, 1994), researchers have found that these benefits pertain across cultures, socioeconomic groupings and various family structures (Amato & Fowler 2002; Grolnick 2003).

Box 8.1 PHILOSOPHICAL DIFFERENCES BETWEEN AUTHORITARIAN AND EGALITARIAN THEORIES OF STUDENT DISCIPLINE

Authoritarian	Egalitarian
By their nature, children will misbehave.	When treated respectfully, children will return the courtesy.
The teacher owns the classroom.	The classroom is owned by all its members.
The teacher is the boss, who wields power.	The teacher is a leader and facilitator, with expertise and wisdom.
Behaviour is controlled from the outside (external locus of causality).	Behaviour is governed internally (internal locus of causality).
Goal of discipline is order, which requires student compliance.	Goal of discipline is considerate behaviour.
Children need limits. The teachers's job is to impose, negiotiate and teach rules.	The 'golden rule' (do as you would be done by) is the only required guideline.
Behavioural errors are inappropriate, unacceptable, misbehaviour	Like academic skills, behavioural skills need practice. Thus, errors are inevitable.
Errors require punishment.	Errors call for teaching more skilful behaviour.
Teacher responses should be consistent.	Teacher responses should wisely reflect the circumstances at the time.
Top-down curriculum.	Constructivist curriculum.
Parents need training.	Collaboration to harness parents' skills and support the wider community.

Resistance to abandoning authoritarianism

Despite the accumulated evidence just presented and despite teachers' personal beliefs in egalitarian discipline, many find that they nevertheless behave in authoritarian ways towards students (Lewis 1997). This raises the question of why the education system is so resistant to changing its authoritarian stance. Perhaps, as Rogers and Freiberg (1994) claim, we distrust democracy as being clumsy and inefficient.

A second possibility is that, by default, authoritarianism is the only style that is familiar to teachers, because their parents raised them that way and the approach is not supplanted during teacher training by information about alternative methods. Meanwhile, students themselves have little experience of egalitarian discipline and do not trust teachers to use it so, in a test of teachers' integrity, may bait them to see if they will revert to authoritarian methods under pressure.

A third possibility is that the use of power-based methods with students is the inevitable consequence of teachers' subordinate place within an education system that dictates to them and places them under pressure to control student outcomes (Deci et al. 1991; Flink et al. 1990). In turn, despite their goodwill and dedication, teachers almost inevitably apply control down the hierarchy to students.

A fourth explanation is that institutions themselves cause inhabitants to fail to question the dominant ethos. This view is supported by a pioneering study whose original purpose was to determine whether psychiatrists could tell that researchers who were faking mental illness were in fact sane, but simultaneously exposed the imposition of power on the defenceless (Rosenhan 1973). When the admitting doctors did not detect the deception, the researchers found themselves confined to mental hospitals for anything from seven to 52 days, whereupon they discovered outright abuses of power but, more insidiously, a depersonalisation of patients and a blatant failure on the part of staff to consider that either the conditions in the institution or the actions of staff might have triggered patients' emotional outbursts. In pondering the reasons for such insularity in staff, Rosenhan (1973: 257) concludes:

> It could be a mistake, and a very unfortunate one, to consider that what happened to us derived from malice or stupidity on the part of the staff. Quite the contrary, our overwhelming impression of them was of people who really cared, who were committed and who were uncommonly intelligent. Where they failed, as they sometimes did painfully, it would be more accurate to attribute those failures to the environment in which they, too, found themselves than to personal callousness. Their perceptions and behavior were controlled by the situation, rather than being motivated by a malicious disposition.

In other words, both staff and their subordinates become institutionalised, perpetuating in schools a power-based system in which there are no demands on anyone—other than students—to change (Curwin & Mendler 1989).

A purely practical explanation could be that, when confronted by apparent threats to their self-efficacy, the resulting stress causes individuals to feel the need to exert control to make others cease behaviour that is distressing them. A cycle develops wherein students react with disruptiveness to a denial of their autonomy, and this behaviour in turn verifies authoritarian teachers' negative predictions of their students and provokes further attempts to control them.

Or, more crucial than any of these reasons, perhaps at the heart of our reluctance to abandon authoritarianism is the belief that has been handed down to us over countless centuries through the Abrahamic religions, that children are bad by nature (Gordon 1991). Such a perspective regards children's opinions as irrelevant or, worse still, purely self-serving and thus not worth accommodating.

Beliefs about children

In lay circles, I commonly hear children being described as attention seeking, manipulative or doing things deliberately to 'get at' their parents. Parents are advised that they can't 'give in' to children and must 'come down hard' on their behaviour because otherwise it will keep happening. In the education sector, this view is translated into the exhortation that a child has *'got to learn'*. The assumption behind this demand is that children will not mature, grow or develop naturally but must be forced to do so *right now*. Similarly sour views of children are often promulgated by even those commentators with credentials that might suggest a more informed opinion, such as the following (which I have embellished with italics):

- 'Kids, when they are little, are—in a way—sort of nuts! They are not born reasonable and unselfish, they are born *unreasonable* and *selfish*' (Phelan 2003: 16).
- 'When students are not given the limits they need, *they will act up* in order *to make the adults around them take notice*' (Canter & Canter 2001: 7).
- 'Children are not born good; they have to be disciplined, otherwise they *are a threat to the rest of society*' (Boyson* in Holland 2004: 75).
- 'If students are given the freedom to do nothing, *that is most likely what they will do*' (Wolfgang et al. 1999: 173).
- 'Today's youth is rotten to the core, it is *evil, godless, and lazy*... It will never be able to preserve our culture' (Watzlawick et al. 1974: 33).

* Sir Rhodes Boyson was an ex-school principal and British Conservative MP advising the government on educational policy, culminating in *The Conservative Education Reform Act* of 1988 (Holland 2004).

It would be comforting if these negative views of young people were all, like the last one, written on clay tablets over 3000 years ago but, as you can see, the previous quotes are far closer in time to this millennium. They clearly imply the belief that children will not choose to put in effort to learn or engage in prosocial behaviour unless forced to do so (Kohn 1996a). To that end, punishment is typically used either to incite people to improve their behaviour in future, or to achieve retribution for a past wrongdoing (Weiner 2000). While the first, utilitarian, purpose might seem the more likely in schools, Weiner reports that punishment is instead commonly applied as retribution, particularly when students' failure is perceived by their teachers to be volitional. Even when punishment is used for utilitarian purposes, Kohn (1996a) questions the underlying assumption that children are so intent on behaving badly that they will not desist unless inflicted with pain.

Thinking of children in these harsh terms inexorably leads to authoritarian attempts to control their behaviour. Paradoxically, seeing children as fragile also leads to the same conclusion, justified by the claim that they 'need' limits to feel secure (see, e.g., Trusty & Lampe 1997). Not only is this ageist (such generalisations would be questioned if applied to adults on the basis of their sex, race or culture), but there is no evidence for the claim. It confuses *limits* with *structure* (Grolnick 2003).

Thus, in the absence of evidence about its truth, humanists reject what Miller (1987) terms this 'poisonous pedagogy' and assume instead that children are equally capable of altruism as they are of being thoughtless. This assumption, although also unprovable, seems logical in the face of statistics that there are more murders of people aged under one year than there are of people aged over one. It would be self-destructive if babies were programmed to threaten the goodwill of the caregivers on whom their survival relies, so it is assumed that they are instead programmed to try to work in with adults.

Effectiveness

Adherents of each theory discussed in Part One of this text believe in their particular approach on the grounds that *it works*. As evidence, researchers typically count how often students perform a negative behaviour prior to an intervention and then demonstrate a decrease during intervention. However, to paraphrase Einstein: 'Not everything that can be counted counts, and not everything that counts can be counted' (Thompson & Rudolph 2000: 215). That is, there is more to effectiveness than merely ending the immediate disruption or gaining compliance, as detailed in Chapter 1. Moreover, that a method works is not an adequate test, for two reasons: first, bias limits the publication of studies where interventions are ineffective; second, cattle prods would effectively suppress disruptive behaviour, but the use of these would be unethical. This demonstrates that proof of mere effectiveness is not enough.

A second standard of proof is to compare outcomes for those who received an intervention with those who did not. Although this is better it is still not ideal, as placebo effects can produce around a 30 per cent improvement despite no treatment being given. Therefore, a higher level of proof is needed—namely to demonstrate that a given method works *better* than its opposing approaches. Very little comparative research is available for behaviour management in general or within schools (Ollendick & King 2000). The parallel literature on counselling approaches (where some comparative research is available) is not very reassuring as it emerges that, while most counselling approaches work better than doing nothing, they all seem to have roughly similar rates of effectiveness (Miller & Berman 1983).

One's theoretical model tends to account for only 15 per cent of different treatment outcomes (Murphy 2006; Murphy & Duncan 1997). Nevertheless, it is still possible that one method is superior to another for particular problems, but this is not known with respect to school-based behavioural difficulties and may never be, given the number of aspects of curricular content, teaching processes and classroom interactions that must be considered and the number of student outcomes that could be measured (Kyriacou & Newson 1982). Furthermore, no intervention can ever be fully validated (Ollendick & King 2000); the fact that a method has been shown to work in a given setting, at that time, with those particular teachers or interventionists and those students does not imply that it will necessarily do so for the student in your classroom today. This is the issue of the transportability of findings, or external validity (Carr 1997). Some reassurance can be provided by cumulative evidence that a method generally works in conditions and with individuals similar to those found in your circumstances; less convincing is evidence on clinical populations who receive one-to-one treatment by highly specialised researchers or clinicians.

Assertive discipline

Despite practitioner support for assertive discipline, there is little research evidence verifying its effectiveness. One well-designed study showed that assertive discipline achieved a decline in off-task behaviour from 12.5 to 7.5 per cent (Canter 1989). Findings from other studies were less positive, with either neutral results or increased referral rates for behavioural difficulties, detentions and truancy (Emmer & Aussiker 1990), with some studies reporting increases in students' negative behaviours and attitudes to school, including lowered student morale.

The major criticism of assertive discipline is its unintended outcomes in areas beyond students' actual behaviour. Critics say that—at best—the program is open to misuse or—at worst—it violates students' emotional and social needs. Canter's defence to such criticisms is that the assertive discipline program is harsh only when not grounded in respectful and supportive student–teacher relationships (Charles & Senter 2005a; Jones & Jones 2004). However, critics claim that the level of control, by definition, is disrespectful and the chances of improper implementation are increased by the approach's lack of an educational theory to guide the use of its techniques: there is no connection between theories of discipline and theories about teaching, motivation or the emotional needs of students (Curwin & Mendler 1989). (The only student need that Canter identifies is the 'need' for limits.) This lack of a theory base neglects the role of inappropriate curricula and teaching methods in provoking behavioural difficulties and inappropriately blames students' shortcomings on poor home backgrounds, when the evidence reviewed in the introductory chapter refutes this.

By imposing consequences on students, it fails to teach them how to think about and solve problems (Carlsson-Paige & Levin 1992). A high degree of teacher control will limit students' learning (Doyle 1986; Honig & Wittmer 1996; McCaslin & Good 1992). Canter believes that it offers students choices, but the approach's critics retort that 'Realistically, the only choice Assertive Discipline offers is, "behave or else!"' (Curwin & Mendler 1989: 83). This choice is otherwise known as 'My way or the highway' (Tileston 2004: 1). This approach defines responsibility as doing as you are told, defines 'good choices' as those that the teacher approves, and defines as 'sincere and meaningful' any feedback that is designed to manipulate students into obedience. In so doing, it fails to address the comprehensively researched question of the difference between internal and external reinforcement (see Chapter 12) and misconstrues the role of feedback in motivation.

Behaviourist methods

A considerable body of research has demonstrated the effectiveness of the methods of applied behaviour analysis (ABA) and functional behavioural assessment (FBA) (Alberto & Troutman 2003; Kaplan & Carter 1995). However, most studies were conducted with atypical individuals displaying atypical problems who were treated in atypical (often clinic) settings with atypically intensive interventions presented by atypical intervention agents (usually researchers and academic psychologists) (Carr 1997; Ervin et al. 2001b; Nelson et al. 1999). There is little evidence that the findings thus generated would be relevant in the natural classroom environment (Doyle 1986; Ervin et al. 2001b; Nelson et al. 1999). As Murphy and Duncan (1997: 88) note: 'The most elaborate and empirically rigorous... measure is useless unless it can be applied by real practitioners to real problems of real people in the real world'.

Atypical subjects

The unrepresentativeness of subjects of most behaviourist research, most being aged under twelve years with severe disabilities, casts into doubt the applicability of the methods to regular students, particularly adolescents when teacher-administered rewards are less likely to be successful and less manageable given the organisational complexity of high schools (Miller 2003).

Atypcial presenting problems

Behaviourist methods have been shown to be effective across a range of clinical behaviours in children, such as the reduction of pica (Piazza et al. 1998, 2002) and other feeding disorders (Ahearn et al. 2001; Buckley & Newchok 2005; Cooper et al. 1995; Kahng et al. 2003; Kelley et al. 2003; Kerwin et al. 1995; Levin & Carr 2001; Luiselli 2000; Piazza et al. 2003; Reed et al. 2004), mouthing of objects (Roane et al. 2003), extreme noise sensitivity associated with Williams syndrome (O'Reilly et al. 2000), social withdrawal (Zanolli & Daggett 1998), general stereotypical behaviours (Kennedy et al. 2000) and specific acts such as hand biting and flapping (Mueller et al. 2001; Van Camp et al. 2000), self-injurious behaviours (Kurtz et al. 2003) and destructive behaviour (Fisher et al. 2000a; Piazza et al. 1997; Roane et al. 2001). These target behaviours are seldom concerns for general education teachers, however.

Other research on behaviours that do commonly concern teachers has focused on students' getting started on tasks (Wehby & Hollahan 2000), improving reading fluency (Eckert et al. 2002), safe use of playground equipment (Heck et al. 2001), aggression (Reynolds & Kelley 1997), reducing elopement (running away from the adult) (Tarbox et al. 2003) and disruptiveness on the school bus (Putnam et al. 2003).

Atypical setting

Even when research focuses on behaviours that concern typical teachers, few studies are conducted in classrooms and, when they are, they focus on only one or a handful of children rather than all students in the group (e.g. Koegel et al. 2001; Musser et al. 2001). Some exceptions include a study with a whole class investigating the relative efficacy of differential reinforcement versus response-cost measures in a preschool (Conyers et al. 2004). Another study, employing the whole-school approach of positive behavioural support (PBS), produced a reduction in school suspensions from 77 in one year to 22 two years later and a massive decline in disciplinary referrals to the school office from 608 incidents to 46 two years later (Scott & Barrett 2004). Much more modest results were achieved in a whole-school intervention by Lewis and colleagues (1998).

Intensive intervention methods

Both the assessments and interventions of ABA and FBA in particular are enormously time consuming. In one study, over 13 000 observations were conducted and still the researchers had insufficient data to judge the function of the target behaviours (McKerchar & Thompson 2004). This expenditure of time is particularly unjustifiable given that traditional ABA approaches seem equally, if not more, effective than the more detailed and rigorous FBA (Nelson et al. 1999). Furthermore, behaviourist assessment overlooks the views of the students themselves, despite the fact that researchers have found that students can contribute more information about antecedents than can their teachers (Wehmeyer et al. 2004). Also, the time taken to complete detailed adult-directed assessments delays intervention, which thereby denies students timely treatment (Gresham et al. 2001) and teachers prompt support, while in the meantime peers could imitate a classmate's disruptive behaviour.

Not only is assessment hugely time consuming, but so too are behaviourist interventions. One study required 93 training sessions (Fisher et al. 2000b); another took in excess of nine months merely to evaluate the differences between differential reinforcement and response-cost procedures in a preschool (Conyers et al. 2004). It would be difficult to scale down the time taken, because the holistic nature of the approaches makes it difficult to discern which components of the program are essential and which might be jettisoned in the interests of efficiency. The time demands calls into question the applicability of such methods to classrooms.

Atypical interventionists

Another threat to the transferability of findings from the research literature into the classroom is the level of expertise required of practitioners. Even its advocates (e.g. Ervin et al. 2001b; Gresham et al. 2001) admit that skilful application of FBA is difficult in school settings, with some contending that it requires doctoral-level expertise (Alberto & Troutman 2003; van Houten et al. 1988; Wolery et al. 1988). Despite such training, analysts judging the functions of behaviours may still achieve low levels of agreement about the contingencies in operation (Gresham et al. 2001; Sterling-Turner et al. 2001).

Interventionists need sufficient expertise to be able to adjust accurately highly technical program variables, such as the manipulation of specific antecedents, the use of high-versus low-probability instructions, adjustment of the schedule of reinforcement (how much time must elapse or how often the target behaviour must be displayed before reinforcement is delivered), changes to the contingency controlling the delivery of positive and negative reinforcers, and varying the quality of the reinforcer. It would take considerable training time to pass on this degree of knowledge and skill to teachers. Although researchers have been able to train teachers to understand the principles of FBA in a single three-hour training session (Wallace et al. 2004), such a low level of training is unlikely to translate into sophisticated classroom-based implementation. Thus, while poor practice is acknowledged to be unethical (Schloss & Smith 1998), it is highly improbable that teachers can accrue the expertise needed for accurate application. Meanwhile, teachers often express distaste for ABA's philosophy (Bailey 1992; Miller 1991; Wolery et al. 1988) and the high level of expertise needed to design interventions tends to exclude their input (Kutsick et al. 1991). Thus, for these and perhaps additional reasons, teachers often refuse to enact behaviourist interventions (Benes & Kramer 1989).

Conclusion

In all cases, behaviourist interventions produced improvements in the target behaviours. However, the outcome criterion is typically children's compliance, which the humanists criticise as being both an illegitimate and inadequate goal in that emotional side-effects or effects on surrounding children are seldom considered. (One exception is Miller (2003), who found that ABA studies in whole special school classrooms produced both improvements in the target children's behaviours and spill-over effects in the form of changed teacher behaviour and improvements in students who were not actually the target of interventions.) Further, there remains minimal evidence that the gains in compliance achieved during intervention are maintained, even when teachers specifically instruct students in skills for generalisation (Ervin et al. 2001b; Kaplan & Carter 1995).

The conclusion is that behaviourism seems to be ineffective with the core 5 to 7 per cent of students with whom teachers most need it to work. These are the students who pose the majority of disciplinary problems in schools, the ones who are repeatedly sent to the principal's office, for whom we have to conclude that if the method were going to work *it would have by now*. It will not work, because reinforcement must be internalised for gains to occur or be maintained (Eslea 1999; Lewis et al. 1998). In other words, students have to *want* to cooperate with the system. But students choose not to learn and to disrupt for intrinsic reasons (such as that the work is 'boring')— in which case, changing extrinsic contingencies is unlikely to be effective (Norwich 1999). Thus, the recidivists at whom most interventions are targeted are the least likely to conform, even under reward and punishment regimes.

Finally, there is evidence that behaviourist parenting programs can increase children's compliance (e.g. Marchant et al. 2004), modestly reduce childhood aggression at least in the short term (Bryant et al. 1999) and improve dysfunctional parenting styles and parents' sense of competence (e.g. Connell et al. 1997; Leung et al. 2003; Sanders 1999;

Sanders et al. 2000). However, the evidence reviewed earlier concludes that egalitarian parenting programs would achieve at least these same results without the attendant risks of behaviourist methods.

Cognitive behaviourism

There is accumulating evidence of modest effectiveness of combined cognitive-behavioural methods with a range of difficulties, from aggression and anger management, social problem solving, antisocial and delinquent behaviour, childhood depression, anxiety and phobias, learning difficulties, impulsivity and adolescent substance use across a range of ages and at various ability levels of students (Alberto & Troutman 2003; Ashman & Conway 1997; Braswell 1995; Kaplan & Carter 1995; Kazdin et al. 1992; Kendall et al. 2000; Kendall & Panichelli-Mindel 1995; Lochman et al. 2000; Miller & Berman 1983; Ollendick & King 2000; Stark et al. 2000; Urbain & Kendall 1980; Yell et al. 2005). Although some studies report improvement in symptoms of the attention deficit disorders (Miranda & Presentación 2000; Robinson et al. 1999; Shechtman 2000), not surprisingly cognitive interventions do not reverse all of the complex array of problems characteristic of these conditions such as children's social difficulties and lowered academic achievement (Hinshaw 2000; Miranda & Presentación 2000).

One review concluded that cognitive training alone was as effective as the combination with behavioural methods (Miller & Berman 1983), while most reviewers conclude that, particularly for the problems of young children, parent training is needed in addition to cognitive training of the child. A promising finding with respect to school-based applications is that rational-emotive behaviour therapy (a subset of the cognitive techniques—see Chapter 4) has been shown to be most effective with the disruptive behaviours of primary-aged children and did not require implementation by mental health professionals (Gonzalez et al. 2004).

Neo-Adlerian theory

Neo-Adlerian theory has little research evidence backing its claims of effectiveness. It relies mainly on practitioners' reports of success, although even these are not well documented. Parenting programs based on this theory (namely, the *Systematic training for effective parenting* programs) have been found to improve family functioning, problem solving, communication and parents' behaviour management (Adams 2001; Allan 1994). Few studies, however, used control groups, other than one by Snow and colleagues (1997), which found that STEP training for parents combined with therapy for adolescents in psychiatric care produced better treatment outcomes for the adolescents than did therapy alone. Even so, the researchers acknowledged that this could have been due to the greater commitment and emotional availability of those parents who attended the parenting program, rather than to its content as such.

Humanism

The majority of the support for humanism comes from the debate that has already been reviewed on egalitarian parenting and teaching. Although the former has been more thoroughly researched than the latter, research into qualities that improve school effectiveness has found that schools with punitive discipline have higher rates of disruptive behaviour than those schools with more egalitarian discipline (Rutter 1983). In line with humanist theory, Rutter (1983: 23) found that:

> in the long run good discipline is achieved by the majority of pupils wanting to participate in the educational process rather than doing so merely through fear of retribution.

This mirrors the findings of my research in centre-based child care which, as reported above, found higher rates of behavioural difficulties under behaviourist than egalitarian disciplinary regimes (Porter 1999).

The strongest findings for Glasser's choice theory have been for individual students who were displaying chronic behavioural difficulties, with most studies reporting immediate positive results in terms of fewer peer disputes, reduced absenteeism and improved on-task rates (Emmer & Aussiker 1990). The application of choice theory reduced the recidivism rate at the Ventura school for delinquent adolescent girls from 90 to 20 per cent in 'a relatively short time' (which is not specified) (Thompson & Rudolph 2000: 116). Emmer and Aussiker's meta-analytic study found that teachers who were trained in choice theory developed more positive attitudes to school and disciplinary issues. They made fewer referrals for behavioural difficulties, perhaps because fewer problems were actually occurring or the teachers simply felt better equipped to cope themselves with any difficulties that arose (Emmer & Aussiker 1990).

These researchers also provide support for Gordon's teacher effectiveness training, which they found achieved improved student attitudes to schooling, to themselves and to their teachers, plus there were achievement gains for students, with some studies also demonstrating positive benefits for teachers (Emmer & Aussiker 1990). Research into the effectiveness of the parallel program for parents (*Parent effectiveness training*) is beset by a lack of rigour, although meta-analyses based on well-designed studies found that PET courses were moderately effective in improving parenting attitudes and behaviour and were increasingly effective over time (after cessation of the training course) at improving child behaviour and parent–child interactions (Cedar & Levant 1990; Krebs 1986; Levant 1983; Root & Levant 1984; Schultz 1981; Schultz & Khan 1982; Schultz & Nystul 1980; Schultz et al. 1980). Gains compared with parents who received no training remained after seven years (Wood & Davidson 1987, 1993). Wood (1985, 2003) compared parents receiving no training with those undertaking a PET course and found considerable improvements in trained parents' use of all three communication skills of listening, assertiveness and conflict resolution and significant qualitative improvements in their self-reported satisfaction in their parenting and parent–child relationships, including reduced stress and increased family harmony.

Solution-focused approach

Evaluation of the effectiveness of approaches based on systems theory is made difficult by the wide range of methods it spawns and how the research defines and then measures therapeutic effectiveness (Nicholson 1989). Many early studies had methodological inadequacies and lacked statistical rigour (Kirkby & Smyrnios 1990; Smyrnios & Kirkby 1989; Smyrnios et al. 1988), although a growing body of more recent studies has demonstrated positive benefits of systemic interventions for a range of difficulties (De Jong & Berg 2002; Duncan et al. 2003; Gingerich & Eisengart 2000; Nichols & Schwartz 1995; Sprenkle & Bischoff 1995). The problems addressed span oppositional and aggressive behaviour in children (Conoley et al. 2003), childhood stealing (Seymour & Epston 1989), conduct disorders, delinquency and emotional disturbances (see Sprenkle & Bischoff 1995). Gains include direct improvement in the presenting problem (Nicholson 1989), cost savings (Thompson & Rudolph 2000) and parents' improved marital satisfaction following resolution of children's behavioural difficulties (Sayger et al. 1993).

Conclusion: Effectiveness

Two conclusions are possible from the above review. First is that, with our present state of knowledge, it is not possible to disentangle which elements of each theory are responsible for generating the reported gains (Emmer & Aussiker 1990). Without this information, as a practitioner, you cannot select components from the various theories in any confidence that you have chosen the most effective features.

Second, you need to be clear about what you are aiming for, so that you can select a theory or combination of theories that shares your goals and has most potential for achieving them (see Box 1.2 on p. 29). You also need to examine which is least likely to produce unintended negative effects. This review has reported that authoritarian interactions with students may have more undesirable side-effects, such as encouraging dependency, competition, powerlessness and alienation from learning (Schmuck & Schmuck 2001).

Practicality of the theories

The practicality of theories is crucial to their success. Schools need speedy change when students' behaviour is seriously disturbing; and students need this also, as it is inhumane to allow them to under-function.

Some critics of the various approaches claim that many are time consuming. This argument is true inasmuch as it takes time for students to learn any new skill, be it behavioural or literacy, for example. The argument is also false, because dealing ineffectively with behavioural disruptions would consume even more teacher time.

Of the theories reviewed here, the behaviourist family of approaches are probably the most time consuming to learn comprehensively and apply accurately. In contrast, the solution-focused approach is tailored to work more quickly than competing approaches (Dicocco et al. 1987). Its proponents say that it promotes efficiency by, first, aiming for only small changes, in the belief that these can spread to all of a student's relationships, both at school and at home. Second, it does not require that parents or teachers learn a new set of jargon. The theory can be used immediately by anyone willing to look at chronic problems in a new way. Nevertheless, skilled application will require some study of its approaches.

Conclusion

The choice of approaches to school discipline must consider not only the impact of recommended practices on student behaviours, but also the secondary impact of practices on students' sense of themselves as worthy, responsible, capable learners who can solve problems and exercise self-control (Curwin & Mendler 1988). Coercive discipline in schools has not helped teachers to feel less burdened or assisted students to learn more or behave better (Manke 1997; Rutter 1983). Therefore, the answer lies in seeing students and teachers as jointly invested in students' learning, which necessitates a sharing of power and responsibility. Education and discipline in schools cannot be things we do *to* students, but must evolve in interaction with students. Part Two of this text describes classroom practices that match this egalitarian stance.

Discussion questions

Select a theory that most interests you, or take each theory in turn, and answer the following questions about it:

1   How well do the philosophical assumptions of the theory stand up to scrutiny from the standpoint of the other theories and from your own knowledge of learning theory?
2   What do you regard as this theory's strengths and weaknesses?
3   How could its weaknesses be overcome? If your answer involves borrowing in approaches from other theories, are the philosophical assumptions and practical recommendations that you have combined compatible with each other?

Suggested further reading

Grolnick, W.S. 2003 *The psychology of parental control: how well-meant parenting backfires* Lawrence Erlbaum, Mahwah, NJ

Part 2 | MOTIVATING ENGAGEMENT AND PROSOCIAL BEHAVIOUR

Effective schools share common characteristics, including student perceptions of high expectations for achievement, effective administrative leadership, a shared mission among teachers and staff, a commitment to appropriate assessments, students' sense of efficacy with respect to learning, and student perceptions of a safe environment in which to learn.

McEvoy & Welker (2000: 135)

The model introduced in Chapter 1 (Figure 1.1—see p. 11) depicts that knowledge of behavioural theories alone is not enough to inform classroom practice; we must also incorporate understandings about teaching and learning. As well as the features mentioned in the above quote, research into effective schools makes clear that the qualities associated with pupil progress include an orderly atmosphere, attractive working environment, student involvement in the management of the school, clear and fair discipline, strong teacher–student relationships, and professional behaviour on the part of teachers (Rutter 1983; Rutter & Maughan 2002). Such findings and self-determination theory (Ryan & Deci 2000) inform Part Two of this book, with each chapter organised according to the student need that it satisfies.

Human needs

Figure II.1 illustrates human needs in a simplification of the humanists' model introduced in Chapter 6. It is amended here to increase its relevance to school-aged populations. The needs posed in the model are distinguishable from mere desires on the criteria that a need is universal (i.e. is found in every culture) and leads to *behaviour* designed

FIGURE II.1   Teaching processes directed at student needs

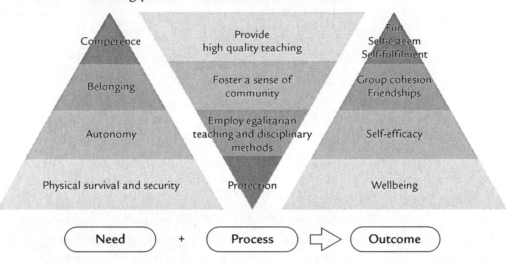

to satisfy it, *cognition* focused on meeting it, and *emotional* benefits from its satisfaction and distress from its non-fulfilment (Baumeister & Leary 1995).

Taking the need for physical and emotional safety as a given, with respect to each emotional need, individuals' requirement for autonomy was first posited by Dewey and Piaget (Kamii 1985). The strongest single line of evidence for it is Seligman's (1975) demonstration that learned helplessness results when individuals feel unable to control their circumstances. This finding is universal (even across species) and incorporates cognitive impairments in the form of an external locus of causality and the affective and behavioural responses typical of depression.

Evidence for the need for belonging is both strong and compelling (Baumeister & Leary 1995). Infants of all cultures form attachments to their parents and parents bond with their infants; thwarting the need to belong leads to many negative outcomes, such as higher rates of physical and emotional illness, suicide and delinquency; the development of new relationships elicits joy, while the dissolution of relationships (e.g. divorce) creates distress; people are more satisfied in relationships characterised by mutual caring and frequent contact; and people think about and seek out new relationships when they feel lonely (Baumeister & Leary 1995).

The need for competence involves both understanding what is needed to attain sought outcomes and feeling empowered to enact requisite strategies (that is, having high self-efficacy) (Deci et al. 1991). Surprisingly, the need for competence is less confirmable through evidence. It is *assumed* by humanism, which believes that all individuals strive to be competent, by the self-esteem literature that posits the need for a healthy self-esteem, which it depicts as a self-evaluation of whether our skills (and personal qualities) meet our ideals, and by motivational theory that examines what features of the task, environment and self contribute to our willingness to put in effort to achieve competence. But these assumptions have little direct evidential backing of a universal *need* for competence. The most explicit line of research perhaps pertains to the importance of intrinsic motivation itself, which is the desire to learn just for the satisfaction of developing competence. Although these lines of evidence are suppositional only, the fact that a need for competence is endorsed by such disparate branches of educational theory suggests that, in the present state of knowledge, we should incorporate it as a fundamental human need until proven otherwise.

Motivation

The notion of a need for competence leads to the question of what motivates individuals to invest time, effort and skills in certain tasks and not others—because, self-evidently, individuals are not motivated to become competent at everything. Historically, motivation has been seen either as variable across tasks or as a fairly stable characteristic of individuals, neither of which is particularly amenable to change (Dörnyei 2000). However, motivation—or a lack of it—is not an inherent part of children's personality, but also depends on the task and social setting. It has three aspects (DiCintio & Gee 1999; Glasser 1998a; Tollefson 2000; Wentzel 1997), which Jones and Jones (2004: 193) depict in the following formula, implying that all three need to be present:

Motivation = Expectation of success × anticipated benefits of success × emotional climate

Expectation of success

Students' expectations that they can be successful on a task require that they experience an optimal (not too high and not too low) degree of challenge, so that they are confident that they can meet demands. Their expectations of success are more crucial to their motivation than are the benefits that they anticipate from achievement. Nevertheless, competence is necessary but insufficient on its own to entice engagement (Deci et al. 1991).

Anticipated benefits of success

Students' assessment of the benefits that success will bring in terms of the fulfilment of their personal needs will cause them to place a value on being successful. Students who are confident of their success and are free to internalise pro-educational values (as opposed to feeling compelled to do so) are more likely to be willing to engage with educational tasks and to anticipate that doing so will benefit them in the future (Berndt & Miller 1990; Deci et al. 1991). Benefits will be both individual and social. Individually, Glasser's theory tells us that all individuals will engage with tasks that meet their needs; socially, students from disadvantaged groups might assess that, even if they work hard in school, this will not pay off for them in adulthood (McCaslin & Good 1992). In other words, discrimination limits the benefits that students can expect to earn from academic engagement and thus can reduce their motivation.

Class and school climate

The third influence on students' motivation is the extent to which they feel supported by their teachers and the wider environment. The term *climate* refers to the learning atmosphere, attitudes, beliefs, values and norms of a school, as these affect teachers' and students' feelings about themselves, each other, their teacher and the subject matter (McEvoy & Welker 2000). It could be said to be the 'personality' of a school (Stanley & McGrath 2006) and is an aggregate of school management, relationships among staff and between students and teachers, the security and condition of school facilities and the school ethos about student achievement (Esposito 1999). School climate has a pervasive influence on students' wellbeing and social skills and, increasingly throughout schooling, on their academic performance, with the student–teacher relationship being the most significant aspect of climate, accounting for 15 per cent of the variance in students' achievements (Esposito 1999). The school climate not only has indirect effects on students' achievement by fostering a sense of being supported, but also direct effects through the encouraging messages delivered by teachers and peers in a supportive setting (Marchant et al. 2001).

A positive classroom tone is reflected in emotionally warm and supportive relationships between you and your students and among the students, open communication between class members and egalitarian teaching that trusts students' contributions to their own learning. These and other features of a positive school climate are listed in Box II.1.

BOX II.1 INFLUENTIAL FEATURES OF SCHOOL CLIMATE
Safety
· How safe students feel from violence.
· Whether they are protected from the behavioural excesses of each other.
· Low levels of drug and alcohol problems.

Autonomy

- Structure—how much you emphasise order for its own sake, versus supplying structure to enable students to achieve.
- Expectations—the extent to which you emphasise rules versus considerateness.
- Control—whether you monopolise control, versus working with students jointly to shape a productive and accepting setting.
- Student decision making—mechanisms for student input into decisions concerning their learning and the school organisation.

Belonging

- Affiliation—how well the students feel that they know each other, how willing they are to assist each other, how much they enjoy working together, the level of interaction between student groups, and absence of gossip, particularly about peers' sexual behaviour.
- Personal involvement with teachers—the level of support or care students receive from teachers.
- Competition—the extent to which students compete with each other for grades and personal recognition in the classroom.
- Acceptance of diversity—signalled by flexible dress codes, acceptance of the use of students' first language at school and inclusive practices across cultures, ability levels and genders.

Competence

- Task orientation—how much emphasis you place on the content of tasks (getting them completed and being correct) compared with a focus on the learning process.
- Engagement—how interested the students are in academic learning and how much they participate.
- Innovation—the extent to which you encourage student creativity and use innovative teaching practices.

Organisational qualities

- Small classes with individual attention.
- The visibility and accessibility of the principal.
- The availability of extracurricular activities.
- The condition of the school's facilities.

Sources: Phelan et al. 1992; Schmuck & Schmuck 2001: 69-70

Conclusion

Disciplinary practices in schools must align with teachers' pedagogical framework, with what they know about how to teach. We cannot teach children to take intellectual risks and be adventurous in their thinking, but then oblige them to sit down and do as they are told when it comes to their behaviour (McCaslin & Good 1992). Our curricular content and teaching and learning processes must safeguard students' dispositions to learn, both to foster students' emotional satisfaction and to enable them to succeed at school. In turn, when they feel that success is not only possible but probable, there will be less cause for them to disrupt classes.

9 SAFEGUARDING STUDENTS:
PHYSICAL AND EMOTIONAL SECURITY

There are many kinds of safety that are required for children to learn. At the most basic level, there is physical safety . . . [This] is not enough, however. Safety also means emotional safety—the safety to be yourself, to be vulnerable, to ask for help, and to be warmly supported . . . [W]hen people are not expending their energy trying to cover up or get by, afraid that someone will find out about their weakness or deficiency, they can learn easily.

Sapon-Shevin (1999: 13)

KEY POINTS

- Learning will not be a high priority for students whose needs for physical and emotional safety are not met.
- To promote a safe school environment, you can take steps to establish an ethos that honours diversity in students and protects them from intimidation by others.

Introduction

Both the egalitarian approaches and evidence from educational research concur that students behave more appropriately and learn more effectively when their basic needs are met in the classroom. When there is tension in the school students become uneasy, watchful, fearful (Phelan et al. 1992), anxious and depressed (Murray & Greenberg 2001), which emotional states are not conducive to engagement with learning and can also lead to behavioural disruptiveness. Students need to feel that their physical and emotional safety are assured and that, if under any threat, they will receive protection. To that end, a nurturing and safe learning community emphasises human interactions based on respect, authenticity, thoughtfulness and integrity (Larrivee 2005).

The physical environment

Naturally, the environment needs to provoke minimal hazards, so that all who use it are protected from avoidable injury. This is an occupational health and safety matter. Beyond this, the environment needs to communicate that people in this place will be safe. When children become stressed by the demands of the classroom, they need a safe place to which to withdraw while they can regain their composure. This needs to be a pleasant area, with comfortable cushions or bean bags, perhaps shrouded in a gauze curtain so they can still see events in the room while being removed from them. This opportunity to withdraw avoids their becoming overwhelmed, with consequent behavioural disruptions.

Those who feel intimidated by the busyness of the playground can also be provided with a form of sanctuary at lunchtime, with structured quiet activities and clubs being provided as an alternative to large-group activities (Doyle 2003).

Emotional safety

The bigger the school and classes, the more difficult it can be to provide students with adequate support and protection (Davies 2005). When students perceive their school as impersonal or unsafe, many will become disaffected (Davies 2005). In contrast, when students feel supported at school they like school more, value learning and are willing to put in effort and take intellectual risks (Goodenow 1993a; Kohn 1996a; Schmuck & Schmuck 2001).

An inclusive curriculum

The concept of inclusiveness is typically applied with respect to race, religion, gender and additional learning needs. Honouring and appreciating students' diversity not only sends them a direct message of acceptance, but also communicates indirectly to those who are different in less identifiable ways that they will be nurtured within this school. In terms of the focus of this book, this acceptance must also be applied to students with behavioural difficulties. Their disruptive behaviour will inevitably attract a negative reputation with their peers, but this must not be added to by teacher reactions to and rejection of them or their difficulties. Even official diagnoses must be employed carefully, as these can highlight labelled students' differences and, in turn, cause them to become neglected by and withdrawn from their peer group (Davies 2005).

Emotional literacy

The school's hidden curriculum needs to be emotionally literate, where 'emotions are recognized, understood and appropriately expressed by adults and children' (Doyle 2003: 264). Students will feel safe when they experience neither blame nor scorn nor humiliation for their weaknesses and when they know that their classmates will delight in their accomplishments (Sapon-Shevin 1999). When they are able to discuss their feelings with each other, this may reveal that they are not alone. When you too accept their feelings and experiences, you demonstrate that emotions are not up for judgment.

Egalitarian discipline

When responding to disruptions, you cannot afford to make scenes and should *never* use sarcasm (Ginott 1972). Disciplining from emotion rather than reason is self-indulgent and unhelpful by reducing students' sense of personal safety (Rogers 1998). Therefore, you will need to remain in control of yourself so that students learn from you how they can manage their own emotions. This will be particularly important for students from violent backgrounds who may find strong emotions terrifying. The methods that you employ must not humiliate miscreants or cause onlookers to feel emotionally vulnerable if in future they were to make a mistake. As Rogers (2002) advises, teachers who disrespect, blame or shame one student will lose not only the cooperation of that young person but also of onlooking peers. Students will also need a procedure for stating and resolving grievances about disciplinary edicts (Algozzine 2002).

Child abuse and protection

Perhaps as many as 70 per cent of children experiencing behavioural problems in schools have suffered child abuse or neglect (Thompson & Wyatt 1999). Although few teachers are trained to help child victims, being attuned to victimisation is crucial as it can have consequences for students' academic performance and behaviour and, of course, emotional wellbeing, both at the time and subsequently. Supporting these children and their families can be complicated by the many other coexisting stressful conditions within abusive families and neighbourhoods, such as poverty, unemployment, welfare reliance, substance abuse or untreated mental illness of parents, family mobility and family isolation (Thompson & Wyatt 1999).

Child maltreatment takes a number of forms: neglect of children's physical or emotional needs; and physical, emotional and sexual abuse. Of these types, neglect constitutes more reported cases than the other forms combined (Haynes-Seman & Baumgarten 1998), although emotional abuse is probably the most pervasive but is more difficult to quantify and thus report (Thompson & Wyatt 1999). Actual rates of child maltreatment are difficult to gauge, not least because so much goes unreported but also because children commonly are victims of more than one type of abuse, making estimation complex.

For sexual abuse, prevalence estimates vary considerably, but the best calculations are that between 22 and 38 per cent of females are sexually abused prior to the age of 18 (Rossman et al. 1998). However, some children can have been sexually abused in early childhood and not know it, because at the time they lacked a cognitive framework to understand what was happening (Haynes-Seman & Baumgarten 1998).

Reported rates for boys seem to be between 9 and 16 per cent—that is, a ratio of 1 male to 2.5 female victims (Bromberg & Johnson 2001; Rossman et al. 1998). A staggering 19 per cent of incidents occur at school (Bromberg & Johnson 2001), with the peak age of onset of sexual abuse being younger than might be expected—for females, from 7 to 8 years of age and for males, prior to puberty (Webster 2001). Abuse commonly persists for in excess of two years.

A profile of perpetrators

Perpetrators of neglect and emotional and physical abuse

Families who are isolated and lacking in support are more prone to child abuse and neglect, while parents' substance abuse is an increasing cause of the neglect of children. Although the use of illicit drugs occurs across all sectors of the community, it is likely to have most impact on those families who are already economically disadvantaged (Hanson & Carta 1995). Combined with poor impulse control or untreated mental illness in parents, lack of support and substance abuse often result in parents' emotional detachment from their children (Thompson & Wyatt 1999). Physical abuse by parents is common in disciplinary encounters, when parents react with frustration and violence to children's inability to comply with developmentally inappropriate expectations.

Sexual abuse perpetrators

Sexual abuse involves the exploitation and coercion of children by someone more powerful than them. Approximately 20 per cent of adult males and 8 per cent of females report having some sexual interest in children, with as many as 7 per cent of males and 3 per cent of females saying that they would engage in sexual activity with children if they could avoid detection (Bromberg & Johnson 2001; Vizard et al. 1995). The factor that translates this high level of sexual interest in children into actual abuse is children's lack of power compared with adults. They trust adults to keep them safe, are not capable of assessing adults' motives and are taught to obey adults (Briggs & McVeity 2000). Coercion, emotional blackmail and subterfuge are typically used by abusers to develop a 'special' relationship that will ensnare their child victim.

This indicates that there are two types of sexual abusers: opportunistic abusers who are sexually attracted to children and molest children within their family or circle of acquaintances; and paedophiles who deliberately seek out places frequented by children with the purpose of locating a victim. Various studies have documented that adult paedophiles molest 150 (Bromberg & Johnson 2001) to 560 times before being caught, across as many as 380 victims (Metzner & Ryan 1995). This figure is the basis for the humanists' contention that we must not teach children to do as adults tell them, as this is how molesters manage to coerce children into such a high number of assaults and then discourage them from reporting the abuse (Briggs & McVeity 2000). Rates for opportunistic abusers are almost certainly lower than this.

Only 6 to 13 per cent of sexual abuse is perpetrated by a stranger to the victim (Briggs & McVeity 2000), with between 20 and 50 per cent of offences (including rape) being committed by adolescents, half of which comprises sibling incest (Bromberg & Johnson 2001; Metzner & Ryan 1995; Vizard et al. 1995). It is startling that in one study, 13 per cent of perpetrators were aged 8–12 years (Vizard et al. 1995). The majority (up to 85 per cent) of perpetrators are male.

Contrary to popular belief, sexual abuse seems unrelated to whether perpetrators were victims themselves as children. The myth arises from research asking adult perpetrators retrospectively whether they were abused as children and the answer is often in the affirmative. But this does not prove causality, as the same answer would likely be given by non-perpetrators. There is also an inherent error in logic in retrospective studies, demonstrated by the fact that when asked, perpetrators would also report that they drink coffee, yet this is clearly unrelated to their later molesting behaviour. When, instead, you follow child victims prospectively, it eventuates that most of them do not progress to being perpetrators—as far as we know (Vizard et al. 1995). This stands to reason, as the majority of victims appear to be female, while the majority of perpetrators are male. Thus, it seems that females and the majority of male victims overcome their early abusive experiences—at least to the extent of not imposing further abuse on the next generation.

The high rates of sexual interest in children and sexual abuse indicate that mental illness and serious dysfunction are not implicated as causes of sexual abuse. Other than their common pattern of socially coercive and manipulative behaviour, perpetrators' characteristics such as socioeconomic status, mental illness, family functioning, developmental delay, delinquency and low self-esteem, are all unrelated to their offending. Other factors that *might* be slightly linked to later sexually abusive offending include low social competence and social isolation, having been subjected to physical *and* heterosexual abuse, and having parents who were molested as children, particularly in cases of adolescent perpetrators of incestuous molestation (Bromberg & Johnson 2001; Vizard et al. 1995).

Effects of abuse

The long-term effects of abuse depend on the type or combinations of abuse to which children are subjected, the age of onset, severity and chronicity of the abuse, the relationship of the perpetrator to the child, the presence of other family and neighbourhood stressors, and the level of support offered to victims upon discovery or disclosure (Eckenrode et al. 1993; Webster 2001). Early neglect or abuse can make children vulnerable later to other forms of abuse, such as sexual abuse, as explained by Haynes-Seman & Baumgarten (1998: 81):

> Neglected children may be more vulnerable to later sexual abuse because, very often, the physical neglect is also accompanied by emotional neglect that makes the child vulnerable to the (sexual) attention of a pedophile or abusive parent.

Physical abuse produces developmental and social-emotional impairments, with children under the age of five years being at more serious risk than older children of injury from physical abuse. Despite this, the effects of neglect and emotional abuse are thought to be more severely damaging than are the actual physical injuries inflicted on children (Bonner et al. 1992; Haynes-Seman & Baumgarten 1998).

The main outcome of sexual abuse seems to be symptoms that resemble post-traumatic stress disorder. This is characterised by physical health complaints and emotional manifestations such as hypervigilance and anxiety (Bromberg & Johnson 2001; Webster 2001). Resulting behaviours can resemble the patterns characteristic of

ADHD or conduct disorders or their opposite, which has been termed *compulsive compliance*, where girls in particular deny, modify or falsify their feelings in order to gain adult approval (Webster 2001). Girls appear to be most negatively affected by sexual abuse, with physical force and threats being associated with greater emotional distress (Webster 2001). However, little research has examined the effects of homosexual abuse on boys, which is probably the least reported category of abuse.

Socially, when parents are the perpetrators, abuse results in children's disturbed attachment to parents—as seen, for example, in 'freezing' in their parent's presence (Haynes-Seman & Baumgarten 1998). Maltreated children often withdraw from the friendly overtures of other caring adults or peers, assault or threaten adults, as they have learned that adults can be dangerous, and behave aggressively towards peers (George & Main 1979; Haynes-Seman & Baumgarten 1998). Neglected children can be withdrawn as a result of learning to avoid relationships; they have few social problem-solving and coping strategies, limited interactions with peers, and they lack empathy for others (Haynes-Seman & Baumgarten 1998; Hoffman-Plotkin & Twentyman 1984; Klimes-Dougan & Kistner 1990).

Emotionally, abused children often have difficulty regulating their anger and aggression—which probably arises from copying their parents' lack of inhibition and because aggression is a common response to feeling under threat (Levin 1994)—while depression and anxiety are other common outcomes (Trickett 1998). Abused children are commonly hostile and uncooperative with adults. In terms of their self-esteem, maltreatment causes children to see themselves in negative terms.

With respect to *learning skills*, children who are suffering sexual abuse typically achieve well at school, which is all the more remarkable given that their anxiety levels must make it difficult to concentrate on academic tasks and that their disorganised home environments, disrupted routines and inadequate child supervision disrupt their ability to complete academic work at home or be fully prepared for the school day. Neglected children are often passive and helpless, give up easily, do not cope well with frustration, are easily distracted, impulsive and lacking in initiative (Haynes-Seman & Baumgarten 1998). In terms of *language skills*, neglect results in a lack of stimulation that causes delays in children's language, particularly expression, and impairment of overall intellectual skills (Haynes-Seman & Baumgarten 1998).

The result of such behaviours is that the children tend to be ignored in school settings—unless they are behaving disruptively, when their interactions with teachers often comprise disciplinary measures (Hoffman-Plotkin & Twentyman 1984). The signs listed in Box 9.1 could alert you to the possibility that students displaying these patterns of behaviours might not be deliberately disruptive, but could have a more distressing reason for their actions.

BOX 9.1 SIGNS AND EFFECTS OF ABUSE

The following effects of abuse can act as signs that can aid its recognition. Many of these signs occur at the time, whereas others have a sleeper effect, not appearing until one or more years after the abuse. After the termination of the assaults, effects tend to persist longer for younger children and those for whom fewer supports are made available upon discovery or disclosure.

Emotional signs

· Abused children can be highly dependent on their parents.
· They have little knowledge of their own or others' feelings.
· They may not regulate anger and aggression.
· They have few emotional coping strategies.
· Many display anxiety, depression, fearfulness or agitation.
· Many have disturbed sleep and frightening or vague nightmares.
· Neglected children in particular, but abused children overall, typically have lowered self-esteem and an external locus of causality (low self-efficacy).

Social skills

· Abused children often withdraw socially and are less responsive to friendly overtures from adults or children.
· Physically abused children in particular have high rates of aggression.
· Some assault or threaten adults in the belief that adults can be dangerous.
· They may not seek comfort from others when distressed.
· They may interact little with peers, and their interactions are often unskilful.
· They exercise few social problem-solving strategies.

Behaviours

When the abuse has just begun, you might see a sudden change in children's behavioural pattern. However, when children have been abused for some time, the link between their behaviour and the abuse can be difficult to detect.

· Their behaviour can regress, whereby they display some demanding patterns that were typical of them some time ago, or they adopt new behaviours not seen before.
· Their behaviour is often impulsive.
· Sexually abused children might begin talking about secrets or of something nasty that is happening to a friend or a doll.
· They might display sexualised behaviour, such as blatant flirting, excessive touching of their own genitals or sexual play with another child.
· They might re-enact the abuse in drawings, play or with their toys.
· They might be reluctant to accompany a particular adult, or adults in general.

- Many have a history of running away from home.
- Some display oppositional behaviour, while others show compulsive compliance.
- Some inflict injury on themselves (in the absence of severe sensory integration dysfunction).

Academic profiles

- Neglected and physically abused children tend to perform at low levels academically. At younger ages this is most pronounced for reading skills, whereas by late primary school the disadvantage is across all subject areas.
- Children experiencing sexual abuse without other forms of abuse do not differ from the norm in their academic skills.
- Children who have been neglected or physically abused are more likely to be suspended from school or drop out early.

Physical signs

- Children enduring physical abuse may have injuries such as bruises, welts, burns or fractures that have no convincing causal explanation.
- They might show little response to pain.
- Those suffering sexual abuse can have injuries or infections to the genital or anal areas or throat.
- Many experience long-term somatic complaints.

Sources: Bonner et al. 1992; Bromberg & Johnson 2001; Haynes-Seman & Baumgarten 1998; Thompson & Wyatt 1999; Webster 2001

Offer child protectiveness training

Programs aimed at preventing child sexual abuse have three weaknesses. The first is that they lack evidence that they empower children to resist abuse (Bevill & Gast 1998). Most were built on the concepts of a stranger-perpetrator and unassertive child victim and thus teach assertiveness skills. However, students both with and without protectiveness training typically can already employ these skills, but may not do so when under threat. Moreover, the skills are less useful and may even further endanger children who are being threatened by a known adult (Ko & Cosden 2001).

The second weakness is that training is more efficient but less effective when delivered in groups as opposed to individually (Johnson et al. 2005). Third, the programs can make children overly suspicious—even terrified—of adults (Bonner et al. 1992; Johnson et al. 2005; Jordan 1993). Perhaps even more damning than these shortcomings is that, by the time children are having to fend off an attack, protective skills will be too little too late. Instead, children need to be immunised against being in abusive situations in the first place by:

- allowing them every day in small ways to be assertive about their needs;
- affirming who they are and that they are valued, so that they are less likely to collude with abuse in an attempt to gain the affectionate contact with adults that they are not receiving otherwise;
- guiding their behaviour in ways that honour their autonomy, so they do not grow accustomed to the subordination to adult power.

Nevertheless, ignorance about their bodies and sexual matters increases children's vulnerability to abuse. Therefore, teaching them about their bodies and empowering them to assert their own needs will offer some protection. To that end, the fundamental principle for keeping children safe is: *It's my body; I get to choose.*

The second aspect of protecting children is to teach them to recognise their feelings and to notice when their feelings are warning them that something is wrong. The guiding rule here is: *If you don't feel safe, you aren't safe.* You might ask young children where in their bodies they feel unsafe feelings—for example, when they are at the top of a high playground slide. You can then highlight the difference between these excited-scared emotions and bad-scared feelings. Children need to be able to take safe risks, have fun and enjoy the challenge of being 'good-scared', but to take steps to protect themselves when they are feeling 'bad-scared'.

Third, you will need to ensure that children know safety strategies, such as seeking adult help by approaching school staff, phoning their parents or calling emergency services. They will need a backup plan for occasions when the first person they would approach is not available. Formal protectiveness training programs get children to draw around their hand and on each finger place a photo or write the names of people they could approach for help. You then explain that they have to persist and talk to every person on their list until they find someone who can assist them.

Report suspected abuse

The sexual assault of children or adults is a criminal offence, so must be reported to police. In many jurisdictions, teachers are legally obliged to report all other forms of child abuse as well. But even when not mandated legally, there is a moral obligation to protect children in your care. Advising parents of this obligation (perhaps at parent information sessions or within a package of information handed out at enrolment) and detailing issues surrounding child abuse will raise awareness of the issue which, in turn, might prevent some abuse, or at least set a foundation for some constructive intervention by school staff on those occasions when abuse is suspected.

The first measure for recognising abuse is to believe that it occurs. Hence the saying: *I wouldn't have seen it if I hadn't believed it.*

In only a few instances will children tell you directly that they are being abused, especially sexually. Perpetrators commonly use threats to make children keep the abuse secret, or claim that the children themselves would be blamed and punished if it were ever disclosed. In the absence of outright reporting, the children might give vague hints or display some of the signs listed in Box 9.1. Do not ignore these signs, as doing so increases the chances that the abuse will recur, both to this child and to others in the perpetrator's life.

Given the huge upsurge in reports of abuse to welfare agencies (probably reflecting increased awareness rather than any increased incidence), you will have to be persistent in following up your report, to ensure that action is taken.

Gain limited information

You need only enough information about the alleged assaults to ascertain whether a report is justified. Your report therefore would not detail the facts, but is a request for welfare personnel to investigate to discover these. You must leave it to specialists to interview the young person, as there is a risk of contaminating the chain of evidence or of being accused of leading the child, thus undermining the credibility of his or her account and, in so doing, limiting the protection that the child receives subsequently (Bromberg & Johnson 2001).

Locate support for yourself

Your outrage and hurt on behalf of a child will be compounded if it reactivates memories of similar trauma in your own life, or when the perpetrators of the abuse are the child's parents. You might be tempted to avoid contact with them for your own physical or emotional protection, or to collude with the family in order to maintain a working relationship with them but, in so doing, could be disregarding the harm that their child has suffered (Harskamp 2002). Given the emotional climate, potential risk of intimidation and the ramifications of malpractice, you will need to access a consultant who can support you in your ongoing contact with parents while their child remains your student and the accusation is being investigated.

Support abused children emotionally

Most abused children tend to be given only the required medical treatment. Thus, it will often fall on school personnel to provide the emotional support these children need to surmount the adversity and injustice that they have endured. Two measures can be particularly helpful.

First, because abuse makes children overly vigilant as they try to read the intentions of an abuser and scan their environment for indications of danger, they will need your support to refocus on their own growth. When they appear to be enjoying an activity, highlight this so that they can get back in touch with life's positive possibilities.

Second, enhancing abused children's self-esteem is especially important. As with adult victims of abuse, children who are ill-treated often lose sight of their own resources. To counteract this, comment on their strengths and encourage their efforts to cope. Survivors of child abuse use tremendous courage and often ingenuity to deal with the abuse, both at the time and into adulthood. At the same time as being empathic to the injustice they have endured, however, it is also important to highlight the parts of them that are 'normal', so they do not come to see themselves as fragile, different or damaged but can use their strengths, interests and passions to experience life in ways that are not connected to their abuse (Berg & Steiner 2003).

Secure services for families

The most successful treatments for child abuse involve supporting and strengthening families. This is likely to be beyond the scope of school personnel, but it might be possible for you to refer the family to agencies that can offer both practical and counselling help. One direct action that schools can take is to invite a supportive relative or family elder of a maltreated child into the school (say, for reading support or to tell stories from his or her culture), whose presence at school can reassure the child or who, with such links formed, can be enlisted to offer specific support outside of school.

Sexualised play

As mentioned in Box 9.1, one sign of child sexual abuse is sexualised play. However, some forms of children's sexual interest are normal and healthy (Essa & Murray 1999). Given that children learn by exploration, normal sexual behaviours are adaptive and educational for children, as their exploration teaches them about how their bodies work and about gender-related adult roles (Rothbaum et al. 1997).

The distinction between unhealthy and healthy sexual play rests on its context and content (Essa & Murray 1999; Rothbaum et al. 1997). An unhealthy interest in sexual play is signalled by:

- sexualised play that is part of an overall pattern of behavioural difficulties, especially social difficulties and poor impulse control;
- anxiety, tension, guilt or shame or, alternatively, lack of emotionality about their sexual play;
- disproportional, preoccupied or compulsive interest in sexual play compared with other play interests;
- inability to redirect children to other forms of activity;
- furtiveness about their sexual activities (in contrast with openness or lack of self-consciousness);
- eroticism in sexual play (in contrast with sensuality and curiosity), as eroticism signals an advanced understanding or knowledge about sexual behaviour;
- purposeful self-stimulation rather than a mere attempt at self-soothing;
- approaches to unfamiliar children rather than friends as sexual partners;
- coercion of or aggression towards partners;
- large differences in age or size of selected play partners;
- complaints from other children about the child's contacts with them;
- penetration of any bodily orifice with a foreign object;
- children's heightened knowledge of sexual matters compared with same-aged peers from a similar economic, social and cultural background.

These distinctions can allow you to judge whether children's sexualised play is natural, is itself abusive of another child or signals that the instigator might have been subjected to sexual abuse.

Physical aggression

Children's safety at school is often compromised by the aggression of their peers. Even when this behaviour is triggered by educational or social disadvantage, surrounding students have a right not to be tormented at school. Thus, while you might understand that individual children are under-functioning with some justification, you would gain less *for* such students if you expected less *of* them, and meanwhile allowing their aggression to go unchecked would be unfair to those around them. Thus, egalitarian discipline will, if necessary, use protective power to safeguard aggressors and victims alike.

Although aggressive children initially approach others often, their overtures are frequently rejected because their approaches tend to be boisterous or aggressive, or they disrupt others' play and are less cooperative, with the result that, over time, the children initiate less often and become increasingly isolated (Dodge 1983). As a result of their behaviour, these children are often disliked by many peers but are liked by and gravitate towards other aggressive children (Arnold et al. 1998; Dodge 1983; Farver 1996; Hartup 1989; Hartup & Moore 1990). Cognitive theory upholds that aggression results from errors at all stages of social problem solving (as depicted in Figure 4.1— see page 77). To teach more prosocial skills, cognitive theory advises teaching children each of these motivational and self-management skills, yielding the following interventions.

- Have at least one adult in the school build a *close relationship* with aggressive children, as their behaviour to date will have alienated their parents, peers and teachers (Blankemeyer et al. 2002; Kelly 1996). This disconnectedness from others will only exacerbate their aggression.
- Using cognitive strategies, teach aggressive children *emotional self-control* to manage their own emotional reactions, so they can behave prosocially with peers without using coercive means that invite further rejection, can enter groups without disrupting others, and can accurately interpret others' social behaviours.
- *Support peers* to be assertive about another's aggression and to negotiate with boisterous peers rather than reject their actions outright (Arnold et al. 1999). Protect peers with follow-up problem-solving efforts if an aggressive peer does not desist.
- *Foster cohesion* within the class group and school, as young people are less likely to be violent towards people whom they know well.
- Give typically aggressive young people an opportunity to *lead prosocially* (not waiting until they have 'earned' this right).
- Ensure that the *curriculum* is engaging, so that young people do not resort to violence in an effort to counteract boredom with some excitement (to 'stir things up a little').
- *Support the parents* of aggressive students. Troubled and isolated children often have troubled and isolated families. Their child's aggressive behaviour often exacerbates their isolation, with not only the child being shunned by peers but the parents also being excluded from interaction with, and support from, other parents. Where possible, recommend social agencies that could help them improve their stressful living conditions, guide parents in egalitarian disciplinary practices to avoid their children reacting aggressively against controlling discipline and encourage parents to provide opportunities for their child to socialise prosocially with peers outside

of school hours (again, because children will be less likely to be aggressive with someone for whom they have affection and because developing at least one friendship will be a buffer against stress, which can lead to aggressive outbursts) (Hartup & Moore 1990).

This advice arises from a cognitive deficit orientation, however. An alternative, post-structuralist, view is that aggressive or other antisocial behaviour of young people attracts adult disapproval and, often, escalated attempts by adults to control them. The resistance they display to these efforts is not a sign of their unwillingness to be nurtured or to submit to limits that will further their interests, but is a reaction to the denial of their autonomy and a way of rejecting the deficit-oriented discourse (or 'collective conversation') that occurs around them and about them (Ungar 2004). This discourse overlooks the fact that, like everyone else, aggressive and delinquent young people are trying to meet their needs for autonomy and connectedness with others, through the only means that are available to them. They refuse to be subjugated to the power of teachers and the institution of schools, or collude with coercive attempts to turn them into 'good students' (Laws & Davies 2000). These nonconformist young people protest violently against perceived injustices to themselves and others. These 'rebels with a cause' (Laws & Davies 2000: 218) need a focus on their 'cause', rather than their rebellion. A solution-focused view, then, would highlight their heroic resistance to injustice and enlarge on the prosocial ways in which they presently enact this, so they can continue to do so without harming others.

Conclusion

Only when students can trust that they are physically and emotionally safe at school will they be empowered to participate in academic work. Both the school ethos and practical measures will promote students' feelings of wellbeing, to the mutual benefit of individuals and the whole school community.

Discussion questions

1 What does your school's physical environment convey to students about how well regarded they are?
2 What measures do you adopt to ensure a positive climate in your classroom?
3 How does the school extend these measures?

4   What measures does your school use to prevent and respond to bullying? How effective are these?

Suggested further reading

Slaby, R.G., Roedell, W.C., Arezzo, D. and Hendrix, K. 1995 *Early violence prevention: tools for teachers of young children* National Association for the Education of Young Children, Washington, DC

Child protection

Briggs, F. and McVeity, M. 2000 *Teaching children to protect themselves* Allen & Unwin, Sydney

10 SATISFYING STUDENTS' NEED FOR AUTONOMY: VOICE AND CHOICE

Students' motivation was significantly associated with the amount of control perceived by them over their learning situations. Students reported being more involved and more competent when they perceived greater control over decisions and choices; conversely, they reported being less bored, less confused, and less interested in doing something else.

DiCintio & Gee (1999: 234)

KEY POINTS

- Fundamental to all human beings is the need to be in control of ourselves.
- You can meet this need in your students, both through how you teach and through your responses to their behaviour.

Introduction

Schools with formal punishment systems have higher rates of delinquency and poorer attendance than those with systems that foster student autonomy (Rutter 1983). The same has been found for centre-based care settings (Porter 1999). School-based behavioural difficulties place students at risk of dropping out, whereas fair disciplinary practices within schools reduce the likelihood that this risk will translate into actual early exit from school (Rumberger 1995).

Autonomy refers to the need to be self-determining or in command of our own lives, to be the origin or initiator of our own actions. It does not imply self-centredness or detachment from others, but instead refers to the exercise of choice or volition (Grolnick 2003; Osterman 2000; Ryan & Deci 2000). It comprises four elements (Wehmeyer et al. 2004; Wheeler & Richey 2005):

- freedom to make choices;
- self-regulation, which entails self-management and working towards self-selected goals;
- self-efficacy, which is the belief that one can control events in one's own life;
- environmental supports to enact these preferences.

The model of human needs presented in the introduction to this section provides the rationale for the inclusion of this topic before discussing what may seem to be the more important social and learning needs of students. Students' need for autonomy is covered first for two reasons. First, declines in students' motivation seem to be related to the lack of opportunities for them to exercise autonomy within the classroom (Cleary & Zimmerman 2004). Second, autonomy is the greatest need for that subgroup of students who are nonconformist—that is, those who pose the greater proportion of disciplinary problems in schools. Authoritarian reactions to their difficulties will only exacerbate their disruptions, while their rejection by mainstream peers will not be repaired until their behaviour improves. And their behaviour will not improve until their need for autonomy is honoured. This can be done through both egalitarian teaching and discipline.

Egalitarian teaching

The egalitarian theorists contend that students will not think for themselves or be motivated to learn in an environment that attempts to control them (DiCintio & Gee 1999). Yet, much of the research into teacher effectiveness in classroom management defines effectiveness in terms of whether teachers' management methods allow them to dominate the flow of the activities (Kohn 1996a). The egalitarian theories argue that this is counterproductive and can provoke behavioural difficulties as students attempt to seize back some of the autonomy that is being denied them.

The teacher as facilitator

The facilitator empowers students to be in command of their own learning and behaviour, giving them practice at exercising initiative, learning cooperatively and communicating accurately (Schmuck & Schmuck 2001). This style of leadership is not to be confused with a laissez-faire style in which, despite having legitimate power, the leader fails to exercise it and instead allows group members to act as they wish (Schmuck & Schmuck 2001). The group will become stressed and disorganised under this type of leadership.

Teachers who are under pressure from the school administration and higher authorities to control student outcomes—when obviously they can only influence, not coerce, these—are more likely to use authoritarian teaching and disciplinary methods with their students (Deci et al. 1991; Flink et al. 1990). However, their own expectations can also affect this tendency. When they believe that their students are capable of exercising autonomy, teachers will provide more opportunities for them to do so than when they believe that students cannot regulate themselves (Deci et al. 1991). Naturally, without being given the opportunity, the students will never demonstrate ability.

Guide students to select personal goals

A basic tenet of cognitive and humanist theory is that students will be more motivated when they can select their own learning goals. This honours their need for autonomy. Therefore, you will need to guide them to establish specific, short-term learning goals (as distinct from performance goals that are aimed at gaining a reward for completed work). Students' decisions may centre on what material to work on, when and how it will be completed and how to monitor their own performance (Jones & Jones 2004).

Provide choice

Students seek opportunities to exercise meaningful choices about the learning content and processes in their classes (Allen 1995). Giving students choice about their activities during lesson time increases their engagement and amount of learning, while reducing disruptive behaviour (Cordova & Lepper 1996; Dunlap et al. 1994), as long as the various options are not fake but offer authentic opportunities for students to select between personally meaningful options (Assor et al. 2002).

At a wider level, students' participation in learning will be fostered by engaging them in decisions about the organisation of their school (Rutter 1983). Opportunities to exert influence foster not only students' individual autonomy, but also a sense of a community within the school (McMillan & Chavis 1986).

Foster self-efficacy

Cognitive theory tells us that individuals' sense of control over their own actions is crucial to success both academically and in life. When individuals believe that they are responsible for the outcomes of their actions (i.e. when they have an internal locus of causality or high self-efficacy), they have a greater incentive to invest effort in tasks and strive for success and are more persistent and more reflective learners (Knight 1995).

You can correct students' maladaptive attributions by coaching them to define failure as *temporary* rather than permanent; as *specific* to the event rather than as a sign of a general or all-pervasive failing on their part; and in terms of their *behaviour*, not personality (Seligman 1995). Specifically, when you hear students blame their personality for failings (e.g. when they say 'I'm hopeless at this') or when they assume that the problem is permanent ('I'll *never* be able to do it'), you can affirm their disappointment but then gently correct their statements with something like: 'You're right: it hasn't worked out. What could you do to fix it?'. Your aim is to teach them to convert self-defeating talk into helpful self-statements (Rogers 2003).

Egalitarian discipline

Chapter 1 listed various forms of leadership, the highest of which were based on students' admiration for teachers' expertise and personal qualities and on close relationships between teachers and students (Schmuck & Schmuck 2001). Under the alternative use of coercive power, disruptions can be ended in the immediate term and groups are thus orderly and productive, but groups will also be more competitive, tensions within the group rise, members are more alienated from learning and, in the long term, onlooking students become more disruptive (Schmuck & Schmuck 2001). The use of coercive power by teachers also establishes a group norm permitting its use by powerful students against their vulnerable peers and thus enables peer bullying within schools.

Establish behavioural guidelines

Most education theorists proclaim that rules are necessary to prevent disruptiveness and to give students the security of knowing what is expected of them and what is not allowed (see, e.g., Arthur et al. 2003; Emmer et al. 2006; Evertson et al. 2003). Having generated a list of rules and consequences for their infraction, teachers are advised to teach and, with younger children, rehearse these so that the students' understanding is assured. Appropriate behaviour, it is said, is taught, not caught (Mathieson & Price 2002).

Being proactive and anticipating disruptions before they occur sounds perfectly in tune with the concept of universal prevention. However, adults in the workplace are not informed on induction that, in this setting, everyone is polite to each other, allows each other to work, and listens respectfully to each other at meetings. It is assumed that adults would know this. I have no trouble assuming that most children will also know such everyday courtesies. It seems disrespectful to assume otherwise, implying that, by their nature, children will naturally be 'naughty' and will need strictures to prevent that. The assumption that they will do their best to work in with everyone is just as viable as the assumption that they won't, but being more positive is likely to engender better practice.

As contended by humanism, the presence of rules instigates the need to police these, thus occasioning authoritarian discipline with all its disadvantages (see Chapter 8). Observance of rules does not ensure moral thinking and activates a rule-driven rather than a value-driven ethos, while violating the educational aims of encouraging independent thinking (Bear et al. 2003; Covaleskie 1992; McCaslin & Good 1992; Wien 2004).

Moral behaviour and rules about morality span three domains: *moral* values, such as justice, respect and consideration for the welfare of others; *conventional* behaviour that abides by rules and social convention; and *personal* behaviour governed by individuals' preferences for dress and other self-referent choices that do not affect others (Bear et al. 2003). Although young people agree on the need for principles governing moral behaviour, they resent adults imposing conformity to non-moral rules or restricting personal choice (Bear et al. 2003; Mayall 2002).

For these reasons, humanism advises no predetermined rules or consequences, but instead the use of problem-solving techniques (individually or at a routine or emergency class meeting). It acknowledges that no one is perfect which means that, in a social world, there *will* be occasions when the needs of two people happen to differ. This will need solving. There *will* also be times when students forget to control themselves and make a mistake. This too needs solving. There will even be a small minority of students who, despite knowing the rules, nevertheless fail to act compassionately, perhaps even intentionally. However, this would not be prevented by teaching rules, as they do not value these. Such students are unlikely to be turned around by rehearsing rules of the 'be nice to each other' variety or by controlling interventions for violations of social niceties. Intervention would not be made any easier by referring to the rule that they have broken and the consequence that their misdemeanour attracts. Instead, the problem needs solving within a personal, rather than an institutional, framework.

The only exception will be that, in its disciplinary policy, the school will need to detail some behaviours (such as illegal acts of drug taking or dealing, assault or intransigent bullying) that will lead to exclusion. These rules, however, need not impinge on everyday classroom practice.

Without rules and without predetermined consequences to administer, the need for consistency abates. Teachers must still consistently (steadfastly) insist that their own rights and those of their students be respected, but *how* conflict is resolved can depend on the circumstances. This allows teachers to exercise the discretion (or wisdom) that befits a professional. Demanding conformity to rigid standards would alienate many students, resulting in behavioural difficulties, whereas appropriate flexibility and informality increase your influence as a leader.

Solve problems

Your response to disruptions must aim to minimise embarrassment and hostility, maximise students' choices about their behaviour, develop and maintain respect, maintain a sense of humour, and ensure follow-up and follow-through (Rogers 1998). It is crucial to respond to disruptions in the most minimalist—and yet effective—way, so that you do not provoke reactive behavioural difficulties, which can be more disturbing than the original behaviour (Porter 1999, 2003, 2006). Sometimes it is necessary to delay dealing with a disruption if you do not have all the facts, when there is not enough time to resolve the issue right then, when it would have to be dealt with in public, or when the student is too upset to respond rationally at the time (Grossman 2004). One of the truisms in life is that you cannot reason with people while they are being unreasonable (Porter 2006).

The following measures can assist with problem solving.

- Develop a warm *relationship* with students, so that they are willing to work with you to solve problems (Kohn 1996a).
- Examine *your own role* in the disruption, both in the immediate circumstances and in the wider context of your relationship with the students and the quality of instruction.
- Be *emotionally supportive* to students, especially those under chronic stress and those in crisis.
- Look for a solution, rather than a culprit (Gordon 1991). In so doing, *listen* to what the students tell you about what is going on, rather than demanding to know in a tone of voice that implies that you simply want to discover who deserves to be punished (Porter 2003, 2006).

- *Defuse conflict* with reflective listening, assertiveness and collaborative problem solving. Signal respect with your posture, tone of voice and gestures. Do not invade students' personal space or adopt an intimidatory manner.
- *Avoid lecturing* students about their mistakes. Without blaming or shaming the perpetrator (so that discouragement does not lead to another outburst), negotiate how he or she could make restitution, maybe through apologising, cleaning up or otherwise restoring any damage (Kohn 1996a). Once a solution has been negotiated, *check back later* to see if it is working (Kohn 1996a).

Promoting the autonomy of stressed students

Young people who are exposed to multiple genetic and environmental stressors are vulnerable to experiencing intellectual, social, emotional and behavioural maladjustment and future negative life events (Rutter 1999). However, positive experiences in school can compensate for, or directly counter, risks posed in other parts of students' lives, insulating them from these detrimental outcomes (Rutter 1999). Resilience—that is, the ability to overcome adversity—can be enhanced when schools promote students' self-efficacy through (Doll & Lyon 1998; Rutter 1999):

- provision of high-quality schooling;
- provision of responsive and supportive adults;
- giving students responsibilities at school;
- fostering prosocial peer friendships;
- connecting students with extracurricular interests;
- teaching coping skills;
- extending supports into families and the community.

Taking each of these protective factors in turn, starting with teaching, young people experiencing multiple disadvantages are likely to need not only a high-quality educational setting but also access to relevant remedial education to offset any educational deficits occasioned by their social disadvantage.

Second, providing emotional support to young people does not need to entail formal counselling. Although this *can* be a part of the services that schools offer, a more naturalistic, and thus more enduring, intervention can be to enhance the quality of relationships between students and adults in the school (Pianta & Walsh 1998). The school must maximise opportunities for teachers and students to maintain warm, supportive and ongoing relationships. One measure might be, therefore, for a class of students to remain with a teacher for consecutive years. Small groupings and self-contained units within larger schools can offer students the responsive relationships needed to support them (Pianta & Walsh 1998). Meanwhile, teachers will need to convey to young people that they honour what they are going through by engaging in respectful interactions with them and giving them feedback that communicates their admiration for the students' 'courage under fire'.

Third, as those most affected by policies in schools, students need to contribute to policy formulation and the oversight of practice, not in a token but in a meaningful way that honours their humanity, needs and preferences and provides due process for resolution of their grievances.

Fourth, as will be discussed in Chapter 11, schools are influential in shaping peer interactions and friendships. These relationships provide a buffer against stress reactions in young people and avoid associations with antisocial peer groups.

Fifth, young people engaged in outside interests and prosocial activities are insulated against stress. These activities can be supported or directly organised by the school.

Sixth, there may be opportunities for teachers to guide young people to appraise challenges realistically and employ coping skills. Coping does not mean feeling no symptoms when experiencing stressful conditions; it means using strategies to *minimise* the impact of the stress on your life, which can entail any of three responses (Compas 1987):

- *problem-focused* action, as its title implies, involves solving the problem that is provoking stress;
- *emotion-focused* strategies involve adjusting our thinking to change our emotional reactions;
- *adjustment* processes involve changing our behaviour so that we can adjust better to circumstances that we cannot change.

In general, children will use problem-focused strategies when they perceive that they have some control over a situation, whereas they will use emotional or behavioural adjustment to deal with issues that they cannot change (Spirito et al. 1991). Even so, as long as they do not rely on ineffective coping mechanisms such as wishful thinking, worrying, blaming themselves or attempting to ignore a problem (Hunter & Boyle 2004; Lewis & Frydenberg 2002), it does not seem to matter *how* children cope but *that* they have a repertoire of positive responses to select from (Rutter 1985, 1999). Responding adaptively both gives them experience of being in command of their lives and stimulates supportive responses from others (Rutter 1999). This implies that it will be important for teachers to ensure that they do not scapegoat stressed students or respond to their provocative behaviour with controlling discipline (Reinke & Herman 2002), as that will only entrench their behavioural problems and may eventually result in their dropping out of school, with all its attendant antisocial sequelae (Rumberger 1995).

Finally, the school can be a hub of services to families and the wider community (Pianta & Walsh 1998). This will not necessarily entail attracting more resources, but perhaps inviting community health professionals to deliver some of their services within the school or under its umbrella (e.g. parenting sessions held on school grounds), so that services can be integrated and parents become accustomed to working with, rather than being separate from, their child's school.

Given that those young people who are most at risk of poor adjustment are those experiencing ongoing, multiple stressors, any school program will need to be multifaceted and sustained (Pianta & Walsh 1998). It will also need to begin early, with children's early childhood and junior primary years of schooling particularly targeted for services (Pianta & Walsh 1998). There is a paradox that students under most stress are the most demanding to work with and most resistant to school-based interventions (Doll & Lyon 1998). Of the above interventions, therefore, those that are indirect may be the most viable for these students.

Conclusion

When we meet students' need for autonomy, they will develop what is variously termed an internal locus of causality, self-efficacy or a sense of personal potency or agency. They will believe in their own ability to shape their lives. This self-belief is essential for academic engagement and for fostering their willingness to regulate their own behaviour.

Discussion questions

1   What is your response to the recommendation that teachers establish no rules for students' behaviour but instead solve problems as they arise?
2   How would egalitarian teaching and discipline transform your role?

11 MEETING STUDENTS' SOCIAL NEEDS: AFFILIATION AND CONNECTION

Classroom groups organized so that students feel liked and respected are more likely to have youngsters acting in ways that warrant the liking and respect of others.

Schmuck & Schmuck (2001: 115)

KEY POINTS

- The need to belong entails *affiliation*. Secure bonds engender trust, self-management and prosocial behaviour whereas broken social bonds contribute to aggression and violence (Cangelosi 2004).
- A feeling of *connection* refers to the extent to which members of the school feel personally accepted, respected, included and supported by others (Goodenow 1993a) and their willingness to give affection in return.
- Both students' and teachers' sense of collegial support enhances their self-efficacy, motivation and wellbeing (Osterman 2000).

Introduction

Young people's social relationships at school influence both their academic progress and their psychological wellbeing, being associated with increased motivation to perform well, higher engagement in learning activities and increased prosocial and reduced antisocial behaviour (Finn et al. 2003; Rutter & Maughan 2002). Indeed, adolescents' sense of connectedness with school is only marginally less influential than family support on aspects of adjustment, including emotional distress and suicidality, involvement in violence, and cigarette, alcohol and other drug use (Resnick et al. 1997). Schools can be particularly vital for students experiencing social disadvantage, who may have limited support from their stressed families and neighbourhoods (Battistich et al. 1995).

The link between belonging and academic achievement is probably due to students' feeling within a supportive setting that they are safe to participate and take intellectual risks as they will receive help if they need it and their worth will not be diminished if they fail (Goodenow 1993b; Osterman 2000). In contrast, when groups are not supportive individuals become stressed which, in turn, results in a decrease in both their effort and output. This effect is particularly apparent for students who are finding the task difficult (Schmuck & Schmuck 2001). Meanwhile, much teacher time becomes expended on suppressing tensions within the group, thus reducing the time and energy available for creative teaching (Schmuck & Schmuck 2001).

Given the importance, then, of the need to belong, we cannot leave to chance that this need will be met by students' family and in recess and lunch breaks at school, but instead need actively to foster a sense of cohesion and friendship within classrooms.

Group cohesion

The school or classroom is not a mere collection of people sharing the same physical space, but an interacting group of individuals who influence each other reciprocally (Schmuck & Schmuck 2001). Thus an important attribute of groups is their cohesiveness. This encompasses a sense of unity or the ability to pull together and feel relaxed and comfortable working together to achieve productively, and affiliation, which is the ability to trust and support one another (Schmuck & Schmuck 2001).

Class groupings must not only support high levels of attainment in members, but must also provide social and emotional support for individuals, such that groups (Finn et al. 2003; McMillan & Chavis 1986; Schmuck & Schmuck 2001):

- promote in members a sense of belonging by welcoming everyone into full membership of the group;
- allow members to experience influence, which is the perception of making a difference to others;
- promote the expectation that their needs will be met by participating in the group;

- foster identification with the group by sharing a common history and experiences;
- ensure self-renewal, which is the capacity of the group to negotiate and adjust its processes to meet changing group or individual needs.

Cohesion can foster voluntary observance of group norms (Osterman 2000). However, these norms may be prosocial or antisocial (Solomon et al. 1996). This implies that cohesion is necessary but not sufficient for classrooms and schools to meet the needs of their members: they also need a sense of community.

Sense of community

A community is a social organisation whose members know, care about and support each other, enjoying a shared commitment and sense of purpose (Solomon et al. 1996). Teachers and students who experience their school as being supportive and caring become committed to the attitudes, values and skills promoted by the school (Solomon et al. 1996). A school environment that is experienced as a community enhances the emotional, social, ethical and intellectual development of all its members, improving teacher satisfaction and feelings of self-efficacy and students' intrinsic motivation, achievement and interpersonal concern (Solomon et al. 1996; Watson et al. 1997). It must be inclusive and foster connection between community members by encouraging high-quality and frequent interaction between them.

Relationships with teachers

Compared with their relationships with peers and their parents, students' relationships with their teachers are the strongest influence on their engagement and interest in learning and sense of belonging in their class (Goodenow 1993b; Osterman 2000; Ryan et al. 1994; Tucker et al. 2002; Wentzel 1998). Throughout the primary years of schooling and beyond, students attach considerable importance to the support that they receive from their teachers, with teachers remaining prominent figures in their emotional and academic lives, supplementing the personal and emotional support provided by their parents and peers (Demaray & Malecki 2002; Demaray & Malecki 2003b; Esposito 1999; Pianta 1999; Pianta & Stuhlman 2004).

Warm relationships and low levels of conflict between teachers and students are effective in preventing risk factors in students' lives being translated into poor academic outcomes, preventing behavioural difficulties and in shaping children's relationships with peers (Larrivee 2005; Pianta 1999). Support from teachers has more influence on the quality of their peer interactions than do parents' relationships with their children (Pianta 1999). Having said this, the direction of effects is not established: it is not clear whether teachers develop warm relationships with able, conforming students who are thus seen to have adjusted well to school, or whether warm relationships with their teachers motivate students to become more engaged, able and conforming to expectations (Birch & Ladd 1997; Blankemeyer et al. 2002).

Nevertheless, when asked, students define teachers as possessing three clusters of desirable characteristics (Allen 1995; Beishuizen et al. 2001; Davies 2005; Jules & Kutnick 1997; Phelan et al. 1992; Schmuck & Schmuck 2001; Wentzel 1997):

- *personal qualities*, such as charisma, kindness, humour, patience and enthusiasm;
- *teaching competence*, spanning content knowledge, pedagogical knowledge (awareness of the level of difficulty of ideas) and curricular knowledge (awareness of different routes through the subject matter), which enables teachers to provide intellectual challenge—that is, have high but realistic expectations of students;
- *emotional support* in the form of nurturing or caring, which comprises caring about students' academic progress, being sensitive to their needs, listening to their ideas and opinions, supporting their emotional communication, dealing fairly with behaviours, providing constructive feedback and interacting democratically.

Peer relationships

When students experience acceptance, they have more favourable attitudes to school and are more likely not only to feel better about themselves, but also to act prosocially towards others (Ladd 1990; Osterman 2000; Wentzel 1998). Peer acceptance assists children's adjustment to school by enhancing their positive attributes and compensating for risk factors that they bring with them at school entry (Ladd 1990).

Whereas cohesiveness is a characteristic of groups, friendship is a voluntary, ongoing bond between *individuals* who have a mutual preference for each other and who share emotional warmth. Although different in this way, cohesiveness and friendships affect each other in that friendships are more likely to develop in cohesive classrooms while, in reverse, classrooms are more likely to be cohesive when every member has at least one close friend (Schmuck & Schmuck 2001).

Despite the fact that peers can make unique and powerful contributions to children's development in many domains (Asher & Parker 1989; Asher & Renshaw 1981; Rubin 1980), peer influence is often regarded with suspicion. Yet friendships enhance young people's engagement with and wellbeing at school, provide a venue for developing and practising social skills, teach children self-control, give them experience at problem solving, provide practice at using language, allow children to exchange skills and information that they do not readily acquire from adults, and teach reciprocity and cooperation (Asher & Parker 1989; Asher & Renshaw 1981; Demaray et al. 2005; Hartup 1979; Johnson & Johnson 1991; Kemple 1991; Kohler & Strain 1993; Perry & Bussey 1984; Rubin 1980; Ryan et al. 1994; Wentzel 1998). These cognitive and social benefits in turn enhance other skill domains (Swetnam et al. 1983). Thus, positive peer relationships are one of the most influential factors in improving student learning outcomes and developing a cohesive school culture (Noble 2006).

On the emotional side, friendships supply reassurance, promote a healthy self-esteem, enhance children's confidence in stressful situations, avoid loneliness, provide fun, and foster individuals' happiness. Friends also offer practical and emotional support by giving information, advice and counsel. By adolescence, peer relationships teach young adults about intimacy, empathy, compassion, loyalty, collaboration, altruism and self-disclosure, as well as give them support for their developing sexuality (Asher & Parker 1989). Such intimacy is necessary to sustain students' drive to excel and contributes significantly to how satisfied they feel about their lives (Gross 1996). These benefits are particularly valuable for students whose home life is strained, when peers can provide the support that parents cannot in order to help them to function positively in school (Schmuck & Schmuck 2001).

Methods to facilitate relationships

Teachers can do much to foster group cohesion, a sense of community, warm relationships with students and supportive peer relationships within the class group.

Personal involvement with students

Teachers' prime motivation for, and satisfaction with, teaching is largely fed by their relationships with students (Oberski et al. 1999; Pianta 1999). Yet, teacher closeness with children declines from the first year of schooling (Pianta & Stuhlman 2004). This largely results from the anonymity of large schools and the limited contact time or 'fragmented interactions' that students have with their many specialist teachers at high school level (Cattley 2004).

Despite this need for personal involvement with students teaching is not a licence to share with students your unfulfilled needs or to become involved in students' lives:

you must be friend*ly* without attempting to be a friend to students. To allow your students to get to know you, you will need to be assertive about both your positive and negative reactions to events that are important to you, while discussing your values and interests. You can use natural events to tell them about who you are, what you stand for and will not stand and what you will and will not be asking them to do (Glasser 1998b). You can write them introductory letters about yourself, allow them to interview you, or participate in their play time, extracurricular events and special activities at school (Jones & Jones 2004). Another option is the 'two truths and a lie' activity, where you tell three stories (two true and one false) about events in your life and have students guess which one is false (Larrivee 2005).

Positive attention

One study found that, on any given day in early childhood settings, nearly one-third of the children received no individual attention from adults (Kontos & Wilcox-Herzog 1997). These children suffer adult neglect, while those with behavioural difficulties often experience adult rejection, receiving four times more negative than positive teacher feedback and receiving fewer positive responses to their contributions during instruction (Stormont 2002; Strein et al. 1999; Tucker et al. 2002). Repeated reprimands of individual students signal to onlookers that the chastised child is less worthy of their friendship, whereas positive teacher comments actively help to recruit peer support for excluded students (Schmuck & Schmuck 2001).

Egalitarian behavioural guidance

So far in Part Two of this text, egalitarian discipline has been advocated as a means to promote student safety and autonomy. Here, its third purpose of fostering social inclusion is the focus. An emphasis on direct instruction and observance of rules does not encourage student openness, whereas informal interactions with students fosters appreciation for diversity (Schmuck & Schmuck 2001). Thus, a formal and impersonal attitude to learning and to discipline, as advocated by the authoritarian theories of discipline, is detrimental to student wellbeing and learning. Group tensions are suppressed and thus never resolved and, as a result of not meeting the personal needs of students, behavioural difficulties surface.

Authoritarian methods such as time out and suspension disconnect students from each other (Noble 2006); in contrast, egalitarian disciplinary methods such as collaborative problem solving and solution-focused approaches have some powerful effects on students' social inclusion. First, egalitarian methods model the communication skills that students will need for relating to others, including listening, assertiveness, collaborative problem solving, understanding another person's point of view, and recognising other people's qualities. Second, they teach students personal attributes that their peers value, such as self-reliance, self-control, exploration, leadership and the ability to solve problems. Third, as well as protecting students from the behavioural excesses of each other, egalitarian discipline also ensures that disruptive students are not scapegoated by how you respond to them, resulting in their further rejection by peers. Finally, egalitarian discipline avoids the contrasting problems of student submission to teacher influence and resulting failure to take initiative versus their resistance to teacher influence, producing antagonism and rebellion.

Finally, children who experience their instructors as supporting their autonomy feel more warmly towards these adults than they do towards controlling adults (Grolnick 2003). In contrast, students who are isolated from their peers and teachers often display their alienation from school in the form of antisocial behaviour, which further jeopardises their relationships (Osterman 2000). Authoritarian responses to these signs of disaffection are likely to exacerbate the students' behavioural difficulties, perhaps culminating in their dropping out of school altogether (Rumberger 1995).

Acquaintance activities

Although they prefer to associate most often with friends, students report that they feel more comfortable at school when they can also mingle with other students (Phelan et al. 1992). When students have numerous opportunities to become acquainted with each other, they will be able to overcome stereotypes about others from backgrounds that differ from their own, make new friends more easily and move between groups with ease (Phelan et al. 1992; Schmuck & Schmuck 2001). Thus, acquaintance activities can help students to get to know each other and bond through their recognition of common interests (Larrivee 2005; Schmuck & Schmuck 2001). These include activities such as having each student create a compact disc of songs and design a cover and label that tell something important about themselves; having them interview each other; having students write an anonymous brief biographical statement about themselves and their interests, following which their classmates have to guess who the account describes.

Looping

Larger schools' potential for impersonality can be avoided by means such as developing relatively autonomous units or departments where more intimate groupings can occur. Another specific option is looping, which is the retention of the same teacher with an intact class for a number of consecutive years. This maintains group stability, avoids the disruption of friendships that occurs when student groupings are rearranged each year and provides continuity for all class members (Charles & Senter 2005b; Pianta 1999).

Limit competition

The emphasis in Western schooling on academic excellence not only belittles the importance of skills in other domains, but also emphasises individual achievement at the expense of others. Not only does this affect the sense of community, but it also creates personal tensions for students (Humphrey & Humphrey 1985). Able students have reported that competition tends to scapegoat them and promote jealousy from classmates (Ford 1989). Thus, competition can actually lower the achievement of even those students who consistently excel (Cropper 1998).

Small classes

Class sizes of under twenty students have been found to be especially beneficial for young and for disadvantaged students, particularly in the teaching of reading and mathematics skills (Finn et al. 2003; Rutter 1983; Rutter & Maughan 2002; Sylva 1994). The main effects are social; in smaller classes, teachers better get to know and interact more often and more positively with their students and the students are more supportive of each other (Finn et al. 2003). Academically, although there is little evidence that teachers vary their instructional methods in smaller classes, students tend to be more engaged and less disruptive, perhaps because a cohesive group pressures each member to cooperate (Blatchford et al. 2001; Finn et al. 2003). When disruptions do occur, teachers' proximity means that they can more readily monitor and intervene because there are fewer students to oversee, they can be more lenient as the contagion effect is less strong in a smaller group, allowing teachers to be more proactive and less reactive in their responses. As a result, they less often need to refer students to outside staff (such as the principal or school counsellor) for discipline (Finn et al. 2003).

Conduct regular class meetings

Groups will repeatedly need to resolve conflict and tension between their members. This is not an indication of malfunction in the group or of individual deficiencies, but is a reality in any social grouping. Gathering together regularly allows the students to see themselves as a group and so develop a sense of community (Honig & Wittmer 1996).

The topic of class meetings was extensively canvassed in Chapters 5 and 6, but it is worth mentioning here that meetings do not always run smoothly, especially when first instigated and particularly when students have little experience with exercising autonomy. In that case, you can use the meetings themselves to solve initial problems, such as students' acting out, outrageous suggestions or resistance to their increased autonomy (Kohn 1996a; Mintz 2003). You can help to share talk time evenly by giving all students a certain number of tokens, one of which must be surrendered each time they have a turn at speaking (Schmuck & Schmuck 2001), and help to have one person talking at a time by passing a stick to the speaker, who is then the only person allowed to talk.

Peer tutoring

In peer tutoring, one child with some expertise instructs a peer with lesser knowledge. The relationship is less unequal than between a student and adult teacher and, compared with being instructed by an adult, the novice may be more willing to ask questions and express ideas—in which case, the interaction would be more mutual (Damon & Phelps 1989). The learner gains through individual guidance, personal care and immediate feedback (Kamps et al. 1994; Topping 1988). Peer tutoring can improve the participation of the learner and enhance the confidence and academic performance of both learner and tutor (Cushing & Kennedy 1997; DuPaul et al. 1998). However, without reciprocity in the tutor and learner roles, some students may resent being one-down to those who are supposed to be their peers, may feel patronised, or may become overly dependent on the helping relationship.

Cross-age tutoring and buddy systems (with an age difference of at least three years between the older and younger student) can overcome the status imbalance of peer tutoring, as the inequalities are inherent in the age difference between tutor and learner rather than in their abilities. Cross-age tutoring and the less structured cross-age grouping for non-academic classes have been shown to produce a wide range of academic, emotional and social gains for both parties (Good & Brophy 2005), although academic gains for the younger children may be no better with peer than with teacher instruction, while the gains for tutors may be less than usual as a result of working with material that they have already mastered (Wright & Cleary 2006). Improved social interactions across the school, including a decrease in stereotypes about and put-downs of students in other age groups, have been reported (Doyle 2003; Stanley & McGrath 2006). However, while friendship can develop between the tutor and learner, acceptance of disliked students is not necessarily guaranteed by the tutoring relationship (García-Vázquez & Ehly 1992).

To ensure that gains exceed the cost to the older tutors, the tutoring needs to be well planned and monitored by the teacher. The system must be voluntary, tutors or buddies have to be well prepared for their role, older mentors must still have time to meet their own needs, they must not be so involved that the younger children do not develop relationships with their own age group, and older students need teacher back-up if they find that they cannot solve a problem of their young charge (Stanley & McGrath 2006).

Small-group learning

Adolescents have the opportunity for only twelve momentary interactions with peers per day, with less popular students having even fewer (Osterman 2000). Small-group learning offers opportunities for more frequent and higher-quality engagement and conversation that connects group members and allows them to experience themselves as part of a community (Cohen 1994; Osterman 2000). However, working in a group does not mean simply seating children in a cluster, but having them work together on a common task. Group-based learning comes in two main forms. The first, *collaborative* activity, entails a pair or small group of students jointly structuring an activity (Wentzel & Watkins 2002). Unlike with peer tutoring, both students share similar status as novices and thus are more equal and their interactions more mutual (Damon & Phelps 1989). The method is best suited to tasks that call for discovery or new insights as it encourages joint experimentation with, and exploration of, new or untested ideas (Damon & Phelps 1989).

The second form of group learning, *cooperative* learning, requires students to work together to achieve a common goal that is typically structured by the teacher in such a way that the group can achieve it if, and only if, each and every member is successful and participates fully (Robinson 1990). This means that cooperative learning is best used for open-ended, conceptual tasks with ill-structured solutions—that is, those requiring higher-level thinking skills, including divergent or creative thinking and problem solving. Lower-level thinking tasks, such as the acquisition of facts and converging on one right answer, are more amenable to individual effort because they can be completed in parallel, rather than in interaction, with other group members (Cohen 1994).

As an alternative to teacher-led instruction, group work aims to produce four types of outcome: higher engagement and productivity of group members; higher-order thinking and deeper understanding occasioned by the members' joint discussion and processes of discovery; equity of status among members; and enhanced self-esteem for participants as a result of being able to contribute (Cohen 1994; Hill & Hill 1990; Hill

& Reed 1989; Johnson et al. 1993). To achieve these outcomes, teachers must structure the following aspects of the cooperative endeavour.

- Clear objectives for the lesson need to be provided, both in terms of students' learning and with respect to their interactions.
- Tasks need to be structured so that they require the resources of each member and thus cannot be achieved without the participation and effort of all (Cohen 1994). Reciprocity can be fostered by allocating roles that focus on the process rather than the task content, such as group facilitator or summariser (Cohen 1994).
- Groups need to be small enough so that members can get to know each other personally, without being so big that some individuals withdraw to work alone or that requests for help are ignored (Webb 1989).
- Groupings should change regularly, so that rivalry does not develop between groups.
- There need to be measures to monitor how the groups are functioning and to evaluate learning outcomes. Each member must contribute and be responsible for the final product, while avoiding redundant effort by individuals. Although some cooperative learning theorists (e.g. Slavin 1991) advocate external rewards for group efforts, humanism asserts that this causes students to compete with each other and thus runs counter to the educational aim of fostering cooperation (Cohen 1994; Damon & Phelps 1989). It also discourages individuals who worked well but whose team does not earn a reward, and seems unnecessary when the task truly requires interdependence and is inherently interesting to students (Cohen 1994).

Most of the difficulties with cooperative learning pertain to the fact that groupings are typically of mixed ability, with those groups with highly disparate skill levels presenting the most challenge (King 1993). With respect to academic outcomes, the less able students may become disengaged or passive and not ask for the help that they need and, as a result, learn little, while the highly able students may dominate or give inadequate or too sophisticated explanations. When the less able students do not understand these, it verifies their own negative self-expectations and compounds the low expectations held of them by their more able peers (Gillies & Ashman 2000; King 1993; Webb 1989). Even when the teacher has allocated specific roles in an effort to balance out the contributions of the group members, the less able students surrender their roles to those who are more capable of fulfilling them (King 1993). On the other hand, the silent (perhaps able but diffident) students may be more outspoken in the smaller groupings, which could then transfer into the larger group setting as they gain confidence (Jules 1991).

In short, the employment of cooperative skills is not automatic in small groups. Explicit training and feedback to the group on their skill use while they are working are necessary for students to employ the cognitive and social skills needed to work together. Cognitive skills include developing understandings of the task, specifying goals, setting up hypotheses, eliciting opinions, sharing ideas and resources, giving explanations, pinpointing differences in members' views, problem solving as a group and evaluating progress. The social skills needed to cooperate with team-mates include giving mutual support, encouraging equal participation, offering and soliciting help, providing constructive feedback and resolving conflict amicably (Cohen 1994; Gillies 2000; Gillies & Ashman 1998; Hill & Hill 1990; Wentzel & Watkins 2002).

Even when group members receive training in these cooperative processes, group learning might not always live up to its promised social benefits of fully including students with learning difficulties, those with low social status, minority cultural members and females (Cohen 1994; Jules 1991). Although cooperative learning expands students' interactive networks, the more able students typically remain dominant and the unpopular students might become more so as a result of their unsuccessful interactions at close quarters with the rest of the group (Jules 1991). This is worrisome for social equity reasons, but also because lack of participation by neglected students is linked to their lesser academic gains (Cohen 1994).

As for the more able students, they have been shown to regress to the level of their less able team-mates (Cohen 1994) or become frustrated if other members of their group are less motivated to participate or do not understand the material (Matthews 1992). The time taken to train them to work cooperatively and then to support their less able peers is criticised by educators of gifted children on the grounds that it shifts instructional attention away from very able learners and restricts their access to more advanced learning (Colangelo & Davis 2003; Robinson 1990, 2003). On the grounds that all students have an equal right to progress from their present skill levels, these critics say that this 'Robin Hood' method of robbing time from able learners amounts to exploitation.

Advocates of cooperative learning answer this with the claim that able learners can gain socially and learn more by leading and teaching the less able children (Slavin 1991). Intellectually, refining their explanations according to the needs of their peers allows them to clarify and reorganise their own understandings (Terwel et al. 2001), although there is little evidence that this advances their learning beyond their capabilities at the outset of the group and may instead cause their confidence to be shaken and their skills to regress (Cohen 1994; Wright & Cleary 2006). Socially, they gain appreciation, it is said, for diversity and have an opportunity to be altruistic (Diamond et al. 1997; Favazza & Odom 1997; Hanson et al. 1998). However, mere contact alone is not enough to ensure improved attitudes to diversity. Interactions between children with and without learning difficulties are not always positive, which requires that teachers highlight how the group could draw on the abilities of low-status students and allocate tasks where their skills could be employed (Cohen 1994). Meanwhile, opportunities to practise altruism are beneficial only as long as the help-giving is not condescending (Stoneman 1993).

The option of grouping students by ability is not the answer to these difficulties, however, because it can entrench the disaffection of the less able and the higher status of the more able students, and would convey a message about the school's lack of inclusivity (Gamoran 1992; Hallinan 1990; Rist 1970; Rutter 1983; Sapon-Shevin 1994). To avoid these academic and social risks, cooperative learning should not entail permanent groupings based on ability, gender, race or any other characteristic that might convey status differentials within the group. However, you might be able to offer tiered tasks, so that the more able students have opportunities to be challenged academically. Tiered tasks take two forms (Montgomery 1996):

- differentiation of *inputs*, whereby you provide different activities that share a common theme with various levels of difficulty;
- differentiation of *outcomes*, whereby you set a common task that children enter at their own level and then respond to according to their level of sophistication.

The students would then self-select which activities suit them, or you could target certain children and support them to attempt the more demanding tasks.

Identify socially isolated students

Most children (around 5 to 10 per cent) will experience some temporary isolation at one time or another during their school lives (Asher & Renshaw 1981), often as a result of being new to a group or having recently lost their best friend. For some students, however, their isolation is protracted (Zettergren 2005), with the result that they lack the relationships within which to practise their skills and so may become less socially able over time. They miss out on the important benefits that friendships offer and are lonelier and less satisfied with those relationships that they do have.

Observations of students can alert you to their isolation, as can structured sociometric assessment. Within schools (in contrast to research applications), this can take two main forms (Asher & Renshaw 1981; Coie et al. 1989; Hops & Lewin 1984):

- Students are asked to nominate those peers with whom they would most (or least) like to be friends or with whom they would most (or least) like to work or play. These *peer nominations* identify the popular children (those with a high number of positive nominations), the rejected children (who receive a high number of negative nominations) and neglected children (those who are ignored and receive few nominations). Shortcomings of this method are that children might nominate other students whom they *want* to be their friends but who in fact are not (Hops & Lewin 1984). Also, different activity criteria yield different nominations, with gifted learners, for example, selected as workmates but not necessarily selected for social groupings, and children with learning disabilities experiencing the reverse pattern (Frederickson & Furnham 2004).

• The *peer rating* method gives students a list of classmates and asks them to rate every individual on a likeability scale. This yields an indication of acceptability or likeability, which is not the same as popularity, and overcomes the problem of some students being forgotten or overlooked with a nomination approach (Hops & Lewin 1984).

You can then use this information to assist the inclusion of isolated students or, in instances where you believe their isolation to be due to a social skill deficit, for social skills training. If, however, you wish to institute targeted rather than universal social skills programs, the above assessment will give you little information about the specific behaviours that have excited the rejection or neglect of particular students (Johnson et al. 1990) and therefore what skills to include in the program.

Teach social skills

A proactive approach for preventing socially referenced disruptive behaviour is to include social skills training as part of the regular curriculum for all children. Long-term, school-wide programs that are delivered to all students are more effective than one-off 'add-on' programs, particularly when social skills curricula are reinforced by measures that develop a cohesive school and classrooms (McGrath 2006; Noble 2006). On the other hand, universal curricular measures tend to be regarded with derision by high school students and so may be less effective in adolescence (Owens et al. 2000a), while at younger ages the programs can seem artificial (Schneider & Blonk 1998) and it must be queried whether the loss of instruction time is justified (Ang & Hughes 2002; Arnold & Hughes 1999).

A second, reactive, approach is to identify individuals with social skill deficits and offer training to these selected children only. This has two disadvantages: when clustered together, young people with serious social difficulties may emulate each other's antisocial behaviour (Kamps & Kay 2002); and any learning that occurs in an adjunct program is less likely to generalise to natural settings (McGrath 1998). That is to say, while students' knowledge of social strategies might improve, this does not necessarily change their actual social behaviour (Arnold & Hughes 1999). On the other hand, targeted interventions can be more manageable within a crowded curriculum, particularly in secondary school.

Meanwhile, it is a mistake to assume that those who act antisocially do so because they lack knowledge of prosocial skills. As the model in Figure 4.1 (see p. 77) showed, some may have the ability but lack the disposition to use prosocial skills, as their aggression or other antisocial behaviour works for them. Other students may possess the appropriate skill but lack the sophistication to judge when to use it, or lack the self-control needed to enact it (Hall et al. 1999). These students do not have a *knowledge* deficit as such, but a *performance* deficit (Schneider 1989). This implies that it is crucial to determine which cluster of skills need teaching, as instruction in a skill that students already possess will inevitably be ineffective.

Consider placement adjustments for developmentally isolated students

Given that individuals choose friends at their ability level, when peers' developmental skills differ significantly from their own, children with developmental disabilities are particularly prone to isolation and social neglect (Guralnick et al. 1995). As a result of their behavioural difficulties, around 30 per cent of children with intellectual disabilities are actively rejected within inclusive settings, while a greater number still are ignored (or neglected) by peers as a result of their social reticence (Odom et al. 1999). This social isolation comes about because, even compared with younger children of an equivalent developmental level, those with intellectual disabilities lack the cognitive and metacognitive skills necessary to read social cues and to instigate and maintain peer relationships, resulting in fewer and less successful initiations of social interaction and fewer positive responses to peers' initiations (Brown et al. 1999; Guralnick & Groom 1987; Hanline 1993; Odom et al. 1999; Reynolds & Holdgrafer 1998). Their social ineptness is largely tolerated by nondisabled peers, however, who reject as workmates only those with disabilities who are disruptive and as playmates only those who are aggressive (Frederickson & Furnham 2004). Thus, reducing their disruptiveness and aggression will assist their social inclusion.

For their part, the majority of moderately gifted children have positive peer relationships, even when they lack intellectual peers (Janos & Robinson 1985). They are generally socially skilful (Freeman 1995; Jones & Day 1996; Moss 1992), which results in most gifted children being socially accepted by their peers (Austin & Draper 1981; Cohen et al. 1994). This picture is not as uniformly positive for highly gifted children, who find it harder to make friends because of the scarceness of highly able intellectual peers (Brody & Benbow 1986; Dauber & Benbow 1990; Janos & Robinson 1985; Janos et al. 1985).

The social inclusion of both types of atypical learners might be assisted by having children with disabilities work alongside younger classmates (see Porter 2002a, 2002b) and those who are gifted working with older peers (see Porter 2005), at least for academic subjects where their skills differ significantly from age mates'. However, any such decision needs to be planned carefully, taking into account many factors of the individual and the social group.

Increased positive teacher interaction

The social difficulties of students who are persistently neglected or rejected by their peers are unlikely to disappear spontaneously (Asher & Parker 1989; Hill & Reed 1989; Schneider 1989). However, teachers can ameliorate their isolation by resisting making negative comments to isolated children that would give permission for onlooking classmates similarly to treat those children with derision. In your positive interactions with isolates, the *content* of your comments can counter any negative reputation that they have developed, while the *process* of positive recognition models to peers an expectation to respect and include all children (Schmuck & Schmuck 2001).

A group solution to isolation

Having identified that a child is isolated, you could use the 'circle of friends' method to engage peers in supporting that child. This method involves conducting a class meeting without the rejected child being in attendance and explaining to the remaining children that this is a special case of talking behind a child's back, made possible only by the permission of the child and his or her parents (Miller 2003). You would then ask the class to describe their absent peer and specify what behaviour he or she displays that gives rise to these negative descriptions. Next, you would explain (and draw) the 'circle of friend' concept—that each of us is surrounded by concentric circles of support comprising those we care about, with family and best friends nearest to us, then good friends, then acquaintances and, at the fourth level, those who are paid to be involved with us, such as teachers and doctors (see Figure 11.1). Next, you would ask how a hypothetical child would feel and act when at school his or her two nearest circles were empty. The aim is for the group to recognise that these behaviours of the hypothetical child are similar to the rejected child's and thus that his or her devalued social behaviour is due to isolation, not to being personally odd. In the final phase of discussion, the class members devise some means to include the isolated child. Later sessions would check that these measures were working.

FIGURE 11.1   Circle of friends

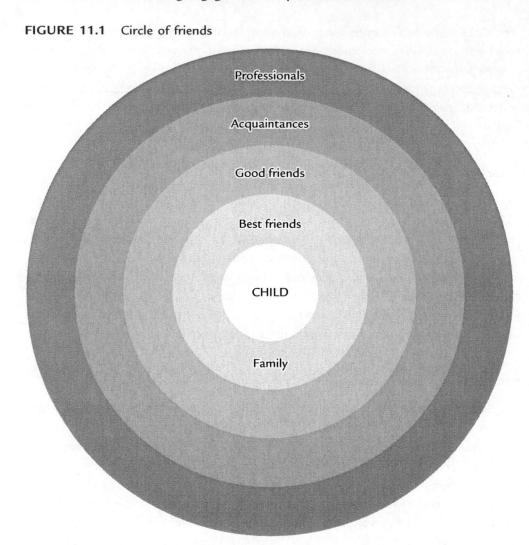

Bullying

Bullying is a form of aggression in which individuals oppress others who are typically younger or weaker than them in gratuitous, unjustified, deliberate and repeated attempts to dominate and inflict hurt (Kochenderfer-Ladd & Ladd 2001; Rigby 2006a; Slee 1995a, 1995b; Slee & Rigby 1994; Smith & Sharp 1994). Bullies typically choose to exercise power over others, not in anger but in what could be termed a 'proactive', rather than reactive, form of aggression (Salmivalli et al. 1998).

For a range of research and definitional reasons, firm rates of bullying are difficult to establish, although figures tend to settle on up to 10 per cent being victims, 13 per cent bullies and 6 per cent being both on a reasonably frequent basis (Espelage & Swearer 2003; Olweus 1993). The consensus is that almost one in five students is subjected to bullying at least once a week in schools and over half experience it during their school lives, with a third of students saying that it makes them feel unsafe at school (Demaray & Malecki 2003a; Pepler et al. 1993; Rigby 1996; Slee 1994b, 1998; Smith & Sharp 1994; Tattum 1993a). Indeed, bullying is so widespread that 'No study of social behaviour in any school anywhere in the world has shown an absence of bullying' (Noble 2006: 68).

Types of bullying

Although early literature on the subject focused mainly on physical bullying, more recent research has examined its more furtive forms. Direct or open bullying comprises *direct physical attacks*, such as pushing, shoving, punching, tripping up, damage to the victim's clothing or possessions, and striking with or without weapons; and *direct verbal attacks*, such as taunting, name calling or using a person consistently as the butt of jokes (O'Moore & Minton 2004). Sending threatening messages by phone or email is a more recent form of verbal bullying. *Extortion* entails the extraction of money or other possessions under threat, or being forced to commit antisocial or illegal acts such as theft or vandalism.

Relational bullying is an attempt to control or manipulate others by constraining their friendship ('You can't be my friend unless…') or by restricting access to social events such as parties (Crick et al. 2001). These methods can entail talking about others behind their backs, using code names for victims, which they suspect refer to themselves, spreading malicious rumours, threatening to expose shared confidences, and leaving anonymous notes or phone messages (Crick et al. 2001; James & Owens 2005; Olweus 1993; Owens et al. 2001; Rigby 1996, 1998; Salmivalli et al. 1998; Slee 1995b; Smith & Sharp 1994; Tattum 1993a). Exclusionary manoeuvres span ignoring someone briefly or for extended periods, hiding from and thus isolating them, excluding them from groupings, to outright prolonged ostracism (Owens et al. 2000a). Public displays of exclusion include using huddles, loud talk and extravagant greetings with only the 'in' members of a clique (Shute et al. 2002). This social bullying is often accompanied by nonverbal signals that are aimed at conveying disgust or anger while asserting one's own power or status (Shute et al. 2002). These include stares, 'bitchy' looks, looking someone up and down in a disparaging manner, rolling the eyes, using a sarcastic tone of voice and tossing the head in 'telegraphic' displays of emotion (Shute et al. 2002).

These nonverbal means, in particular, ensure that relational bullying remains covert, allowing perpetrators to disguise their aggressive intentions and give deniability (James & Owens 2004). The bullying has maximum effect on the victim with minimum risk to the perpetrator, as any reaction or report can be met with accusations that the victim is paranoid. Further relational bullying can be inflicted on the victim in retaliation for reporting.

A final form of bullying is *sexual harassment*. This involves sexually toned verbal comments about girls' physical appearance, circulation of rumours affecting girls' sexual reputation, physical touch, and visual harassment such as using pornography or defacing school posters of women to embarrass or intimidate girls (Drouet 1993; Owens et al. 2005b). Girls may be required to perform favours (not necessarily sexual) at the threat of having sexual rumours spread about them. Whereas most perpetrators of such forms of heterosexual harassment are males who use these acts to gain status with their male peers, while regarding their taunts as jokes or as flattering to females, their victims find them threatening and they may feel obliged to avoid areas in which males congregate (Owens et al. 2005b).

A particular class of sexual harassment focuses on the recipient's sexual orientation, with gay, lesbian and particularly bisexual adolescents suffering up to double the usual rate of verbal and physical bullying (Murdock & Bolch 2005; Rivers 2001). They often endure not only the interpersonal bullying of school peers but also mobbing by unknown assailants and continuous sociocultural harassment from overt and covert negative messages about their sexual orientation (Henning-Stout et al. 2000). The combination of a homophobic school climate, low teacher support and victimisation reduces these students' psychological sense of belonging within their school and results in poorer academic performance and increased behavioural difficulties (Murdock & Bolch 2005).

These forms of bullying arise when students have superior psychological strength to their victims. This same condition commonly applies in relationships between teachers and students. Thus, although usually spoken of with reference to peers, it is important to highlight that *teachers* can also be the perpetrators of bullying in schools (Rigby 2003). Finally, we also need to be aware of the bullying of teachers by colleagues or by their students (Rigby 2003; Terry 1998).

Age trends

As they age, children are less likely to be victimised physically and more likely to be recipients of verbal and relational bullying (Olweus 1993). This is probably because bullies' social and verbal skills become more sophisticated with age (James & Owens

2004; Owens et al. 2005a). It appears that bullying is most prevalent towards the end of primary school and the beginning of secondary school (Espelage & Swearer 2003; Marsh et al. 2004; Rigby 1996; Slee 1994a; Slee 1994b). Meanwhile, the tendency to bully remains fairly constant (Olweus 1993), suggesting the need to interrupt the pattern early in the life of bullies lest it persist throughout their schooling years (and beyond).

Although in the early childhood years (under five years of age) young children can be aggressive in reaction to immediate events, they tend to lack the premeditation required for proactive bullying of individual targets (Crick et al. 2001). Common to this age range, however, are exclusionary manoeuvres (e.g. 'You can't come to my birthday party'), which are intended to hurt but, again, are an immediate reaction to a peer's perceived transgression (Crick et al. 1999; Porter 1999). When nothing is done to prevent it, however, by the ages of five to seven years, rates of bullying and victimisation resemble the incidence for older children (Alsaker & Valkanover 2001; Kochenderfer & Ladd 1996).

Gender differences

It is unclear whether boys and girls are socially aggressive at similar rates (as found by Crick & Grotpeter 1995) or boys remain more prone both to bullying and victimisation (as found by Marsh et al. 2004). It is certainly clear that boys of all ages are more likely than girls to be both perpetrators and victims of physical bullying. It also appears that, from the age of eight years, boys reduce their relational aggression (Henington et al. 1998) whereas, in keeping with their more intimate social groupings, girls increase theirs (Crick et al. 2001; Owens 1996; Owens & MacMullin 1995; Owens et al. 2001, 2005a; Perry et al. 2001; Salmivalli et al. 1998). By adolescence, heterosexual relational bullying involves both male–female (romantic) pairs as well as the single-sex pairings characteristic of younger ages (Crick et al. 2001).

Location of bullying

Most bullying takes place in the playground, with one-third occurring on the way to and from school, although this usually involves those who are being bullied in school as well (Boulton 1997; Olweus 1993). When both physical and relational bullying are considered, both girls and boys report being bullied more in coeducational than in single-sex schools, with girls in coeducational settings also being sexually harassed more than in single-sex schools (Rigby 1993, 1998).

Effects of bullying

As young people seldom report to adults that they are victims or perpetrators of bullying, the immediate effects of bullying as listed in Box 11.1 can signal the need for investigation. At the time of direct or covert attacks, victims are likely to feel confusion at why they have been targeted, followed by covering up or denying the reality of their victimisation (Owens et al. 2000c) or, perhaps less adaptively, blaming themselves for it (Juvonen et al. 2000). Subsequently, they may admit to their misery, which spans loneliness, hurt, fear, loss of self-esteem (particularly with respect to peer relationships), anxiety and fear for future relationships (Egan & Perry 1998; Juvonen et al. 2000; Marsh et al. 2004; Owens et al. 2000c). They might next seek to escape by joining other friendship groups or alternatively may retaliate, but this can exacerbate—and be seen to justify—peers' subsequent victimisation of them (Owens et al. 2000c). In turn, these effects create a vicious cycle in which their sensitive demeanour causes others to see them as 'easy marks' and thus repeat their abuses.

Long-term outcomes of bullying vary. Some victims report few long-lasting effects (Juvonen et al. 2000), whereas others experience ongoing maladjustment (Kochenderfer-Ladd & Ladd 2001). Some have few lasting effects socially, but enduring emotional effects (Olweus 2001; Rivers 2001).

Prolonged harassment is likely to lead to absenteeism from school (with 10 to 15 per cent of persistent absentees giving bullying as their reason), or leaving a school altogether; increased health complaints (possibly because stress undermines immune system functioning); impaired capacity to relate to others; and emotional effects, including anxiety, low self-esteem, impaired self-efficacy, depressive tendencies, feelings of isolation, unhappiness and loneliness, and suicidal ideation (Espelage & Swearer 2003; Hunter & Boyle 2004; Kochenderfer-Ladd & Ladd 2001; Owens et al. 2000c; Rigby 1996, 1999, 2001, 2006a; Slee 1995a, 1995b; Slee & Rigby 1994; Smith et al. 2004). At the same time, victims' learning can suffer (Rigby 1996, 2001). Finally, as might be expected, victims become intimidated and lack confidence and therefore are less likely to seek social support or report the abuse to adults (Hunter & Boyle 2004).

Although students typically recover from the emotional effects of short-lived bullying (Juvonen et al. 2000), protracted victimisation has an added and perhaps more persistent *social* impact, characterised by social mistrust and alienation (Kochenderfer-Ladd & Ladd 2001). Reactions to extended bullying can be similar to those found in post-traumatic stress (Mynard et al. 2000), with effects persisting even after victims of extended harassment have escaped the abusive setting (Kochenderfer-Ladd & Ladd 2001).

BOX 11.1 SIGNS OF VICTIMISATION FROM BULLYING

Physical signs

- unexplained physical injuries
- unexplained damage to clothing and property
- disappearance of money
- somatic complaints
- sleeping difficulties, resulting in tiredness at school
- loss of appetite
- are unusually ravenous when they come home from school (having had their lunch stolen)

Social signs

- involvement in quarrels or fights in which they appear defenceless
- victims of constant teasing
- isolation at play and lunch times
- try to stay close to adults at play and lunch times
- lack of out-of-school-hours contact with classmates
- few invitations to social gatherings of peers

Emotional signs

- appear distressed, anxious, subdued, unhappy or tearful, but refuse to say what is wrong
- changes in mood and behaviour
- explosive anger
- low self-esteem
- fear of going to school
- requests to leave the school

Academic signs

- sudden difficulty asking or answering questions in class
- decline in school performance (output) and/or processes such as concentration
- reduced participation in class activities
- absenteeism

Sources: Field & Carroll 2006; Olweus 1993; O'Moore & Minton 2004

Explanations for bullying

Tattum (1993a: 3) does not mince words when he calls bullying 'the most malicious and malevolent form of antisocial behaviour practised in our schools'. While a perfectly natural human reaction, this view gives rise to demonising its perpetrators, yielding a range of ineffective responses within schools.

Behaviourism

The authoritarian theories (notably behaviourism) advocate a zero-tolerance policy, with clear anti-bullying rules and consequences for their violation. To ensure detection of incidents, this approach advocates more 'visible and vigilant' playground supervision (Boulton 1994; McGrath & Stanley 2006b; Olweus 1993). However, as most bullying goes on behind teachers' backs, schools would need saturation coverage of the playground, bus stops, lunch areas and toilets to make even a dent in the incidence. Even if the school could afford the associated expense, this would result in a siege mentality across the school, which would be detrimental to its climate (McEvoy & Welker 2000).

Thus, although you must protect students, for a range of reasons most researchers favour non-punitive (non-behaviourist) approaches to bullying (McGrath & Stanley 2006a). First, those who do not share the school values will not be won over by rules of the 'be nice to each other' variety (see, e.g., Orpinas et al. 2003). Second, if you define bullying as a breach of school rules, it will be impossible to specify and thus respond to nonverbal and other subtle forms of bullying. Third, it can be difficult to glean sufficient facts to determine who is at fault. Fourth, blaming and punishing perpetrators will not prompt their empathy or repentance nor deter future bullying, and may provoke bullies into subsequently exacting revenge on their victim. Last, a more philosophical objection is that the imposition of power over bullies simply replicates and reinforces their use of power over their peers.

Cognitive theory

The cognitive perspective holds great sway on this issue, with much research focusing on the presumed social skill deficits of victims (e.g. Fox & Boulton 2005; Perry et al. 2001). However, other than being physically less equipped to fend off attacks, victims differ little from non-victims (Marsh et al. 2004). Non-aggressive victims do have friends at school—albeit sometimes other victims, who thus offer little protection from harassment (Pellegrini et al. 1999), and their friendship skills outside of school (Smith et al. 2004) and their social skills after the cessation of the attacks are normal (Olweus 1993, 2001). Therefore general social skills training seems unwarranted.

A second cluster of skills sometimes thought lacking in victims is their inability to be assertive under threat (Hodges & Perry 1999; Schwartz et al. 2001). This hypothesis is based on their observed tendency either to submit or to react aggressively to attacks, neither of which is effective and both of which signal emotional distress that invites further torment (Fox & Boulton 2005; Pellegrini et al. 1999).

A third possibility arises from awareness that, while aggressive children initially direct their hostility towards many group members, they soon focus consistently on those peers whose sensitivity, non-aggression and lack of friendships make them high-risk targets (Kochenderfer & Ladd 1996; Olweus 1993). This leads to the hypothesis that victims' low self-esteem leads to these characteristics and, in turn, causes their failure to deter future bullying (Marsh et al. 2004). However, it seems clear that these emotional effects are, in large part, the *result* of the bullying, rather than being its cause. Evidence for this view is provided by the research finding that young children's school adjustment was normal prior to bullying, but deteriorated once bullying began (Kochenderfer & Ladd 1996).

Other evidence that these hypotheses may be in error is that curricula aimed at remediating the assumed skill deficiencies of victims have achieved little success. Few gains were noted by Fox and Boulton (2003), perhaps because an individual focus on victims that ignores the dynamics of the peer group is unlikely to be successful.

Naturally, the victims—even if socially or emotionally vulnerable—would not be victimised unless others behaved antisocially. This leads cognitivists into an examination of the deficiencies of perpetrators, fed by awareness that the tendency to bully is a fairly stable characteristic across time and is associated with many types of maladjustment, including academic underachievement, school drop-out, and aggression towards teachers, school property and siblings. In later life, bullies also tend to have higher rates of delinquency, criminality and perhaps depression, with greater likelihood of becoming abusive spouses and parents and of being abused themselves (Elinoff et al. 2004; Marsh et al. 2004; Olweus 1993, 2001; Rigby 1996; Slee 1995b, 1998; Smith & Sharp 1994; Tattum 1993a, 1993b). Deficit orientations uphold that bullies are impulsive, believe in dominance and in being manipulative or violent to gain status (Olweus 1993; Smith & Sharp 1994; Tattum 1993a), or that they lack commitment to acting morally and the moral sensitivity and reasoning needed to make moral decisions (Marsh et al. 2004; Sanders 2004).

This view, as operationalised in the form of social skills packages teaching perpetrators the likes of cooperation, anger management and conflict resolution skills, has achieved modest effects at reducing aggression and bullying in early to middle primary school (see Leff et al. 2001; Samples 2004; Smith et al. 2004) and at improving attitudes to bullying, even into the high school years (Van Schoiack-Edstrom et al. 2002). However, these social skills packages make little impact on bullying *behaviour* in high school (Stevens et al. 2000), and adolescents are contemptuous of efforts to include such curricula at their level (Owens et al. 2000a).

This is probably because bullies reject the implied view of themselves as socially incompetent. Indeed, many proactive aggressors are outgoing and confident, enjoying a wide base of peer support both within and beyond their aggressive clique (Pelligrini et al 1999; Rodkin & Hodges 2003). Rather than being socially inept, their broad popularity gives them the 'social authority' to control the peer relationships around them (Crick & Grotpeter 1995). They understand people very well and use this information to their own advantage (Espelage & Swearer 2003). These findings and the unlikelihood, given the high rate of bullying, that so many individuals could be maladjusted, suggest that bullying persists not because of the malice of its perpetrators, but because it *works*. Manipulation of who is 'in' and the exclusion of outsiders establish, maintain and strengthen bonds within one's peer group, while differentiating one's group from others (Bukowski & Sippola 2001; McMillan & Chavis 1986; Nishina 2004; Owens et al. 2000b).

As well as enhancing group cohesion, bullying also appears to be a strategy for establishing power or dominance within groups (Pellegrini 2004). This is verified by research showing that the incidence of dominance and bullying coincided (Long & Pellegrini 2003). The dominant gain access to resources: in early childhood, to toys; by later adolescence, access to peer status and to heterosexual relationships (Pellegrini 2004). Other reasons that adolescents have given for social bullying include to alleviate boredom, create excitement or as revenge for gossiping or for the poaching of same-sex friends or boyfriends (Owens et al. 2000b).

The third explanation for bullying rests on the fact that half of all bullying involves a group of students with a ringleader harassing a single peer (Olweus 1993, 2001). Individual perpetrators in these 'mobs' are not socially impaired, but the group setting results in the diffusion of responsibility, which allows individuals to evade personal awareness of their part in causing the victim's distress (Olweus 1993; Pikas 2002). Some hold no malice against the victim—and may even feel shame for their actions—but participate in the bullying to avoid becoming victims themselves or to elevate their own status within the peer group (James & Owens 2005; Owens et al. 2000b; Rigby 1996).

Egalitarian views

The inadequacy of cognitive conceptions of the skills deficits of victims and perpetrators gives rise to the egalitarian perspective. This recognises that bullying is a complex behaviour that is embedded in systems (family, classroom and school) that inadvertently model, maintain and reinforce domination and intimidation (Pepler et al. 1993; Tattum 1993b). Whereas bullying has been thought to prevail more in larger schools, city schools and in those whose communities experience socioeconomic disadvantage, racial discrimination or high rates of violence, it is now apparent that, even when schools have similar structural characteristics or student populations, the rate of bullying in one school can be up to four times higher than in another, while students in classes with high rates of aggression become more aggressive themselves over time (Olweus 1993; Rigby 2006a; Rodkin & Hodges 2003). These differences have been attributed to the school ethos and teacher practices. School factors that allow bullying to occur include status differences between students and teachers and among the various grade levels of the student population (Nishina 2004), neglect of victims within schools, lack of intervention with bullying, and a school ethos that does not question oppression (Olweus 1993), which includes the oppression of students by authoritarian teaching. In such a climate, there will be too few countervailing forces to dissuade students from using their power in antisocial ways against vulnerable peers.

Safe school (anti-bullying) programs

An egalitarian approach to bullying recognises that students are likely to resist and even be contemptuous of adult-imposed, authoritarian interventions (Rodkin & Hodges 2003). Thus, anti-bullying measures need to be nestled within a communal school organisation that fosters supportive relations, common goals and norms, and collaboration and involvement across all sectors of the school (Payne & Gottfredson 2004).

Slee (2001, 2006) proposes that schools enact a five-phase anti-bullying program described by the acronym PEACE:

P   represents the *preparation* stage of collecting data about bullying in your school and gathering resources to inform an anti-bullying program;
E   stands for *education* about what is meant by bullying and which procedures to use to deal with it;
A   means taking *action* at all levels;
C   stands for helping victims to *cope*. However, because in lay understanding the word *coping* implies 'putting up' with adversity, I shall replace this term with O'Moore and Minton's (2004) term, *countering* strategies;
E   stands for *evaluation* of the effectiveness of the program.

Preparation

In the preliminary phases, a small working party of teachers, parents, students and community representatives needs to be convened to gather data and resource materials for future dissemination across the school. Given that teachers in secondary school spend little time with students individually or in their peer groups, and given that the covert nature of relational bullying makes it difficult to detect, teachers may be aware of less than half of the bullying that is occurring at their school (Leff et al. 1999). Therefore, the administration of sociometric measures within classrooms can help identify students who are neglected or rejected, while questionnaires to all teachers, parents and students about bullying can give the school information and thus the impetus to adjust its responses to bullying (Noble 2006; Rigby 2001; Rodkin & Hodges 2003).

Education

Teachers, parents and students need to receive some straightforward information about the various forms of bullying, its signs and its effects on victims. At the same time, misinformation needs to be countered, such as myths that bullying is an inescapable part of life, that it toughens people up, that some students 'ask' for it, or that words cannot harm us (O'Moore & Minton 2004). Nevertheless, while education will win over empathic bystanders, it will be less influential with perpetrators and therefore must be supplemented by other measures.

Action

The first form of action entails *primary prevention* strategies. These are aimed at changing those aspects of the school environment that are permitting the victimisation of others. The place to start is suggested by the contention of the egalitarian theories that, when teachers relate fairly with students, they in turn are more likely to do so with each other and more likely to seek and welcome teacher support in their conflicts. A cohesive school and class community (from the principal and teachers down) that is based on prosocial interactions will create a climate of acceptance in which injustice towards others is less tolerated. Some specific primary preventive measures include the following.

- Schools will need to enrich playgrounds and offer structured activities at breaks to give students something productive to do (Boulton 1994; James & Owens 2005; Leff et al. 2003; Olweus 1993; Owens et al. 2000b; Whitney et al. 1994).
- Teachers can avoid the isolation and consequent victimisation of vulnerable individuals and orchestrate higher levels of peer acceptance by displaying warmth and care towards all students (Rodkin & Hodges 2003).
- Although curricular *measures* have been shown to have little effect, primary schools in particular might include anti-bullying themes within regular subject areas, in class meetings or within a 'caring community' program. In the context of other measures to enhance social cohesion in classrooms and across the school, information conveyed naturalistically might mobilise the large numbers of peers who feel empathic towards victims, helping them to resist colluding and even enabling them to come to the aid of victims without inflaming the situation or endangering themselves or the victim (Rigby & Bagshaw 2006).

Secondary preventive measures entail giving both victims and perpetrators emotional as well as practical support (Hunter et al. 2004). This is particularly necessary for those students who are both victimised *and* instigators of bullying ('bully-victims'), as their aggression is often seen by teachers to justify their victimisation, with the result that they receive low levels of teacher support (Demaray & Malecki 2003a). Emotional support will help victims to feel better, while instrumental support is designed to help them during an incident and to deter future attacks (Demaray & Malecki 2003a).

Interventions form the third layer of action. One disturbing feature of bullying is the perception of 25 to 60 per cent of students that teachers seldom act to protect them (Olweus 1993; Slee 1994a). Pikas (2002) asserts that, notwithstanding the laudable aims of primary and secondary preventive measures, these are expensive in terms of time and resources, sometimes to the point of being impractical. He argues that, instead, the most appropriate way to prevent bullying is to be supremely effective at responding to incidents and thus avoiding a repetition. Taking action will require that you be receptive to students' complaints of bullying, particularly its subtle forms such as nonverbal manipulation (Shute et al. 2002). It will also require a non-punitive response that accepts victims, perpetrators, bully-victims and onlookers alike, while clearly repudiating their behaviour.

At younger ages (below nine years), and for individual rather than gang bullying, simply telling the bully to stop might be effective (Smith et al. 1994). For students aged over nine, various approaches have been reported for dealing with perpetrators. These include Pikas's (2002) method of shared concern employed for gang bullying, Maines and Robinson's no-blame approach (McGrath & Stanley 2006a), restorative responses (Armstrong & Thorsborne 2006) and counselling of victims and their parents (Fuller 2006).

All these approaches share a recognition that, although perpetrators are responsible for their actions and for their effect on victims, the aim is to solve the problem rather than punish the perpetrators. The steps involved in these methods differ slightly but, in essence, they aim to repair relationships by listening to victims and dispassionately conveying their feelings to perpetrators and any colluders, either individually or as a group. This explains that victims are in a bad situation, without accusing perpetrators or asking them to admit guilt. Pikas (2002) also aims to support collaborators so that they do not need to fear retribution or worry that they will become the next victim. Thus empowered and with their empathy aroused, you invite perpetrators to suggest ways in which they could help improve the victims' circumstances and ask for a commitment to these measures. In follow-up meetings, you would check that these were working. Perhaps even less confronting to perpetrators is the solution-focused approach described in Chapter 7 and outlined in Vignette 11.1.

VIGNETTE 11.1 A SOLUTION-FOCUSED APPROACH TO HELP VICTIMS OF BULLYING

Preamble

Interview the victim, starting with non-problem talk, such as what the child would be doing right now if not talking with you. Find out some of the child's interests.

Statement of the problem

Young people will be reluctant to say that they are being bullied, so instead you can bring up the problem by stating that you, another teacher or the child's parent is worried about him or her. You can follow this up with the question 'Are they right to be worried about you?'

Having received assent that the worry is justified, you will need to state that answers to the next three questions will not get anyone into trouble. These questions are:

- 'Who do you find difficult to deal with at the moment?' There is no need to ask what the named students are doing, as this can make the conversation deteriorate into problem-saturated talk.
- 'Who else is around when (named peer) is being difficult?' This allows you to identify bystanders who could be recruited to help.
- 'Who are your friends?' or, for those who are now completely isolated from their peer group, 'Who would you like to be your friend?'

Explain to the victim that you will be recruiting those named to work together to help the child be happier at school.

Garner support

Meet as a group with the children named by the victim, explaining that you have chosen them because you know that they can help to make the victim happier at school. Do not mention bullying or talk about the events, as this could degenerate into accusations of fault and blame. Instead, discuss with them times when they have been unhappy at school and express empathy that it is not easy to be so. Then ask for their suggestions of what can be done to help the focus child. As they raise suggestions, you can compliment those that seem promising but check that they are realistic: 'That's a good idea. Would that be difficult or easy for you to do?' When they volunteer that it would not be difficult, you can compliment them on their kindness. While not asking them to be friends with the focus child or demanding a commitment to carrying out the suggestions, you can end this session with a comment that you think their plan will work to make the victim happier at school.

Review

A week later, meet with the victim to hear what has been better over the past week and ask how he or she managed to make that happen (e.g. responding to or trusting the friendlier overtures of the former bullies). Also contact the child's parents for their feedback about his or her progress.

Next, meet with the support group (of former perpetrators, bystanders and potential or actual friends) and ask what each has done over the previous week to make the focus child happier at school. There is no need to refer back to their original suggestions as it does not matter if they employed those particular strategies, only that they did something to make the situation improve for the victim. Congratulate them personally and as a group for a job well done and ask if they would like to continue for another week.

Conduct one more review and, if no further problems surface, cease the intervention.

Comment

Young (2001) reports that the advantage of this method is that the bullies are not punished, which prevents their retaliating against the victim for disclosing the abuse and ensures that no injustice occurs in instances where the victim is also provocative or a bully at other times. Most parties are relieved not to have to discuss the actual bullying behaviour but focus instead on finding a solution. Once that is achieved, the details of who did what to whom become irrelevant anyway.

Source: Young (2001)

Peer mediation, which trains students to help their peers to negotiate an agreed solution to conflict between them, may be beyond the capabilities of younger children and may be inappropriate for the complex issues posed by bullying. However, it could be suitable during adolescence, when adolescents' imperatives to belong and be popular—which give rise to the problem—can also generate its solution. Peer mediation at this age may be more successful than interventions by teachers, particularly given adolescents' belief that teachers should stay out of their conflicts (James & Owens 2004; Owens et al. 2001; Shute et al. 2002). However, selection, training and supervision of mediators must be handled sensitively, so that mediators are not exploited or undermined when antisocial peers denigrate them for colluding with the 'establishment' (Smith & Daunic 2002).

Taking action will also entail collaborating with parents of both bullies and victims. Parents of bullies need to be told about their child's behaviour, without their child being condemned and without themselves being criticised. To avoid angry parents punishing their children at home, it will be crucial to communicate that this is a school-based problem that the school intends to solve. Solution-focused interventions may be useful if parents of bullies attempt to convince parents of other perpetrators to ostracise victims or their parents (Field & Carroll 2006), if parents of bully-victims overlook their child's culpability in the bullying and claim victim status only, or if parents of victims feel powerless to help their child or may inflame the situation by confronting the bullies or their parents themselves. The strength of the solution-focused approach is that it does not require unanimous agreement about the facts of the bullying, but just an acknowledgment that victims are having a difficult time.

Action will also involve the use of support services, such as school counsellors, outside health professionals or the police. Finally, for intractable bullying, the school must reserve a final option of suspension of bullies. Although isolating perpetrators is a violation of community cohesion, so too is their behaviour, and the physical and psychological health of victims must take precedence in those rare cases where perpetrators have had every chance to cease their harassment but have been unwilling to do so. While there are some legal remedies for victims of bullying—such as provided by anti-stalking legislation or the imposition of apprehended violence orders, violation of which is a criminal offence (Nicholson 2006)—once parents and victims have needed to resort to the criminal courts to protect themselves, the school should have suspended the offenders.

Countering strategies

Given that preventive and interventive methods will never, sadly, eliminate bullying, it will continue to be necessary to enfranchise victims to resist harassment (Fuller 2006). This, then, is the fourth aspect of the PEACE plan (Slee 2001, 2006). As Rigby (2001) affirms, the most successful intervention is to help children to help themselves. As already outlined, social skills training seems unnecessary in most cases, although victims can be apprised of the most effective strategies for handling an incident. In the junior primary years, the most successful strategies can be to enlist the support of a friend; by late primary school, conflict-resolution skills, such as assertiveness in the form of 'brave talk', can be useful in countering bullying (Rigby 1996, 2006b; Sharp & Cowie 1994). An 'invisibility' strategy of avoiding those areas where most bullying occurs can be useful in the interim (Fuller 2006). Subsequently, students need to know how and to whom they can report incidents and to feel confident that their report will be met with empathy (O'Moore & Minton 2004). Solution-focused interventions could highlight these and other resiliency skills that victims already employ.

Evaluation

Once your policy and procedures are in place, you must check whether they are working—that is, helping victims to feel safer. Your measures can then be formalised into a whole-school policy on bullying, which will be part of an overall 'safe school' policy about aggression and discipline in general and be guided by your social justice, pastoral care and protective behaviours policies (Rigby 1996; Roland 1993; Sharp & Thompson 1994). Your bullying policy will have the same components as any of these others, beginning with a definition, then a series of statements proclaiming that (McGrath & Stanley 2006b):

- bullying is an issue for all members of the school community;
- everyone has a right to feel safe;
- all school members are responsible not to take part in bullying;
- all are responsible to report bullying;
- the school is committed to preventing, minimising and responding to bullying.

Conclusion

Perceived caring and connectedness to others at school and within their families are crucial to students' involvement in their learning and attitude to themselves as learners (Phelan et al. 1992). Both teacher and peer support is fundamental to students' liking for school. Enjoying warm relationships with teachers insulates students against the effects of isolation from peers (Wentzel & Asher 1995), attesting to teachers' ongoing value as supports to students throughout the school years. Teachers can both directly and indirectly influence the quality of their interactions with students and of students' relationships with each other. Bullying can activate both preventive measures to enhance the sense of the school as a community and interventions that demonstrate how to solve problems justly.

Discussion questions

1   Think about schools in which you have taught or that you attended as a student. In what ways do they foster in young people, teachers and parents a sense of ownership of and belonging in their school?
2   What measures do you adopt to facilitate group cohesion in your classroom?

3   How could you go about teaching a social skills program to students in the age group in which you specialise? With which social tasks do they have the most difficulty?

4   Which measures does your school use to prevent and respond to bullying? How effective are these?

Suggested further reading

Detailed suggestions about cooperative learning

Johnson, D.W. and Johnson, R.T. 1991 *Learning together and alone* 3rd edn, Allyn & Bacon, Boston, MA

Johnson, D.W., Johnson, R.T. and Holubec, E.J. 1993 *Circles of learning: cooperation in the classroom* 4th edn, Interaction Books, Edina, MN

Practical suggestions for establishing a socially inclusive classroom

McGrath, H. and Noble, T. 1993 *Different kids, same classroom: making mixed ability classes really work* Longman, Melbourne

Sapon-Shevin, M. 1999 *Because we can change the world: a practical guide to building cooperative, inclusive classroom communities* Allyn & Bacon, Boston, MA

Programs and activities for social skills training in schools

Cartledge, G. and Milburn, J.F. (eds) 1995 *Teaching social skills to children and youth: innovative approaches* 3rd edn, Allyn & Bacon, Boston, MA

McGrath, H. 1997 *Dirty tricks: classroom games for teaching social skills* Longman, South Melbourne

McGrath, H. and Francey, S. 1991 *Friendly kids; friendly classrooms* Longman Cheshire, Melbourne

Petersen, L. and Ganoni, A. 1989 *Teacher's manual for training social skills while managing student behaviour* ACER, Melbourne

Early childhood practitioners

Kostelnik, M.J., Whiren, A.P., Soderman, A.K. and Gregory, K. 2006 *Guiding children's social development: theory to practice* 5th edn, Thomson Delmar, New York

School approaches to bullying

McGrath, H. & Noble, T. (eds) 2006 *Bullying solutions: evidence-based approaches to bullying in Australian schools* Pearson Longman, Sydney

O'Moore, M. and Minton, S.J. 2004 *Dealing with bullying in schools: a training manual for teachers, parents and other professionals* Paul Chapman, London

Rigby, K. 1996 *Bullying in schools: and what to do about it* ACER, Melbourne

——2003 *Stop the bullying: a handbook for schools* 2nd edn, ACER, Melbourne

Slee, P.T. 2001 *The PEACE pack: a program for reducing bullying in our schools* 3rd edn, Flinders University, Adelaide, SA

Sharp, S. and Smith, P.K. (eds) 1994 *Tackling bullying in your school: a practical handbook for teachers* Routledge, London

Early childhood teachers

Sprung, B., Froschl, M. and Hinitz, B. 2005 *The anti-bullying and teasing book for preschool classrooms* Gryphon House, Beltsville, MD

Websites

National Coalition Against Bullying: <www.ncab.org.au>

Child and Adolescent Psychological and Educational Resources (CAPER): <www.caper.com.au>

Ken Rigby's site: <www.education.unisa.edu.an/bullying>

12 FACILITATING LEARNING:
COMPETENCE AND CONFIDENCE

When tasks are meaningful to students, when students have authority over their learning, and when mistakes are considered as part of the learning process, [this] would encourage students to display more on-task behaviours and would arouse less anxiety, and therefore less disruptive behaviour.

Kaplan et al. (2002: 195)

KEY POINTS

- Students will be motivated to participate in learning and to behave considerately when they anticipate that they can be successful at school.
- When they become competent at worthwhile skills their self-esteem will rise which, in turn, will make them more willing to take intellectual risks in future.
- Feedback that informs them about their achievements is more likely to encourage continued effort than are judgments about them or their work products.

Introduction

Although learning is the core business of schools and therefore this chapter might seem to be better placed as the first in Part Two of this text, research shows that students' sense of safety, of autonomy and of support from teachers, peers and the school at large have to be in place first before they will be motivated academically and behaviourally (Marchant et al. 2001; Rutter 1983).

In the first section of this chapter I shall summarise some core classroom management skills that, although being your bread-and-butter competencies as a teacher, deserve summarising to highlight their significance, not only in fostering learning, but also in avoiding disruptiveness. These fundamental skills are widely endorsed and uncontroversial, so will be covered only briefly. In the second part of the chapter, I will focus on the effects of students' goal orientations and intrinsic versus extrinsic motivation on student engagement and behaviour.

Structured teaching

Egalitarian teaching combines low levels of control with clear structure, so that students can autonomously observe routines that allow them to devote maximal time to learning. A conducive classroom climate is supported by teaching that is efficient and has a clear purpose, with appropriately structured lessons that engage students' interest and convey appropriately high expectations of students' academic performance (Rutter & Maughan 2002).

Physical setting

The environment refers to the physical structure of a setting, its organisation and its social climate. Within an ecological perspective, the environment is seen as the 'third teacher'—with the first being the students themselves and the second being their social relationships with teachers and peers (Fraser & Gestwicki 2002).

As Fraser and Gestwicki (2002: 100) observe 'Space does indeed speak'. The first message that school buildings can convey to those who use them is that they and the activities that go on there are valued. To that end, the school's facilities must be well maintained and aesthetically pleasing. Well-maintained buildings also attract less vandalism (Rutter 1983). Second, the space communicates a welcome to children, families, educators and visitors and signals their ownership of the space by reflecting their personal interests and requirements (Fraser & Gestwicki 2002). Third, physical arrangements convey to students and teachers what they can do in that space. Therefore, the structure should help students to feel safe, allow them to exercise choice, invite investigation, permit them to use ideas creatively and access materials readily, thus giving them confidence that they can have control of their learning (Fraser & Gestwicki 2002; Robson 1996; Smidt 1998). Fourth, the physical layout allows the program to flow smoothly—such as by keeping thoroughfares free of congestion, minimising distractions for students who find it difficult to concentrate, and allowing teachers to monitor and thus respond to students who need support.

Finally, the organisation of the school and individual classrooms is an unspoken comment about the power relations existing there, depending on whether teachers dictate the arrangement of the setting or whether students are engaged in making such decisions as well (Manke 1997). Within a classroom, one significant structural decision is about desk configurations. The preferred desk arrangement will depend on whether students will be working alone or cooperatively. When desks are arranged in rows, the centre and front rows receive most communication from the teacher, with students on the periphery sometimes feeling left out and receiving mostly public communication (Doyle 1986; Good & Brophy 2005). Therefore, if using this seating arrangement, disengaged or distractable students and those with hearing or vision difficulties might be best located in the middle and front rows.

Efficient procedures

The second element of effective teaching is enacting procedures to prevent disruptive behaviour that can arise from unnecessary delays and confusion for students about what they should be doing. The aim of these procedures is not to enforce student compliance, but to make it easier for students *to learn* (Kohn 1996a).

- Have an efficient system for handing out assignments and other materials.
- There must be a procedure for students to get started without delay. For example, in high schools, rather than giving an instruction to the whole group once everyone has assembled and thus delaying those who arrive to class promptly, you might hand out instruction cards to individual students as they become seated (Cangelosi 2004).
- Another essential procedure is how students are to signal that they need help. To avoid their hand being raised for extended periods or their becoming disruptive because they cannot proceed, you might institute a system such as having them place a card on a corner of their desk and working on something else until you can get to them.

- Have a system for giving students efficient help so that you do not delay getting to others who are also uncertain. Jones and colleagues (2000) advise that you give help by acknowledging what the student has achieved thus far, then follow with a brief prompt about what to do next. Making sure that you do not 'over-service' students' needs in this way conveys confidence in their ability to proceed.
- Plan how those who finish individual tasks early can be productively engaged. It is unwise simply to give them more work to do, as they will learn to work slowly to avoid having to do extra.

Instruction

The third element of appropriately structured classrooms and lessons is clarity of instructions. To improve children's engagement and ability to follow reasonable directives it will be important to give calm, concise and precise instructions that contain a verb that specifies what you want students to do (rather than what they are not to do) (Matheson & Shriver 2005). It can also be important to use visual cues for those students who learn better by visualising concepts than by listening to sequential information (Silverman 2002). Before giving an instruction for visual learners, it will pay to gain eye contact (where culturally appropriate) or use a predetermined cue to signal for them to change out of picturing mode into listening made (e.g. pointing to your own ears) and then use visual language. For example, rather than saying 'Get your maths book from your locker', try 'Picture your locker. Can you see where your maths book is at the moment? Okay, get it'.

Having engaged students through well-structured lessons and clear instructions, you will need to maintain their involvement with an appropriate pace. Lessons can lose momentum when you repeat instructions or information that students have already understood, or dwell on behaviour (process) rather than content. Students' nonverbal cues will give you information about when you need to pick up the pace or are proceeding too quickly. Short breaks can help students to remain on-task during longer lessons.

You will need to supply enough activity for students to be able to operate quietly when necessary. Science has verified what folklore has long upheld—namely, that boys typically need to be more physically active than girls. While the exact biological causes of this difference are not yet known, it is part and parcel of boyhood (Gilbert 2000). Rather than interpreting this as boys' domination of the space, instead we should affirm and accommodate their need. Physical activity gives students confidence in their ability to control their bodies, exercises both the body and the brain (thus enhancing academic success), teaches children that they can meet physical challenges and, as long as it does not become another avenue for serious competition, offers an outlet for stress.

Finally, to maintain students' interest, your teaching will need variety. You can vary the content, presentation method, materials used, study group configuration and instructional approach (direct instruction, individual work or group work).

Relevant curriculum

The above structural measures are aimed at making it *easier* for students to engage; relevance is aimed at making them more *willing* both to engage and sustain their involvement. With top-down curricula, the teacher decides what counts as knowledge and thus what is worth learning (Manke 1997). Some see this as inevitable; others see it as an oppression, particularly of those who are not part of the dominant culture (Manke 1997). Egalitarian theory sees it as impossible, because students can resist learning by disengaging from work that does not interest them, 'losing' the resources (such as pens and books) that they need for tasks, refusing to complete assignments, disrupting lessons, or feigning incomprehension—all of which will block the transmission of the teacher's agenda. Thus, in line with humanist and cognitive theories, we need to keep in mind that students will be more motivated to learn—and correspondingly less motivated to disrupt in class—when they value what they are being asked to do; that is, when it is relevant to their lives. Humanism tells us that being off-task is not a behavioural issue but an educational one that calls for an educational response, one that draws on motivation theory for ways to enhance students' engagement.

Many of the recommendations for enhancing task relevance posed by humanism (see Chapter 6) have been supported by educational research. For example, research has verified the importance of detailing the rationale for tasks (Assor et al. 2002) and has confirmed that, for younger children in particular, teachers should heighten the appeal (or 'fun') inherent in tasks by embellishing them with fantasy (Cordova & Lepper 1996; Parker & Lepper 1992). Research has also verified the need to match task difficulty to students' abilities. This is because tasks that are too difficult or too easy will be seen by students as irrelevant and thus will reduce both engagement and completion rates (Umbreit et al. 2004). While some challenge is necessary to excite learning, students who experience less pressure to excel report enjoying tasks more and experiencing less tension while completing them (Deci et al. 1994). When students believe that the task demands exceed their resources, they can experience anxiety (fear of failure), worrisome thoughts and physical symptoms of stress (Silverman et al. 1995). This stress syndrome will reduce their motivation to invest energy in the tasks, compromise their learning and show itself in processes such as procrastination (avoidance) and attempts to escape task demands (Chan 1996; DiCintio & Gee 1999; Milgram & Toubiana 1999; Vallerand et al. 1994).

Foster a mastery orientation

Students with *mastery* goals apply themselves to tasks in order to gain skill and competence; in contrast, those who seek to excel compared with others are said to have *performance* goals. The last category can be further divided into those who approach tasks in order to demonstrate their superiority, versus those who avoid tasks so that their relative inferiority is not exhibited. Although many individuals have a mixture of both mastery and performance orientations, students who emphasise comparative performance tend to be more disruptive in class (Kaplan et al. 2002; Sylva 1994). Both mastery and performance-approach orientations are associated with high engagement and achievement (Dweck & Leggett 1988; Kavussanu & Harnisch 2000; Pintrich 2000). However, this holds only under two conditions. The first is that the students must have what is known as an incremental belief about ability (Dweck & Leggett 1988; Kavussanu & Harnisch 2000), which perceives ability as an internal, specific, controllable and temporary capacity that increases with effort. Ability is thus seen to be malleable (Sylva 1994). In contrast, an entity view sees ability as an internal, general, uncontrollable and stable trait—one can be endowed with more or less ability, which cannot be changed. Under the entity perspective, the need to put in effort signals a lack of ability (Tollefson 2000; Weiner 2000). However, it is clear that 'Effort will surpass talent when talent makes no effort' (Porter 2005: 220).

Second, performance and mastery orientations produce similar engagement and self-esteem levels only as long as performance-oriented students experience themselves as being more successful than others. This is a risky stance, because it is obviously impossible for everyone to be above average in their performances. When these students perceive themselves as failing (which is a subjective impression based on a comparison with others), their engagement, effort and performance decline along with a corresponding increase in negative affect (Dweck & Leggett 1988; Sylva 1994). Thus, as depicted in Figure 12.1, those who are below average in abilities are likely to attempt to preserve their dignity by giving up, avoiding challenge and becoming off-task, which is an avoidance orientation (Covington & Müeller 2001). Meanwhile, in what has been termed the 'big-fish-little-pond effect', able students with a performance orientation—who seek to *be* the best rather than to *do* their best—will suffer reduced self-esteem when placed within a very able peer group or school, as in that setting they will not excel compared with others (Chan 1988; Coleman & Fults 1982; Craven & Marsh 1997; Gross 1997; Hoge & Renzulli 1993; Marsh & Craven 1998; Marsh et al. 1995; Moon et

FIGURE 12.1   Goal orientations of students

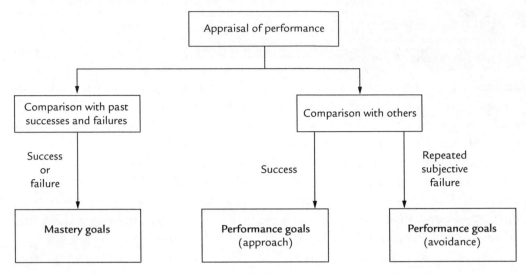

al. 2002; Olszewski et al. 1987; Rutter & Maughan 2002; Schneider et al. 1989; Wright & Leroux 1997). No such effect of relative failure is found for mastery-oriented students. As depicted in Figure 12.1, students with a mastery orientation will interpret both success and failure as a reflection of their strategy use and, when failing, will change strategy.

Students' personal orientation is complemented by the orientation of their teachers. Kaplan and colleagues (2002) found that when teachers emphasise demonstrating high ability and conformity to teachers' goals, the level of disruptive behaviour is higher than in classrooms where teachers emphasise the value of learning, understanding and improving over past performances. Mastery-oriented teachers foster more active engagement of students, tolerate their higher activity levels (Kaplan et al. 2002) and minimise competitiveness between students, the benefits of which were described in Chapter 11.

Finally, the peer group also fosters individuals' goal orientations. Highly achieving students pursue academic goals, whereas low-achieving students are less willing to conform to the school's achievement norms (Wentzel & Wigfield 1998). This is a strong justification for universal prevention efforts aimed at adjusting the achievement norms for a whole class, as this will be more effective than a targeted (secondary) intervention aimed at changing the individual goals of lower achievers within a social context that continues to pressure for high achievement.

Taking these two elements together and drawing on cognitive theory (see Chapter 4), you will need to guide your students to compare their progress to their own past achievements, rather than to their peers'. Second, you will need to teach them to attribute outcomes to the strategy they have employed, rather than to an uncontrollable trait such as inherent ability. As will be discussed shortly, the form of your feedback can help students to be less preoccupied with comparing their performances with their peers' and instead to use their own progress as the index of their achievement (Wentzel & Wigfield 1998). This will directly influence their engagement and behaviour in the classroom and contribute indirectly to a more robust self-esteem (Bong & Skaalvik 2003).

Maintain high expectations of students

It is crucial that you encourage students to take risks by setting goals for themselves that extend their skills. This will be enabled by your own and by the school's ethos of high expectations for students. Low expectations of students' ability can become a self-fulfilling prophecy—that is, can result in your acting in ways that cause low abilities to be displayed (Good & Brophy 2005). A second expectation is called a sustaining expectation, whereby teachers anticipate that students' past behavioural patterns will persist (Good & Brophy 2005). In other words, students' reputations endure. Both self-fulfilling and sustained expectations of students' low performances can result in teachers assigning less challenging tasks to students whom they believe to be of low ability, calling on less able students infrequently, giving them only brief periods in which to formulate their answers and being less positive in their feedback to them. In contrast, positive self-fulfilling prophecies are powerful at stimulating improved performances from lower-ability students in particular (Good & Brophy 2005). Naturally, teacher expectations cannot deny the reality of students' skill levels, but can communicate through authentic feedback that all can make progress. This feedback should not patronise low achievers with positive feedback about ordinary performances, but instead give specific information that will explain what they can do to increase their skills.

Eliminate compulsory homework

A penetrating review of research into the benefits of homework found that the minimal gains it produces in students' achievement levels are found only in high school (Trautwein & Köller 2003). Even the modest demonstrated benefits at that age could be due to the fact that the most able students are in the most academic classes, where most homework is assigned and teaching is typically of a higher quality (Gamoran & Berends

1987), making it impossible to separate the effects of homework from these other teaching practices.

The coercion required to enforce homework completion and the fact that young people resent its intrusion into their private lives (Mayall 2002), as do many parents, plus the humanists' criticisms of its contribution to lower-quality learning and student stress, all lead to the conclusion that the imposition of compulsory homework should cease. By the last years of high school, students will be capable of judging what extra work they need to do to pass their final examinations. The imposition of homework on them in the meantime makes it no more likely that they will do so, while eating into relaxation time and time for extracurricular activities that act as a buffer against stress.

Offer remedial education

Alienation from school is more a function of low school achievement than of economic disadvantage (Reinke & Herman 2002). Working memory deficits have been implicated in low academic achievement (Gathercole & Pickering 2000) and ADHD (Tannock 2004), while as many as two-thirds of students who have been excluded from school for behavioural difficulties have been later discovered to have unrecognised language difficulties, particularly impaired auditory working memory (Ripley & Yuill 2005). Language impairments interfere with students' abilities to understand what is being asked of them, create frustration in communicating with others, block the development of supportive peer relationships and, perhaps even more importantly with respect to their behaviour, impair children's self-talk or inner speech, which can help them to guide and regulate their own behaviour and manage their emotions. This can result, among other things, in impulsive and often aggressive behaviour, poor frustration tolerance, poor peer interaction skills and impaired task orientation (McCabe 2005), which together often become labelled as a behavioural difficulty while the underlying language deficit is overlooked.

Sequential processing deficits may account for some instances where young people with diagnosed emotional or behavioural difficulties also display below-average performance in spelling and mathematics (Reid et al. 2004). Difficulties with processing sequential information could contribute to their low academic skills, while also being implicated in their impulsive and reckless behaviour that arises from impaired means–end thinking, whereby they fail to anticipate the outcome of their actions.

To many students with such learning or attention difficulties the curriculum seems inaccessible and irrelevant, and thus does not motivate them to engage with it. Their resulting academic failure leads to alienation from school (McEvoy & Welker 2000). This sense of futility is often displayed as absenteeism and task evasion through antisocial or disruptive behaviour. When schools problematise these behaviours rather than remediate the learning difficulty, a cycle of failure and coercive discipline is often perpetuated (Davies 2005; Kerr & Nelson 2006). As we saw in Chapter 10, authoritarian discipline is likely to exacerbate rather than repair their disaffection with school (Rumberger 1995). Instead, rather than a disciplinary response, schools need to fashion an educational intervention that entails negotiating with students what they need to learn, honours how they learn best, and supports them to take command of their own learning (Davies 2005).

Egalitarian discipline

Structured teaching will make it *easier* for students to learn, while egalitarian discipline will make them more *willing* to do so. The previous three chapters gave recommendations to use egalitarian discipline on the grounds that it safeguards students, fosters student autonomy and enhances social relationships within the classroom. The fourth and final reason is that it enhances student learning. With high autonomy support, young people engage with tasks more, perform better, are more creative and, as we shall see shortly, feel better about themselves as learners (Grolnick 2003; Grolnick et al. 2002; Kamins & Dweck 1999). When, in contrast, children are induced to learn through teacher control—even rewards—learning becomes only a means to an end. The reduced focus on the task itself results in less acquisition and reduced retention of knowledge, particularly on more complex tasks (Grolnick 2003).

Give authentic feedback

A core component of egalitarian disciplinary practice is feedback to students about their accomplishments and behaviour. Praise to children comprises two distinct elements, each with opposing effects. The first element is a judgment of students, their work product or the processes that they used to achieve it. An extensive body of research has detailed the following negative outcomes of such evaluations.

- Person praise lowers students' subsequent evaluations of themselves and their work products and leads to more negative affect and helpless reactions to errors (Kamins & Dweck 1999). Children become less persistent and more self-critical in the face of setbacks.
- Praise for high ability promotes in children a stable rather than an incremental view of ability, producing even in those who are typically successful a performance-

avoidance orientation whereby they choose safe tasks and avoid challenge, do not persist and experience less task enjoyment and declining performance (Mueller & Dweck 1998).

- Meanwhile, those students who seldom earn rewards also develop a performance-avoidance goal orientation, which will similarly disadvantage them academically and emotionally while increasing their behavioural disruptiveness.
- The delivery of praise or other rewards for achievement reduces children's intrinsic motivation for the task (Deci et al. 1991, 1999a, 2001a; Ryan & Deci 1996, 2000). This has consistently been found to be particularly true for children, for females, within controlling interpersonal climates, and for those whose relatively poorer performances result in their not earning an equivalent reward to their peers (Deci et al. 1999a, 2001a; Ryan & Deci 1996, 2000).

The second element of feedback is specific information that helps students to recognise what they have achieved and what their next goal may be. In contrast to the above effects, such *informative* feedback fosters considerate behaviour, promotes a healthy self-esteem and sets a positive tone for the classroom. It helps students feel more competent and enhances their intrinsic motivation (Grolnick 2003), promotes a mastery rather than a performance goal orientation and fosters an incremental rather than an entity view of ability (Möller 2005).

The differential outcomes of judgmental versus informative feedback probably arise for two reasons. To explain the first reason, I shall divert for a moment into a brief description of self-esteem. Speaking generally, it is an amalgam of comparisons across various skill domains between how we see ourselves (our self-concept) and how we would like to be (our ideals). This is depicted in Figure 12.2. Children's appraisal (or self-concept) of their academic abilities is largely a *result* of their past successes or failures (Bouffard et al. 2003; Chapman et al. 1990; McCoach & Siegle 2003; Muijs 1997). If these appraisals are unduly pessimistic—if children deprecate their own skills and thus their self-concept is impoverished—or if their expectations of themselves are unrealistically high, their self-esteem will be lowered.

Judgmental praise generates both inaccurate self-appraisals and unduly demanding ideals. It implies to children that their self-worth is contingent on maintaining their achievements and desired behaviours. In short, praise of the person imposes an obligation to continue to act in a praiseworthy manner (Farson 1963, in Grolnick 2003). Doubting their ability to attain this ideal, their cognitions, affect and behaviour all mimic helplessness, with consequent reduction in their engagement and work quality (Kamins & Dweck 1999).

FIGURE 12.2   Self-esteem as the overlap between self-concept and ideal self

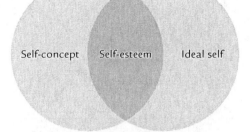

A second explanation attributes the above negative outcomes to the controlling nature of praise. When used to induce students to repeat a behaviour of which we approve, it detracts from students' sense of autonomy. Many writers believe that this loss of autonomy is directly responsible for students' subsequent reduced engagement, arguing that autonomy is essential to human motivation (Deci et al. 1991, 1999a, 2001a; Ryan & Deci 1996, 2000). This is verified by the considerable body of research on the effects of egalitarian parenting reviewed in Chapter 8.

In sum, these research findings tell us that praise and other rewards can have detrimental effects on students' attitude to learning and to themselves as learners. Observations in classrooms add another argument against the use of praise—namely, that it is typically administered so inaccurately that it cannot function as a reinforcer (in applied behaviour analysis terms) for appropriate academic or behavioural skills (Brophy 1981). Box 12.1 lists many common uses and misuses of praise within classrooms. Given that malpractice is so widespread, it is unlikely that so many teachers are incompetent rewarders of students' performances, but that classroom settings make it difficult to administer praise appropriately.

BOX 12.1 COMMON USES (AND MISUSES) OF PRAISE IN CLASSROOMS
- Praise may be delivered as *recognition* for academic achievement. However, it is often given to low-ability students even when their work is incorrect—in which case, if it functioned as a reinforcer, it would be reinforcing poor-quality performances.
- Praise is often intended as a *reinforcement* for desirable behaviour. However, for this purpose it is a weak, or even ineffectual, reinforcer as it is typically delivered noncontingently or indiscriminately, may be accompanied by

negative nonverbal behaviour that contradicts the positive verbal message, and occurs too rarely to be effective. It is particularly ineffective beyond the junior primary years, when it is usually neutral or negative in its effects on student achievement and behaviour.

· Sometimes praise is a *spontaneous expression of surprise or admiration*. This is probably the most reinforcing for students, although your surprise could communicate that you believe that a praised student is ordinarily less competent.

· Praise may be used in an attempt to *offset earlier criticism*. To the extent that this has undertones of 'I told you that you could do better', praise may actually be punitive.

· Praise is sometimes used to *induce onlookers to emulate a praised student*. However, model students are seldom popular—in which case, others will not choose to emulate them and may even reject them further. Praise delivered in public in this way is also more likely to be detrimental for recipients, particularly for adolescents and those whose cultures shun having individuals singled out for accolade.

· Praise can be used *to set a positive tone*, so that you do not feel that you are always nagging and issuing commands.

· Praise in the form of compliments is sometimes used to *make contact with alienated students*.

· Sometimes praise is given as a form of *student-elicited stroking*. Some students will approach you for praise, but knowing that they 'pulled' it may make it less potent for them.

· Praise may be used as a *transition ritual* in which you comment positively on students' work as a way to indicate that they have finished that task and can now move on to the next. Students are unlikely to attribute this sort of praise to anything special that they have done and so it will have little effect on their perceptions of themselves as learners.

· Finally, some praise is a *consolation prize* for the least able or most discouraged students. However, in a paradoxical effect, effusive praise for ordinary performances humiliates recipients and lowers their self-esteem, as it communicates that you believe that they can do no better (Möller 2005).

Sources: Brophy 1981; Good & Brophy 2005; Schmuck & Schmuck 2001

The shared conclusion of the neo-Adlerians, humanists and many educational researchers is that, while it is essential that students receive feedback about their performances, specific informative feedback will be at least as beneficial as praise and other rewards, without any of the risks posed by the delivery of judgments (Brophy 1981; Dev 1997; Kohn 1996b; Porter 2003, 2006). Naturally, behaviourists (e.g. Cameron & Pierce 1994, 1996; Eisenberger & Armeli 1997) disagree with this summation, largely because they interpret abandoning evaluative feedback as meaning the elimination of *all* feedback. They claim that when students are discouraged, are failing or find tasks uninteresting, difficult, tedious or complex, they will need extrinsic reinforcers to motivate them to engage and persist, after which their success will cause intrinsic satisfaction to take over (Cameron 2001). The competing view merely reiterates that informative feedback would be equally effective in such circumstances. Behaviourists also contest the claim that rewards violate children's autonomy, citing that students can choose by their behaviour to earn a reward or not (Eisenberger et al. 1999). A rebuttal by the original researchers is that knowing how to get the environment to reward you represents (in the terms introduced in Chapter 4) an internal *locus* of control but, given that outsiders rather than yourself *cause* reinforcement regimes to be implemented, this is not an internal locus of causality (i.e. self-efficacy) as conceptualised by cognitive theory (Deci et al. 1999b).

Thus, the conclusion remains: children need specific feedback that describes but does not judge what they have achieved. Attributional theory (as described in Chapter 4) reminds us that informative feedback will be particularly beneficial when students are given specific information about their strategy use or about their progress over time (rather than compared with peers'). Some strategies that can be highlighted through feedback include three sets of thinking skills and a cluster of emotional dispositions (Gagné 2003; Lambert & Clyde 2000; Perkins et al. 1993; Ritchhart 2001).

- The *creative* thinking processes include imaginativeness, exploration, being open to new ideas and experiences, curious and adventurous with tolerance for ambiguity, being playful and seeking alternatives.
- *Reflective* skills include the use of metacognitive strategies of self-awareness, self-control (including impulse control) and self-monitoring to regulate one's own thinking.
- *Critical* thinking skills include planning and being strategic, investigative, inquiring, intellectually rigorous and logical (seeking truth, reason and evidence).
- *Emotional* dispositions include the motivational cluster, such as interest, confidence and enthusiasm for learning, and the goal-directed behaviours, which include engagement, persistence, patience, independence, cooperativeness and delay of gratification.

A second form of feedback can be to start, first, with students' own assessments. This can be as basic as asking them what they think of what they have done, to having them allocate a grade to their own work (when grading is unavoidable). This not only gives information that will enlarge their self-concept, but noticing their accomplishments gives them practice at monitoring their own behaviour as well—which, as posited by cognitivists, is a core component of self-discipline.

Grades

Grades have both personal and social effects within a classroom, affecting (as do other forms of rewards) the intrinsic motivation, goal orientation and academic engagement of both individuals and the group as a whole (Wentzel & Wigfield 1998). Giving high grades and awards at a class or school level to the most able students makes ability more salient than effort, increases competitiveness between students (as normative grading means that only the top quartile will achieve high grades) and runs the risks of discouraging those who know that they will never measure up, causing them to develop a performance-avoidant goal orientation (Covington & Müeller 2001; Wentzel & Wigfield 1998). Individual students' self-worth comes to rely on their attainment of high grades, but as these are scarce in competitive settings their self-esteem is at risk (Covington & Müeller 2001). Adding to these research findings are the humanists' criticisms of teacher-imposed grades. For these reasons and others, the humanists advise that grades should be abandoned or, if imposed on you, that they should be awarded by the students in negotiation with you. Any such grades should not be relative to others in the class but reflect the personal progress of each individual student. This will foster a mastery orientation. It will, however, need to be explained to the students themselves (lest they still compare grades with each other) and to parents so that, when children have learning difficulties but are still earning good grades, parents do not misconstrue this as meaning that their child is achieving at age level.

Conclusion

The need to feel competent is the last of the triumvirate of emotional needs examined in this section. Like its companion requirements for autonomy and relatedness, it is promoted by egalitarian teaching and discipline that provide structured support for students' learning while upholding their need to be self-directive. In turn, students' improved self-reliance will meet their personal needs, while at the same time enhancing their achievement and lessening the necessity for adult surveillance of their behaviour.

Discussion questions

1 In your view, what is the link between students' competence, their self-esteem, their academic motivation and their behaviour at school?
2 Do you agree that informative and evaluative feedback would be equally successful with the students whom you teach? Is there an argument for the retention of praise and other rewards within classrooms and schools?

Suggested further reading

Cangelosi, J.S. 2004 *Classroom management strategies: gaining and maintaining students' cooperation* 5th edn, Wiley, New York

Charles, C.M. and Senter, G.W. 2005 *Elementary classroom management* 4th edn, Pearson Allyn & Bacon, Boston MA

Good, T.L. and Brophy, J.E. 2005 *Looking in classrooms* 9th edn, Longman, New York

Jones, V.F. and Jones, L.S. 2004 *Comprehensive classroom management: creating communities of support and solving problems* 7th edn, Pearson Allyn & Bacon, Boston, MA

Early childhood

Arthur, L., Beecher, B., Death, E., Dockett, S. and Farmer, S. 2005 *Programming and planning in early childhood settings* 3rd edn, Thomson, Melbourne

MacNaughton, G. and Williams, G. 1998 *Techniques for teaching young children: choices in theory and practice* Longman, Sydney

Part 3 | BEYOND THE CLASSROOM

At this point in your personal and professional life, you have solved many problems and have developed numerous skills. You have a personal and professional style that provides you with a useful foundation for finding solutions to chronic problems... We encourage you to do a capacity analysis of yourself, your classroom, your school, and the community your school serves and... amplify the knowledge and skills that are already available to you.

Molnar & Lindquist (1989: 164–5)

As Seeley (1985, in Christenson 2004) points out, educational outcomes (student learning) are not produced by schools, but by students. In order to learn, young people need the help and support of parents, schools and peers. These three influences will be more useful when they are coordinated. Thus, teaching involves more than working with students within the four walls of your classroom. Going it alone in the face of difficulties would trap you in an impossible situation of making you accountable for everything that your students do, while lacking adequate resources to solve problems.

A constructivist approach to education that honours the skills of students also implies that you do not have to possess the solutions to all problems. Particularly when problems arise, you need to be able to draw on the resources of those around you, including your parent group, colleagues, and students themselves. Your group of consultants thus becomes anyone affected by a problem or with expertise to contribute to its solution.

As is the case with egalitarian teaching, collaboration with parents and colleagues entails sharing power with them. The egalitarian stance of teacher-as-facilitator means that this is no threat to your status, however, as your standing is earned through your expertise, not your power. And your expertise—your effectiveness—can only be enhanced by drawing on the resources of those who possess skills that can complement your own.

To that end, the final chapter of this section and book details a process for enshrining in policy both actual disciplinary measures and the expectation that teachers will be able to draw on support from across the school community to assist them in resolving school-based behavioural difficulties.

13 COLLABORATING WITH PARENTS AND OTHER EXPERTS TO RESOLVE SCHOOL-BASED DIFFICULTIES

When a teacher talks to parents about their children, he [or she] inevitably intrudes on family dreams . . . What the teacher says about the child touches on deep feelings and hidden fantasies. A concerned teacher is aware of the impact of his [or her] words. He [or she] consciously avoids comments that may casually kill dreams.

Ginott (1972: 277–8)

KEY POINTS

- Collaboration with parents and other professionals is more a state of mind than yet another additional task to add to your many others.
- The goal of collaboration is to enfranchise parents to act in their children's interests, to enable you to meet their needs at school and to empower students to contribute to problem solving.
- The solution-focused approach introduced in Chapter 7 informs this chapter. It acknowledges that parents have skills and knowledge to contribute to their children's education in general and to resolving their school-based behavioural difficulties.

Introduction

When the term *parent* is used in this chapter, it is meant to encompass any caregivers who are significant to young people in schools, regardless of whether these adults are the children's actual parents. In many families, grandparents or other extended family members have a crucial role either as an elder or as a major or supplementary care provider for a child.

Students' school adjustment relies, at least in part, on the practical and emotional resources made available to them over the years from home, school and the wider community (Christenson 2004). Parents' educational aspirations for their children and the educational involvement of both mothers and fathers are linked to their children's and adolescents' improved attitudes to school and better academic outcomes and emotional adjustment (Demaray & Malecki 2002; Demaray et al. 2005; Flouri et al. 2002; Gonzalez-DeHass et al. 2005; Marcon 1999; Miedel & Reynolds 1999; Paulson 1994). These effects could be due to increases in students' perceived control and competence, the sense that parents value both them and their schooling, or the internalisation of parents' values about effort and education (Gonzalez-DeHass et al. 2005; Marchant et al. 2001). However, parents' aspirations and involvement may not *cause* improved academic outcomes for their sons and daughters, as their involvement is likely just one of many effective parenting practices that they employ. Nevertheless, it is clear that, in order to optimise young people's performance at school, families and parents cannot work in isolation; parents need schools and educators need parents (Christenson 2004).

Relationships between parents and schools

Schools and families share the common task of educating young people (Adams & Christenson 2000). However, relationships between teachers and parents are often ones of concealed power, with educators having power by virtue of their expertise, being part of the system and, in the case of children with disabilities or behavioural difficulties, the ones who confer diagnoses (Fylling & Sandvin 1999). Meanwhile, the stigma of having a troublesome child detracts from parents' power and makes it difficult for them to garner support from the wider parent body for fear of being socially devalued in the process (Fylling & Sandvin 1999). Within this frame of reference, parents are often regarded as the *source of children's problems*, particularly when their family is disadvantaged socially or has a structure other than the idealised nuclear family (Fylling & Sandvin 1999). Sometimes this view is softened into a conceptualisation of parents as clients, which regards them as joint victims with their child. This tends to regard parents as somewhat fragile and in need of 'empowerment', when in reality you cannot give people skills that they are incapable of performing; all they need is enfranchisement to use the skills that they already have (Murphy 2006).

Another view sees parents within schools as *passive recipients* of advice. Early in their professionalisation, teachers were considered to have expertise that exceeded parents' (rather than expertise that *differs from* or *complements* parents') and parents did not question their judgment.

A more active role for parents entails acting as volunteers on nominal activities such as canteen work or fundraisers or as classroom assistants. In special education, it translates into parents delivering remedial activities to their children at home. This *associative* relationship between parents and educators is more reciprocal than a one-way flow of information from the school to home, although parents' roles tend to be defined mainly by educators who perform assessments and determine the child's priorities and program, with minimal input or decision making by parents (Fylling & Sandvin 1999).

In regular education, parents' contribution is often termed 'involvement', which can entail valuing, mentoring, helping and doing (Scott-Jones 1995). The 'doing' can take five forms: participation in school activities; providing intellectually stimulating activities that assist children's academic functioning; being personally or emotionally involved by keeping abreast of what is happening for their child at school; collaborating to make educational decisions concerning their children; and contributing to the development of school policies (Grolnick et al. 1997; Raffaele & Knoff 1999). This more active role has been found to benefit children, unless the parents are intrusive or controlling—in which case, the children's school grades, motivation and attitude to school deteriorate (Ginsberg & Bronstein 1993; Gottfried et al. 1994; Parker et al. 1999).

Nevertheless, it is clear that a partnership with parents encompasses more than active parental involvement. True collaboration is a process of direct and voluntary interaction between parties of equal status engaged in shared decision making towards a common goal (Friend & Cook 2003). It entails both equal status and parity, which refers to a valuing and blending of each partner's ideas and expertise (Christenson 2004). Parents' participation at this level does not necessarily mean day-to-day involvement in a school, because many parents will be unavailable for this. Instead, collaboration is a philosophical stance of openness to parents that implies a shared responsibility for the education of their children.

However, it can sometimes be tinged with the sense that schools are 'giving' parents equality, rather than that equality is their entitlement (Roffey 2002). Thus, this chapter proceeds one step beyond reciprocity in its recognition that parents are the experts in their children's and family's needs and have experience at resolving their issues. Parents employ you for your expertise as an educator, much as they might employ a doctor for advice on medical matters. They pay your salary by way of private school fees or taxes. Therefore, children's education is to be steered by their parents, rather than directed by teachers. Although this stance may feel as though your authority is threatened, from an egalitarian point of view your authority comes from your expertise rather than your power.

Impediments to collaboration

A wide variety of factors affect parents' participation in their son or daughter's school. The most crucial of these is parents' perceptions of the school's receptivity to them (Overstreet et al. 2005). Whereas early childhood education explicitly encourages collaboration, parents' contact with teachers declines progressively from the first year of school (Adams & Christenson 2000; Rimm-Kaufman & Pianta 1999). This will be partly because older children are more reliable informants about the happenings at school and because parents are attempting to give their older sons and daughters increasing autonomy. However, it also reflects diminishing invitations by the school. In one study, 60 per cent of parents reported that their child's school had not requested from them information about their child, 65 per cent reported that they had not been given information about their child's progress at school and 70 per cent had not been invited to volunteer at school (Spera 2005). From teachers' perspectives, this can be due to the lack of resources in schools for collaboration and to diminishing everyday contacts with parents (Rimm-Kaufman & Pianta 1999). By the middle years of high school, a purely practical problem is the sheer number of students, and thus parents, with whom teachers must form relationships, while parents must develop trust in many teachers (Adams & Christenson 2000). This almost inevitably results in a lessened focus on parent–teacher interactions and, in turn, less support of students themselves (Cattley 2004).

Even when schools overcome these impediments, inviting parental involvement will not guarantee that parents will attend. A common perception by teachers is that those parents whom you most want to reach are the ones who absent themselves from school meetings. Many parent, child and school-based factors operate to block parents' ability to take up the school's invitations to become involved. Parent factors include parents' dread of school and lack of confidence acquired from their own schooling history (Miller 2003; Roffey 2002). Those with low self-efficacy will doubt their ability to solve their child's problems or to influence their child's educational trajectory, even if they did become involved (Grolnick et al. 1997). Some parents regard their child's behaviour at school as your domain, particularly when they believe that the behaviours are incited or exacerbated by difficult work demands or unfair disciplinary or teaching practices at school (Roffey 2002).

Of the child factors that limit parents' engagement at school, the most influential is how difficult the child is to deal with (Grolnick et al. 1997). Parents might distance themselves from a difficult child or might simply be embarrassed to discuss with teachers their perceived failures with parenting such children.

Next, family stress, impoverishment and single parenting (Grolnick et al. 1997; McWayne et al. 2004) and purely practical problems (e.g. transport, babysitters and shift work) all limit the flexibility and resources that would enable parents' involvement. Nevertheless, these impediments may limit only their presence but not their emotional interest and personal involvement in their child's school life (Grolnick et al. 1997).

Finally, interaction styles between teachers and parents can deter parental involvement. Teachers' use of a top-down model and directive style with their students can unwittingly extend into their interactions with parents, while being accustomed to isolation within your classroom can cause you to overlook opportunities to gain support from parents (Friend & Cook 2003). Parents from low-income families in particular, but all parents in general, report that they find schools more formal and less welcoming than early childhood centres and that they experience a more judgmental attitude towards themselves and an increasingly negative focus during teacher–parent interactions, particularly over children's behavioural difficulties (Rimm-Kaufman & Pianta 1999).

Thus, while many parents will be willing to assist with solving their child's school-based difficulties, some will be constrained by the many other functions that they must perform in their families and the external pressures that they must navigate. This means that you will need to negotiate with them what role they would like to adopt in solving their child's school-based problem.

Collaborative practices

Parents see their job as being their child's advocate. They want him or her to be happy at school and to that end they value teachers acting professionally but in ways that protect, nurture and encourage their child (Roffey 2002). For your part, you will have the child as your focus, but will also be concerned for the smooth functioning of the class overall. Despite these different focuses, you and children's parents share a common bond: you both want what is best for their son or daughter. This is the first basis for common ground between you, upon which the remaining measures can build.

An inviting school climate

Building meaningful connections with parents begins with establishing an inviting school climate or family-centred ethos (Christenson 2004; Raffaele & Knoff 1999). Sustained administrative commitment will be essential for fostering connections with families. The precise nature of services can be in response to a survey of parents' needs and may include the provision of a parent lounge or drop-in centre to promote informal contacts or more structured parent support groups, or bringing in community health specialists to practise on the school grounds so that their efforts and the school's can be coordinated (Raffaele & Knoff 1999).

Routine communication

Mutual trust between parents and educators cannot develop in a vacuum and is even more difficult to establish during crises, when emotions are likely to be running high. Instead, it must be engendered through frequent, ongoing, everyday, responsive communication with parents (Adams & Christenson 2000). Regular communication with parents about classroom learning activities and their child's progress and ideas for supporting their child academically contribute to students' intrinsic motivation (Gonzalez-DeHass et al. 2005) and can cement cooperation between parents and teachers by helping each become familiar with the other's expectations (Raffeale & Knoff 1999). If all that parents receive from school is a barrage of complaints about their child, they will become defensive (Roffey 2002). There are many occasions when you can exchange positive information with parents, including orientation visits before their child starts at the school or in a new classroom, during everyday informal contacts, in brochures about the school's policies and procedures, at meetings to review students' progress, in newsletters, on bulletin boards, and in a letter to parents and students at the beginning of the school year to introduce yourself, your philosophy about education, the curriculum at that grade level and your aims for the year, while also asking parents for their feedback about their own goals for their son or daughter (Jones & Jones 2004).

As the year progresses, personal contact with parents over positive events at school is a powerful communication both for them and for students (Miller 2003; Miller et al. 2002). Against such a backdrop of ongoing positive communication, problem solving with parents will be more successful.

Collaborative problem solving

The recursive interactions between students and teachers over disruptive behaviour that were illustrated in Figure 7.1 (see p. 157) can also occur between parents and teachers, with each accusing the other of incompetence and the result that both feel unsupported. As reported in Chapter 1, teachers tend to blame students' behavioural difficulties on home or child factors while overlooking the teaching context (Bibou-Nakou et al. 2000; Miller 2003), whereas students and parents tend to blame teacher unfairness and student vulnerability, although parents do also recognise certain disadvantaging home factors (Miller et al. 2002).

At the same time, we must respect that parents will have been co-opted somewhat involuntarily into discussing their child's behaviour with you. While wanting the best for their child, and thus being willing to be involved, they would prefer not to have the problem in the first place. They will not relish the prospect of yet another encounter with school personnel about their child's behaviour. The fact that previous efforts at solving chronic problems have been unsuccessful means that parents' self-assurance may have been compromised and they may feel sceptical and lack hope about the chances of success of any new intervention. Furthermore, their child's failure at school may mirror their own unsuccessful school career—in which case, they are likely to approach you with suspicion and distrust.

Nevertheless, as already mentioned, you both share a common interest in their child's wellbeing and, when it comes to collaborating over their child's behavioural difficulties at school, you both want the problem to be resolved. No matter how pessimistic parents might feel about the possibility for a solution, like you they do want relief from the problem.

With this as your starting point, four principles inform how you engage with parents when their son or daughter is displaying disruptive behaviour at school. First, you must recognise that this is a school-based problem and therefore the school must be the one to solve it, not the parents. Even when parents do instigate disciplinary measures at home, these have little impact on their child's behaviour at school (Miller 2003). This is because the behaviour happens in the school context and therefore it is in this setting that the problem must be resolved.

Second, your purpose in collaborating is not to have the parents punish their child at home for behavioural incidents at school. You would not punish a child at school for something that happened at home.

The third principle is that all parents from all backgrounds want to be proud of their children, to give them educational and other opportunities that they themselves might not have had and to have a good relationship with their children (Berg & Steiner 2003). They want to have hope for their children. When collaborating with parents to resolve school-based behavioural difficulties it is your task, then, to restore parents' pride in their children.

Finally, it is self-evident that you will be working with parents at times when there is a problem to be solved, rather than when all is going well. At such times of stress, it could be easy to fall into a trap of judging parents or assuming that their personal or parenting deficiencies are the cause of their children's difficulties. However, school pressure for students to perform more satisfactorily can stress even a well-functioning family and can add intolerable pressure to an already strained family. Thus, the source of the stress can be beyond the family's influence—as with poverty—or even a product of the problem itself. This implies that the final key ingredient of collaborating with parents is to bear in mind that the child (or family) is not the problem: *the problem is the problem* (Winslade & Monk 1999).

Engage parents' expertise

Given that they see their children in a wide variety of contexts and over a longer time period than teachers, that children behave differently at home than they do at school, and that parents have intimate knowledge of their children's emotional wellbeing, they can be more accurate than teachers at describing their child's characteristic behaviours (Lindsay & Dockrell 2000). This expertise can inform solutions. Additionally, collaborating with parents to solve their son or daughter's school-based behavioural difficulty can fulfil the following many supportive functions (Freeman et al. 1997).

- Parents can give examples and enlarge on stories that enrich the descriptions of their child's problem and of exceptions to it.
- They can brainstorm ideas and solutions.
- They can become co-conspirators or part of the child's 'team', helping him or her to outwit, combat or oppose the problem.
- They form an audience that can highlight and celebrate their child's mastery over the problem.

This embracing of parents' expertise can be a significant reversal of the pattern of uncooperative and unproductive relationships between families and school that can become entrenched when students have ongoing behavioural difficulties (Lindquist et al. 1987; Lusterman 1985).

Negotiate who to involve

As those most affected by the outcome of any meeting between you and their parents, students have a right to be involved in discussions concerning them. More than this, however, children are the experts on their own problems and can advise adults how to respond. Therefore, they will need to be involved in the process of solution finding. If their attendance at meetings would mean that they were heavily outnumbered by adults, they can invite a best friend along for moral support or as adviser to the adults. If the friend cannot attend or students decline to invite a peer, you can allocate an empty seat on which you place the friend's name and participants at the meeting can speak hypothetically to the friend in his or her absence, by posing questions such as 'I wounder what Shara would advise us about this?'.

Phase 1: Define the problem

Following the sequence of steps illustrated in Figure 7.2 (see p. 160), the solution-focused approach tells us that we need to define behavioural difficulties in ways that suggest change, rather than hopelessness. However, when parents have had previous contact with health professionals, they may be wedded to a diagnosis that implies that their child cannot change. In such cases, it will be vital while listening to their explanations to use progressive questions that highlight the potential for improvement.

If, rather than feeling helpless about their child, parents feel helpless about themselves, it will be important to deflect their self-criticism. To that end, Freeman and colleagues (1997) suggest literally presenting parents with a list of possible self-accusations, so that they can confirm which ones they have believed about their own culpability for their child's difficulties. This list could include self-accusations that they are too lenient/too strict, left/didn't leave their violent spouse, were too young/old as a parent, overindulged the child/did not give him or her enough, are overreacting/should have done something sooner, and so on. This process of acknowledging parents' inevitable self-accusations allows these to be confronted and neutralised, enabling you thereafter to move towards finding a solution to the child's behavioural difficulties (Freeman et al. 1997).

Phase 2: Map the problem's influence

Defining the problem is accompanied by empathising that it has been pushing the whole family (and perhaps even teachers) around for a long time. To map how it has influenced them, inquire how it makes the child behave (at home and at school) and ask how parents respond when the child behaves in this way. You can report similar information about how teachers respond. Mapping how the difficulty has influenced all those involved sets the scene for exploring (in phase 4) how each person has influenced the difficulty.

Phase 3: Set goals collaboratively

The solution-focused approach tells us that parents have expertise about solving problems of their family members. Therefore, your role is not to know more than they do, but to listen so you can discern and then highlight what the family already knows. However, some parents can be so oppressed by what seems to be the intractability of their child's school problems that they find it difficult to identify any optimistic goals. The exploration of exceptions can assist with this.

Phase 4: Explore exceptions

As detailed in Chapter 7, the next phase of solution finding is to map exceptions to the problems and discover what those involved did to make these happen. Exceptions are occasions when the problem did not occur or was less severe than at other times. Resiliency questions ask family members to talk about previous occasions when they have overcome adversity or solved this or other issues for their family. What skills and strategies have parents been using that have prevented their son's or daughter's behaviour from getting worse than it is now? (Selekman 1997).

When parents are so paralysed by their child's or their own problems that they cannot notice exceptions or their role in enabling these, future-oriented questions can help. You can begin by asking them, in their child's presence, how they know that he or she can do better (Berg & Steiner 2003). When young people hear that their parents believe that they have some fine qualities, they will experience the care and support that they cannot ask for outright. Next, you can ask those involved to picture a time a few months hence when this problem is resolved and to imagine what they have been doing to achieve this. What has the child been doing differently to achieve this imagined success? What have you (parents or teacher) or other adults or peers been doing that contributed to the improvement? If even these future-oriented questions do not assist the parents and child in identifying goals and their capacity to attain these, you can externalise the problem as outlined in Chapter 7. This allows the problem to be the villain, rather than the child.

Phase 5: Plan and implement solutions

In the next phase of problem solving, solutions need to be enacted. These will entail enlarging on the students' actions that have already been successful at generating exceptions, or perhaps actions that parents have considered but held back because they thought those actions might not work (Selekman 1997). Other solutions can be suggested by having students themselves (or their friend) act as advisers to the adults. Reversal questions invite children to give their parents advice about how to respond to their behaviour at home, or to suggest how teaching staff should handle it at school. Alternatively, consultancy questions can explicitly capitalise on parents' knowledge: 'Given that you know your child better than anyone else, what suggestions do you have for us to help her at school?' (Murphy 2006); 'You've spoken to your child's previous teachers about this in the past. What have we all missed so far that could help? ... If I have another child with similar issues in my class in future, what could you tell me about how I might help that child? ... If there was one useful question about your child's behaviour that I could ask, what would that question be?' (Selekman 1997).

As discussed in Chapter 7, tasks can be a useful bridge between how things happen now and how they will be when the problem is solved. Some tasks were described in that earlier chapter but, in summary, for parents who can identify aspects of their own behaviour that contribute to exceptions, you could suggest *behavioural* tasks of doing more of those behaviours that bring about their goals, or behaving as if the problem were solved. In contrast, for those who want others to change (say, when they want their son's or daughter's behaviour to improve) or who feel powerless to make a difference in their own lives, you can give *observational* tasks, such as discerning what aspects of their life they want to have continue, which events tell them that this problem can be solved or, at a time their child is behaving better, what they are doing differently that might be inducing the improved behaviour.

When two parents disagree on a solution, it is clear that they are both committed to solving the child's difficulties and both want what is best for the child. Therefore, you cannot take sides with one or the other. Instead, you can suggest that each morning they flip a coin, with heads signalling that the mother is in charge for the day and tails denoting that the father is. The one who is in charge enacts his or her solution for the day, while the other notices what works about the other's approach (De Jong & Berg 2002). This undermines the either/or thinking that upholds that one parent is right and the other is wrong about how to solve the problem, allows them to save face with the other and almost inevitably results in their collaborating to build a new solution (De Jong & Berg 2002).

Phase 6: Notice and highlight change

As noted in Chapter 7, at subsequent meetings you will inquire what has changed since the previous meeting. In response, those involved could report that there has been some improvement, no change, a deterioration in the child's behaviour, or different members could have mixed opinions. For each of these four scenarios, Selekman (1997) advises the following.

When *improvements* have been recognised, you can ask about and highlight what each person has done to bring those about. You can then all agree to continue using more of these successful strategies.

When there appears to all those involved to have been *no change* in the student's behaviour, parents who are stuck doing 'more of the same' could be given the advice that their child is finding them too predictable. Therefore, they need to do something different to surprise the child. This, in turn, will provoke a change in his or her behaviour. Other options are to recommend pattern interruption or to externalise the problem (see Chapter 7). Giving adults the task of observing the child for any signs of non-problematic behaviour can also be a way to help them notice small improvements that otherwise they might overlook in their discouragement.

When the problem appears *worse* than before, you will need to listen to the parents' despondency without permitting their desperation to become contagious and without blaming them for their feelings (Freeman et al. 1997). Instead, empathising with their despair is more likely to uncover the underlying love and worry for their child. You can ask 'What does your desperate worry for your son's/daughter's future tell you about your feelings for him/her?'. Their declarations of love can be newsworthy for onlooking children. Next, you can begin to highlight their skills by asking why they have not given up, what keeps them hanging in there and trying, or how they have prevented the problem from becoming worse than it is. Another possibility is to suggest to parents that, despite not knowing in advance how it might help, they do the opposite of what they have been trying so far (Selekman 1997).

When progress reports are *mixed*, with some individuals reporting improvement while others are still pessimistic, begin by highlighting the improvements. This can help sceptics to rise above their pessimism. At the same time, however, acknowledge their caution, agreeing that it is only sensible, given how long they have been battling their child's behaviour.

Refer on

No one knows everything about everything, even within their field of expertise. Furthermore, a teacher's role is typically not one of counselling students or parents. Therefore, on occasion it will be necessary to refer parents to specialist counsellors. In order to do so, you will need to find out about available services, including details of waiting time, costs and contact phone numbers. The more specific your information, the easier it will be for parents to follow up your concerns promptly.

Responding to parental complaints

So far, this chapter has dealt with how to enlist parents' advice for solving their child's school-based behavioural difficulties. A second occasion when you need to collaborate with parents is when they have approached you with a complaint, such as about how their child's behaviour has been dealt with by the school. As consumers of an important (and in terms of private school fees or tax contributions, an expensive) service, parents would be irresponsible if they did not closely question what you offer their child (Greenman & Stonehouse 1997). This means that, regardless of their manner, you need to meet with courtesy the questions that they ask and the demands that they make. Even 'difficult' parents are not being demanding just to make you jump through hoops; they both *need* and have a *right* to ask questions.

Any expression of strong emotions of blame or hopelessness is a sign that parents care deeply about their child. Although strong emotions can be intimidating, it will help not to take their behaviour personally but to remember that it is being triggered by their situation (not by you) and that from their perspective the parents feel that they have a valid reason for their feelings and behaviour. All animals become feral when their young are under threat. Thus, you will need to listen, acknowledge their frustration or anger and reflect what they are saying.

Nevertheless, if parents become belligerent, uncooperative, abusive or otherwise disrespectful, offensive or overpowering, you will need them to moderate how they are talking to you. It might help to direct them to what they want to accomplish (Jones & Jones 2004). For example: 'I accept that you are angry that Simon was sent out of class. Perhaps now we can focus on what you would like to see happen next time so that his behaviour doesn't hurt others but he still feels that he has been listened to?'.

When your time is limited, it will help to advise the parents of this at the outset and suggest that all you can do now is make a start on solving the problem, but can schedule another meeting for later. On occasion, it can be useful to impose a time limit deliberately, to give yourself time to evaluate their complaint. A delay will also give them time to calm down. They will not be able to listen to even the most reasonable explanation while they are angry. Therefore, you could take the information, offer to think about it or to gather more facts from others who were involved, and then get back to the parents for a follow-up conversation. In the meantime, you can invite the parents to speak with the principal about their concerns. This deflects their anger from you, while being granted access to someone in higher authority can satisfy them that the matter is being taken seriously.

In most instances, listening to the feeling behind parents' manner will effectively avoid a confrontation. However, your school will also need a policy for protecting staff when parents are physically threatening. You will need specific procedures for withdrawing to a safe location within the school or for requesting backup from a colleague or even police or other security personnel.

Cross-cultural collaboration

The term *culture* encompasses demographic characteristics such as race, gender, country of origin, language and socioeconomic status, as well as less explicit features such as individuals' beliefs, values and attitudes (Sheridan 2000). With respect to behaviour in schools, it also refers to the norms and customs of institutions. In these settings within the dominant culture's frame of reference, a student's behaviour might be interpreted as problematic, but it may be appropriate within the child's family culture (Ramirez et al. 1998) or be a natural reaction to social disadvantage or disempowerment. Thus, cultural sensitivity applies not only to how we interact with parents to solve a problem, but also to how we frame problems in the first place.

Cultural literacy begins with developing awareness of our own cultural biases. Learning about oneself precedes attempting to understand others (Ramirez et al. 1998). Professional development, multicultural experiences, reading about other cultures and personal and professional contacts with individuals who bridge cultures can help you as a member of the dominant culture to become aware of its implicit assumptions, biases and values, being sensitive to the fact that these are not universally shared (Lynch & Hanson 1996).

A next measure to enhance cross-cultural collaboration is developing awareness of others' cultural perspectives. Adopting a 'colour-blind' stance that other people's culture is irrelevant would disrespect its deep significance to them, while stereotyping people on the basis of their culture would disrespect their individuality (Ramirez et al. 1998). Therefore, as we cannot possibly know the nuances of every culture and as there is considerable variation in beliefs and practices within any cultural group, the most useful stance when working with parents from other cultures is one taken by the solution-focused approach—that is, a posture of 'not-knowing' (Berg & Steiner 2003). When collaborating cross-culturally to resolve children's behavioural difficulties at school, you will need to ask parents specifically about their values and preferred practices concerning discipline (Phoenix 2002). The solution-focused approach reminds us that we do not have to accept parents' values (cultural or otherwise), but merely recognise that they believe that their perceptions are the proper and logical way to understand and respond to the problem.

Third, you will need cultural empathy. This facet of cross-cultural work calls for an understanding of the impact of the dominant culture on others (Ingraham 2000; Ramirez et al. 1998). When consulting with parents from a culture other than your own, you could invite them to bring along to the meeting a member of their own community or extended family. Or, if you have a teacher on staff from their culture, you could ask if they would like you to invite that person to attend. This has to be their choice entirely, because in some cultures the presence of an outsider would be experienced as supportive, while in others it would cause parents to lose face. If they choose to see you without a cultural advocate or none is available, you can check with them whether they are willing to discuss with you the concerns over their son or daughter despite your cultural differences. Your openness about discussing cultural differences is fundamental to developing trust between you (M. Rogers 1998).

While it will never be possible to walk in another person's shoes and understand how others experience the social oppression that often accompanies their cultural membership, cross-cultural empathy can be informed by an awareness of the distinction between voluntary and involuntary minority groups. Some families migrate voluntarily to a country in search of more opportunities. Despite having chosen to migrate and thus surmount its challenges, when they confront educational dilemmas about their child their migrant status can disenfranchise them, as they are more likely to be living in poverty and to have little access to support from social services (Salend & Taylor 1993). Furthermore, the fact that they were educated elsewhere, and thus do not know the local education system, can mean that they are reluctant to engage with educators or join parent groups, which results in their being particularly isolated (Marion 1980).

In contrast, involuntary minorities were brought to a country against their will (e.g. African Americans) or were invaded (e.g. Native Americans, Australian Aborigines and the New Zealand Māori peoples) (Borland & Wright 2000). The history of oppression and ongoing negative contact between involuntary minorities and the dominant culture generate repeated disadvantage and may give rise to oppositional coping mechanisms, including a resistance to 'acting white' via school success (Borland & Wright 2000). For these groups, school learning is often perceived not as *adding* to their lives but as *detracting from* their own cultural values, traditions and attitudes, while effort during the school years is less likely to be rewarded in their working life. Educators therefore need to find a way of convincing these children and their families that academic achievement will be good for them, their families and their communities (Kerr & Cohn 2001). This points to the need to promote pluralism (in contrast with assimilationism), so that children from minority cultures feel that they can preserve their own cultural heritage at the same time as acquiring the knowledge and skills that are necessary for success in the majority culture (Maker & Schiever 1989).

Inclusive day-to-day practices within your classroom will communicate more effectively than any other means that you honour diversity. Particularly in the face of the traditional silencing of minorities, when you are a member of the majority culture you will need to listen to students, their families and members of other cultures to find out how to make learning culturally meaningful and relevant for these children (Ford & Trotman 2001). Among other measures, this will entail prohibiting discrimination within your classroom and the school and respecting students' use of dialects and their home languages (Ford 2003; Ford & Harris 2000; Ford et al. 2000; Harmon 2002). Meanwhile, an anti-bias curriculum must not perpetuate stereotypes through a 'tourist curriculum' that focuses on a culture's exotic customs (Derman-Sparks & the ABC Task Force 1989), but must recognise how the various cultural groups that make up a society have contributed to how it has been shaped as a collective (Ford 2003; Ford & Harris 2000; Ford et al. 2000).

Cross-cultural problem solving

When collaborating with parents from other cultures to solve their child's school-based behavioural difficulties, their cultural values can influence their aspirations for their child, their expectations of their own role in solving the problem, their expectations of your role, perceptions of your status and nonverbal communication styles. You will need to ask about these aspects, which of course requires parents to feel confident of their English skills. Lack of communication can deny you vital information about their child while limiting how much information parents can receive from you as, even when they can use everyday language, they might have difficulty comprehending more technical educational terms (Rosin 1996; Salend & Taylor 1993). Therefore, it can be essential to locate a translator for formal conversations or invite a community volunteer to accompany non-English-speaking parents on a regular basis at drop-off or collection times, so that you can pass on day-to-day information about their child's experiences. It is wise to avoid using their son or daughter as a translator, as that burdens a child with inappropriate responsibility, while the use of translators who are children or family friends can lead to discomfort when they are exposed to information that parents regard as personal (Lynch & Hanson 1996; Salend & Taylor 1993).

A solution-focused approach, as outlined here and in Chapter 7, is ideal for working cross-culturally because, in having parents generate their own definitions of problems, determine their own goals and design interventions based on their own past successes, necessarily these will match their perspectives (cultural and otherwise). In turn, this congruence with their values will contribute to trust between you and to their openness to solutions. While respecting that there are differences among people, adopting the parents' perspective also upholds that, regardless of cultural or ethnic differences between educators and parents, their core similarity is that (Berg & Steiner 2003: 9):

> All people want to be treated with respect, want to be valued and accepted, loved, and cherished, and made to feel they are making important contributions to society and that their wishes and desires are heard and respected.

Supporting disadvantaged families

Functioning under the burden of chronic poverty is linked with other risk factors that are detrimental to children—such as poor housing, limited social supports from equally stressed neighbours, inadequate health care, and low-quality child care and educational services (Schaffer 1998). In response, parents might neglect their children's needs as they become caught up in their own issues of survival; inadequate monitoring can lead children to develop undesirable peer relationships (Schaffer 1998); parents themselves might develop mental illnesses in response to their trying circumstances (or a mental illness may be the cause of their poverty); and the parents' relationship can be strained.

Having said this, we have to guard against stereotypes because, while awareness of the difficulties under which children and families are functioning can sensitise us to their needs, it can also cause us to lower our expectations of them (Spicker et al. 1987). When you compare *groups* across the full range of socioeconomic status (SES), although family SES does correlate with children's academic achievement, it has very little impact on *individual* children's academic achievement either across or within groups of similar SES. Instead, parents' ability to manage family crises, their encouragement of their children's learning and the quality of their parenting skills—which are independent of family income—are most influential (Robinson et al. 2002; Sirin 2005; White 1982). In other words, it is not family status but family *processes* that predict student achievement (Raffaele & Knoff 1999). Given that teachers can do little to raise the socioeconomic status of impoverished families or neighbourhoods, this fact is liberating, because school programs and teaching quality can do much to help parents fulfil their various functions (Raffaele & Knoff 1999; Sirin 2005).

A solution-focused approach is the same for families experiencing multiple problems as for those who are more advantaged: find out from them which problem is their priority and assist them in solving that (Fisch & Schlanger 1999). This will relieve the most stress and might open the way for spontaneous improvement in other troubling aspects of their lives, or their early success might enfranchise them to solve their next problem.

At a deeper level, solution-focused approaches openly acknowledge social forces that oppress cultural minorities, women and those living in poverty, to name but a few disadvantaged groups. Although you are powerless to control these external factors, you can challenge the message that they often convey to parents about their personal worth. The first step will be to acknowledge the special stressors that they face in bringing up young people within a subculture of deprivation, violence and (where relevant) racism. You can ask these parents what it is like for them to have to function under oppression. Does it cause them to believe that they cannot raise healthy children? Do they feel criticised and believe that they have to be perfect to counter stereotypes about single parents/people from their culture? How do they manage to raise their children in such a loving way in an environment characterised by poverty, prejudice, disadvantage or violence? (De Jong & Berg 2002).

In instances where purely practical assistance is needed, it may not be your role to deliver this yourself, but you can advise parents of agencies that can help improve their living circumstances through providing access to better housing, financial support or other community services such as translators. Nevertheless, you must not attempt to secure for them services that they are not asking for, as that would compound their helplessness.

Consultation in schools

Consultation in schools entails one professional who has specialist knowledge—often a special educator, educational psychologist, social worker or the like—assisting another with generalist knowledge (i.e. a teacher) to orchestrate services that will improve the functioning of individual students (Friend & Cook 2003). The specialist and teacher share responsibility for jointly planning interventions, although teachers have the ultimate authority to determine what is practicable. The typical expectation of consultants in schools is that they adopt a clinical style of assessment to diagnose a cause for children's school-based difficulties in order to generate a prescription detailing what teachers and parents can do about it (Wagner & Gillies 2001). However, this can degenerate into the administration of increasingly detailed assessments to find more and more obscure names for conditions that ultimately prove to be untreatable. Meanwhile, teachers are frustrated by the delay in gaining support to help the student concerned.

Furthermore, this approach represents a top-down rather than collaborative style that violates the basic tenets of egalitarian thinking, which respects the wisdom and expertise of teachers just as it respects the expertise of parents and young people.

Instead, a solution-oriented assessment involving observation of the child will not yield a 'laundry list' of what is going wrong, but will examine exceptions to the problem and what occasions those (McGlone 2001). Subsequent consultative problem solving with teachers will begin in the same way as any solution-building approach. It will start with listening to their concerns and asking in what ways they hope the consultation will be useful. Goals are clarified by asking what they want to see changed (perhaps employing the miracle question) and who will be doing what differently when the miracle has eventuated.

Next follows an examination of what is working. This gives you an opportunity to reflect to the child, parents and teacher what your observations tell you they each are doing to enable those exceptions. You will inquire about what they have done in the past that has worked. Useful questions include: 'When faced with this kind of behaviour before, what did you do that worked? What effects did you notice? How do you explain those? How could you do that again?' (Wagner & Gillies 2001). Having them rating the difficulty (on a scale of 1 to 10) aids reflection about exceptions by imposing some distance between the teacher's perceptions and the often emotionally charged difficulties (Wagner & Gillies 2001). At the close of the discussion, the consultant can ask (Wagner & Gillies 2001: 156):

- How close are we to making a plan?
- What else do we need to consider?
- What would it take to put these ideas into action?
- If you were to do this as an experiment, what would you do?

In the period between consultations, teachers can experiment with new ways of responding to the student's behaviour and notice exceptions, observing what they and the student are doing differently when these occur. As mentioned in Chapter 7, follow-up consultations will be guided by the acronym EARS (Wagner & Gillies 2001: 157):

- Elicit what has worked and the exceptions: What has gone well?
- Amplify the changes: How did you manage to do that?
- Reinforce success: Who else has noticed this improvement?
- Start on the next problem—if necessary.

Conclusion

Students' behavioural and academic difficulties will not disappear with a single intervention, but can be improved only through ongoing supportive interaction between teachers and parents, both across all sectors of the school and across time (Christenson 2004). A solution-focused approach is particularly valuable for solving school-based behavioural difficulties in collaboration with parents, as it does not set you up as the expert and does not require specialist counselling skills other than being curious and listening and questioning. This is important as counselling, after all, is not your job. However, as Molnar and Lindquist (1989) observe, you have a successful history of solving both personal and professional problems, which expertise you can combine with that of parents and students themselves to arrive at solutions that perhaps none of you could devise alone.

Discussion questions

1   When you have collaborated with parents to resolve their son's or daughter's behavioural difficulties at school, what helped make those approaches effective for you? For the parent/s? For the student?
2   What supports do you need within the school for working with parents?

Suggested further reading

Bolton, R. 1993 *People skills* Simon & Schuster, Sydney
Friend, M. and Cook, L. 2003 *Interactions: collaboration skills for school professionals* 4th edn, Allyn & Bacon, Boston, MA
Roffey, S. 2002 *School behaviour and families: frameworks for working together* David Fulton, London
Rosenberg, M.B. 2003 *Nonviolent communication: a language of life* 2nd edn, Puddle Dancer Press, Encinitas, CA

14 FORMULATING A DISCIPLINE POLICY

> As long as the management of students' challenging behaviours focuses solely on correction techniques, teachers will continue to experience failure and frustration. Teachers should spend as much time developing positive, proactive behavior management plans as they spend developing instructional lesson plans.
>
> Maag (2001: 182)

KEY POINTS

- Whether at a classroom or a school-wide level, a policy on discipline in schools needs to have clear philosophy, goals, theory base and guidelines for practice.
- Proactive measures will be given most emphasis in such a policy, because the prevention of problems is both more humane and more effective than correction.
- Policies must be broadly canvassed so that they take into account the requirements of teachers, students, parents and school administrators.

Introduction

Student outcomes are better when school staff agree on and collaborate over disciplinary issues (Rutter 1983). This can be facilitated by the development of a school disciplinary policy that provides a framework for preventing and intervening with disruptions and for offering collegial support to teachers. A school-wide policy on discipline enshrines a strategic vision for the school that embodies capable leadership and attendance to the needs of students, teachers and parents.

In general, policies are statements about what services you will offer and how you will deliver them. A school disciplinary policy expresses how school members are expected to behave towards each other so that they can work productively together (Cowin et al. 1990). Although formulating policy is time consuming, the process has many benefits.

- A policy can provide a means for all members of the school community to communicate their sense of shared purpose (Mathieson & Price 2002).
- It offers students, teachers and parents safeguards and clear expectations of their roles, rights and responsibilities (Stonehouse 1991).
- The process of formulating a policy allows you to plan how to respond to disruptiveness rather than having to make hasty reactive decisions.
- A policy can be the basis for staff development (Mathieson & Price 2002).
- It clarifies for teachers how to procure support to deal with demanding behaviours.
- A policy can provide practical information for inexperienced, temporary or new teachers to the school. At the same time, it must still allow teachers some autonomy, as befits their professionalism (Cangelosi 2004).

For these benefits to eventuate, you cannot simply import the policy of a sister school or revamp an old policy document, as it is the process of discussing and understanding nuance, not the final document, that is the potent aspect of policy formulation.

Discipline is a process for helping students to learn and to gain personal skills; it is not an end in itself. Therefore, a policy statement about student behaviour must include far more than a direct focus on intervening with disruptive behaviour. The model presented in Chapter 1 (Figure 1.1—see page 11) details four core components that will contribute to your disciplinary practices and can be encompassed in your policy. These are your philosophy or beliefs, your values, your knowledge of theories of discipline, and your knowledge of teaching and learning theory. Your repertoire of potential responses will be expanded by enabling features of the school and community and limited by its constraints. This model can provide a framework for developing your personal or school-wide policy on student discipline.

Pre-planning

Before you can proceed with formulating a policy, decisions will have to be made about who will steer the process, whether staff will need some professional development to inform their options, how and whom you will consult, and timelines for doing all this. Typically, an action group or steering committee will be appointed to start the process. As illustrated in Figure 14.1, their first step will be to collate the present policy and others that affect it, such as the school's inclusive education policy and directives of the school's governing bodies. Next, they will gather resources needed to inform them of their options (such as texts on teaching and behaviour management) or source some professional development training on the topic. The third step will be to survey teachers, students and parents about the aspects of the current procedures that are working and not working.

This information will then be presented back to the wider staff group who, over a series of meetings, will discuss each of the elements of policy—its philosophy, goals and preventive and interventive practices. The action group will record the group's decisions in the form of a draft document for subsequent discussion and ultimate ratification by all stakeholders. At this stage, you will need to consider how you will take account of differences in individuals' views and whether you expect consensus by the majority or 100 per cent endorsement by all staff. This decision will have implications for implementation and will dictate whether you will need procedures for incorporating different disciplinary styles of staff.

Wide consultation with teachers, students and parents throughout this process will ensure that they do not feel that the policy has been imposed on them from above. Their inclusion will, in turn, increase the chances that they will both understand and support the policy and its procedures. Naturally, the people most affected by the policy will be students themselves and thus they need to be active participants in its formulation, both because there is a moral obligation to consult them and also because doing so improves policy effectiveness (Davies 2005).

Philosophical beliefs

A policy will be useless—and perhaps even obstructive—when it is inconsistent with the culture of the school (Miller 2003). A school's culture is comprised of its norms, members' roles, structures and procedures, with most of these informal or covert (Schmuck & Schmuck 2001). The process of debating the assumptions behind a discipline policy and the active engagement of all members of the school community can enfranchise them to expose, and even challenge, covert cultural beliefs and practices, ultimately resulting in a transformation of these.

Therefore, this section of your policy needs to make explicit your beliefs about children, their relative status compared with adults and about the reasons for disruptions

FIGURE 14.1   Process of policy development

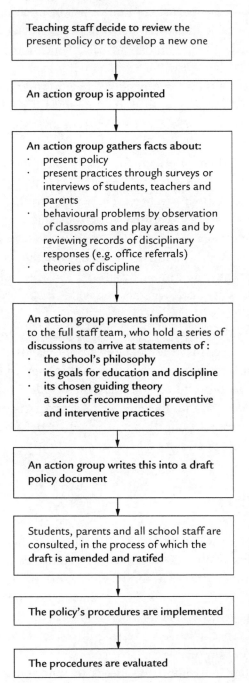

in schools. You will then need to take a stance on the question of whether individuals' control is located internally or externally. This stance needs to be consistent with recommendations in your *Practices* section, with the administration of rewards and punishments consistent with an external locus of causality and solution-focused approaches aligning with an internal locus.

More than other sections of the document, this philosophy statement is prone to two traps. First, you should avoid 'motherhood' statements such as 'We strive for excellence'. Given that no school is likely to proclaim that it strives for mediocrity, this statement is meaningless. It may be an attractive motto for public relations purposes, but it cannot be operationalised—that is, it does not imply what staff, students or parents will actually *do*.

The second trap is that many schools express an egalitarian disciplinary philosophy and yet detail authoritarian interventions (Lewis 1997; R. Slee 1995). To avoid this, once subsequent sections of your policy are written you should compare them with this philosophy statement to ensure that your practices align with what you say you believe.

Values

A school policy will need to take account of teachers' personal and particularly professional values, which might include (Charles & Senter 2005a):

- a pleasant physical environment in which to work;
- a measure of order in the classroom;
- courteous behaviour between all members of the school;
- job satisfaction;
- parental and collegial support.

As noted in Chapter 1, these values cannot be imposed on students and neither can teachers be required to reach consensus on these. However, together with individuals' beliefs, their values contribute to their goals, about which some agreement will be necessary.

Goals

A solution-focused perspective asks you to imagine how your class and school would be operating after a miracle occurred. If all its present challenges were eliminated, what would endure in their place? (Davis & Osborn 2000). What would teachers be doing differently? What would students be doing? These post-miracle qualities and the small signs of progress towards them are your goals. They are not meant to imply that you will achieve perfection.

In light of teachers' professional values, the school's disciplinary policy must specify its educational goals for students' intellectual, social, emotional, physical and cultural growth. The main focus here is what you want your students to achieve as members of the classroom and of the wider society (McCaslin & Good 1992). Such goals might include:

- provision of a safe and caring physical and emotional environment that supports and protects the rights of all students to learn and grow personally and that safeguards the rights of teachers to teach;
- facilitation of students' success by providing a meaningful curriculum;
- recognition of students' achievements (which will involve making a judgment about the debate on the use of intrinsic versus external reinforcers);
- student participation in all aspects of school life;
- maintaining collaborative relationships with parents.

Your third cluster of goals will be disciplinary. In general, your overall aim will probably be to create a well-disciplined environment in which you can work and students can learn. The specifics, however, must match your broad philosophical stance (outlined in the previous section) and your educational goals (just enunciated). As listed in Box 1.2 (see p. 29), the range of potential goals for you to select from include: establishing, maintaining and restoring order; facilitating students' self-discipline (with internalised compliance distinguished from the exercise of autonomous ethics); teaching emotional regulation; fostering cooperation; and encouraging what may be variously termed self-efficacy, a sense of agency or potency.

Theory

The next section of your policy will have two parts. First, it will describe which theories of discipline will guide your practice. When selecting a guiding theory, you will need to evaluate its assumptions and practices on the basis of whether they are consistent with your views about children and their education and whether they are known to be both effective and ethical. Although you might combine theories, you will need to achieve a coherent synthesis rather than an atheoretical compilation of incompatible ideas. As mentioned in Chapter 1, a useful guide might be that only those theories from the same category (authoritarian, mixed or egalitarian) or one step either side of it can be blended coherently.

The second part of your theory section will detail your educational theory. You can select from a top-down or teacher-directed model of education or a constructivist, child-centred model. Given that your disciplinary aims cannot contradict your educational ones, these two aspects of theory need to be analysed for consistency.

This analysis can inform a definition of behavioural 'problems', differentiating between those behaviours that you will regard as disciplinary or educational issues. It could also include a statement about your collective attitude to behavioural mistakes as distinct from academic ones (see Box 1.1), on the understanding that a view of mistakes as inevitable may engender more egalitarian responses.

This principle of not defining normal behaviours as inappropriate can be especially useful when a school's disciplinary policy is authoritarian but your personal policy for your own classroom is egalitarian. In that case, although you must abide by the school's edict that you respond punitively to inappropriate behaviour, you can simply define none of the behaviours you face as 'inappropriate'. As a teacher of, say, nine year olds, you can choose to define their disruptions as typical of nine year olds or as inevitable mistakes. In this way you violate neither your principles nor the school's directives.

Enabling and constraining aspects of the school

You will require support to implement the disciplinary methods to be selected in the subsequent section of your policy. Therefore, you will need to conduct an audit to determine if the necessary resources and supports are indeed available. You will need to find ways to surmount constraints such as a nonconducive physical environment, large school size or the socioeconomic disadvantage of the student population, so that your recommended practices are realistic.

Practice

Next, in wide consultation across the school community, you will need to detail some efficient, self-sustaining procedures for achieving your goals. Procedures will focus on how you can organise your school or classroom so that most behavioural difficulties are prevented and those that do occur receive a constructive response (Cowin et al. 1990). As prevention is far more powerful than intervention, this aspect will be the largest part of your practices section.

Monitoring and assessment methods

As a universal preventive measure, you will need to plan procedures to monitor students' behaviour so that you will know when problems are arising and can respond promptly (Rutter & Maughan 2002). Secondary prevention will entail assessing individual students' behaviour in an effort to judge if a targeted intervention is necessary.

Recognition of considerate behaviour

In this section, you will need to determine your collective view about the use of informative versus judgmental feedback for students' achievements and prosocial behaviour. This will lead into a declaration of your intentions whether to employ public awards and grades and other personal rewards to students.

Layered responses to disruptions

As depicted in Figure I.1 (see p. 6), your policy must incorporate three levels of disciplinary action: universal prevention, secondary prevention and solutions, in that order of magnitude. Primary, or *universal*, prevention strategies are supportive measures that recognise that facilitating the success of each individual student is a responsibility for the whole school, not just that child's teacher (Doyle 2003). They might include strategies to build an inclusive and cohesive school community, develop peer support systems (Roffey 2004), reduce class sizes (Finn et al. 2003), keep classes intact over consecutive years, enact anti-bullying (or 'safe school') programs, improve academic instruction (Miller et al. 1998), and establish pastoral care programs, to name a few. Primary measures can also widen their focus to supporting parents and the wider community. This can prevent student absenteeism and form a foundation for solving problems collaboratively with parents.

Secondary, or *supportive*, interventions aimed at avoiding future disruptions by at-risk students might include conducting class meetings, social skills training and the provision of remedial education and self-restraint training (see Chapter 4). Secondary prevention will also entail conducting comprehensive educational assessments for students whose behavioural difficulties could be the expression of learning problems. This might require referring students to specialists.

The third level of practice comprises short- and long-term *solutions* to emergent difficulties. Depending on your theoretical orientation, solutions can range from the authoritarian theories' use of punishment (when this level of procedures is known as *corrective* measures) through to the communication approach of humanism, or solution building. Whatever solutions are recommended, this section of your policy should be the smallest.

Finally, sanctions would need to be reserved for extremely serious infractions, such as criminal behaviour (including sexual assault or drug use or dealing), stalking, intransigent bullying or violence. Enunciating these banned behaviours and stating that their breach would result in suspension or expulsion provides legal protection from being sued for wrongful suspension (Nicholson 2006).

Student participation

The content of the policy will detail ways for students to participate in school decision making about their behaviour and learning. You should specify their rights and responsibilities, particularly that they have a right to due process in the case of infractions (Knight 1991). This means that students should be presumed innocent until proven guilty, permitted to state their side of events, and have available channels of appeal against what they might perceive to be injustices.

Parental participation

The policy will need to enunciate systematic procedures for eliciting parents' advice and support with academic and behavioural issues when these arise. This should extend beyond informing parents about the school and their child's conduct there, but instead will encompass a collaborative exchange of information (see Chapter 13).

Collegial support

Collegial support provides a buffer against stress in teachers, with high levels of organisational stress being a better predictor of burn-out in teachers than actual teaching challenges (Friedman 2003; Griffith et al. 1999; Nelson et al. 2001). A successful school culture offers the following forms of support to teachers (Gamman 2003; Nelson et al. 2001):

- openness about disciplinary challenges;
- willingness by staff to give time to each other to help solve behavioural difficulties;
- strong relationships with the principal;
- teachers' contribution to decisions;
- respectful relationships among the various levels of staff within the school;
- recognition of colleagues' efforts and achievements.

Primary or proactive measures—particularly principals' interest and presence in classrooms—are crucial for communicating to teachers that their efforts are valued (Gamman 2003). Such respect throughout the staff hierarchy in turn becomes a feature of teachers' relationships with students (Gamman 2003). Therefore, your policy needs to enunciate the means whereby staff can support each other to empower their problem solving (Gamman 2003). Rogers (2002) details some key forms of such support, including the induction of new staff to the school, mentoring novice teachers and providing support for relief (or 'supply') teachers.

Secondary forms of collegial support can be provided in the immediate aftermath of a disciplinary incident, of which there are three phases: release, reflect and rebuild (Gamman 2003). During the immediate aftermath of a stressful incident, teachers need to release some emotional energy, with a useful part of this being the opportunity to vent to colleagues. Next, they will need to talk through the incident to reflect on what happened and why. Finally, in the rebuilding phase, there is a need to develop a plan for dealing in future with similar situations, based on a judgment about what did or did not help in the present incident.

Tertiary measures can include problem solving in a one-to-one relationship to help a troubled colleague to analyse a problem, set goals and develop a plan to solve the problem, followed by the provision of descriptive feedback about his or her efforts (Rogers 2002). A second option is collaborative problem solving with a group of teachers. In primary schools, typically one teacher has the main responsibility for individual students; however, by high school many teachers will be in contact with a given student. Each could be facing similar difficulties with individual students, with each making little headway or inadvertently undermining what another teacher is putting in place. To develop a single, coherent plan, Roffey (2004) recommends routine 'cause for concern' meetings, where all teachers involved with given students can discuss the issues that concern them and how these might be solved.

A last form of tertiary support is the provision of emergency time away for teachers, which can entail taking over their class on the pretence that they must 'retrieve a message' from the front office, or temporarily removing some troublesome students so that their teacher can regain control of those students who remain in class.

One specific case for collegial support is the bullying or harassment of teachers, to which inexperienced teachers may be particularly vulnerable (Terry 1998). As is true for student victims, bullying of teachers needs a rapid response, which will be enabled when they feel confident of collegial support rather than feeling that they risk criticism for being victimised (Rogers 2002). Mentioning the topic in the school's discipline policy gives teachers confidence to expose harassment when it occurs.

Use of consultants

It would be useful to include in your policy a statement about the use of consultants—when, how and to whom to refer students for assessment and support. To that end, the school can collate a list of social service agencies that can support needy children and families.

Special issues

It will be useful for the school policy on discipline to cover specific issues such as catering for students with additional learning needs, preventing and responding to sexual harassment and bullying (whether perpetrated by teachers or students on either student or teacher victims) and child protection and abuse. The preponderance of boys as recipients of disciplinary measures might warrant a special focus on helping them adjust to schooling, particularly those made more vulnerable by socioeconomic or learning difficulties, as early intervention can prevent the later emergence of academic and behavioural problems (Sbarra & Pianta 2001). Issues to consider with respect to girls' behaviour might include how to equalise their access to special education services which, while an inclusion issue and thus part of a separate policy on that topic, is also a universal method to prevent disruptive behaviour. Finally, if the school plans to use suspension for serious behavioural infractions, you will need procedures for continuing to deliver an education to students during their exclusion.

Evaluation

The final section of your policy will detail how and by whom its procedures are to be evaluated. Specific measures of the effectiveness of practices might entail tallying the number of times that particular interventions have been invoked. Depending on which corrective measures are advocated within the policy, these could include numbers of referrals to the principal, peer mediation sessions, time outs or suspensions. Such tallies need to be interpreted in light of the school's special circumstances, however. For example, with highly mobile student populations, there might be little change in the number of disruptions or disciplinary referrals, which could either mean that the practices are ineffective or that they are being invoked most with new initiates to the school (McConaughy & Leone 2002). Or the total number of interventions might decrease, but the same students are referred repeatedly or the same teachers are the source of most referrals, signifying that for these individuals at least the measures are not working.

Other options to assess the effectiveness of practices include direct observations of classrooms, or questionnaires or interviews of teachers, students and parents about their satisfaction with the school's disciplinary methods. Teacher focus groups or surveys could also assess their morale, stress levels or perceived levels of work satisfaction. Of these, direct observation is difficult without extra staff time being made available for this purpose, which has budgetary implications.

A more general procedure could be to ask school staff, parents and students the following questions, negative answers to which will indicate a need to change practices (Borland 2003; Cowin et al. 1990; Sharp & Thompson 1994).

- Is your discipline plan consistent with your philosophy and theory?
- Are the procedures being enacted as originally conceived? Do your recommendations reflect actual practice or are they a 'wish list'?
- Are the outcomes congruent with what you set out to accomplish—that is, your original goals?
- Are there other, important, unanticipated outcomes?
- Are there students for whom the procedures are more or less successful than others?
- What additional resources (including materials and personnel) are necessary to make the policy more effective? Are these available?

As well as assessing these outcomes, you will need to evaluate the effectiveness of inputs—such as the resources being used, the efficient use of teachers' time and the involvement of parents (Davis & Rimm 2004). Although such evaluation may seem burdensome, it can be professionally fulfilling to be able to demonstrate to yourself—if to no one else—that what you are doing is effective. Reflection on your practice can only enhance your skills.

Conclusion

Above all, the policy that you arrive at has to be a living document—one that is relevant, owned, communicated, practised and regularly reviewed (Drifte 2004; Roffey 2004). It will need to be adjusted to reflect changes in the school community brought about by staff turnover and the enrolment of new students (Mathieson & Price 2002).

The result of minimising disruptiveness and maximising student engagement will be improved teacher morale. Policy formulation can enshrine reasonable work demands, clarify teachers' roles and responsibilities, improve coordination and communication across the school and harness support for teachers from senior school staff and parents

(Hart et al. 2000; Rutter 1983). These outcomes make it easier for teachers to teach well and for students to profit from that teaching (Rutter 1983).

Discussion questions

1   What are your beliefs about the purpose of discipline? How are these influenced by your understanding of childhood and how children learn, the reasons for disruptive behaviour, and the status of teachers with respect to students? What do these imply for your role as a teacher?
2   What goals would you seek to include in your discipline policy?
3   Which theory (or blend of theories) of discipline is consistent with your beliefs?
4   Which practices would you consider to be ideal in your present or intended teaching context?
5   What constraints can you identify that may affect the use or success of those practices?
6   If your school (or a school you attended on placement) adopted the policy that you espouse, would its present practices change? If so, in what ways?

Suggested further reading

Roffey, S. 2004 *The new teacher's survival guide to behaviour* Paul Chapman, London
Rogers, B. 1995 *Behaviour management: a whole-school approach* Ashton Scholastic, Gosford, NSW
——1998 '*You know the fair rule' and much more: strategies for making the hard job of discipline and behaviour management in school easier* ACER, Melbourne
——2002 *Classroom behaviour: a practical guide to teaching, behaviour management and colleague support* Paul Chapman, London

BIBLIOGRAPHY

Achenbach, T.M., Dumenci, L. and Rescorla, L.A. 2002 'Is American student behavior getting worse?: teacher ratings over an 18-year period' *School Psychology Review* vol. 31, no. 3, pp. 428–42

Adams, J.F. 2001 'Impact of parent training on family functioning' *Child and Family Behavior Therapy* vol. 23, no. 1, pp. 29–42

Adams, K.S. & Christenson S.L. 2000 'Trust and the family–school relationship: examination of parent–teacher differences in elementary and secondary grades' *Journal of School Psychology* vol. 38, no. 5, pp. 477–97

Adler, A. 1957 *Understanding human nature* Fawcett, New York

Agran, M. and Martin, J.E. 1987 'Applying a technology of self-control in community environments for individuals who are mentally retarded' in *Progress in behavior modification* eds M. Hersen, R. Eisler & P. Miller, SAGE, Newbury Park, CA, pp. 105–51

Ahearn, W.H., Kerwin, M.E., Eicher, P.S. and Lukens, C.T. 2001 'An ABAC comparison of two intensive interventions for food refusal' *Behavior Modification* vol. 25, no. 3, pp. 385–405

Ajmal, Y. 2001 'Introducing solution-focused thinking' in *Solutions in schools* eds Y. Ajmal & I. Rees, BT Press, London, pp. 10–29

Albert, L. 2003 *Cooperative discipline: teacher's handbook* AGS Publishing, Circle Pines, MN

Alberto P.A. and Troutman, A.C. 2003 *Applied behavior analysis for teachers* 6th edn, Merrill Prentice Hall, Upper Saddle River, NJ

Algozzine, B. 2002 'Building effective preventive practices' in *Preventing problem behaviors: a handbook of successful prevention strategies* eds B. Algozzine & P. Kay, Corwin Press, Thousand Oaks, CA, pp. 220–34

Algozzine, B. and Kay. P. 2002 'Promising practices for preventing problem behaviors' in *Preventing problem behaviors: a handbook of successful prevention strategies* eds B. Algozzine & P. Kay, Corwin Press, Thousand Oaks, CA, pp. 1–10

Allan, J. 1994 'Parenting education in Australia' *Children and Society* vol. 8, no. 4, pp. 344–59

Allen, J. 1995 'Friends, fairness, fun, and the freedom to choose: hearing student voices' *Journal of Curriculum and Supervision* vol. 10, no. 4, pp. 286–301

Alsaker, F.D. and Valkanover, S. 2001 'Early diagnosis and prevention of victimization in kindergarten' in *Peer harassment in school: the plight of the vulnerable and victimized* eds J. Juvonen & S. Graham, Guilford, New York, pp. 175–95

Amatea, E.S. 1988 'Brief strategic intervention with school behavior problems: a case of temper tantrums' *Psychology in the Schools* vol. 25, no. 2, pp. 174–83

Amatea, E.S. and Sherrard, P.A.D. 1989 'Reversing the school's response: a new approach to resolving persistent school problems' *The American Journal of Family Therapy* vol. 17, no. 1, pp. 15–26

——1991 'When students cannot or will not change their behavior: using brief strategic intervention in the school' *Journal of Counseling and Development* vol. 64, no. 4, pp. 341–3

Amato, P.R. and Fowler, F. 2002 'Parenting practices, child adjustment, and family diversity' *Journal of Marriage and Family* vol. 64, no. 3, pp. 703–16

Anastopoulos, A.D. and Barkley, R.A. 1992 'Attention deficit-hyperactivity disorder' in *Handbook of clinical child psychology* 2nd edn, eds C.E. Walker & M.C. Roberts, John Wiley and Sons, New York, pp. 413–30

Ang, R.P. and Hughes, J.N. 2002 'Differential benefits of skills training with antisocial youth based on group composition: a meta-analytic investigation' *School Psychology Review* vol. 31, no. 2, pp. 164–85

Ansbacher, H.L. and Ansbacher, R.R. 1956 *The individual psychology of Alfred Adler* Basic Books, New York

Armstrong, M. and Thorsborne, M. 2006 'Restorative responses to bullying' in *Bullying solutions: evidence-based approaches to bullying in Australian schools* eds H. McGrath & T. Noble, Pearson Longman, Sydney, pp. 175–88

Arnold, D.H., Homrok, S., Ortiz, C. and Stowe, R.M. 1999 'Direct observation of peer rejection acts and their temporal relation with aggressive acts' *Early Childhood Research Quarterly* vol. 14, no. 2, pp. 183–96

Arnold, D.H., McWilliams, L. and Arnold, E.H. 1998 'Teacher discipline and child misbehavior in day care: untangling causality with correlational data' *Developmental Psychology* vol. 34, no. 2, pp. 276–87

Arnold, L.E. 1996 'Sex differences in ADHD: conference summary' *Journal of Abnormal Child Psychology* vol. 24, no. 5, pp. 555–69

Arnold, M.E. and Hughes, J.N. 1999 'First do no harm: adverse effects of grouping deviant youth for skills training' *Journal of School Psychology* vol. 37, no. 1, pp. 99–115

Arthur, L., Beecher, B., Death, E., Dockett, S. and Farmer, S. 2005 *Programming and planning in early childhood settings* 3rd edn, Thomson, Melbourne

Arthur, M., Gordon, C. and Butterfield, N. 2003 *Classroom management: creating positive learning environments* Thomson, Melbourne

Asher, S.R. 1983 'Social competence and peer status: recent advances and future directions' *Child Development* vol. 54, pp. 1427–34

Asher, S.R. and Parker, J.G. 1989 'Significance of peer relationship problems in childhood' in *Social competence in developmental perspective* eds B.H. Schneider, G. Attili, J. Nadel & R.P. Weissberg, Kluwer Academic Publishers, Dordrecht, pp. 5–23

Asher, S.R. and Renshaw, P.D. 1981 'Children without friends: social knowledge and social-skill training' in *The development of children's friendships* eds S.R. Asher & J.M. Gottman, Cambridge University Press, Cambridge, UK, pp. 273–96

Ashman, A. and Conway, R.N.F. 1989 *Cognitive strategies for special education* Routledge, London

——1997 *An introduction to cognitive education: theory and applications* Routledge, London

Assor, A., Kaplan, H. and Roth, G. 2002 'Choice is good, but relevance is excellent: autonomy-enhancing and suppressing teacher behaviours predicting students' engagement in schoolwork' *British Journal of Educational Psychology* vol. 72, no. 2, pp. 261–78

Austin, A.B. and Draper, D.C. 1981 'Peer relationships of the academically gifted: a review' *Gifted Child Quarterly* vol. 25, no. 3, pp. 129–33

Australian Early Childhood Association 1991 'Australian Early Childhood Association code of ethics' *Australian Journal of Early Childhood* vol. 16, no. 1, pp. 3–6

Axelrod, S. 1977 *Behaviour modification for the classroom teacher* McGraw Hill, New York

Bailey, J. and Pyles, D. 1989 'Behavioral diagnostics' in *The treatment of severe behavior disorders: behavior analysis approaches* ed E. Cipani, The American Association on Mental Retardation, Washington, DC, pp. 85–107

Bailey, J.S. 1991 'Marketing behavior analysis requires different talk' *Journal of Applied Behavior Analysis* vol. 24, no. 3, pp. 445–8

——1992 'Gentle teaching: trying to win friends and influence people with euphemism, metaphor, smoke, and mirrors' *Journal of Applied Behavior Analysis* vol. 25, no. 4, pp. 879–83

Balson, M. 1992 *Understanding classroom behaviour* 3rd edn, ACER, Melbourne

——1994 *Becoming better parents* 4th edn, ACER, Melbourne

Bandura, A. 1986 *Social foundations of thought and action* Prentice Hall, Englewood Cliffs, NJ

——2001 'Social cognitive theory: an agentic perspective' *Annual Review of Psychology* vol. 52, pp. 1–26

Barkley, R.A. 1988 'Attention deficit disorder with hyperactivity' in *Behavioral assessment of childhood disorders* 2nd edn, eds E.J. Mash & L.G. Terdal, Guilford, New York, pp. 69–104

Battistich, V., Solomon, D., Kim, D., Watson, M. & Schaps, E. 1995 'Schools as communities, poverty levels of student populations, and students' attitudes, motives, and performance: a multilevel analysis' *American Educational Research Journal* vol. 32, no. 3, pp. 627–58

Baumeister, R.F. and Leary, M.F. 1995 'The need to belong: desire for interpersonal attachments as a fundamental human motivation' *Psychological Bulletin* vol. 117, no. 3, pp. 497–529

Baumrind, D. 1967 'Child care practices anteceding three patterns of preschool behavior' *Genetic Psychology Monographs* vol. 75, pp. 43–88

——1971 'Current patterns of parental authority' *Developmental Psychology Monograph* vol. 4, no. 1, pp. 1–103

Bear, G.G., Manning, M.A. and Izard, C.E. 2003 'Responsible behavior: the importance of social cognition and emotion' *School Psychology Quarterly* vol. 18, no. 2, pp. 140–57

Beishuizen, J.J., Hof, E., van Putten, C.M., Bouwmeester, S. and Asscher, J.J. 2001 'Students' and teachers' cognitions about good teachers' *British Journal of Educational Psychology* vol. 71, no. 2, pp. 185–201

Benes, K.M. and Kramer, J.J. 1989 'The behavioral tradition in schools (and miles to go before we sleep)' in *Cognitive-behavioral psychology in the schools* eds J.N. Hughes & R.J. Hall, Guilford, New York, pp. 15–36

Berg, I.K. and Steiner, S. 2003 *Children's solution work* Norton, New York

Berk, L.E. and Landau, S. 1993 'Private speech of learning disabled and normally achieving children in classroom academic and laboratory contexts' *Child Development* vol. 64, no. 2, pp. 556–71

Berk, L.E. and Potts, M.K. 1991 'Development and functional significance of private speech among attention-deficit hyperactivity disordered and normal boys' *Journal of Abnormal Child Psychology* vol. 19, no. 3, pp. 357–77

Bernard, M.E. 1986 *Becoming rational in an irrational world: Albert Ellis and rational-emotive therapy* McCulloch, Melbourne

Berndt, T.J. and Miller, K.E. 1990 'Expectancies, values, and achievement in junior high school' *Journal of Educational Psychology* vol. 82, no. 2, pp. 319–26

Bevill, A.R. and Gast, D.L. 1998 'Social safety for young children: a review of the literature on safety skills instruction' *Topics in Early Childhood Special Education* vol. 18, no. 4, pp. 222–34

Bibou-Nakou, I., Kiosseoglou, G. and Stogiannidou, A. 2000 'Elementary teachers' perceptions regarding school behavior problems: implications for school psychological services' *Psychology in the Schools* vol. 37, no. 2, pp. 123–34

Biederman, G.B., Davey, V.A., Ryder, C. and Franchi, D. 1994 'The negative effects of positive reinforcement in teaching children with developmental delay' *Exceptional Children* vol. 60, no. 5, pp. 458–65

Binder, L.M., Dixon, M.R. and Ghezzi, P.M. 2000 'A procedure to teach self-control to children with attention deficit hyperactivity disorder' *Journal of Applied Behavior Analysis* vol. 33, no. 2, pp. 233–7

Birch, S.H. and Ladd, G.W. 1997 'The teacher–child relationship and children's early school adjustment' *Journal of School Psychology* vol. 35, no. 1, pp. 61–79

Blankemeyer, M., Flannery, D.J. and Vazsonyi, A.T. 2002 'The role of aggression and social competence in children's perceptions of the child–teacher relationship' *Psychology in the Schools* vol. 39, no. 3, pp. 293–304

Blatchford, P., Baines, E., Kutnick, P. and Martin, C. 2001 'Classroom contexts: connections between class size and within class grouping' *British Journal of Educational Psychology* vol. 71, no. 2, pp. 283–302

Bolton, R. 1993 *People skills* Simon & Schuster, Sydney

Bong, M. & Skaalvik, E.M. 2003 'Academic self-concept and self-efficacy: how different are they really?' *Educational Psychology Review* vol. 15, no. 1, pp. 1–40

Bonner, B.L., Kaufman, K.L., Harbeck, C. and Brassard, M.R. 1992 'Child maltreatment' in *Handbook of clinical child psychology* 2nd edn, eds C.E. Walker & M.C. Roberts, John Wiley & Sons, New York, pp. 967–1008

Borland, J.H. 2003 'Evaluating gifted programs: a broader perspective' in *Handbook of gifted education* 2nd edn, eds N. Colangelo & G.A. Davis, Allyn & Bacon, Boston, MA, pp. 293–307

Borland, J.H. and Wright, L. 2000 'Identifying and educating poor and under-represented gifted students' in *International handbook of giftedness and talent* 2nd edn, eds K.A. Heller, F.J. Mönks, R.J. Sternberg & R.F. Subotnik, Pergamon, Oxford, UK, pp. 587–94

Bouffard, T., Marcoux, M-F., Vezeau, C. and Bordeleau, L. 2003 'Changes in self-perceptions of competence and intrinsic motivation among elementary schoolchildren' *British Journal of Educational Psychology* vol. 73, no. 2, pp. 171–86

Boulton, M.J. 1994 'Understanding and preventing bullying in the junior school playground' in *School bullying: insights and perspectives* eds P.K. Smith & S. Sharp, Routledge, London, pp. 132–59

——1997 'Teachers' views on bullying: definitions, attitudes and ability to cope' *British Journal of Educational Psychology* vol. 67, no. 2, pp. 223–33

Braswell, L. 1995 'Cognitive-behavioral approaches in the classroom' in *Understanding and managing children's classroom behavior* ed S. Goldstein, Wiley, New York, pp. 319–55

Briggs, F. and McVeity, M. 2000 *Teaching children to protect themselves* Allen & Unwin, Sydney

Brody, L.E. and Benbow, C.P. 1986 'Social and emotional adjustment of adolescents extremely talented in verbal or mathematical reasoning' *Journal of Youth and Adolescence* vol. 15, no. 6, pp. 1–18

Bromberg, D.S. and Johnson, B.T. 2001 'Sexual interest in children, child sexual abuse, and psychological sequelae for children' *Psychology in the Schools* vol. 38, no. 4, pp. 343–55

Brophy, J. 1981 'Teacher praise: a functional analysis' *Review of Educational Research* vol. 51, no. 1, pp. 5–32

Brown, W.H., Odom, S.L., Li, S. and Zercher, C. 1999 'Ecobehavioral assessment in early childhood programs: a portrait of preschool inclusion' *The Journal of Special Education* vol. 33, no. 3, pp. 138–53

Bryant, D., Vizzard, L.H., Willoughby, M. and Kupersmidt, J. 1999 'A review of interventions for preschoolers with aggressive and disruptive behavior' *Early Education and Development* vol. 10, no. 1, pp. 47–68

Buckingham, D. 2000 *After the death of childhood: growing up in the age of electronic media* Polity Press, Cambridge, UK

Buckley, S.D. and Newchok, D.K. 2005 'An evaluation of simultaneous presentation and differential reinforcement with response cost to reduce packing' *Journal of Applied Behavior Analysis* vol. 38, no. 3, pp. 405–9

Bukowski, W.M. and Sippola, L.K. 2001 'Groups, individuals, and victimization: a view of the peer system' in *Peer harassment in school: the plight of the vulnerable and victimized* eds J. Juvonen & S. Graham, Guilford, New York, pp. 355–77

Burden, R.L. and Fraser, B.J. 1993 'Classroom environment assessments' *Psychology in the Schools* vol. 30, no. 3, pp. 232–40

Butler-Por, N. 1993 'Underachieving gifted students' in *International handbook of research and development of giftedness and talent* eds K.A. Heller, F.J. Mönks & A.H. Passow, Pergamon, Oxford, UK, pp. 649–68

Bye, L. and Jussim, L. 1993 'A proposed model for the acquisition of social knowledge and social competence' *Psychology in the Schools* vol. 30, no. 2, pp. 143–61

Cameron, J. 2001 'Negative effects of reward on intrinsic motivation—a limited phenomenon: comment on Deci, Koestner, and Ryan (2001)' *Review of Educational Research* vol. 71, no. 1, pp. 29–42

Cameron, J. and Pierce, W.D. 1994 'Reinforcement, reward, and intrinsic motivation: a meta-analysis' *Review of Educational Research* vol. 64, no. 3, pp. 363–423

——1996 'The debate about rewards and intrinsic motivation: protests and accusations do not alter the results' *Review of Educational Research* vol. 66, no. 1, pp. 39–51

Cangelosi, J.S. 2004 *Classroom management strategies: gaining and maintaining students' cooperation* 5th edn, Wiley, New York

Canter, L. 1989 'Assertive discipline: a response' *Teachers College Record* vol. 90, no. 4, pp. 631–8

Canter, L. and Canter, M. 1976 *Assertive discipline: a take charge approach for today's educator* Lee Canter & Associates, Los Angeles, CA

——1992 *Assertive discipline: positive behavior management for today's classroom* Lee Canter & Associates, Santa Monica, CA

——2001 *Assertive discipline: positive behavior management for today's classroom* Canter and Associates, Los Angeles, CA

Caplan, M.Z. and Weissberg, R.P. 1989 'Promoting social competence in early adolescence' in *Social competence in developmental perspective* eds B.H. Schneider, G. Attili, J. Nadel & R.P. Weissberg, Kluwer Academic Publishers, Dordrecht, pp. 371–85

Carey, M. 1999 'Escaping the effects of violence: therapeutic gatherings with mothers and their children' in *Once upon a time...narrative therapy with children and their families* ed A. Morgan, Dulwich Centre Publications, Adelaide, SA, pp. 109–24

Carey, M. and Russell, S. 2003 'Re-authoring: some answers to commonly asked questions' *The International Journal of Narrative Therapy and Community Work* vol. 3, pp. 60–71

Carlsson-Paige, N. and Levin, D.E. 1992 'Making peace in violent times: a constructivist approach to conflict resolution' *Young Children* vol. 48, no. 1, pp. 4–13

Carr, E.G. 1997 'Invited commentary: the evolution of applied behavior analysis into positive behavior support' *Journal of the Association for Persons with Severe Handicaps* vol. 22, no. 4, pp. 208–9

Carter, J.F. 1993 'Self management: education's ultimate goal' *Teaching Exceptional Children* vol. 25, no. 3, pp. 28–32

Cartledge, G. and Milburn, J.F. (eds) 1995 *Teaching social skills to children and youth: innovative approaches* 3rd edn, Allyn & Bacon, Boston, MA

Cattley, G. 2004 'The impact of teacher-parent-peer support on students' well-being and adjustment to the middle years of schooling' *International Journal of Adolescence and Youth* vol. 11, no. 4, pp. 269–82

Cedar, R.B. and Levant, R.F. 1990 'A meta-analysis of the effects of Parent Effectiveness Training' *American Journal of Family Therapy* vol. 18, no. 4, pp. 373–84

Chan, L.K.S. 1988 'The perceived competence of intellectually talented students' *Gifted Child Quarterly* vol. 32, no. 3, pp. 310–14

——1996 'Motivational orientations and metacognitive abilities of intellectually gifted students' *Gifted Child Quarterly* vol. 40, no. 4, pp. 184–94

Chapman, J.W., Lambourne, R. and Silva, P.A. 1990 'Some antecedents of academic self-concept: a longitudinal study' *British Journal of Educational Psychology* vol. 60, part 1, pp. 142–52

Charles, C.M. and Senter, G.W. 2005a *Building classroom discipline* 8th edn, Pearson Allyn & Bacon, Boston, MA

——2005b *Elementary classroom management* 4th edn, Pearson Allyn & Bacon, Boston MA

Chew, A.L. 1998 *A primer on Adlerian psychology: behavior management techniques for young children* Humanics, Lake Worth, FL

Chibucos, T.R., Leite, R.W. and Weis, D.L. 2005 *Readings in family theory* SAGE, Thousand Oaks, CA

Childs, G. and McKay, M. 2001 'Boys starting school disadvantaged: implications from teachers' ratings of behaviour and achievement in the first two years' *British Journal of Educational Psychology* vol. 71, no. 2, pp. 303–14

Christenson, S.L. 2004 'The family–school partnership: an opportunity to promote the learning competence of all students' *School Psychology Review* vol. 33, no. 1, pp. 83–104

Cleary, T.J. and Zimmerman, B.J. 2004 'Self-regulation empowerment program: a school-based program to enhance self-regulated and self-motivated cycles of student learning' *Psychology in the Schools* vol. 41, no. 5, pp. 537–50

Cohen, E.G. 1994 'Restructuring the classroom: conditions for productive small groups' *Review of Educational Research* vol. 64, no. 1, pp. 1–35

Cohen, R., Duncan, M. and Cohen, S.L. 1994 'Classroom peer relations of children participating in a pull-out enrichment program' *Gifted Child Quarterly* vol. 38, no. 1, pp. 33–7

Coie, J.D., Christopoulos, C., Terry, R., Dodge, K.A. and Lochman, J.E. 1989 'Types of aggressive relationships, peer rejection, and developmental consequences' in *Social competence in developmental persective* eds B.H. Schneider, G. Attili, J. Nadel & R.P. Weissberg, Kluwer Academic Publishers, Dordrecht, pp. 223–37

Colangelo, N. and Davis, G.A. (eds) 2003 *Handbook of gifted education* 3rd edn, Allyn & Bacon, Boston, MA

Coleman, J.M. and Fults, B.A. 1982 'Self-concept and the gifted classroom: the role of social comparison' *Gifted Child Quarterly* vol. 26, no. 3, pp. 116–20

Combrinck-Graham, L. 1991 'On technique with children in family therapy: how calculated should it be?' *Journal of Marital and Family Therapy* vol. 18, no. 4, pp. 373–7

Compas, B.E. 1987 'Coping with stress during childhood and adolescence' *Psychological Bulletin* vol. 101, no. 3, pp. 393–403

Connell, S., Sanders, M.R., and Markie-Dadds, C. 1997 'Self-directed behavioral family intervention for parents of oppositional children in rural and remote areas' *Behavior Modification* vol. 21, no. 4, pp. 379–408

Conoley, C.W., Graham, J.M., Neu, T., Craig, M.C., O'Pry, A., Cardin, S.A., Brossart, D.F. and Parker, R.I. 2003 'Solution-focused family therapy with three aggressive and oppositional-acting children: an N=1 empirical study' *Family Process* vol. 42, no. 3, pp. 361–74

Conyers, C., Miltenberger, R., Maki, A., Barenz, R., Jurgens, M., Sailer, A., Haugen, M. and Kopp, B. 2004 'A comparison of response cost and differential reinforcement of other behavior to reduce disruptive behavior in a preschool classroom' *Journal of Applied Behavior Analysis* vol. 37, no. 3, pp. 411–15

Cooper, L.J., Wacker, D.P., McComas, J.J., Brown, K., Peck, S.M., Richman, D., Drew, J., Frischmeyer, P. and Millard, T. 1995 'Use of component analyses to identify active variables in treatment packages for children with feeding disorders' *Journal of Applied Behavior Analysis* vol. 28, no. 2, pp. 139–53

Cooper, P. and Upton, G. 1991 'Controlling the urge to control: an ecosystemic approach to problem behaviour in schools' *Support for Learning* vol. 6, no. 1, pp. 22–6

Cordova, D.I. and Lepper, M.R. 1996 'Intrinsic motivation and the process of learning: beneficial effects of contextualization, personalization, and choice' *Journal of Educational Psychology* vol. 88, no. 4, pp. 715–30

Corey, G. 1996 *Theory and practice of counseling and psychotherapy* 5th edn, Brooks/Cole, Monterey, CA

Covaleskie, J.F. 1992 'Discipline and morality: beyond rules and consequences' *The Educational Forum* vol. 56, no. 2, pp. 173–83

Covington, M.V. and Müeller, K.J. 2001 'Intrinsic versus extrinsic motivation: an approach/avoidance reformulation' *Educational Psychology Review* vol. 13, no. 2, pp. 157–76

Cowin, M., Freeman, L., Farmer, A., James, M., Drent, A. and Arthur, R. 1990 *Positive school discipline: a practical guide to developing policy* rev edn Narbethong Publications, Boronia, Vic.

Craven, R.G. and Marsh, H.W. 1997 'Threats to gifted and talented students' self-concepts in the big pond: research results and educational implications' *The Australasian Journal of Gifted Education* vol. 6, no. 2, pp. 7–17

Crick, N.R., Casas, J.F. and Hyon-Chin, K. 1999 'Relational and physical forms of peer victimization in preschool' *Developmental Psychology* vol. 35, no. 2, pp. 376–85

Crick, N.R. and Grotpeter, J.K. 1995 'Relational aggression, gender, and social-psychological adjustment' *Child Development* vol. 66, no. 3, pp. 710–22

Crick, N.R., Nelson, D.A., Morales, J.R., Cullerton-Sen, C., Casas, J.F. and Hickman, S.E. 2001 'Relational victimization in childhood and adolescence: I hurt you through the grapevine' in *Peer harassment in school: the plight of the vulnerable and victimized* eds J. Juvonen & S. Graham, Guilford, New York, pp. 196–214

Crockenberg, S. and Litman, C. 1990 'Autonomy as competence in 2-year-olds: maternal correlates of child defiance, compliance, and self-assertion' *Developmental Psychology* vol. 26, no. 6, pp. 961–71

Cropper, C. 1998 'Is competition an effective classroom tool for the gifted student?' *Gifted Child Today* vol. 21, no. 3, pp. 28–31

Cullen, K. and Ramoutar, L. 2003 'Building fresh perceptions of a class: turning "horrors into lovelies"' *Educational and Child Psychology* vol. 20 no. 4, pp. 116–30

Curwin, R.L. and Mendler, A.N. 1988 'Packaged discipline programs: let the buyer beware' *Educational Leadership* vol. 46, no. 2, pp. 68–71

——1989 'We repeat, let the buyer beware: a response to Canter' *Educational Leadership* vol. 46, no. 6, p. 83

Cushing, L.S. and Kennedy, G.H. 1997 'Academic effects of providing peer support in general education classrooms on students without disabilities' *Journal of Applied Behavior Analysis* vol. 30, no. 1, pp. 139–51

Dahlberg, G., Moss, P. and Pence, A. 1999 *Beyond quality in early childhood education and care: postmodern perspectives* Routledge Falmer, London

Dallos, R. and Draper, R. 2005 *An introduction to family therapy: systemic theory and practice* 2nd edn, Open University Press, Maidenhead, UK

Damon, W. and Phelps, E. 1989 'Critical distinctions among three approaches to peer education' *International Journal of Educational Research* vol. 13, no. 1, pp. 9–19

Dauber, S.L. and Benbow, C.P. 1990 'Aspects of personality and peer relations of extremely talented adolescents' *Gifted Child Quarterly* vol. 34, no. 1, pp. 10–14

Davies, J.D. 2005 'Voices from the margins: the perceptions of pupils with emotional and behavioural difficulties about their educational experiences' in *Handbook of emotional and behavioural difficulties* eds P. Clough, P. Garner, J.T. Pardeck & F. Yuen, SAGE, London, pp. 299–316

Davis, G.A. and Rimm, S.B. 2004 *Education of the gifted and talented* 5th edn, Pearson Allyn & Bacon, Boston, MA

Davis, T.E. and Osborn, C.J. 2000 *The solution-focused school counselor: shaping professional practice* Brunner-Routledge, New York

De Jong, P. and Berg, I.K. 2002 *Interviewing for solutions* 2nd edn, Brooks/Cole Thomson, Pacific Grove, CA

de Shazer, S. 1988 *Clues: investigating solutions in brief therapy* Norton, New York

——1993 'Creative misunderstanding: there is no escape from language' in *Therapeutic conversations* eds S. Gilligan & R. Price, W.W. Norton & Co, New York, pp. 81–135

de Shazer, S., Berg, I.K., Lipchik, E., Nunnally, E., Molnar, A., Gingerich, W. and Weiner-Davis, M. 1986 'Brief therapy: focused solution development' *Family Process* vol. 25, no. 2, pp. 207–22

Deci, E.L., Driver, R.E, Hotchkiss, L., Robbins, R.J. and Wilson, I.M. 1993 'The relation of mothers' controlling vocalizations to children's intrinsic motivation' *Journal of Experimental Child Psychology* vol. 55, no. 2, pp. 151–62

Deci, E.L., Eghrari, H., Patrick, B.C. and Leone, D.R. 1994 'Facilitating internalization: The self-determination theory perspective' *Journal of Personality* vol. 62, no. 1, pp. 119–42

Deci, E.L., Koestner, R. and Ryan, R.M. 1999a 'A meta-analytic review of experiments examining the effects of extrinsic rewards on intrinsic motivation' *Psychological Bulletin* vol. 125, no. 6, pp. 627–68

——1999b 'The undermining effect is a reality after all—extrinsic rewards, task interest, and self-determination: reply to Eisenberger, Pierce, and Cameron (1999) and Lepper, Henderlong, and Gingras (1999)' *Psychological Bulletin* vol. 125, no. 6, pp. 692–700

——2001 'Extrinsic rewards and intrinsic motivation in education: reconsidered once again' *Review of Educational Research* vol. 71, no. 1, pp. 1–27

Deci, E.L., Vallerand, R.J., Pelletier, L.G. and Ryan, R.M. 1991 'Motivation and education: the self-determination perspective' *Educational Psychologist* vol. 26, nos 3 & 4, pp. 325–46

Dekovic, M., Janssens, J.M.A.M. and Van As, N.M.C. 2003 'Family predictors of antisocial behavior in adolescence' *Family Process* vol. 42, no. 2, pp. 223–35

Demaray, M.K. and Malecki, C.K. 2002 'The relationship between perceived social support and maladjustment for students at risk' *Psychology in the Schools* vol. 39, no. 3, pp. 305–16

——2003a 'Perceptions of the frequency and importance of social support by students classified as victims, bullies, and bully/victims in an urban middle school' *School Psychology Review* vol. 32, no. 3, pp. 471–89

——2003b 'Importance ratings of socially supportive behaviors by children and adolescents' *School Psychology Review* vol. 32, no. 1, pp. 108–31

Demaray, M.K., Malecki, C.K., Davidson, L.M., Hodgson, K.K. and Rebus, J. 2005 'The relationships between social support and student adjustment: a longitudinal analysis' *Psychology in the Schools* vol. 42, no. 7, pp. 691–706

Derman-Sparks, L. and the A.B.C. Task Force 1989 *Anti-bias curriculum: tools for empowering young children* National Association for the Education of Young Children, Washington, DC

Dev, P.C. 1997 'Intrinsic motivation and academic achievement: what does their relationship imply for the classroom teacher?' *Remedial and Special Education* vol. 18, no. 1, pp. 12–19

Diamond, K.E., Hestenes, L.L., Carpenter, E.S. and Innes, F.K. 1997 'Relationships between enrollment in an inclusive class and preschool children's ideas about people with disabilities' *Topics in Early Childhood Special Education* vol. 17, no. 4, pp. 520–36

Diaz, R.M. and Berk, L.E. 1995 'A Vygotskian critique of self-instructional training' *Development and Psychopathology* vol. 7, no. 2, pp. 369–92

DiCintio, M.J. and Gee, S. 1999 'Control is the key: unlocking the motivation of at-risk students' *Psychology in the Schools* vol. 36, no. 3, pp. 231–7

Dicocco, N.E., Chalfin, S.R. and Olson, J.M. 1987 'Systemic family therapy goes to school' *Social Work in Education* vol. 9, no. 4, pp. 209–21

Dinkmeyer, D. and Dreikurs, R. 1963 *Encouraging children to learn: the encouragement process* Prentice Hall, Englewood Cliffs, NJ

Dinkmeyer, D. and McKay, G. 1989 *Systematic training for effective parenting* 3rd edn, American Guidance Service, Circle Pines, MN

Dinkmeyer, D., McKay, G. and Dinkmeyer, D. 1980 *Systematic training for effective teaching* American Guidance Service, Circle Pines, MN

Dinkmeyer, D. Sr, McKay, G.D., Dinkmeyer, J.S., Dinkmeyer, D. Jr, McKay, J.L. 1997 *Parenting young children: systematic training for effective parenting (STEP) of children under six* American Guidance Service, Circle Pines, MN

Dixon, M.R., Hayes, L.J., Binder, L.M., Manthey, S., Sigman, C. and Zdanowski, D.M. 1998 'Using a self-control training procedure to increase appropriate behaviour' *Journal of Applied Behavior Analysis* vol. 31, no. 2, pp. 203–9

Dobson, J. 1970 *Dare to discipline* Anzea Books, Sydney

——1992 *The new dare to discipline* Tyndale House, Wheaton, IL

Docking, J. 1982 'The impact of control and management styles on young children in the early years of schooling' *Early Child Development and Care* vol. 8, pp. 239–52

Dodge, K.A. 1983 'Behavioral antecedents of peer social status' *Child Development* vol. 54, pp. 1386–99

Doherty-Derkowski, G. 1995 *Quality matters: excellence in early childhood programs* Addison-Wesley, Don Mills, Ontario

Doll, B. and Lyon, M.A. 1998 'Risk and resilience: implications for the delivery of educational and mental health services in schools' *School Psychology Review* vol. 27, no. 3, pp. 348–63

Dornbusch, S.M., Ritter, P.L., Liederman, P.H., Roberts, D.F. and Fraleigh, M.J. 1987 'The relation of parenting style to adolescent school performance' *Child Development* vol. 58, no. 5, pp. 1244–57

Dörnyei, Z. 2000 'Motivation in action: towards a process-oriented conceptualization of student motivation' *British Journal of Educational Psychology* vol. 70, no. 4, pp. 519–38

Doyle, R. 2003 'Developing the nurturing school: spreading nurture groups and principles into mainstream classrooms' *Emotional and Behavioural Difficulties* vol. 8, no. 4, pp. 252–66

Doyle, W. 1986 'Classroom organization and management' *Handbook of research on teaching* 3rd edn, ed M.C. Wittrock, Macmillan, New York, pp. 392–431

Dreikurs, R. and Cassel, P. 1990 *Discipline without tears* 2nd edn, Dutton, New York

Drifte, C. 2004 *Encouraging positive behaviour in the early years: a practical guide* Paul Chapman, London

Drouet, D. 1993 'Adolescent female bullying and sexual harassment' in *Understanding and managing bullying* ed D. Tattum, Heinemann Educational, Oxford, UK, pp. 173–88

Ducharme, D.E. and Holborn, S.W. 1997 'Programming generalization of social skills in preschool children with hearing impairments' *Journal of Applied Behavior Analysis* vol. 30, no. 4, pp. 639–51

Duncan, B.L., Miller, S.D. and Sparks, J.A. 2003 'Interactional and solution-focused brief therapies: evolving concepts of change' in *Handbook of family therapy: the science and practice of working with families and couples* eds T.L. Sexton, G.R. Weeks & M.S. Robbins, Brunner-Routledge, New York, pp. 101–23

Dunlap, G., dePerczel, M., Clarke, S., Wilson, D., Wrights, S., White, R. and Gomez, A. 1994 'Choice making to promote adaptive behavior for students with emotional and behavioral challenges' *Journal of Applied Behavior Analysis* vol. 27, no. 3, pp. 505–18

DuPaul, G.J., Ervin, R.A., Hook, C.L. and McGoey, K.E. 1998 'Peer tutoring for children with attention deficit hyperactivity disorder: effects on classroom behavior and academic performance' *Journal of Applied Behavior Analysis* vol. 31, no. 4, pp. 579–92

Durrant, M. 1995 *Creative strategies for school problems* Eastwood Family Therapy Centre, Epping, NSW/Norton, New York

Dweck, C.S. and Leggett, E.L. 1988 'A social-cognitive approach to motivation and personality' *Psychological Review* vol. 95, no. 2, pp. 256–73

Eckenrode, J., Laird, M. and Doris, J. 1993 'School performance and disciplinary problems among abused and neglected children' *Developmental Psychology* vol. 29, no. 1, pp. 53–62

Eckert, T.L., Ardoin, S.P., Daly, E.J. III and Martens, B.K. 2002 'Improving oral reading fluency: a brief experimental analysis of combining an antecedent intervention with consequences' *Journal of Applied Behavior Analysis* vol. 35, no. 3, pp. 271–81

Edwards, C.H. and Watts, V. 2004 *Classroom discipline and management: an Australian perspective* Wiley, Milton, QLD

Egan, S.K. and Perry, D.G. 1998 'Does low self-regard invite victimization?' *Developmental Psychology* vol. 34, no. 2, pp. 299–309

Eisenberger, R. and Armeli, S. 1997 'Can salient reward increase creative performance without reducing intrinsic creative interest?' *Journal of Personality and Social Psychology* vol. 72, no. 3, pp. 652–63

Eisenberger, R., Pierce, W.D. and Cameron, J. 1999 'Effects of reward on intrinsic motivation: comment on Deci, Koestner, and Ryan (1999)' *Psychological Bulletin* vol. 125, no. 6, pp. 677–91

Elinoff, M.J., Chafouleas, S.M. and Sassu, K.A. 2004 'Bullying: considerations for defining and intervening in school settings' *Psychology in the Schools* vol. 41, no. 8, pp. 887–97

Elkind, D. 2001 *The hurried child: growing up too fast too soon* 3rd edn, Perseus Books, Cambridge, MA

Ellis, A. 1962 *Reason and emotion in psychotherapy* Lyle Stuart, Secaucus, NJ

——2005 'Rational emotive behavior therapy' in *Current psychotherapies* 7th edn, eds R.J. Corsini & D. Wedding, Thomson Brooks/Cole, Belmont, CA, pp. 166–201

Emmer, E.T. and Aussiker, A. 1990 'School and classroom discipline programs: how well do they work?' in *Student discipline strategies: research and practice* ed O.C. Moles, State University of New York Press, Albany, NY, pp. 129–66

Emmer, E.T., Evertson, C.M. and Worsham, M.E. 2006 *Classroom management for middle and high school teachers* 7th edn, Pearson Allyn & Bacon, Boston, MA

Ervin, R.A., Ehrhardt, K.E. and Poling, A. 2001 'Functional assessment: old wine in new bottles' *School Psychology Review* vol. 30, no. 2, pp. 173–9

Ervin, R.A, Radford, P.M., Bertsch, K., Piper, A.L., Ehrhardt, K.E. and Poling, A. 2001 'A descriptive analysis and critique of the empirical literature on school-based functional assessment' *School Psychology Review* vol. 30, no. 2, pp. 193–210

Eslea, M. 1999 'Attributional styles in boys with severe behaviour problems: a possible reason for lack of progress on a positive behaviour programme' *British Journal of Educational Psychology* vol. 69, no. 1, pp. 33–45

Espelage, D.L. and Swearer, S.M. 2003 'Research on school bullying and victimization: what have we learned and where do we go from here?' *School Psychology Review* vol. 32, no. 3, pp. 365–83

Esposito, C. 1999 'Learning in urban blight: school climate and its effect on the school performance of urban, minority, low-income children' *School Psychology Review* vol. 28, no. 3, pp. 365–77

Essa, E.L. and Murray, C.I. 1999 'Sexual play: when should you be concerned?' *Childhood Education* vol. 75, no. 4, pp. 231–4

Evertson, C.M., Emmer, E.T. and Worsham, M.E. 2003 *Classroom management for elementary teachers* 6th edn, Pearson Allyn & Bacon, Boston, MA

Faber, A., Mazlish, E., Nyberg, L. and Templeton, R.A. 1995 *How to talk so kids can learn at home and in school* Fireside, New York

Farver, J.M. 1996 'Aggressive behavior in preschoolers' social networks: do birds of a feather flock together?' *Early Childhood Research Quarterly* vol. 11, no. 3, pp. 333–50

Favazza, P.D. and Odom, S.L. 1997 'Promoting positive attitudes of kindergarten-age children toward people with disabilities' *Exceptional Children* vol. 63, no. 3, pp. 405–18

Field, E. and Carroll, P. 2006 'Effective ways to work with parents' in *Bullying solutions: evidence-based approaches to bullying in Australian schools* eds H. McGrath & T. Noble, Pearson Longman, Sydney, pp. 209–25

Fields, M. and Boesser, C. 2002 *Constructive guidance and discipline* 3rd edn, Merrill Prentice Hall, Upper Saddle River, NJ

Finn, J.D., Pannozzo, G.F.M. and Achilles, C.M. 2003 'The "why's" of class size: student behavior in small classes' *Review of Educational Research* vol. 73, no. 3, pp. 321–68

Fisch, R. and Schlanger, K. 1999 *Brief therapy with intimidating cases: changing the unchangeable* Jossey-Bass, San Francisco, CA

Fisch, R., Weakland, J.H. and Segal, L. 1982 *The tactics of change: doing therapy briefly* Jossey-Bass, San Francisco, CA

Fisher, W.W., O'Connor, J.T., Kurtz, P.F., DeLeon, I.G. and Gotjen, D.L. 2000a 'The effects of noncontingent delivery of high- and low-preference stimuli on attention-maintained destructive behavior' *Journal of Applied Behavior Analysis* vol. 33, no. 1, pp. 79–83

Fisher, W.W., Thompson, R.H., Hagopian, L.P., Bowman, L.G. and Krug, A. 2000b 'Facilitating tolerance of delayed reinforcement during functional communication training' *Behavior Modification* vol. 24, no. 1, pp. 3–29

Flink, C., Boggiano, A.K. and Barrett, M. 1990 'Controlling teaching strategies: undermining children's self-determination and performance' *Journal of Personality and Social Psychology* vol. 59, no. 5, pp. 915–26

Flouri, E., Buchanan, A. and Bream, V. 2002 'Adolescents' perceptions of their fathers' involvement: significance to school attitudes' *Psychology in the Schools* vol. 39, no. 5, pp. 575–82

Ford, D.Y. 2003 'Equity and excellence: culturally diverse students in gifted education' in *Handbook of gifted education* 3rd edn, eds N. Colangelo & G.A. Davis, Allyn & Bacon, Boston, MA, pp. 506–20

Ford, D.Y. and Harris, J.J. III 2000 'A framework for infusing multicultural curriculum into gifted education' *Roeper Review* vol. 23, no. 1, pp. 4–10

Ford, D.Y., Howard, T.C., Harris, J.J. III and Tyson, C.A. 2000 'Creating culturally responsive classrooms for gifted African American students' *Journal for the Education of the Gifted* vol. 23, no. 4, pp. 397–427

Ford, D.Y. and Trotman, M.F. 2001 'Teachers of gifted students: suggested multicultural characteristics and competencies' *Roeper Review* vol. 23, no. 4, pp. 235–9

Ford, M.A. 1989 'Students' perceptions of affective issues impacting the social emotional development and school performance of gifted/talented youngsters' *Roeper Review* vol. 11, no. 3, pp. 131–4

Fox, C.L. and Boulton, M.J. 2005 'The social skills problems of victims of bullying: self, peer and teacher perceptions' *British Journal of Educational Psychology* vol. 75, no. 2, pp. 313–28

Fox, H. 2003 'Using therapeutic documents: a review' *The International Journal of Narrative Therapy and Community Work* vol. 4, pp. 26–36

Foxx, R. 1982 *Decreasing behaviors of severely retarded and autistic persons* Research Press, Champaign, IL

Fraser, S. and Gestwicki, C. 2002 *Authentic childhood: exploring Reggio Emilia in the classroom* Delmar, Albany, NY

Frederickson, N.L. and Furnham, A.F. 2004 'Peer-assessed behavioural characteristics and sociometric rejection: differences between pupils who have moderate learning difficulties and their mainstream peers' *British Journal of Educational Psychology* vol. 74, no. 3, pp. 391–410

Freeman, J. 1995 'Annotation: recent studies of giftedness in children' *Journal of Child Psychology and Psychiatry* vol. 36, no. 4, pp. 531–47

——1996 *Highly able girls and boys* Department for Education and Employment, London

Freeman, J., Epston, D. and Lobovits, D. 1997 *Playful approaches to serious problems: narrative therapy with children and their families* Norton, New York

Friedman, I.A. 2003 'Self-efficacy and burnout in teaching: the importance of interpersonal-relations efficacy' *Social Psychology of Education* vol. 6, no. 3, pp. 191–215

Friend, M. and Cook, L. 2003 *Interactions: collaboration skills for school professionals* 4th edn, Allyn & Bacon, Boston, MA

Fuller, A. 2006 'A resilience-based approach to helping victims of bullying and their families' *Bullying solutions: evidence-based approaches to bullying in Australian schools* eds H. McGrath & T. Noble, Pearson Longman, Sydney, pp. 161–73

Fylling, I. and Sandvin, J.T. 1999 'The role of parents in special education: the notion of partnership revised' *European Journal of Special Needs Education* vol. 14, no. 2, pp. 144–57

Gagné, F. 2003 'Transforming gifts into talents: the DMGT as a developmental theory' in *Handbook of gifted education* 3rd edn, eds N. Colangelo & G.A. Davis, Allyn & Bacon, Boston, MA, pp. 60–74

Gamman, R. 2003 'Sharing the load, supporting the staff: collaborative management of difficult behaviour in primary schools' *Emotional and Behavioural Difficulties* vol. 8, no. 3, pp. 217–29

Gamoran, A. 1992 'Is ability grouping equitable?' *Educational Leadership* vol. 50, no. 2, pp. 11–17

Gamoran, A. and Berends, M. 1987 'The effects of stratification in secondary schools: synthesis of survey and enthnographic research' *Review of Educational Research* vol. 57, no. 4, pp. 415–35

García-Vázquez, E. and Ehly, S.W. 1992 'Peer tutoring effects on students who are perceived as not socially accepted' *Psychology in the Schools* vol. 29, no. 3, pp. 256–66

Gartrell, D. 1987a 'Assertive discipline: unhealthy for children and other living things' *Young Children* vol. 42, no. 2, pp. 10–11

——1987b 'Punishment or guidance?' *Young Children* vol. 42, no. 3, pp. 55–61

——2003 *A guidance approach for the encouraging classroom* 3rd edn, Delmar, New York

Gathercole, S.E. and Pickering, S.J. 2000 'Working memory deficits in children with low achievement in the national curriculum at 7 years of age' *British Journal of Educational Psychology* vol. 70, no. 2, pp. 177–94

George, C. and Main, M. 1979 'Social interactions of young abused children: approach, avoidance, and aggression' *Child Development* vol. 50, no. 2, pp. 306–18

Gesten, E.L., De Apodaca, R.F., Rains, M., Weissberg, R.P. and Cowen, E.L. 1979 'Promoting peer-related social competence in schools' in *Social competence in children* eds M.W. Kent & J.E. Rolf, University Press of New England, Hanover, NH, pp. 220–47

Gilbert, S. 2000 *A field guide to boys and girls* Quill, New York

Gillies, R.M. 2000 'The maintenance of cooperative and helping behaviours in cooperative groups' *British Journal of Educational Psychology* vol. 70, no. 1, pp. 97–111

Gillies, R.M. and Ashman, A.F. 1998 'Behavior and interactions of children in cooperative groups in lower and middle elementary grades' *Journal of Educational Psychology* vol. 90, no. 4, pp. 746–57

——2000 'The effects of cooperative learning on students with learning difficulties in the lower elementary school *The Journal of Special Education* vol. 34, no. 1, pp. 19–27

Gingerich, W.J. and Eisengart, S. 2000 'Solution-focused brief therapy: a review of the outcome research' *Family Process* vol. 39, no. 4, pp. 477–98

Ginott, H.G. 1972 *Teacher and child* Macmillan, New York

Ginott, H.G., Ginott, A. and Goddard, H.W. 2003 *Between parent and child* 2nd edn, Three Rivers Press, New York

Ginsberg, G.S. and Bronstein, P. 1993 'Family factors related to children's intrinsic/extrinsic motivational orientation and academic performance' *Child Development* vol. 64, no. 5, pp. 1461–74

Glasser, W. 1969 *Schools without failure* Harper & Row, New York

——1988 *Choice theory in the classroom* rev edn, HarperCollins, New York

——1992a *The quality school: managing students without coercion* 2nd edn, Harper Perennial, New York

——1992b 'The quality school curriculum' *Phi Delta Kappan* vol. 73, no. 9, pp. 690–4

——1998a *The quality school: managing students without coercion*, HarperPerennial, New York

——1998b *The quality school teacher*, HarperPerennial, New York

——1998c *Choice theory: a new psychology of personal freedom* HarperCollins, New York

Goldenberg, I. and Goldenberg, H. 2005 'Family therapy' in *Current psychotherapies* 7th edn, eds R.J. Corsini & D. Wedding, Thomson Brooks/Cole, Belmont, CA, pp. 372–404

Goldstein, A.P., Sprafkin, R.P. and Gershaw, N.J. 1995 'Teaching the adolescent: social skills training through skillstreaming' in *Teaching social skills to children and youth: innovative approaches* 3rd edn, eds G. Cartledge & J.F. Milburn, Allyn & Bacon, Boston, MA, pp. 291–327

Goldstein, S. 1995 'Attention deficit hyperactivity disorder' in *Understanding and managing children's classroom behavior* ed S. Goldstein, John Wiley & Sons, New York, pp. 56–78

Gonzalez, J.E., Nelson, J.R., Gutkin, T.B., Saunders, A., Galloway, A. and Shwery, C.S. 2004 'Rational emotive therapy with children and adolescents: a meta-analysis' *Journal of Emotional and Behavioral Disorders* vol. 12, no. 4, pp. 222–35

Gonzalez-DeHass, A.R., Willems, P.P. and Holbein, M.F.D. 2005 'Examining the relationship between parental involvement and student motivation' *Educational Psychology Review* vol. 17, no. 2, pp. 99–123

Good, T.L. and Brophy, J.E. 2005 *Looking in classrooms* 9th edn, Longman, New York

Goodenow, C. 1993a 'The psychological sense of school membership among adolescents: scale development and educational correlates' *Psychology in the Schools* vol. 30, no. 1, pp. 79–90

——1993b 'Classroom belonging among early adolescent students: relationships to motivation and achievement' *Journal of Early Adolescence* vol. 13, no. 1, pp. 21–43

Goodman, J. 1992 *Elementary schooling for critical democracy* State University of New York Press, Albany, NY

Gordon, T. 1970 *Parent effectiveness training* Plume, New York

——1974 *Teacher effectiveness training* Peter H. Wyden, New York

——1991 *Teaching children self-discipline at home and at school* Random House, Sydney

Gottfried, A.E., Fleming, J.S. and Gottfried, A.W. 1994 'Role of parental motivational practices in children's academic intrinsic motivation and achievement' *Journal of Educational Psychology* vol. 86, no. 1, pp. 104–13

Greenman, J. and Stonehouse, A. 1997 *Prime times: a handbook for excellence in infant and toddler programs* Longman, South Melbourne

Gresham, F.M., Watson, T.S. and Skinner, C.H. 2001 'Functional behavioral assessment: principles, procedures, and future directions' *School Psychology Review* vol. 30, no. 2, pp. 156–72

Griffith, J., Steptoe, A. and Cropley, M. 1999 'An investigation of coping strategies associated with job stress in teachers' *British Journal of Educational Psychology* vol. 69, no. 4, pp. 517–31

Grolnick, W.S. 2003 *The psychology of parental control: how well-meant parenting backfires* Lawrence Erlbaum, Mahwah, NJ

Grolnick, W.S., Benjet, C., Kurowski, C.O. and Apostoleris, N.H. 1997 'Predictors of parent involvement in children's schooling' *Journal of Educational Psychology* vol. 89, no. 3, pp. 538–48

Grolnick, W.S., Bridges, L.J. and Connell, J.P. 1996 'Emotion regulation in two-year-olds: strategies and emotional expression in four contexts' *Child Development* vol. 67, no. 3, pp. 928–41

Grolnick, W.S., Frodi, A. and Bridges, L.J. 1984 'Maternal control style and the mastery motivation of one-year-olds' *Infant Mental Health Journal* vol. 5, pp. 72–82

Grolnick, W.S., Gurland, S.T., DeCourcey, W. and Jacob, K. 2002 'Antecedents and consequences of mothers' autonomy support: an experimental investigation' *Developmental Psychology* vol. 38, no. 1, pp. 143–55

Grolnick, W.S. and Ryan, R.M. 1989 'Parent styles associated with children's self-regulation and competence in school' *Journal of Educational Psychology* vol. 81, no. 2, pp. 143–54

Gross, M.U.M. 1996 'The pursuit of excellence or the search for intimacy: the forced-choice dilemma for gifted youth' in *Gifted children: the challenge continues: a guide for parents and teachers* eds A. Jacob & G. Barnsley, New South Wales Association for Gifted and Talented Children, Sydney, pp. 111–20

——1997 'How ability grouping turns big fish into little fish—or does it?: of optical illusions and optimal environments' *The Australasian Journal of Gifted Education* vol. 6, no. 2, pp. 18–30

Grossman, H. 2004 *Classroom behavior management for diverse and inclusive schools* 3rd edn, Rowman & Littlefield, Lanham, MD

Grusec, J.E. and Goodnow, J.J. 1994 'Impact of parental discipline methods on the child's internalization of values: a reconceptualization of current points of view' *Developmental Psychology* vol. 30, no. 1, pp. 4–19

Guralnick, M.J. and Groom, J.M. 1987 'The peer relations of mildly delayed and nonhandicapped preschool children in mainstreamed playgroups' *Child Development* vol. 58, no. 6, pp. 1556–72

Guralnick, M.J., Connor, R.T., Hammond, M., Gottman, J.M. and Kinnish, K. 1995 'Immediate effects of mainstreamed settings on the social interactions and social integration of preschool children' *American Journal on Mental Retardation* vol. 100, no. 4, pp. 359–77

Haley, J. 1980 *Leaving home: the therapy of disturbed young people* McGraw-Hill, New York

Hall, C.W., Peterson, A.D., Webster, R.E., Bolen, L.M. and Brown, M.B. 1999 'Perception of nonverbal social cues by regular education, ADHD, and ADHD/LD students' *Psychology in the Schools* vol. 36, no. 6, pp. 505–14

Hallahan, D.P. and Kauffman, J.M. 2003 *Exceptional learners: introduction to special education* 9th edn, Allyn & Bacon, Boston, MA

Hallinan, M.T. 1990 'The effects of ability grouping in secondary schools: a response to Slavin's best-evidence synthesis' *Review of Educational Research* vol. 60, no. 3, pp. 501–4

Hammel, B. 1989 'So good at acting bad' in *Control theory in the practice of reality therapy* ed N. Glasser, Harper & Row, New York, pp. 205–23

Hanline, M.F. 1993 'Inclusion of preschoolers with profound disabilities: an analysis of children's interactions' *Journal of the Association for Persons with Severe Handicaps* vol. 18, no. 1, pp. 28–35

Hanson, M.J. and Carta, J.J. 1995 'Addressing the challenges of families with multiple risks' *Exceptional Children* vol. 62, no. 3, pp. 201–12

Hanson, M.J., Wolfberg, P., Zercher, C., Morgan, M., Gutierrez, S., Barnwell, D. and Beckman, P. 1998 'The culture of inclusion: recognizing diversity at multiple levels' *Early Childhood Research Quarterly* vol. 13, no. 1, pp. 185–209

Harker, M. 2001 'How to build solutions at meetings' in *Solutions in schools* eds Y. Ajmal & I. Rees, BT Press, London, pp. 30–44

Harmon, D. 2002 'They won't teach me: the voices of gifted African American inner-city students' *Roeper Review* vol. 24, no. 2, pp. 68–75

Harris, T.A. 1969 *I'm OK; you're OK* Harper & Row, New York

Harrison, J. 2004 *Understanding children: foundations for quality* 3rd edn, ACER, Melbourne

Harskamp. A. 2002 'Working with parents who harm their children' in *School behaviour and families* ed S. Roffey, David Fulton, London, pp. 77–92

Hart, P.M., Wearing, A.J., Conn, M., Carter, N.L. and Dingle, R.K. 2000 'Development of the School Organisational Health Questionnaire: a measure for assessing teacher morale and school organisational climate' *British Journal of Educational Psychology* vol. 70, no. 2, pp. 211–28

Hartup, W.W. 1979 'Peer relations and social competence' in *Social competence in children* eds M.W. Kent & J.E. Rolf, University Press of New England, Hanover, NH, pp. 150–70

——1989 'Social relationships and their developmental significance' *American Psychologist* vol. 44, no. 2, pp. 120–6

Hartup, W.W. and Moore, S.G. 1990 'Early peer relations: developmental significance and prognostic implications' *Early Childhood Research Quarterly* vol. 5, no. 1, pp. 1–17

Haynes-Seman, C. and Baumgarten, D. 1998 'The victimization of young children' in *Multiple victimization of children: conceptual, developmental, research, and treatment issues* eds B.B.R. Rossman & M.S. Rosenberg, Haworth Press, New York, pp. 67–86

Heck, A., Collins, J. and Peterson, L. 2001 'Decreasing children's risk taking on the playground' *Journal of Applied Behavior Analysis* vol. 34, no. 3, pp. 349–52

Heins, T. 1988 'Relearning childthink' *Australian and New Zealand Journal of Family Therapy* vol. 9, no. 3, pp. 143–9

Henington, C., Hughes, J.N., Cavell, T.A. and Thompson, B. 1998 'The role of relational aggression in identifying aggressive boys and girls' *Journal of School Psychology* vol. 36, no. 4, pp. 457–77

Henning-Stout, M. 1998 'Assessing the behavior of girls: what we see and what we miss' *Journal of School Psychology* vol. 36, no. 4, pp. 433–55

Henning-Stout, M., James, S. and Macintosh, S. 2000 'Reducing harassment of lesbian, gay, bisexual, transgender, and questioning youth in schools' *School Psychology Review* vol. 29, no. 2, pp. 180–91

Hill, S. and Hill, T. 1990 *The collaborative classroom: a guide to cooperative learning* Eleanor Curtin, Melbourne

Hill, S. and Reed, K. 1989 'Promoting social competence at preschool: the implementation of a cooperative games programme' *Australian Journal of Early Childhood* vol. 14, no. 4, pp. 25–31

Hinshaw, S.P. 2000 'Attention-deficit/hyperactivity disorder: the search of viable treatments' in *Child and adolescent therapy: cognitive-behavioral procedures* 2nd edn, ed P.C. Kendall, Guilford, New York, pp. 88–128

Hitz, R. and Driscoll, A. 1988 'Praise or encouragement?: new insights into praise: implications for early childhood teachers' *Young Children* vol. 43, no. 5, pp. 6–13

Hodges, E.V.E. and Perry, D.G. 1999 'Personal and interpersonal antecedents and consequences of victimization by peers' *Journal of Personality and Social Pyschology* vol. 76, no. 4, pp. 677–85

Hoffman-Plotkin, D. and Twentyman, C.T. 1984 'A multimodal assessment of behavioral and cognitive deficits in abused and neglected preschoolers' *Child Development* vol. 55, no. 3, pp. 794–802

Hoge, R.D. and Renzulli, J.S. 1993 'Exploring the link between giftedness and self-concept' *Review of Educational Research* vol. 63, no. 4, pp. 449–65

Holland, P. 2004 *Picturing childhood: the myth of the child in popular imagery* I.B. Tauris, London

Honig, A.S. and Wittmer, D.S. 1996 'Helping children become more prosocial: ideas for classrooms, families, schools and communities' *Young Children* vol. 51, no. 2, pp. 62–70

Hops, H. and Lewin, L. 1984 'Peer sociometric forms' in *Child behavioral assessment* eds T.H. Ollendick & M. Hersen, Pergamon, New York, pp. 124–47

Humphrey, J.H. and Humphrey, J.N. 1985 *Controlling stress in children* Charles C. Thomas, Springfield, IL

Hunter, S.C. and Boyle, J.M.E. 2004 'Appraisal and coping strategy use in victims of school bullying' *British Journal of Educational Psychology* vol. 74, no. 1, pp. 83–107

Hunter, S.C., Boyle, J.M.E. and Warden, D. 2004 'Help seeking amongst child and adolescent victims of peer-aggression and bullying: the influence of school-stage, gender, victimisation, appraisal, and emotion' *British Journal of Educational Psychology* vol. 74, no. 3, pp. 375–90

Huntley, J. 1999 'A narrative approach to working with students who have "learning difficulties"' in *Once upon a time... narrative therapy with children and their families* ed A. Morgan, Dulwich Centre Publications, Adelaide, SA, pp. 35–49

Ingraham, C.L. 2000 'Consultation through a multicultural lens: multicultural and cross-cultural consultation in schools' *School Psychology Review* vol. 29, no. 3, pp. 320–43

James, V. and Owens, L.D. 2004 'Peer victimization and conflict resolution among adolescent girls in a single-sex South Australian school' *International Education Journal* vol. 5, no. 1, pp. 37–49

——2005 '"They turned around like I wasn't there": an analysis of teenage girls' letters about their peer conflicts' *School Psychology International* vol. 26, no. 1, pp. 71–88

Janos, P.M., Marwood, K.A. and Robinson, N.M. 1985 'Friendship patterns in highly intelligent children' *Roeper Review* vol. 8, no. 1, pp. 46–53

Janos, P.M. and Robinson, N.M. 1985 'Psychosocial development in intellectually gifted children' in *The gifted and talented: developmental perspectives* eds F.D. Horowitz & M. O'Brien, American Psychological Association, Washington, DC, pp. 149–96

Johnson, B.M., Miltenberger, R.G., Egemo-Helm, K., Jostad, C.M., Flessner, C. and Gatheridge, B. 2005 'Evaluation of behavioral skills training for teaching abduction-prevention skills to young children' *Journal of Applied Behavior Analysis* vol. 38, no. 1, pp. 67–78

Johnson, B., Whitington, V. and Oswald, M. 1994 'Teachers' views on school discipline: a theoretical framework' *Cambridge Journal of Education* vol. 24, no. 2, pp. 261–76

Johnson, D.W. and Johnson, R.T. 1991 *Learning together and alone* 3rd edn, Allyn & Bacon, Boston, MA

Johnson, D.W., Johnson, R.T. and Holubec, E.J. 1993 *Circles of learning: cooperation in the classroom* 4th edn, Interaction Books, Edina, MN

Johnson, J.H., Jason, L.A. and Betts, D.M. 1990 'Promoting social competencies through educational efforts' in *Developing social competency in adolescence* eds T.P. Gullotta, G.R. Adams & R. Montemayor, SAGE, Newbury Park, CA, pp. 139–68

Johnston, J.M. 1972 'Punishment of human behavior' *American Psychologist* vol. 27, no. 11, pp. 1033–54

Jones, F.H., Jones, P. and Jones, J.L. 2000 *Tools for teaching: discipline, instruction, motivation* Fredric H. Jones and Associates, Santa Cruz, CA

Jones, K. and Day, J.D. 1996 'Cognitive similarities between academically and socially gifted students' *Roeper Review* vol. 18, no. 4, pp. 270–3

Jones, S.M. and Dindia, K. 2004 'A meta-analytic perspective on sex equity in the classroom' *Review of Educational Research* vol. 74, no. 4, pp. 443–71

Jones, V.F. and Jones, L.S. 2004 *Comprehensive classroom management: creating communities of support and solving problems* 7th edn, Pearson Allyn & Bacon, Boston, MA

Jordan, N.H. 1993 'Sexual abuse prevention programs in early childhood education: a caveat' *Young Children* vol. 48, no. 6, pp. 76–9

Joy, M. 1999 'Shame on who?: consulting with children who have experienced sexual abuse' in *Once upon a time . . . narrative therapy with children and their families* ed A. Morgan, Dulwich Centre Publications, Adelaide, SA, pp. 145–72

Jules, V. 1991 'Interaction dynamics of cooperative learning groups in Trinidad's secondary schools' *Adolescence* vol. 26, no. 104, pp. 931–49

Jules, V. and Kutnick, P. 1997 'Student perceptions of a good teacher: the gender perspective' *British Journal of Educational Psychology* vol. 67, no. 4, pp. 497–511

Juvonen, J., Nishina, A. and Graham, S. 2000 'Peer harassment, psychological adjustment, and school functioning in early adolescence' *Journal of Educational Psychology* vol. 92, no. 2, pp. 349–59

Kahng, S.W., Boscoe, J.H. and Byrne, S. 2003 'The use of an escape contingency and a token economy to increase food acceptance' *Journal of Applied Behavior Analysis* vol. 36, no. 3, pp. 349–53

Kamii, C. 1985 'Autonomy: the aim of education envisioned by Piaget' *Australian Journal of Early Childhood* vol. 10, no. 1, pp. 3–10

Kamins, M.L. and Dweck, C.S. 1999 'Person versus process praise and criticism: implications for contingent self-worth and coping' *Developmental Psychology* vol. 35, no. 3, pp. 835–47

Kamps, D.M. 2002 'Preventing problems by improving behavior' in *Preventing problem behaviors: a handbook of successful prevention strategies* eds B. Algozzine & P. Kay, Corwin Press, Thousand Oaks, CA, pp. 11–36

Kamps, D.M., Barbetta, P.M., Leonard, B.R. and Delquadri, J. 1994 'Classwide peer tutoring: an integration strategy to improve reading skills and promote peer interactions among students with autism and general education peers' *Journal of Applied Behavior Analysis* vol. 27, no. 1, pp. 49–61

Kamps, D.M. and Kay, P. 2002 'Preventing problems through social skills instruction' in *Preventing problem behaviors: a handbook of successful prevention strategies* eds B. Algozzine & P. Kay, Corwin Press, Thousand Oaks, CA, pp. 57–84

Kaplan, A., Gheen, M. and Midgley, C. 2002 'Classroom goal structure and student disruptive behaviour' *British Journal of Educational Psychology* vol. 72, no. 2, pp. 191–211

Kaplan, J.S. and Carter, J. 1995 *Beyond behavior modification: a cognitive-behavioral approach to behavior management in the school* 3rd edn, Pro-Ed, Austin, TX

Katsurada, E. and Sugawara, A.I. 1998 'The relationship between hostile attributional bias and aggressive behavior in preschoolers' *Early Childhood Research Quarterly* vol. 13, no. 4, pp. 623–36

Katz, L. 1995 *Talks with teachers of young children* Ablex, Norwood, NJ

Kavussanu, M. and Harnisch, D.L. 2000 'Self-esteem in children: do goal orientations matter?' *British Journal of Educational Psychology* vol. 70, no. 2, pp. 229–42

Kay, M. 2001 'A thoughtful process' in *Solutions in schools* eds Y. Ajmal & I. Rees, pp. 135–46, BT Press, London

Kazdin, A.E., Siegel, T.C. and Bass, D. 1992 'Cognitive problem-solving skills training and parent management training in the treatment of antisocial behavior in children' *Journal of Consulting and Clinical Psychology* vol. 60, no. 5, pp. 733–47

Kelley, M.E., Piazza, C.C., Fisher, W.W. and Oberdorff, A.J. 2003 'Acquisition of cup drinking using previously refused foods as positive and negative reinforcement' *Journal of Applied Behavior Analysis* vol. 36, no. 1, pp. 89–93

Kelly, B. 1996 'The ecology of peer relations' *Early Child Development and Care* vol. 115, no. 1, pp. 99–114

Kemple, K.M. 1991 'Preschool children's peer acceptance and social interaction' *Young Children* vol. 46, no. 5, pp. 47–54

Kendall, P.C. (ed) 2000 *Child and adolescent therapy: cognitive-behavioral procedures* 2nd edn, Guilford, New York

Kendall, P.C., Chu, B.C., Pimentel, S.S. and Choudhury, M. 2000 'Treating anxiety disorders in youth' in *Child and adolescent therapy: cognitive-behavioral procedures* 2nd edn, ed P.C. Kendall, Guilford, New York, pp. 235–87

Kendall, P.C. and Panichelli-Mindel, S.M. 1995 'Cognitive-behavioral treatments' *Journal of Abnormal Child Psychology* vol. 23, no. 1, pp. 107–24

Kennedy, C.H., Meyer, K.A., Knowles, T. and Shukla, S. 2000 'Analyzing the multiple functions of stereotypical behavior for students with autism: implications for assessment and treatment' *Journal of Applied Behavior Analysis* vol. 33, no. 4, pp. 559–71

Kerr, B.A. 1996 *Smart girls two: a new psychology of girls, women and giftedness* Hawker Brownlow Education, Melbourne

——1997 'Developing talents in girls and young women' in *Handbook of gifted education* 2nd edn, eds N. Colangelo & G.A. Davis, Allyn & Bacon, Boston, MA, pp. 483–97

Kerr, B.A. and Cohn, S.J. 2001 *Smart boys: talent, manhood, and the search for meaning* Great Potential Press, Scottsdale, AZ

Kerr, M.M. and Nelson, C.M. 2006 *Strategies for addressing behavior problems in the classroom* 5th edn, Pearson Merrill Prentice Hall, Upper Saddle River, NJ

Kerwin, M.E., Ahearn, W.H., Eichers, P.S. and Burd, D.M. 1995 'The costs of eating: a behavioral economic analysis of food refusal' *Journal of Applied Behavior Analysis* vol. 28, no. 3, pp. 245–60

King, L.H. 1993 'High and low achievers' perceptions and cooperative learning in two small groups' *The Elementary School Journal* vol. 93, no. 4, pp. 399–416

Kirkby, R.J. and Smyrnios, K.X. 1990 'Child-oriented family therapy outcome research: comparisons between brief family therapy and an alternative treatment' *Australian and New Zealand Journal of Family Therapy* vol. 11, no. 2, pp. 75–84

Klimes-Dougan, B. and Kistner, J. 1990 'Physically abused preschoolers' responses to peers' distress' *Developmental Psychology* vol. 26, no. 4, pp. 599–602

Kline, B.E. and Short, E.B. 1991 'Changes in emotional resilience: gifted adolescent females' *Roeper Review* vol. 13, no. 3, pp. 118–21

Knight, B.A. 1995 'The influence of locus of control on gifted and talented students' *Gifted Education International* vol. 11, no. 1, pp. 31–3

Knight, T. 1991 'Democratic schooling: basis for a school code of behaviour' in *Classroom discipline* eds M.N. Lovegrove & R. Lewis, Longman Cheshire, Melbourne, pp. 117–44

Ko, S.F. and Cosden, M.A. 2001 'Do elementary school-based child abuse prevention programs work?: a high school follow-up' *Psychology in the Schools* vol. 38, no. 1, pp. 57–66

Kochenderfer, B.J. and Ladd, G.W. 1996 'Peer victimization: cause or consequence of school maladjustment?' *Child Development* vol. 67, no. 4, pp. 1305–17

Kochenderfer-Ladd, B. and Ladd, G.W. 2001 'Variations in peer victimization: relations to children's maladjustment' in *Peer harassment in school: the plight of the vulnerable and victimized* eds J. Juvonen & S. Graham, Guilford, New York, pp. 25–48

Koegel, L.K., Koegel, R.L., Frea, W.D. and Fredeen, R.M. 2001 'Identifying early intervention targets for children with autism in inclusive school settings' *Behavior Modification* vol. 25, no. 5, pp. 745–61

Kohler, F.W. and Strain, P.S. 1993 'The early childhood social skills program' *Teaching Exceptional Children* vol. 25, no. 2, pp. 41–2

Kohn, A. 1996a *Beyond discipline: from compliance to community* Association for Supervision and Curriculum Development, Alexandria, VA

——1996b 'By all available means: Cameron and Pierce's defense of extrinsic motivators' *Review of Educational Research* vol. 66, no. 1, pp. 1–4

——1999 *Punished by rewards: the trouble with gold stars, incentive plans, A's, praise and other bribes* 2nd edn, Houghton Mifflin, Boston, MA

——2004 'From degrading to de-grading' in *What does it mean to be well educated?* ed A. Kohn, Beacon Press, Boston, MA, pp. 75–92

Kontos, S. and Wilcox-Herzog, A. 1997 'Teachers' interactions with children: why are they so important?' *Young Children* vol. 52, no. 2, pp. 4–12

Kowalski, K. 1990 'The girl with the know-how: finding solutions to a school problem' *Family Therapy Case Studies* vol. 5, no. 1, pp. 3–14

Kral, R. and Kowalski, K. 1989 'After the miracle: the second stage in solution focused brief therapy' *Journal of Strategic and Systemic Therapies* vol. 8, no. 2, pp. 73–6

Krebs, L.L. 1986 'Current research on theoretically based parenting programs' *Individual Psychology* vol. 42, no. 3, pp. 375–87

Kurtz, P.F., Chin, M.D., Huete, J.M., Tarbox, R.S.F., O'Connor, J.T., Paclawskyj, T.R. and Rush, K.S. 2003 'Functional analysis and treatment of self-injurious behavior in young children: a summary of 30 cases' *Journal of Applied Behavior Analysis* vol. 36, no. 2, pp. 205–19

Kutsick, K.A., Gutkin, T.B. and Witt, J.C. 1991 'The impact of treatment development process, intervention type, and problem severity on treatment acceptability as judged by classroom teachers' *Psychology in the Schools* vol. 28, no. 4, pp. 325–31

Kyriacou, C. and Newson, G. 1982 'Teacher effectiveness: a consideration of research problems' *Educational Review* vol. 34, no. 1, pp. 3–12

Ladd, G.W. 1990 'Having friends, keeping friends, making friends, and being liked by peers in the classroom: predictors of children's early school adjustment?' *Child Development* vol. 61, no. 4, pp. 1081–100

Lambert, E.B. and Clyde, M. 2000 *Re-thinking early childhood theory and practice* Social Science Press, Katoomba, NSW

Larrivee, B. 2002 'The potential perils of praise in a democratic interactive classroom' *Action in Teacher Education* vol. 23, no. 4, pp. 77–88

——2005 *Authentic classroom management: creating a learning community and building reflective practice* 2nd edn, Pearson Allyn & Bacon, Boston, MA

Laws, C. and Davies, B. 2000 'Poststructuralist theory in practice: working with "behaviourally disturbed" children' *Qualitative Studies in Education* vol. 13, no. 3, pp. 205–21

Le Messurier, M. 2004 *Cognitive behavioural training: a how-to guide for successful behaviour* Hawker Brownlow, Melbourne

LeCroy, C.W. 1983 'Social skills training with adolescents: a review' in *Social skills training for children and youth* ed C.W. LeCroy, pp. 91–116, Haworth Press, New York

Lee, N. 2001 *Childhood and society: growing up in an age of uncertainty* Open University Press, Buckingham, UK

Leff, S.S., Kupersmidt, J.B., Patterson, C.J. and Power, T.J. 1999 'Factors influencing teacher identification of peer bullies and victims' *School Psychology Review* vol. 28, no. 3, pp. 505–17

Leff, S.S., Power, T.J., Costigan, T.E. and Manz, P.H. 2003 'Assessing the climate of the playground and lunchroom: implications for bullying prevention programming' *School Psychology Review* vol. 32, no. 3, pp. 418–30

Leff, S.S., Power, T.J., Manz, P.H., Costigan, T.E. and Nabors, L.A. 2001 'School-based aggression prevention programs for young children: current status and implications for violence prevention' *School Psychology Review* vol. 30, no. 3, pp. 344–62

Lerman, D.C. and Iwata, B.A. 1996 'Developing a technology for the use of operant extinction in clinical settings: an examination of basic and applied research' *Journal of Applied Behavior Analysis* vol. 29, no. 3, pp. 345–82

Lerman, D.C, Iwata, B.A. and Wallace, M.D. 1999 'Side effects of extinction: prevalence of bursting and aggression during the treatment of self-injurious behavior' *Journal of Applied Behavior Analysis* vol. 32, no. 1, pp. 1–8

Lerman, D.C. and Vorndran, C.M. 2002 'On the status of knowledge for using punishment: implications for treating behavior disorders' *Journal of Applied Behavior Analysis* vol. 35, no. 4, pp. 431–64

Leung, C., Sanders, M.R., Leung, S., Mak, R. and Lau, J. 2003 'An outcome evaluation of the implementation of the Triple P-Positive Parenting Program in Hong Kong' *Family Process* vol. 42, no. 4, pp. 531–44

Levant, R.F. 1983 'Client-centered skills-training programs for the family: a review of the literature' *The Counseling Psychologist* vol. 11, no. 3, pp. 29–46

Levin, D.E. 1994 'Building a peaceable classroom: helping young children feel safe in violent times' *Childhood Education* vol. 70, no. 5, pp. 267–70

Levin, L. and Carr, E.G. 2001 'Food selectivity and problem behavior in children with developmental disabilities: analysis and intervention' *Behavior Modification* vol. 25, no. 3, pp. 443–70

Lewis, R. 1997 *The discipline dilemma: control, management, influence* 2nd edn, ACER, Melbourne

Lewis, R. and Frydenberg, E. 2002 'Concomitants of failure to cope: what we should teach adolescents about coping' *British Journal of Educational Psychology* vol. 72, no. 3, pp. 419–31

Lewis, T.J., Powers, L.J., Kelk, M.J. and Newcomer, L.L. 2002 'Reducing problem behaviors on the playground: an investigation of the application of schoolwide positive behavior supports' *Psychology in the Schools* vol. 39, no. 2, pp. 181–90

Lewis, T.J., Sugai, G. and Colvin, G. 1998 'Reducing problem behavior through a school-wide system of effective behavioral support: investigation of a school-wide social skills training program and contextual interventions' *School Psychology Review* vol. 27, no. 3, pp. 446–59

Lindquist, B., Molnar, A. and Brauchmann, L. 1987 'Working with school related problems without going to school: considerations for systemic practice' *Journal of Strategic and Systemic Therapies* vol. 6, no. 4, pp. 44–50

Lindsay, G. and Dockrell, J. 2000 'The behaviour and self-esteem of children with specific speech and language difficulties' *British Journal of Educational Psychology* vol. 70, no. 4, pp. 583–601

Little, E. 2003 *Kids behaving badly: teacher strategies for classroom behaviour problems* Pearson Prentice Hall, Sydney

Lochman, J.E., Whidby, J.M. and FitzGerald, D.P. 2000 'Cognitive-behavioral assessment and treatment with aggressive children' in *Child and adolescent therapy: cognitive-behavioral procedures* 2nd edn, ed P. Kendall, Guilford, New York, pp. 31–87

Loeb, R.C. and Jay, G. 1987 'Self-concept in gifted children: differential impact in boys and girls' *Gifted Child Quarterly* vol. 31, no. 1, pp. 9–14

Long, J.D. and Pellegrini, A.D. 2003 'Studying change in dominance and bullying with linear mixed models' *School Psychology Review* vol. 32, no. 3, pp. 401–17

Lowe, R. 2005 'Structured methods and striking moments: using question techniques in "living" ways' *Family Process* vol. 44, no. 1, pp. 65–75

Luiselli, J.K. 2000 'Cueing, demand fading, and positive reinforcement to establish self-feeding and oral consumption in a child with chronic food refusal' *Behavior Modification* vol. 24, no. 3, pp. 348–58

Lusterman, D. 1985 'An ecosystemic approach to family-school problems' *The American Journal of Family Therapy* vol. 13, no. 1, pp. 22–30

Lynch, E.W. and Hanson, M.J. 1996 'Ensuring cultural competence in assessment' in *Assessing infants and preschoolers with special needs* 2nd edn, eds M. McLean, D.B. Bailey Jr & M. Wolery, Merrill, Englewood Cliffs, NJ, pp. 69–95

Maag, J.W. 2001 'Rewarded by punishment: reflections on the disuse of positive reinforcement in schools' *Exceptional Children* vol. 67, no. 2, pp. 173–86

Maag, J.W., Reid, R. and DiGangi, S.A. 1993 'Differential effects of self-monitoring attention, accuracy and productivity' *Journal of Applied Behavior Analysis* vol. 26, no. 3, pp. 329–44

McCabe, P.C. 2005 'Social and behavioral correlates of preschoolers with specific language impairment' *Psychology in the Schools* vol. 42, no. 4, pp. 373–87

McCaslin, M. and Good, T.L. 1992 'Compliant cognition: the misalliance of management and instructional goals in current school reform' *Educational Researcher* vol. 21, no. 3, pp. 4–17

McClun, L.A. and Merrell, K.A. 1998 'Relationship of perceived parenting styles, locus of control orientation, and self-concept among junior high age students' *Psychology in the Schools* vol. 35, no. 4, pp. 381–90

McCoach, D.B. and Siegle, D. 2003 'The structure and function of academic self-concept in gifted and general education students' *Roeper Review* vol. 25, no. 2, pp. 61–5

McConaughy, S.H. and Leone, P.E. 2002 'Measuring the success of prevention programs' in *Preventing problem behaviors: a handbook of successful prevention strategies* eds B. Algozzine & P. Kay, Corwin Press, Thousand Oaks, CA, pp. 183–219

McDonnell, A.P. 1993 'Ethical considerations in teaching compliance to individuals with mental retardation' *Education and Training in Mental Retardation* vol. 28, no. 1, pp. 3–12

Mace, F.C. and Wacker, D.P. 1994 'Toward greater integration of basic and applied behavioral research: an introduction' *Journal of Applied Behavior Analysis* vol. 27, no. 4, pp. 569–74

McEvoy, A. and Welker, R. 2000 'Antisocial behavior, academic failure, and school climate: a critical review' *Journal of Emotional and Behavioral Disorders* vol. 8, no. 3, pp. 130–40

McGlone, C. 2001 'Wrapping new narratives in golden paper: solution-focused work with pupils, teachers and parents in mainstream primary schools' in *Solutions in schools* eds Y. Ajmal & I. Rees, BT Press, London, pp. 122–34

McGrath, H. 1998 'An overview of prevention and treatment programmes for developing positive peer relations' in *Children's peer relations* eds P.T. Slee & K. Rigby, pp. 229–41, Routledge, London

——2006 'What research tells us about whole-school programs for preventing bullying' in *Bullying solutions: evidence-based approaches to bullying in Australian schools* eds H. McGrath & T. Noble, Pearson Longman, Sydney, pp. 49–66

McGrath, H. and Francey, S. 1991 *Friendly kids; friendly classrooms* Longman Cheshire, Melbourne

McGrath, H. and Stanley, M. 2006a 'A comparison of two non-punitive approaches to bullying' in *Bullying solutions: evidence-based approaches to bullying in Australian schools* eds H. McGrath & T. Noble, Pearson Longman, Sydney, pp. 189–208

——2006b 'A safe school (anti-bullying) template for schools' in *Bullying solutions: evidence-based approaches to bullying in Australian schools* eds H. McGrath & T. Noble, pp. 229–78, Pearson Longman, Sydney

Macht, J. 2005 'Functional behavioral assessment' in *Behavior management: applications for teachers* 4th edn, ed T.J. Zirpoli, Pearson Merrill Prentice Hall, Upper Saddle River, NJ, pp. 172–85

McKerchar, P.M. and Thompson, R.H. 2004 'A descriptive analysis of potential reinforcement contingencies in the preschool classroom' *Journal of Applied Behavior Analysis* vol. 37, no. 4, pp. 431–44

McLeod, W. 1989 'Minor miracles or logical processes?: therapeutic interventions and techniques' *Journal of Family Therapy* vol. 11, no. 3, pp. 257–80

McMillan, D.W. and Chavis, D.M. 1986 'Sense of community: a definition and theory' *Journal of Community Psychology* vol. 14, no. 1, pp. 6–23

MacMullin, C., Aistrope, D., Brown, J.L., Hannaford, D. and Martin, M. 1992 *The Sheidow Park social problem solving program* Flinders University of South Australia, Adelaide, SA

MacNaughton, G. 2003 *Shaping early childhood learners, curriculum and contexts* Open University Press, Berkshire, UK

McWayne, C., Hampton, V., Fantuzzo, J., Cohen, H.L. and Sekino, Y. 2004 'A multivariate examination of parent involvement and the social and academic competencies of urban kindergarten children' *Psychology in the Schools* vol. 41, no. 3, pp. 363–77

Maker, C.J. and Schiever, S.W. 1989 'Purpose and organization of the volume' in *Critical issues in gifted education: defensible programs for cultural and ethnic minorities* eds C.J. Maker & S.W. Schiever, Pro-Ed, Austin, TX, pp. xv-xix

Manke, M.P. 1997 *Classroom power relations: understanding student–teacher interaction* Lawrence Erlbaum Associates, Mahwah, NJ

Manning, M.L. and Bucher, K.T. 2003 *Classroom management: models, applications, and cases* Merrill Prentice Hall, Upper Saddle River, NJ

Marchant, G.J., Paulson, S.E. and Rothlisberg, B.A. 2001 'Relations of middle school students' perceptions of family and school contexts with academic achievement' *Psychology in the Schools* vol. 38, no. 6, pp. 505–19

Marchant, M., Young, K.R. and West, R.P. 2004 'The effects of parental teaching on compliance behavior of children' *Psychology in the Schools* vol. 41, no. 3, pp. 337–50

Marcon, R.A. 1999 'Positive relationships between parent school involvement and public school inner-city preschoolers' development and academic progress' *School Psychology Review* vol. 28, no. 3, pp. 395–412

Marion, R.L. 1980 'Communicating with parents of culturally diverse exceptional children' *Exceptional Children* vol. 46, no. 8, pp. 616–23

Marsh, H.W. and Craven, R.G. 1998 'The big fish little pond effect, optimal illusions, and misinterpretations: a response to Gross (1997)' *The Australasian Journal of Gifted Education* vol. 7, no. 1, pp. 6–15

Marsh, H.W., Chessor, D., Craven, R. and Roche, L. 1995 'The effects of gifted and talented programs on academic self-concept: the big fish strikes again' *American Educational Research Journal* vol. 32, no. 2, pp. 285–319

Marsh, H.W., Parada, R.H., Craven, R.G. and Finger, L. 2004 'In the looking glass: a reciprocal effects model elucidating the complex nature of bullying, psychological determinants, and the central role of self-concept' in *Bullying: implications for the classroom* eds C.E. Sanders & G.D. Phye, Elsevier, San Diego, CA, pp. 63–109

Martin, A.J., Linfoot, K. and Stephenson, J. 1999 'How teachers respond to concerns about misbehavior in their classroom' *Psychology in the Schools* vol. 36, no. 4, pp. 347–58

Martin, G. and Pear, J. 2003 *Behavior modification: what it is and how to do it* 7th edn, Prentice Hall, Upper Saddle River, NJ

Maslow, A.H. 1968 *Toward a psychology of being* 2nd edn, Van Nostrand, Princeton, NJ

Matheson, A.S. and Shriver, M.D. 2005 'Training teachers to give effective commands: effects on student compliance and academic behaviors' *School Psychology Review* vol. 34, no. 2, pp. 202–19

Mathieson, K. and Price, M. 2002 *Better behaviour in classrooms: a framework for inclusive behaviour management* Routledge/Falmer, London

Matthews, M. 1992 'Gifted students talk about cooperative learning' *Educational Leadership* vol. 50, no. 2, pp. 48–50

Mayall, B. 2002 *Towards a sociology of childhood: thinking from children's lives* Open University Press, Buckingham, UK

Metzner, J.L. and Ryan, G.D. 1995 'Sexual abuse perpetration' in *Conduct disorders in children and adolescents* ed G.P. Sholevar, American Psychiatric Press, Washington, DC, pp. 119–42

Meyers, A.W., Cohen, R. and Schleser, R. 1989 'A cognitive-behavioral approach to education: adopting a broad-based perspective' in *Cognitive-behavioral psychology in the schools* eds J.N. Hughes & R.J. Hall, Guilford, New York, pp. 62–84

Miedel, W.T. and Reynolds, A.J. 1999 'Parent involvement in early intervention for disadvantaged children: does it matter?' *Journal of School Psychology* vol. 37, no. 4, pp. 379–402

Milgram, N. and Toubiana, Y. 1999 'Academic anxiety, academic procrastination, and parents' involvement in students and their parents' *British Journal of Educational Psychology* vol. 69, no. 3, pp. 345–61

Milgram, S. 1963 'Behavioral study of obedience' *Journal of Abnormal and Social Psychology* vol. 67, no. 4, pp. 371–8

Miller, A. 1987 *For your own good: the roots of violence in child-rearing* Virago Press, London

——2003 *Teachers, parents and classroom behaviour: a psychosocial approach* Open University Press, Maidenhead, UK

Miller, A., Ferguson, E. and Byrne, I. 2000 'Pupils' causal attributions for difficult classroom behaviour' *British Journal of Educational Psychology* vol. 70, no. 1, pp. 85–96

Miller, A., Ferguson, E. and Moore, E. 2002 'Parents' and pupils' causal attributions for difficult classroom behaviour' *British Journal of Educational Psychology* vol. 72, no. 1, pp. 27–40

Miller, G. and de Shazer, S. 2000 'Emotions in solution-focused therapy: a re-examination' *Family Process* vol. 39, no. 1, pp. 5–23

Miller, G.E., Brehm, K. and Whitehouse, S. 1998 'Reconceptualizing school-based prevention for antisocial behavior within a resiliency framework' *School Psychology Review* vol. 27, no. 3, pp. 364–79

Miller, L.K. 1991 'Avoiding the countercontrol of applied behavior analysis' *Journal of Applied Behavior Analysis* vol. 24, no. 4, pp. 645–7

Miller, R.C. and Berman, J.S. 1983 'The efficacy of cognitive behavior therapies: a quantitative review of the research evidence' *Psychological Bulletin* vol. 94, no. 1, pp. 39–53

Mintz, J. 2003 *No homework and recess all day: how to have freedom and democracy in education* Bravura, New York

Miranda, A. and Presentación, M.J. 2000 'Efficacy of cognitive-behavioral therapy in the treatment of children with ADHD, with and without aggressiveness' *Psychology in the Schools* vol. 37, no. 2, pp. 169–82

Möller, J. 2005 'Paradoxical effects of praise and criticism: social, dimensional and temporal comparisons' *British Journal of Educational Psychology* vol. 75, no. 2, pp. 275–95

Molnar, A. and de Shazer, S. 1987 'Solution-focused therapy: toward the identification of therapeutic tasks' *Journal of Marital and Family Therapy* vol. 13, no. 4, pp. 349–58

Molnar, A. and Lindquist, B. 1989 *Changing problem behavior in schools* Jossey-Bass, San Francisco, CA

Montgomery, D. 1996 *Educating the able* Cassell, London

Montgomery, H. 2003 'Childhood in time and place' in *Understanding childhood: an interdisciplinary approach* eds M. Woodhead & H. Montgomery, Open University Press, Milton Keynes, UK, pp. 45–83

Moon, S.M., Swift, M. and Shallenberger, A. 2002 'Perceptions of a self-contained class for fourth- and fifth-grade students with high to extreme levels of intellectual giftedness' *Gifted Child Quarterly* vol. 46, no. 1, pp. 64–79

Morgan, A. (ed) 1999 *Once upon a time... narrative therapy with children and their families* Dulwich Centre Publications, Adelaide, SA

——2000 *What is narrative therapy?: an easy-to-read introduction* Dulwich Centre Publications, Adelaide, SA

Morgensen, G. 1989 'Act your age: a strategic approach to helping children change' *Journal of Strategic and Systemic Therapies* vol. 8, nos 2 & 3, pp. 52–4

Mortimore, P., Sammons, P., Stoll, L., Ecob, R. and Lewis, D. 1988 'The effects of school membership on pupils' outcomes' *Research Papers in Education* vol. 3, no. 1, pp. 3–26

Mosak, H.H. 2005 'Adlerian psychotherapy' in *Current psychotherapies* eds R.J. Corsini & D. Wedding, 7th edn, Thomson Brooks/Cole, Belmont, CA, pp. 52–95

Moss, E. 1992 'Early interactions and metacognitive development of gifted preschoolers' in *To be young and gifted* eds P.S. Klein & A.J. Tannenbaum, Ablex, Norwood, NJ, pp. 278–318

Mueller, C.M. and Dweck, C.S. 1998 'Praise for intelligence can undermine children's motivation and performance' *Journal of Personality and Social Psychology* vol. 75, no. 1, pp. 33–52

Mueller, M.M., Sterling-Turner, H.E. and Scattone, D. 2001 'Functional assessment of hand flapping in a general education classroom' *Journal of Applied Behavior Analysis* vol. 34, no. 2, pp. 233–6

Muijs, R.D. 1997 'Symposium: self perception and performance: predictors of academic achievement and academic self-concept: a longitudinal perspective' *British Journal of Educational Psychology* vol. 67, no. 3, pp. 263–77

Murdock, T.B. and Bolch, M.B. 2005 'Risk and protective factors for poor school adjustment in lesbian, gay, and bisexual (LGB) high school youth: variable and person-centered analyses' *Psychology in the Schools* vol. 42, no. 2, pp. 159–72

Murphy, J.J. 1994 'Brief therapy for school problems' *School Psychology International* vol. 15, pp. 115–31

——2006 *Solution-focused counseling in middle and high schools* Pearson Merrill Prentice Hall, Upper Saddle River, NJ

Murphy, J.J. and Duncan, B.L. 1997 *Brief intervention for school problems: collaborating for practical solutions* Guilford, New York

Murray, C. and Greenberg, M.T. 2001 'Relationships with teachers and bonds with school: social emotional adjustment correlates for children with and without disabilities' *Psychology in the Schools* vol. 38, no. 1, pp. 25–41

Musser, E.H., Bray, M.A., Kehle, T.J. and Jenson, W.R. 2001 'Reducing disruptive behaviors in students with serious emotional disturbance' *School Psychology Review* vol. 30, no. 2, pp. 294–304

Myers, C.L. and Holland, K.L. 2000 'Classroom behavioral interventions: do teachers consider the function of the behavior?' *Psychology in the Schools* vol. 37, no. 3, pp. 271–80

Mynard, H., Joseph, S. and Alexander, J. 2000 'Peer-victimisation and posttraumatic stress in adolescents' *Personality and Individual Differences* vol. 29, no. 5, pp. 815–21

Napier, R. and Gershenfeld, M. 2004 *Groups: theory and experience* 7th edn, Houghton & Mifflin, Boston, MA

National Association for the Education of Young Children 1983 'Four components of high quality early childhood programs: staff–child interaction, child–child interaction, curriculum, and evaluation' *Young Children* vol. 38, no. 6, pp. 46–52

Neef, N.A., Bicard, D.F. and Endo, S. 2001 'Assessment of impulsivity and the development of self-control in students with attention deficit hyperactivity disorder' *Journal of Applied Behavior Analysis* vol. 34 no. 4, pp. 397–408

Neef, N.A., Mace, F.C. and Shade, D. 1993 'Impulsivity in students with serious emotional disturbance: the interactive effects of reinforcer rate, delay, and quality' *Journal of Applied Behavior Analysis* vol. 26, no. 1, pp. 37–52

Nelsen, J., Erwin, C. and Duffy, R. 1998 *Positive discipline for preschoolers: for their early years—raising children who are responsible, respectful, and resourceful* rev 2nd edn, Prima Publishing, Rocklin, CA

Nelsen, J., Lott, L. and Glenn, H.S. 2000 *Positive discipline in the classroom* 3rd edn, Prima Publishing, Roseville, CA

Nelson, J.R., Maculan, A., Roberts, M.L. and Ohlund, B.J. 2001 'Sources of occupational stress for teachers of students with emotional and behavioral disorders' *Journal of Emotional and Behavioral Disorders* vol. 9, no. 2, pp. 123–30

Nelson, J.R., Roberts, M.L., Mathur, S.R. and Rutherford, R.B. Jr 1999 'Has public policy exceeded our knowledge base?: a review of the functional behavioral assessment literature' *Behavioral Disorders* vol. 24, no. 2, pp. 169–79

Nelson, W.M. III and Finch, A.J. Jr 2000 'Managing anger in youth: a cognitive-behavioral approach' in *Child and adolescent therapy: cognitive-behavioral procedures* 2nd edn, ed P. Kendall, Guilford, New York, pp. 129–70

Newell, S. and Jeffery, D. 2002 *Behaviour management in the classroom: a transactional analysis approach* David Fulton, London

Newman, L. and Pollnitz, L. 2005 *Working with children and families: professional, legal and ethical issues* Pearson Prentice Hall, Sydney, NSW

Nichols, M.P. and Schwartz, R.C. 1995 *Family therapy: concepts and methods* 3rd edn, Allyn & Bacon, Boston, MA

Nicholson, A. 2006 'Legal perspectives on bullying' in *Bullying solutions: evidence-based approaches to bullying in Australian schools* eds H. McGrath & T. Noble, Pearson, Sydney, pp. 17–45

Nicholson, S. 1989 'Outcome evaluation of therapeutic effectiveness' *Australian and New Zealand Journal of Family Therapy* vol. 10, no. 2, pp. 77–83

Nishina, A. 2004 'A theoretical review of bullying: can it be eliminated?' in *Bullying: implications for the classroom* eds C.E. Sanders & G.D. Phye, Elsevier, San Diego, CA, pp. 35–62

Noble, T. 2006 'Core components of a school-wide safe schools curriculum' in *Bullying solutions: evidence-based approaches to bullying in Australian schools* eds H. McGrath & T. Noble, Pearson Longman, Sydney, pp. 67–83

Northup, J. & Gulley, V. 2001 'Some contributions of functional analysis to the assessment of behaviors associated with attention deficit hyperactivity disorder and the effects of stimulant medication' *School Psychology Review* vol. 30, no. 2, pp. 227–38

Norwich, B. 1999 'Pupils' reasons for learning and behaving and for not learning and behaving in English and maths lessons in a secondary school' *British Journal of Educational Psychology* vol. 69, no. 4, pp. 547–69

Oberski, I., Ford, K., Higgins, S. and Fisher, P. 1999 'The importance of relationships in teacher education' *Journal of Education for Teaching* vol. 25, no. 2, pp. 135–50

Odom, S.L., McConnell, S.R., McEvoy, M.A., Peterson, C., Ostrosky, M., Chandler, L.K., Spicuzza, R.J., Skellenger, A., Creighton, M. and Favazza, P.C. 1999 'Relative effects of interventions supporting the social competence of young children with disabilities' *Topics in Early Childhood Special Education* vol. 19, no. 2, pp. 75–91

O'Leary, K.D. 1972 'Behavior modification in the classroom: a rejoinder to Winett and Winkler' *Journal of Applied Behavior Analysis* vol. 5, no. 4, pp. 505–11

Ollendick, T.H. and King, N.J. 2000 'Empirically supported treatments for children and adolescents' in *Child and adolescent therapy: Cognitive-behavioral procedures* 2nd edn, ed P.C. Kendall, Guilford, New York, pp. 386–425

Olszewski, P., Kulieke, M.J. and Willis, G. 1987 'Changes in the self-perceptions of gifted students who participate in rigorous academic programs' *Journal for the Education of the Gifted* vol. 10, no. 4, pp. 287–303

Olweus, D. 1993 *Bullying at school: what we know and what we can do* Blackwell, Oxford, UK

——2001 Peer harassment: a critical analysis and some important issues' in *Peer harassment in school: the plight of the vulnerable and victimized* eds J. Juvonen & S. Graham, Guilford, New York, pp. 3–20

O'Moore, M. and Minton, S.J. 2004 *Dealing with bullying in schools: a training manual for teachers, parents and other professionals* Paul Chapman, London

O'Reilly, M.F., Lacey, C. and Lancioni, G.E. 2000 'Assessment of the influence of background noise on escape-maintained problem behavior and pain behavior in a child with Williams syndrome' *Journal of Applied Behavior Analysis* vol. 33, no. 4, pp. 511–14

Orpinas, P., Horne, A.M. and Staniszewski, D. 2003 'School bullying: changing the problem by changing the school' *School Psychology Review* vol. 32, no. 3, pp. 431–44

Osler, A. and Vincent, K. 2003 *Girls and exclusion: rethinking the agenda* RoutledgeFalmer, London

Osterman, K.F. 2000 'Students' need for belonging in the school community' *Review of Educational Research* vol. 70, no. 3, pp. 323–67

Overstreet, S., Devine, J., Bevans, K. and Efreom, Y. 2005 'Predicting parental involvement in children's schooling within an economically disadvantaged African American sample' *Psychology in the Schools* vol. 42, no. 1, pp. 101–11

Owens, L.D. 1996 'Sticks and stones and sugar and spice: girls' and boys' aggression in schools' *Australian Journal of Guidance and Counselling* vol. 6, pp. 45–55

Owens, L., Daly, A. and Slee, P. 2005a 'Sex and age differences in victimisation and conflict resolution among adolescents in a South Australian school' *Aggressive Behavior* vol. 31, no. 1, pp. 1–12

Owens, L.D. and MacMullin, C.E. 1995 'Gender differences in aggression in children and adolescents in South Australian schools' *International Journal of Adolescence and Youth* vol. 6, no. 1, pp. 21–35

Owens, L., Shute, R. and Slee, P. 2000a '"Guess what I just heard!": indirect aggression among teenage girls in Australia' *Aggressive Behavior* vol. 26, no. 1, pp. 67–83

——2000b '"I'm in and you're out...": explanations for teenage girls' indirect aggression' *Psychology, Evolution and Gender* vol. 2, no. 1, pp. 19–46

——'"It hurts a hell of a lot...": the effects of indirect aggression on teenage girls' *School Psychology International* vol. 21, no. 4, pp. 359–76

——2001 'Victimization among teenage girls: what can be done about indirect harassment?' in *Peer harassment in school: the plight of the vulnerable and victimized* eds J. Juvonen & S. Graham, Guilford, New York, pp. 215–41

——2005b '"In the eye of the beholder...": girls', boys' and teachers' perceptions of boys' aggression to girls' *International Education Journal* vol. 5, no. 5, pp. 142–51

Parker, F.L., Boak, A.Y., Griffin, K.W., Ripple, C. and Peay, L. 1999 'Parent–child relationship, home learning environment, and school readiness' *School Psychology Review* vol. 28, no. 3, pp. 413–25

Parker, L.E. and Lepper, M.R. 1992 'Effects of fantasy contexts on children's learning and motivation: making learning more fun' *Journal of Personality and Social Psychology* vol. 62, no. 4, pp. 625–33

Parpal, M. and Maccoby, E.E. 1985 'Maternal responsiveness and subsequent child compliance' *Child Development* vol. 56, no. 5, pp. 1326–34

Paulson, S.E. 1994 'Relations of parenting style and parental involvement with ninth-grade students' achievement' *Journal of Early Adolescence* vol. 14, no. 2, pp. 250–67

Paulson, S.E., Marchant, G.J. and Rothlisberg, B.A. 1998 'Early adolescents' perceptions of patterns of parenting, teaching, and school atmosphere: implications for achievement' *Journal of Early Adolescence* vol. 18, no. 1, pp. 5–26

Payne, A.A. and Gottfredson, D.C. 2004 'Schools and bullying: school factors related to bullying and school-based bullying interventions' in *Bullying: implications for the classroom* eds C.E. Sanders & G.D. Phye, Elsevier, San Diego, CA, pp. 159–76

Pellegrini, A.D. 2004 'Bullying during the middle school years' in *Bullying: implications for the classroom* eds C.E. Sanders & G.D. Phye, Elsevier, San Diego, CA, pp. 177–202

Pellegrini, A.D., Bartini, M. and Brooks, F. 1999 'School bullies, victims, and aggressive victims: factors relating to group affiliation and victimization in early adolescence' *Journal of Educational Psychology* vol. 91, no. 2, pp. 216–24

Pepler, D., Craig, W., Ziegler, S. and Charach, A. 1993 'A school-based anti-bullying intervention: preliminary evaluation' in *Understanding and managing bullying* ed D. Tattum, Heinemann Educational, Oxford, UK, pp. 76–91

Perkins, D.N., Jay, E. and Tishman, S. 1993 'Beyond abilities: a dispositional theory of thinking' *Merrill Palmer Quarterly* vol. 39, no. 1, pp. 1–21

Perkins, D., Tishman, S., Ritchhart, R., Donis, K. and Andrade, A. 2000 'Intelligence in the wild: a dispositional view of intellectual traits' *Educational Psychology Review* vol. 12, no. 3, pp. 269–93

Perry, D. and Bussey, K. 1984 *Social development* Prentice Hall, Englewood Cliffs, NJ

Perry, D.G., Hodges, E.V.E. and Egan, S.K. 2001 'Determinants of chronic victimization by peers: a review and a new model of family influence' in *Peer harassment in school: the plight of the vulnerable and victimized* eds J. Juvonen & S. Graham, Guilford, New York, pp. 73–104

Perry, L. 1999 'Mitakuyu Oyasin—all of my relations: exploring metaphors of connectedness' in *Once upon a time... narrative therapy with children and their families* ed A. Morgan, Dulwich Centre Publications, Adelaide, SA, pp. 125–44

Petersen, L. and Ganoni, A. 1989 *Teacher's manual for training social skills while managing student behaviour* ACER, Melbourne

Phelan, P., Davidson, A.L. and Cao, H.T. 1992 'Speaking up: students' perspectives on school' *Phi Delta Kappan* vol. 73, no. 9, pp. 695–704

Phelan, T.W. 2003 *1–2–3-magic: effective discipline for children 2–12* 3rd edn, ParentMagic Inc, Glen Ellyn, IL

Phoenix, A. 2002 'Working with diverse communities' in *School behaviour and families* ed S. Roffey, David Fulton, London, pp. 125–39

Pianta, R.C. 1999 *Enhancing relationships between children and teachers* American Psychological Association, Washington, DC

Pianta, R.C. and Stuhlman, M.W. 2004 'Teacher–child relationships and children's success in the first years of school' *School Psychology Review* vol. 33, no. 3, pp. 444–58

Pianta, R.C. and Walsh, D.J. 1998 'Applying the construct of resilience in schools: cautions from a developmental systems perspective' *School Psychology Review* vol. 27, no. 3, pp. 407–17

Piazza, C.C., Adelinis, J.D., Hanley, G.P., Goh, H.-L. and Delia, M.D. 2000 'An evaluation of the effects of matched stimuli on behaviors maintained by automatic reinforcement' *Journal of Applied Behavior Analysis* vol. 33, no. 1, pp. 13–27

Piazza, C.C., Fisher, W.W., Hanley, G.P., LeBlanc, L.A., Worsdell, A.S., Lindauer, S.E. and Keeney, K.M. 1998 'Treatment of pica through multiple analyses of its reinforcing functions' *Journal of Applied Behavior Analysis* vol. 31, no. 2, pp. 165–89

Piazza, C.C., Fisher, W.W., Hanley, G.P., Remick, M.L., Contrucci, S.A. and Aitken, T.L. 1997 'The use of positive and negative reinforcement in the treatment of escape-maintained destructive behavior' *Journal of Applied Behavior Analysis* vol. 30, no. 2, pp. 279–98

Piazza, C.C., Patel, M.R., Gulotta, C.S., Sevin, B.M. and Layer, S.A. 2003 'On the relative contributions of positive reinforcement and escape extinction in the treatment of food refusal' *Journal of Applied Behavior Analysis* vol. 36, no. 3, pp. 309–24

Piazza, C.C., Roane, H.S., Keeney, K.M., Boney, B.R. and Abt, K.A. 2002 'Varying response effort in the treatment of pica maintained by automatic reinforcement' *Journal of Applied Behavior Analysis* vol. 35, no. 3, pp. 233–46

Piercy, F.P., Lipchik, E. and Kiser, D. 2000 'Commentary: Miller and de Shazer's article on "Emotions in solution-focused therapy"' *Family Process* vol. 39, no. 1, pp. 25–8

Pikas, A. 2002 'New developments of the shared concern method' *School Psychology International* vol. 23, no. 3, pp. 307–26

Pintrich, P.R. 2000 'Multiple goals, multiple pathways: the role of goal orientation in learning and achievement' *Journal of Educational Psychology* vol. 92, no. 3, pp. 544–55

Porter, L. 1999 'Behaviour management practices in child care centres' unpublished doctoral dissertation, University of South Australia, Adelaide, SA

——(ed) 2002a *Educating young children with additional needs* Allen & Unwin, Sydney

——(ed) 2002b *Educating young children with special needs* Paul Chapman, London/SAGE, Thousand Oaks, CA

——2003 *Young children's behaviour: practical approaches for caregivers and teachers* 2nd edn, Elsevier, Sydney/Paul Chapman, London/Brookes, Baltimore, MD

——2005 *Gifted young children: a guide for teachers and parents* 2nd edn, Allen & Unwin, Sydney/ Open University Press, Buckingham, UK

——2006 *Children are people too: a parent's guide to young children's behaviour* 4th edn, East Street Publications, Adelaide, SA

Putallaz, M. and Gottman, J.M. 1981 'An interactional model of children's entry into peer groups' *Child Development* vol. 52, no. 3, pp. 986–94

Putallaz, M. and Wasserman, A. 1990 'Children's entry behavior' in *Peer rejection in childhood* eds S.R. Asher & J.D. Coie, Cambridge University Press, Cambridge, UK, pp. 60–89

Putnam, R.F., Handler, M.W., Ramirez-Platt, C.M. and Luiselli, J.K. 2003 'Improving student bus-riding behavior through a whole-school intervention' *Journal of Applied Behavior Analysis* vol. 36, no. 4, pp. 583–90

Raffaele, L.M. and Knoff, H.M. 1999 'Improving home–school collaboration with disadvantaged families: organizational principles, perspectives, and approaches' *School Psychology Review* vol. 28, no. 3, pp. 448–66

Ramirez, S.Z., Lepage, K.M., Kratochwill, T.R. and Duffy, J.L. 1998 'Multicultural issues in school-based consultation: conceptual and research considerations' *Journal of School Psychology* vol. 36, no. 4, pp. 479–509

Raskin, N.J. and Rogers, C.R. 2005 'Person-centered therapy' in *Current psychotherapies* 7th edn, eds R.J. Corsini & D. Wedding, Thomson Brooks/Cole, Belmont, CA, pp. 130–65

Reed, G.K., Piazza, C.C., Patel, M.R., Laver, S.A., Bachmeyer, M.H., Bethke, S.D. and Gutshall, K.A. 2004 'On the relative contributions of noncontingent reinforcement and escape extinction in the treatment of food refusal' *Journal of Applied Behavior Analysis* vol. 37, no. 1, pp. 27–42

Reid, R., Gonzalez, J.E., Nordness, P.D., Trout, A. and Epstein, M.H. 2004 'A meta-analysis of the academic status of students with emotional/behavioral disturbance' *The Journal of Special Education* vol. 38, no. 3, pp. 130–43

Reid, R. and Harris, K.R. 1993 'Self-monitoring of attention versus self-monitoring of performance: effects on attention and academic performance' *Exceptional Children* vol. 60, no. 1, pp. 29–40

Reinke, W.M. and Herman, K.C. 2002 'Creating school environments that deter antisocial behaviors in youth' *Psychology in the Schools* vol. 39, no. 5, pp. 549–59

Reis, S.M. and Callahan, C.M. 1989 'Gifted females: they've come a long way—or have they?' *Journal for the Education of the Gifted* vol. 12, no. 2, pp. 99–117

Rekers, G.A. 1984 'Ethical issues in child behavioral assessment' in *Child behavioral assessment* eds T.H. Ollendick & M. Hersen, Pergamon, New York, pp. 244–62

Resnick, M.D., Bearman, P.S., Blum, R.W., Bauman, K.E., Harris, K.M., Jones, J., Tabor, J., Beuhring, T., Sieving, R.E., Shew, M., Ireland, M., Bearinger, L.H. and Udry, J.R. 1997 'Protecting adolescents from harm: findings from the national longitudinal study on adolescent health' *Journal of the American Medical Association* vol. 278, no. 10, pp. 823–32

Reynolds, E. 2001 *Guiding young children: a problem-solving approach* 3rd edn, Mayfield, Mountain View, CA

Reynolds, L.K. and Kelley, M.L. 1997 'The efficacy of a response cost-based treatment package for managing aggressive behavior in preschoolers' *Behavior Modification* vol. 21, pp. 216–30

Reynolds, M.A. and Holdgrafer, G. 1998 'Social-communicative interactions of preschool children with developmental delays in integrated settings: an exploratory study' *Topics in Early Childhood Special Education* vol. 18, no. 4, pp. 235–42

Rhodes, J. 1993 'The use of solution-focused brief therapy in schools' *Educational Psychology in Practice* vol. 9, no. 1, pp. 27–34

Rigby, K. 1993 'Countering bullying in schools' *CAFHS Forum* vol. 1, no. 2, pp. 19–22

——1996 *Bullying in schools: and what to do about it* ACER, Melbourne

——1998 'Gender and bullying in schools' in *Children's peer relations* eds P.T. Slee & K. Rigby, Routledge, London, pp. 47–59

——1999 'Peer victimisation at school and the health of secondary school students' *British Journal of Educational Psychology* vol. 69, no. 1, pp. 95–104

——2001 'Health consequences of bullying and its prevention in schools' in *Peer harassment in school: the plight of the vulnerable and victimized* eds J. Juvonen & S. Graham, Guilford, New York, pp. 310–31

——2003 *Stop the bullying: a handbook for schools* 2nd edn, ACER, Melbourne

——2006a 'What international research tells us about bullying' in *Bullying solutions: evidence-based approaches to bullying in Australian schools* eds H. McGrath & T. Noble, Pearson Longman, Sydney, pp. 3–15

——2006b 'An overview of approaches to managing bully/victim problems' in *Bullying solutions: evidence-based approaches to bullying in Australian schools* eds H. McGrath & T. Noble, Pearson Longman, Sydney, pp. 149–60

Rigby, K. and Bagshaw, D. 2006 'Using educational drama and bystander training to counteract bullying' in *Bullying solutions: evidence-based approaches to bullying in Australian schools* eds H. McGrath & T. Noble, Pearson Longman, Sydney, pp. 133–45

Rimm-Kaufman, S.E. and Pianta, R.C. 1999 'Patterns of family-school contact in preschool and kindergarten' *School Psychology Review* vol. 28, no. 3, pp. 426–38

Ripley, K. and Yuill, N. 2005 'Patterns of language impairment and behaviours in boys excluded from school' *British Journal of Educational Psychology* vol. 75, no. 1, pp. 37–50

Rist, R.C. 1970 'Student social class and teacher expectations: the self-fulfilling prophecy in ghetto education' *Harvard Educational Review* vol. 40, no. 3, pp. 411–51

Ritchhart, R. 2001 'From IQ to IC: a dispositional view of intelligence' *Roeper Review* vol. 23, no. 3, pp. 143–50

Rivers, S. 2001 'The bullying of sexual minorities at school: its nature and long-term correlates' *Educational and Child Psychology* vol. 18, no. 1, pp. 32–46

Roane, H.S., Fisher, W.W. and Sgro, G.M. 2001 'Effects of a fixed-time schedule on aberrant and adaptive behavior' *Journal of Applied Behavior Analysis* vol. 34, no. 3, pp. 333–6

Roane, H.S., Kelly, M.L. and Fisher, W.W. 2003 'The effects of noncontingent access to food on the rate of object mouthing across three settings' *Journal of Applied Behavior Analysis* vol. 36, no. 4, pp. 579–82

Robertson, J.S. 2000 'Is attribution training a worthwhile classroom intervention for K–12 students with learning difficulties?' *Educational Psychology Review* vol. 12, no. 1, pp. 111–34

Robinson, A. 1990 'Cooperation or exploitation?: the argument against cooperative learning for talented students' *Journal for the Education of the Gifted* vol. 14, no. 1, pp. 9–27

——2003 'Cooperative learning and high ability students' in *Handbook of gifted education* 3rd edn, eds N. Colangelo & G.A. Davis, Allyn & Bacon, Boston, MA, pp. 282–92

Robinson, N.M., Lanzi, R.G., Weinberg, R.A., Ramey, S.L. and Ramey, C.T. 2002 'Family factors associated with high academic competence in former Head Start children at third grade' *Gifted Child Quarterly* vol. 46, no. 4, pp. 278–90

Robinson, T.R., Smith, S.W., Miller, M.D. & Brownell, M.T. 1999 'Cognitive behavior modification of hyperactivity-impulsivity and aggression: a meta-analysis of school-based studies' *Journal of Educational Psychology* vol. 91, no. 2, pp. 195–203

Robson, S. 1996 'The physical environment' in *Education in early childhood: first things first* eds S. Robson & S. Smedley, David Fulton, London, pp. 153–71

Rodd, J. 1996 *Understanding young children's behaviour* Allen & Unwin, Sydney

Rodkin, P.C. and Hodges, E.V.E. 2003 'Bullies and victims in the peer ecology: four questions for psychologists and school professionals' *School Psychology Review* vol. 32, no. 3, pp. 384–400

Roffey, S. 2002 *School behaviour and families: frameworks for working together* David Fulton, London

——2004 *The new teacher's survival guide to behaviour* Paul Chapman, London

Roffey, S. and O'Reirdan, T. 2001 *Young children and classroom behaviour: needs, perspectives and strategies* David Fulton, London

——2003 *Plans for better behaviour in primary school: management and intervention* David Fulton, London

Rogers, B. 1998 *'You know the fair rule' and much more: strategies for making the hard job of discipline and behaviour management in school easier* ACER, Melbourne

——2002 *Classroom behaviour: a practical guide to teaching, behaviour management and colleague support* Paul Chapman, London

——2003 *Behaviour recovery: practical programs for challenging behaviour* 2nd edn, ACER, Melbourne

——2004 'Essential principles and practices that enable us to make a difference with individual children and classroom groups' in *How to manage children's challenging behaviour* ed B. Rogers, Paul Chapman, London, pp. 97–112

Rogers, C. 1951 *Client-centred therapy* Constable, London

——1978 *On personal power* Constable, London

Rogers, C.R. and Freiberg, H. 1994 *Freedom to learn* 3rd edn, Merrill, New York

Rogers, M.R. 1998 'The influence of race and consultant verbal behavior on perceptions of consultant competence and multicultural sensitivity' *School Psychology Quarterly* vol. 13, no. 4, pp. 265–80

Rogers, N. 1994 'Foreword' in *Freedom to learn* 3rd edn, eds C.R. Rogers & H. Freiberg, Merrill, New York, pp. iii-vii

Rogers, W.S. 2003 'What is a child?' in *Understanding childhood: an interdisciplinary approach* eds M. Woodhead & H. Montgomery, Open University Press, Milton Keynes, UK, pp. 1–43

Roland, E. 1993 'Bullying: a developing tradition of research and management' in *Understanding and managing bullying* ed D. Tattum, Heinemann Educational, Oxford, UK, pp. 15–30

Root, R.W. and Levant, R.F. 1984 'An evaluation of Parent Effectiveness Training for rural parents' *Journal of Rural Community Psychology* vol. 5, no. 2, pp. 45–54

Rosenberg, M.B. 2003 *Nonviolent communication: a language of life* 2nd edn, Puddle Dancer Press, Encinitas, CA

Rosenhan, D.L. 1973 'On being sane in insane places' *Science*, vol. 179, no. 4070, pp. 250–58

Rosin, P. 1996 'Parent and service provider partnerships in early intervention' in *Partnerships in family-centred care: a guide to collaborative early intervention* eds P. Rosin, A.D. Whitehead, L.I. Tuchman, G.S. Jesien, A.L. Begun & L. Irwin, Paul H. Brookes, Baltimore, MD, pp. 65–79

Rossman, B.B.R., Hughes, H.M. and Hanson, K.L. 1998 'The victimization of school-age children' in *Multiple victimization of children: conceptual, developmental, research, and treatment issues* eds B.B.R. Rossman & M.S. Rosenberg, Haworth Press, New York, pp. 87–106

Rothbaum, F., Grauer, A. and Rubin, D.J. 1997 'Becoming sexual: differences between child and adult sexuality' *Young Children* vol. 52, no. 6, pp. 22–8

Rubin, Z. 1980 *Children's friendships* Harvard University Press, Boston, MA

Rumberger, R.W. 1995 'Dropping out of middle school: a multilevel analysis of students and schools' *American Educational Research Journal* vol. 32, no. 3, pp. 583–625

Russell, A., Petit, G.S. and Mize, J. 1998 'Horizontal qualities in parent–child relationships: parallels with and possible consequences for children's peer relationships' *Developmental Review* vol. 18, no. 3, pp. 313–52

Rutter, M. 1983 'School effects on pupil progress: research findings and policy implications' *Child Development* vol. 54, no. 1, pp. 1–29

——1985 'Resilience in the face of adversity: protective factors and resistance to psychiatric disorder' *British Journal of Psychiatry* vol. 147, pp. 598–611

——1990 'Psychosocial resilience and protective mechanisms' in *Risk and protective factors in the development of psychopathology* eds J. Rolf, A.S. Masten, D. Cicchetti, K.H. Nuechterlein & S. Weintraub, Cambridge University Press, New York, pp. 181–214

——1999 'Resilience concepts and findings: implications for family therapy' *Journal of Family Therapy* vol. 21, no. 2, pp. 119–44

Rutter, M. and Maughan, B. 2002 'School effectiveness findings 1979–2002' *Journal of School Psychology* vol. 40, no. 6, pp. 451–75

Ryan, R.M. and Deci, E.L. 1996 'When paradigms clash: comments on Cameron and Pierce's claim that rewards do not undermine intrinsic motivation' *Review of Educational Research* vol. 66, no. 1, pp. 33–8

——2000 'Self-determination theory and the facilitation of intrinsic motivation, social development, and well-being' *American Psychologist* vol. 55, no. 1, pp. 68–78

Ryan, R.M., Stiller, J.D. and Lynch, J.H. 1994 'Representations of relationships to teachers, parents, and friends as predictors of academic motivation and self-esteem' *Journal of Early Adolescence* vol. 14, no. 2, pp. 226–49

Salend, S.J. and Taylor, L. 1993 'Working with families: a cross-cultural perspective' *Remedial and Special Education* vol. 14, no. 5, pp. 25–32

Salmivalli, C., Kaukiainen, A. and Lagerspetz, K. 1998 'Aggression in the social relations of school-aged girls and boys' in *Children's peer relations* eds P.T. Slee & K. Rigby, Routledge, London, pp. 60–75

Samples, F.L. 2004 'Evaluating curriculum-based intervention programs: an examination of preschool, primary, and elementary school intervention programs' in *Bullying: implications for the classroom* eds C.E. Sanders & G.D. Phye, Elsevier, San Diego, CA, pp. 203–27

Sanders, C.E. 2004 'What is bullying?' in *Bullying: implications for the classroom* eds C.E. Sanders & G.D. Phye, Elsevier, San Diego, CA, pp. 1–18

Sanders, M.R. 1999 'Triple P—Positive Parenting Program: towards an empirically validated multilevel parenting and support strategy for the prevention of behaviour and emotional problems in children' *Clinical Child and Family Psychology Review* vol. 2, no. 2, pp. 71–90

Sanders, M.R., Markie-Dadds, C., Tully, L.A. and Bor, W. 2000 'The Triple P—Positive Parenting Program: a comparison of enhanced, standard, and self-directed behavioral family intervention for children with early onset conduct problems' *Journal of Consulting and Clinical Psychology* vol. 68, no. 4, pp. 624–40

Sapon-Shevin, M. 1994 *Playing favorites: gifted education and the disruption of community* State University of New York, Albany, NY

——1996 'Beyond gifted education: building a shared agenda for school reform' *Journal for the Education of the Gifted* vol. 19, no. 2, pp. 194–214

——1999 *Because we can change the world: a practical guide to building cooperative, inclusive classroom communities* Allyn & Bacon, Boston, MA

Sayger, T.V., Horne, A.M. and Glaser, B.A. 1993 'Marital satisfaction and social learning family therapy for child conduct problems: generalisation of treatment effects' *Journal of Marital and Family Therapy* vol. 19, no. 4, pp. 393–402

Sbarra, D.A. and Pianta, R.C. 2001 'Teacher ratings of behavior among African American and Caucasian children during the first two years of school' *Psychology in the Schools* vol. 38, no. 3, pp. 229–38

Schaffer, H.R. 1998 *Making decisions about children: psychological questions and answers* 2nd edn, Blackwell, Oxford, UK

Schlick, M. 1966 'When is man responsible?' in *Free will and determinism* ed B. Berofsky, Harper & Row, New York, pp. 54–63

Schloss, P.J. and Smith, M.A. 1998 *Applied behavior analysis in the classroom* 2nd edn, Allyn & Bacon, Boston, MA

Schmuck, R.A. and Schmuck, P.A. 2001 *Group processes in the classroom* 8th edn, McGraw Hill, Boston, MA

Schneider, B.H. 1989 'Between developmental wisdom and children's social skills training' in *Social competence in developmental persective* eds B.H. Schneider, G. Attili, J. Nadel & R.P. Weissberg, Kluwer Academic Publishers, Dordrecht, pp. 339–53

Schneider, B.H. and Blonk, R.W.B. 1998 'Children's comments about their social skills training' in *Children's peer relations* eds P.T. Slee & K. Rigby, Routledge, London, pp. 272–87

Schneider, B.H., Clegg, M.R., Byrne, B.M., Ledingham, J.E. and Crombie, G. 1989 'Social relations of gifted children as a function of age and school program' *Journal of Educational Psychology* vol. 81, no. 1, pp. 48–56

Schultz, C.L. 1981 'The family and Parent Effectiveness Training' *Australian Journal of Sex, Marriage and Family* vol. 2, no. 3, pp. 135–42

Schultz, C.L. and Khan, J.A. 1982 'Mother–child interaction behaviour and Parent Effectiveness Training' *Australian Journal of Sex, Marriage and Family* vol. 3. no. 3, pp. 133–8

Schultz, C.L. and Nystul, M.S. 1980 'Mother–child interaction behavior as an outcome of theoretical models of parent group education' *Journal of Individual Psychology* vol. 36, no. 1, pp. 3–15

Schultz, C.L., Nystul, M.S. and Law, H.G. 1980 'Attitudinal outcomes of theoretical models of parent group education' *Journal of Individual Psychology* vol. 36, no. 1, pp. 16–28

Schwartz, D., Proctor, L.J. and Chien, D.H. 2001 'The aggressive victim of bullying: emotional and behavioral dysregulation as a pathway to victimization by peers' in *Peer harassment in school: the plight of the vulnerable and victimized* eds J. Juvonen & S. Graham, Guilford, New York, pp. 147–74

Schwartz, R.C. and Johnson, S.M. 2000 'Does couple and family therapy have emotional intelligence?' *Family Process* vol. 29, no. 1, pp. 29–33

Scott, T.M. and Barrett, S.B. 2004 'Using staff and student time engaged in disciplinary procedures to evaluate the impact of school-wide PBS' *Journal of Positive Behavior Interventions* vol. 6, no. 1, pp. 21–7

Scott-Jones, D. 1995 'Parent–child interactions and school achievement' in *The family–school connection: theory, research, and practice* eds B.A. Ryan, G.R. Adams, T.P. Gullotta, R.P. Weissbeerg & R.L. Hampton, SAGE, Thousand Oaks, CA, pp. 75–107

Scott-Little, M.C. and Holloway, S.D. 1992 'Child care providers' reasoning about misbehaviors: relation to classroom control strategies and professional training' *Early Childhood Research Quarterly* vol. 7, no. 4, pp. 595–606

Selekman, M.D. 1997 *Solution-focused therapy with children* Guilford, New York

Seligman, M.E.P. 1975 *Helplessness: on depression, development and death* W.H. Freeman & Co, San Francisco, CA

——1995 *The optimistic child* Random House, Sydney

Seymour, F.W. and Epston, C. 1989 'An approach to childhood stealing with evaluation of 45 cases' *Australian and New Zealand Journal of Family Therapy* vol. 10, no. 3, pp. 137–43

Shapiro, E.S. 1984 'Self-monitoring procedures' in *Child behavioral assessment* eds T.H. Ollendick & M. Hersen, Pergamon, New York, pp. 148–65

Sharp, S. and Cowie, H. 1994 'Empowering pupils to take positive action against bullying' in *School bullying: insights and perspectives* eds P.K. Smith & S. Sharp, Routledge, London, pp. 108–31

Sharp, S. and Thompson, D. 1994 'The role of whole-school policies in tackling bullying behaviour in schools' in *School bullying: insights and perspectives* eds P.K. Smith & S. Sharp, Routledge, London, pp. 57–83

Shechtman, Z. 2000 'An innovative intervention for treatment of child and adolescent aggression: an outcome study' *Psychology in the Schools* vol. 37, no. 2, pp. 157–82

Sheridan, S.M. 2000 'Considerations of multiculturalism and diversity in behavioral consultation with parents and teachers' *School Psychology Review* vol. 29, no. 3, pp. 344–53

Shriver, M.D., Anderson, C.M. and Proctor, B. 2001 'Evaluating the validity of functional behaviour assessment' *School Psychology Review* vol. 30, no. 2, pp. 180–92

Shute, R., Owens, L. and Slee, P. 2002 '"You just stare at them and give them daggers": nonverbal expressions of social aggression in teenage girls' *International Journal of Adolescence and Youth* vol. 10, no. 4, pp. 353–72

Silverman, L.K. 2002 *Upside-down brilliance: the visual-spatial learner* DeLeon, Denver, CO

Silverman, W.K., La Greca, A.M. and Wasserstein, S. 1995 'What do children worry about?: worries and their relation to anxiety' *Child Development* vol. 66, pp. 671–86

Sirin, S.R. 2005 'Socioeconomic status and academic achievement: a meta-analytic review of research' *Review of Educational Research* vol. 75, no. 3, pp. 417–53

Skinner, C.H., Pappas, D.N. and Davis, K.A. 2005 'Enhancing academic engagement: providing opportunities for responding and influencing students to choose to respond' *Psychology in the Schools* vol. 42, no. 4, pp. 389–403

Skinner, C.H., Williams, R.L. and Neddenriep, C.E. 2004 'Using interdependent group-oriented reinforcement to enhance academic performance in general education classrooms' *School Psychology Review* vol. 33, no. 3, pp. 384–97

Sklare, G.B. 2005 *Brief counseling that works: a solution-focused approach for school counselors and administrators* 2nd edn, Corwin Press, Thousand Oaks, CA

Slavin, R.E. 1991 'Are cooperative learning and "untracking" harmful to the gifted?: response to Allan' *Educational Leadership* vol. 48, no. 6, pp. 68–71

Slee, P.T. 1994a 'Life at school used to be good: victimisation and health concerns of secondary school students' *Young Studies Australia* Dec, pp. 20–23

——1994b 'Situational and interpersonal correlates of anxiety associated with peer victimisation' *Journal of Child Psychiatry and Human Development* vol. 25, no. 2, pp. 97–107

——1995a 'Peer victimisation and its relationship to depression among Australian primary school students' *Journal of Personality and Individual Differences* vol. 18, no. 1, pp. 57–62

——1995b 'Bullying: health concerns of Australian secondary school students' *International Journal of Adolescence and Youth* vol. 5, no. 4, pp. 215–24

——1998 'Bullying amongst Australian primary school students: some barriers to help-seeking and links with sociometric status' in *Children's peer relations* eds P.T. Slee & K. Rigby, Routledge, London, pp. 205–14

——2001 *The PEACE pack: a program for reducing bullying in our schools* 3rd edn, Flinders University, Adelaide, SA

——2006 'The P.E.A.C.E. Pack: a whole-school program for reducing school bullying' in *Bullying solutions: evidence-based approaches to bullying in Australian schools* eds H. McGrath & T. Noble, Pearson Longman, Sydney, pp. 85–99

Slee, P.T. and Rigby, K. 1994 'Peer victimisation at school' *Australian Journal of Early Childhood* vol. 19, no. 1, pp. 3–10

Slee, R. 1995 *Changing theories and practices of discipline* Falmer, London

Smidt, S. 1998 *Guide to early years practice* Routledge, London

Smith, P.K., Cowie, H. and Sharp, S. 1994 'Working directly with pupils involved in bullying situations' in *School bullying: insights and perspectives* eds P.K. Smith & S. Sharp, Routledge, London, pp. 193–212

Smith, P.K. and Sharp, S. 1994 'The problem of school bullying' in *School bullying: insights and perspectives* eds P.K. Smith & S. Sharp, Routledge, London, pp. 1–19

Smith, P.K., Talamelli, L., Cowie, H., Naylor, P. and Chauhan, P. 2004 'Profiles of non-victims, escaped victims, continuing victims and new victims of school bullying' *British Journal of Education Psychology* vol. 74, no. 4, pp. 565–81

Smith, S.W. and Daunic, A.P. 2002 'Using conflict resolution and peer mediation to support positive behavior' in *Preventing problem behaviors: a handbook of successful prevention strategies* eds B. Algozzine & P. Kay, Corwin Press, Thousand Oaks, CA, pp. 142–61

Smyrnios, K.X. and Kirkby, R.J. 1989 'A review of brief, child-oriented family therapy outcome research: descriptive reports and single group studies' *Australian and New Zealand Journal of Family Therapy* vol. 10, no. 3, pp. 151–9

Smyrnios, K.X., Kirkby, R.J. and Smyrnios, S.M. 1988 'Brief family therapy: a critique of Kinston and Bentovim' *Australian and New Zealand Journal of Family Therapy* vol. 9, no. 3, pp. 139–42

Snow, J.N., Kern, R.M. and Penick, J. 1997 'The effects of STEP on patient progress in an adolescent day hospital' *Individual Psychology: Journal of Adlerian theory, research and practice* vol. 53, no. 4, pp. 388–95

Solomon, D., Watson, M., Battistich, V., Schaps, E. and Delucci, K. 1996 'Creating classrooms that students experience as communities' *American Journal of Community Psychology* vol. 24, no. 6, pp. 719–48

Spera, C. 2005 'A review of the relationship among parenting practices, parenting styles, and adolescent school achievement' *Educational Psychology Review* vol. 17, no. 2, pp. 125–46

Spicker, H.H., Southern, W.T. and Davis, B.I. 1987 'The rural gifted child' *Gifted Child Quarterly* vol. 31, no. 4, pp. 155–7

Spirito, A., Stark, L.J., Grace, N. and Stamoulis, D. 1991 'Common problems and coping strategies reported in childhood and early adolescence' *Journal of Youth and Adolescence* vol. 20, no. 5, pp. 531–44

Sprenkle, D.H. and Bischoff, R.J. 1995 'Research in family therapy: trends, issues and recommendations' in *Family therapy: concepts and methods* 3rd edn, eds M.P. Nichols & R.C. Schwartz, Allyn & Bacon, Boston, MA, pp. 542–80

Stanley, M. and McGrath, H. 2006 'Buddy systems: peer support in action' in *Bullying solutions: evidence-based approaches to bullying in Australian schools* eds H. McGrath & T. Noble, Pearson Longman, Sydney, pp. 101–22

Stark, K.D., Sander, J.B., Yancy, M.G., Bronik, M.D. and Hoke, J.A. 2000 'Treatment of depression in childhood and adolescence: cognitive-behavioral procedures for the individual and family' in *Child and adolescent therapy: cognitive-behavioral procedures* 2nd edn, ed P.C. Kendall, Guilford, New York, pp. 173–234

Steinberg, L., Elmen, J.D. and Mounts, N.S. 1989 'Authoritative parenting, psychosocial maturity, and academic success among adolescents' *Child Development* vol. 60 no. 6, pp. 1424–36

Steinberg, L., Lamborn, S.D., Darling, N., Mounts, N.S. and Dornbusch, S.M. 1994 'Over-time changes in adjustment and competence among adolescents from authoritative, authoritarian, indulgent, and neglectful families' *Child Development* vol. 65, no. 3, pp. 754–70

Steinberg, L., Lamborn, S.D., Dornbusch, S.M. and Darling, N. 1992 'Impact of parenting practices on adolescent achievement: authoritative parenting, school involvement, and encouragement to succeed' *Child Development* vol. 63, no. 5, pp. 1266–81

Sterling-Turner, H.E., Robinson, S.L. and Wilczynski, S.M. 2001 'Functional assessment of distracting and disruptive behaviors in the school setting' *School Psychology Review* vol. 30, no. 2, pp. 211–26

Sterling-Turner, H. and Watson, T.S. 1999 'Consultant's guide for the use of time-out in the preschool and elementary classroom' *Psychology in the Schools* vol. 36, no. 2, pp. 135–48

Stevens, V., De Bourdeauhuij, I. and Van Oost, P. 2000 'Bullying in Flemish schools: an evaluation of anti-bullying intervention in primary and secondary schools' *British Journal of Educational Psychology* vol. 70, no. 2, pp. 195–210

Stonehouse, A. 1991 *Our code of ethics at work* Australian Early Childhood Association, Watson, ACT

Stoneman, Z. 1993 'The effects of attitude on preschool integration' in *Integrating young children with disabilities into community programs: ecological perspectives on research and implementation* eds C.A. Peck, S.L. Odom & D.D. Bricker, Paul H. Brookes, Baltimore, MD, pp. 223–48

Stormont, M. 2002 'Externalizing behavior problems in young children: contributing factors and early intervention' *Psychology in the Schools* vol. 39, no. 2, pp. 127–38

Strein, W., Simonson, T. and Vail, L. 1999 'Convergence of views: self-perceptions of African American and White kindergartners' *Psychology in the Schools* vol. 36, no. 2, pp. 125–34

Strike, K.A. and Soltis, J.F. 2004 *The ethics of teaching* 4th edn, Teachers College Press, New York

Stuhlman, M.W. and Pianta, R.C. 2001 'Teachers' narratives about their relationships with children: associations with behavior in classrooms' *School Psychology Review* vol. 31, no. 2, pp. 148–63

Sulzer-Azaroff, B. and Mayer, G.R. 1991 *Behavior analysis for lasting change* Holt, Rinehart & Winston, Fort Worth, TX

Swetnam, L., Peterson, C.R. and Clark, H.B. 1983 'Social skills development in young children: preventive and therapeutic approaches' in *Social skills training for children and youth* ed C.W. LeCroy, Haworth Press, New York, pp. 5–27

Sylva, K. 1994 'School influences of children's development' *Journal of Child Psychology and Psychiatry and Related Disciplines* vol. 35, no. 1, pp. 135–70

Tannock, R. 2004 'What is ADHD?' Keynote address to the ADD Association Queensland conference *Removing the barriers to learning* 30 July 2004, Brisbane, QLD

Tarbox, R.S.F., Wallace, M.D. and Williams, L. 2003 'Assessment and treatment of elopement: a replication and extension' *Journal of Applied Behavior Analysis* vol. 36, no. 2, pp. 239–44

Tattum, D. 1993a 'What is bullying?' in *Understanding and managing bullying* ed D. Tattum, Heinemann Educational, Oxford, UK, pp. 3–14

——1993b 'Child, school and family' in *Understanding and managing bullying* ed D. Tattum, Heinemann Educational, Oxford, UK, pp. 153–60

Terry, A.A. 1998 'Teachers as targets of bullying by their pupils: a study to investigate incidence' *British Journal of Educational Psychology* vol. 68, no. 2, pp. 255–68

Terwel, J., Gillies, R.M., van den Eeden, P. and Hoek, D. 2001 'Co-operative learning processes of students: a longitudinal multilevel perspective' *British Journal of Educational Pyschology* vol. 71, no. 4, pp. 619–44

Thompson, C.L. and Rudolph, L.B. 2000 *Counseling children* 5th edn, Brooks/Cole, Belmont, CA

Thompson, R.A. and Wyatt, J.M. 1999 'Current research on child maltreatment: implications for educators' *Educational Psychology Review* vol. 11, no. 3, pp. 173–201

Tileston, D.W. 2004 *What every teacher should know about classroom management and discipline* Corwin Press, Thousand Oaks, CA

Tollefson, N. 2000 'Classroom applications of cognitive theories of motivation' *Educational Psychology Review* vol. 12, no. 1, pp. 63–83

Topping, K. 1988 *The peer tutoring handbook: promoting co-operative learning* Croom Helm, London

Trautwein, U. and Köller, O. 2003 'The relationship between homework and achievement—still much of a mystery' *Educational Psychology Review* vol. 15, no. 2, pp. 115–45

Trawick-Smith, J. 1988 '"Let's say you're the baby, OK?": play leadership and following behavior of young children' *Young Children* vol. 43, no. 5, pp. 51–9

Trickett, P.K. 1998 'Multiple maltreatment and the development of self and emotion regulation' in *Multiple victimization of children: conceptual, developmental, research and treatment issues* eds B.B.R. Rossman & M.S. Rosenberg, Haworth Press, New York, pp. 171–87

Trusty, J. and Lampe, R.E. 1997 'Relationship of high-school seniors' perceptions of parental involvement and control to seniors' locus of control' *Journal of Counseling and Development* vol. 75, no. 5, pp. 375–84

Tucker, C.M., Zayco, R.A., Herman, K.C., Reinke, W.M., Trujillo, M., Carraway, K., Wallack, C. and Ivery, P.D. 2002 'Teacher and child variables as predictors of academic engagement among low-income African American children' *Psychology in the Schools* vol. 39, no. 4, pp. 477–88

Ullman, L.P. and Krasner, L. 1975 *A psychological approach to abnormal behavior* 2nd edn, Prentice Hall, Englewood Cliffs, NJ

Umbreit, J., Lane, K.L. and Dejud, C. 2004 'Improving classroom behavior by modifying task difficulty: effects of increasing the difficulty of too-easy tasks' *Journal of Positive Behavior Interventions* vol. 6, no. 1, pp. 13–20

Ungar, M. 2004 'The importance of parents and other caregivers to the resilience of high-risk adolescents' *Family Process* vol. 43, no. 1, pp. 23–41

Urbain, E.S. and Kendall, P.C. 1980 'Review of social-cognitive problem-solving interventions with children' *Psychological Bulletin* vol. 88, no. 1, pp. 109–43

Vallerand, R.J., Gagné, F., Senécal, C. and Pelletier, L.G. 1994 'A comparison of the school intrinsic motivation and perceived competence of gifted and regular students' *Gifted Child Quarterly* vol. 38, no. 4, pp. 172–5

Van Camp, C.M., Lerman, D.C., Kelley, M.E., Roane, H.S., Contrucci, S.A. and Vorndran, C.M. 2000 'Further analysis of idiosyncratic antecedent influences during the assessment and treatment of problem behavior' *Journal of Applied Behavior Analysis* vol. 33, no. 2, pp. 207–21

van Houten, R., Axelrod, S., Bailey, J.S., Favell, J.E., Foxx, R.M., Iwata, B.A. and Lovaas, O.I. 1988 'The right to effective treatment' *Journal of Applied Behavior Analysis* vol. 21, no. 4, pp. 381–4

Van Schoiack-Edstrom, L., Frey, K.S. and Beland, K. 2002 'Changing adolescents' attitudes about relational and physical aggression: an early evaluation of a school-based intervention' *School Psychology Review* vol. 31, no. 2, pp. 201–16

Vizard, E., Monck, E. and Misch, P. 1995 'Child and adolescent sex abuse perpetrators: a review of the research literature' *Journal of Child Psychology and Psychiatry* vol. 36, no. 5, pp. 731–56

Vollmer, T.R., Iwata, B.A., Zarcone, J.R., Smith, R.G. and Mazaleski, J.L. 1993 'The role of attention in the treatment of attention-maintained self-injurious behavior: noncontingent reinforcement and differential reinforcement of other behavior' *Journal of Applied Behavior Analysis* vol. 26, no. 1, pp. 9–21

Vollmer, T.R., Roane, H.S., Ringdahl, J.E. and Marcus, B.A. 1999 'Evaluating treatment challenges with differential reinforcement of alternative behavior' *Journal of Applied Behavior Analysis* vol. 32, no. 1, pp. 9–23

Wagner, P. and Gillies, E. 2001 'Consultation: a solution-focused approach' in *Solutions in schools* eds Y. Ajmal & I. Rees, BT Press, London, pp. 147–62

Wagner, P. and Watkins, C. 2005 'Narrative work in schools' in *Narrative therapies with children and their families: a practitioner's guide to concepts and approaches* eds A. Vetere & E. Dowling, Routledge, London, pp. 239–53

Walker, J.E., Shea, T.M. and Bauer, A.M. 2004 *Behavior management: a practical approach for educators* 8th edn, Pearson Merrill Prentice Hall, Upper Saddle River, NJ

Wallace, M.D., Doney, J.K., Mintz-Resudek, C.M. and Tarbox, R.S.F. 2004 'Training educators to implement functional analyses' *Journal of Applied Behavior Analysis* vol. 37, no. 1, pp. 89–92

Warnes, E.D., Sheridan, S.M., Geske, J. and Warnes, W.A. 2005 'A contextual approach to the assessment of social skills: identifying meaningful behaviors for social competence' *Psychology in the Schools* vol. 42, no. 2, pp. 173–87

Watson, M., Battistich, V. and Solomon, D. 1997 'Enhancing students' social and ethical development in schools: an intervention program and its effects' *International Journal of Educational Research* vol. 27, no. 7, pp. 571–86

Watzlawick, P., Weakland, J. and Fisch, R. 1974 *Change: principles of problem formation and problem resolution* W.W. Norton, New York

Webb, N.M. 1989 'Peer interaction and learning in small groups' *International Journal of Educational Research* vol. 13, no. 1, pp. 21–39

Webster, R.E. 2001 'Symptoms and long-term outcomes for children who have been sexually assaulted' *Psychology in the Schools* vol. 38, no. 6, pp. 533–47

Wehby, J.H. and Hollahan, M.S. 2000 'Effects of high-probability requests on the latency to initiate academic tasks' *Journal of Applied Behavior Analysis* vol. 33, no. 2, pp. 259–62

Wehmeyer, M.L., Baker, D.J., Blumberg, R. and Harrison, R. 2004 'Self-determination and student involvement in functional assessment: innovative practices' *Journal of Positive Behavior Interventions* vol. 6, no. 1, pp. 29–35

Weiner, B. 2000 'Interpersonal and intrapersonal theories of motivation from an attributional perspective' *Educational Psychology Review* vol. 22, no. 1, pp. 1–14

Wentzel, K.R. 1994 'Family functioning and academic achievement in middle school: a social-emotional perspective' *Journal of Early Adolescence* vol. 14, no. 2, pp. 268–91

——1997 'Student motivation in middle school: the role of perceived pedagogical caring' *Journal of Educational Psychology* vol. 89, no. 3, pp. 411–19

——1998 'Social relationships and motivation in middle school: the role of parents, teachers, and peers' *Journal of Educational Psychology* vol. 90, no. 2, pp. 202–9

Wentzel, K.R. and Asher, S.R. 1995 'The academic lives of neglected, rejected, popular, and controversial children' *Child Development* vol. 66, no. 3, pp. 754–63

Wentzel, K.R. and Watkins, D.E. 2002 'Peer relationships and collaborative learning as contexts for academic enablers' *School Psychology Review* vol. 31, no. 3, pp. 366–77

Wentzel, K.R. and Wigfield, A. 1998 'Academic and social motivational influences on students' academic performance' *Educational Psychology Review* vol. 10, no. 2, pp. 155–75

Wheeler, J.J. and Richey, D.D. 2005 *Behavior management: principles and practices of positive behavior support* Pearson Merrill Prentice Hall, Upper Saddle River, NJ

Whedall, K. and Merrett, F. 1984 *Positive teaching: the behavioural approach* Allen & Unwin, London

White, K.R. 1982 'The relation between socioeconomic status and academic achievement' *Psychological Bulletin* vol. 91, no. 3, pp. 461–81

Whitman, T.L., Scherzinger, M.L. and Sommer, K.S. 1991 'Cognitive instruction and mental retardation' in *Child and adolescent therapy: cognitive-behavioral procedures* ed P.C. Kendall, Guilford, New York, pp. 276–315

Whitney, I., Rivers, I., Smith, P.K. and Sharp, S. 1994 'The Sheffield project: methodology and findings' in *School bullying: insights and perspectives* eds P.K. Smith & S. Sharp, Routledge, London, pp. 20–56

Wien, C.A. 2004 'From policing to participation: overturning the rules and creating amicable classrooms' *Young Children* vol. 59, no. 1, pp. 34–40

Winett, R.A. and Winkler, R.C. 1972 'Current behavior modification in the classroom: be still, be quiet, be docile' *Journal of Applied Behavior Analysis* vol. 5, no. 4, pp. 499–504

Winslade, J. and Monk, G. 1999 *Narrative counseling in schools* Corwin Press, Thousand Oaks, CA

Wolery, M., Bailey, D.B. and Sugai, G.M. 1988 *Effective teaching: principles and procedures of applied behavior analysis with exceptional students* Allyn & Bacon, Boston, MA

Wolfgang, C.H., Bennett, B.J. and Irvin, J.L. 1999 *Strategies for teaching self-discipline in the middle grades* Allyn & Bacon, Boston, MA

Wood, C.D. 1985 *A study of Parent Effectiveness Training* Unpublished Diploma in Psychology thesis, University of Tasmania, Hobart, TAS

——2003 *How we talk to our children: an evaluation of parent effectiveness training for the development of emotional competence* Unpublished doctoral thesis, University of Tasmania, Hobart, TAS

Wood, C.D. and Davidson, J.A. 1987 'PET: an outcome study' *Australian Journal of Sex, Marriage and Family* vol. 8, no. 3, pp. 131–41

——1993 'Conflict resolution in the family: a PET evaluation study' *Australian Psychologist* vol. 28, no. 2, pp. 100–4

Wragg, J. 1989 *Talk sense to yourself: a program for children and adolescents* A.C.E.R., Melbourne

Wright, J. and Cleary, K.S. 2006 'Kids in the tutor seat: building schools' capacity to help struggling readers through a cross-age peer-tutoring program' *Psychology in the Schools* vol. 43, no. 1, pp. 99–107

Wright, P.B. and Leroux, J.A. 1997 'The self-concept of gifted adolescents in a congregated program' *Gifted Child Quarterly* vol. 41, no. 3, pp. 83–94

Yell, M.L., Busch, T. and Drasgow, E. 2005 'Cognitive behavior modification' in *Behavior management: applications for teachers* 4th edn, ed T.J. Zirpoli, Pearson Merrill Prentice Hall, Upper Saddle River, NJ, pp. 226–66

Yoon, J.S., Hughes, J.N., Cavell, T.A. and Thompson, B. 2000 'Social cognitive differences between aggressive-rejected and aggressive-nonrejected children' *Journal of School Psychology* vol. 38, no. 6, pp. 551–70

Young, M.E. 1992 *Counseling methods and techniques: an eclectic approach* Merrill, New York

Young, S. 2001 'Solution focused anti-bullying' in *Solutions in schools* eds Y. Ajmal & I. Rees, BT Press, London, pp. 86–96

Zanolli, K. and Daggett, J. 1998 'The effects of reinforcement rate on the spontaneous social initiations of socially withdrawn preschoolers' *Journal of Applied Behavior Analysis* vol. 31, no. 1, pp. 117–25

Zarcone, J.R., Iwata, B.A., Mazaleski, J.L. and Smith, R.G. 1994 'Momentum and extinction effects on self-injurious escape behavior and noncompliance' *Journal of Applied Behavior Analysis* vol. 27, no. 4, pp. 649–58

Zettergren, P. 2005 'Childhood peer status as predictor of midadolescence peer situation and social adjustment' *Psychology in the Schools* vol. 42, no. 7, pp. 745–57

Zirpoli, T.J. 2005 *Behavior management: applications for teachers* 4th edn, Pearson Merrill Prentice Hall, Upper Saddle River, NJ